The Stowe Debate

# THE STOWE DEBATE

•

Rhetorical Strategies in

## *UNCLE TOM'S CABIN*

*Edited by*

## Mason I. Lowance, Jr.
## Ellen E. Westbrook
## R. C. De Prospo

_____

University of Massachusetts Press    *Amherst*

Copyright © 1994 by
The University of Massachusetts Press

All rights reserved

Printed in the United States of America

LC 94-12254

ISBN 0-87023-951-1; 952-X (pbk.)

Designed by David Ford

Set in Walbaum by Keystone Typesetting, Inc.

Printed and bound by Thomson-Shore, Inc.

Library of Congress Cataloging-in-Publication Data
The Stowe debate : rhetorical strategies in Uncle Tom's cabin / edited
by Mason I. Lowance, Jr., Ellen E. Westbrook, and R. C. De Prospo.
    p.   cm.
    Includes bibliographical references and index.
    ISBN 0-87023-951-1 (alk. paper). — ISBN 0-87023-952-X (pbk.:
alk. paper)
    1. Stowe, Harriet Beecher, 1811–1896.   Uncle Tom's cabin.
2. Rhetoric—Social aspects—United States—History—19th century.
3. Stowe, Harriet Beecher, 1811–1896—Technique.   4. Southern
States—In literature.   5. Race relations in literature.   6. Slavery
in literature.   7. Slaves in literature.   8. Narration (Rhetoric)
9. Fiction—Technique.   I. Lowance, Mason I., 1938–   .
II. Westbrook, Ellen E., 1952–   .   III. De Prospo, R. C., 1949–
PS2954.U53S76   1994
813′.3—dc 20                                                    94-12254
                                                                    CIP

British Library Cataloguing in Publication data are available.

•

# Contents

## Contents

### III

*Religious Rhetoric and Biblical Influences on Stowe*

### IV

*Race and Slavery in* Uncle Tom's Cabin

# The Stowe Debate

•

# Introduction

The title of this volume refers to three very distinct and separate arenas of debate that have been generated by Harriet Beecher Stowe's 1852 publication of *Uncle Tom's Cabin*. The first and most obvious is the controversy the book started by highlighting the moral outrage readers felt toward the "peculiar institution" of slavery. Abolitionists and antislavery critics the world over joined the chorus of voices that resulted from Stowe's inflammatory volume. At the same time, proslavery objections to her work were filled with invective and attacks not only against the book, but also on Stowe's character. The second debate to which the title refers is the professional critical controversy that commenced in March 1852, the month the book was first published as a complete volume. *The Stowe Debate* also embraces a third set of conflicts: the often heated discussions that dominate contemporary theoretical discourse, including the disagreements that take place within the pages of our volume.

*Uncle Tom's Cabin* was an instant best-seller; it was also instantly controversial and the focal point of a long discourse about the nature of slavery and the character of those who embraced it as a way of life. We employ the terms *rhetoric* and *discourse* frequently in these essays, and the words suggest a powerful dialogue taking place in mid-nineteenth-century American culture concerning the slavery issue, the dominant argument of the English-speaking world on both sides of the Atlantic. Rhetoric

1

and discourse also suggest the significance of language, that is, the rhetorical strategies that Stowe employed in creating the most rhetorically powerful document to emerge in antebellum American treatment of the slavery issue. What gave the book this power? How do issues of voice, public ideology and sentiment, cultural value and response relate to Stowe's influence as a critic of culture at a time when women and chattel slaves were both emerging from conditions of repression? The essayists here respond to these and other crucial questions as they examine an author's role in a society that was divided over the rights of both women and slaves. By observing the cultural conditions out of which *Uncle Tom's Cabin* was developed, and the literary conventions Stowe appropriated to give her critique a particularly powerful voice for the emancipation of women as well as slaves, the contributors to this volume seek to illuminate both the book itself and the responses it generated.

*Uncle Tom's Cabin* was much more than a successful narrative. It came to embody the moral force of freedom in an experimental democratic culture. Originally intended by Stowe to be a vigorous response to the Compromise of 1850 and particularly to the Fugitive Slave Law, the book emerged as a mirror of the times, a graphic reminder to the American people of the horror they had created by embracing slavery while professing that "all men were created equal." As Eric Sundquist has noted, "By giving flesh-and-blood reality to the inhuman system for which the Fugitive Slave Law now required the North, as well as the South, to be responsible, it became a touchstone for antislavery sentiment. Stowe was hardly the first to call attention to slavery's destruction of both black and white families, but her novel perfectly combined the tradition of the sentimental novel and the rhetoric of antislavery polemic. In scene after scene, the fragmentation of black households and the corrosive moral effect on white conscience is her focal point" (Sundquist, *New Essays* 8).

Academic and public response since 1852 has acknowledged the cultural significance of *Uncle Tom's Cabin*. The first edition (Boston, March 20, 1852) of 5,000 copies sold out only two days after it appeared. Within a year, 300,000 copies had been sold in America and 150,000 in England. Before September 1853, a dramatization of the story was produced in Troy, New York, commencing a long tradition of dramatic representation of the powerfully emotional narrative. Theatrical performances were soon followed by minstrel show parody, and during the 1850s, New York City hosted hundreds of stage versions, most of which were severely edited to produce the maximum sentimental effect. In 1859, four separate stage companies were performing the work simultaneously, each giving as many as three shows daily. The text itself has been one of the world's leading best-sellers, rivaled only by the Bible. It has been translated into sixty languages, including Welsh and Bengali. However, Stowe realized little of the publishing profits because her initial negotiations with the publisher, Jewett and Company of Boston, excluded royalties on foreign sales.[1] Instead, the rewards for Stowe were instant recognition as a leading opponent of slavery in all its forms, and Abraham Lincoln exaggerated only slightly when he greeted her at the White House, in 1863, with the words, "So this is the little lady who started this great big war." *Uncle Tom's Cabin* as a cultural phenomenon and the rhetorical strategies that made it so powerful are the subject of this book. The larger cultural debate about slavery had prepared the way for the enthusiastic reception enjoyed by the book, and these essays relate the discourses *within* the narrative to those that lie without it.

In the twentieth century, dramatizations on film superseded stage productions, but the dramatic force of the horrors of slavery and its brutal treatment of blacks by whites continues to attract audiences in large numbers. Hollywood is never far behind when conditions are so conducive to audience appeal, and in 1935 and 1936 the child star Shirley Temple portrayed little Eva in *The Littlest Rebel* and *Dimples.* In these versions of the story, character stereotypes were more the focus than was any historical guilt over slavery, and music often added to the already pervasive nostalgia about the Old South. Judy Garland played Topsy in blackface in *Everybody Singing* in 1938, and the comedians Abbott and Costello parodied Simon Legree and Eva in *The Naughty Nineties* in 1945 (Sundquist, *New Essays* 5).

But the issues generated by the original Stowe debate of the 1850s persisted into the 1930s and after. As recently as 1936, upon the publication of *Gone with the Wind*, Margaret Mitchell stated that she was pleased to present to the world a more accurate and less negative portrait of the antebellum South than Harriet Beecher Stowe had written almost a century earlier. Mitchell's modest objections were mild indeed when compared to the vituperative rantings of Stowe's contemporary proslavery advocates like George Fitzhugh, who published *A Sociology for the South* in 1854 and *Cannibals All!* in 1856. Both works argued for the essential value of slavery as an institution and denounced morally sentimental portrayals of slavery in works like *Uncle Tom's Cabin.* The slavery issue and the various debates surrounding it clearly show the relationship of rhetoric to action, morality to argument, and discourse or dialogue to the rhetorical techniques employed to frame them. Stowe's narrative is a challenging call to action cast in epic and biblical terms, so that individual readers who shared the author's religious and moral values and attitudes, even in part, could not escape the demands for action contained in the novel's rhetorical inventions.

The professional or critical debate about the book also began before the book was published as a volume in 1852, but its circulation in parts in the *National Era* did not generate the level of discourse provoked by the novel in its completed form. Responses to the volume were heated, both positive and negative. As a work of art, the book received mixed reviews. Charles Dickens found Stowe's novel pedestrian and overly sentimental. Frederick Douglass, who had not cooperated with Stowe in the development of her data base of slave narrative materials, nevertheless found the completed work to be of tremendous political and social significance. Many reviewers addressed Stowe's excessive use of sentimental tropes and paradigms, such as the death of little Eva, as well as the more politically and racially sensitive issues, such as Stowe's stereotyping of black characters. Of particular note is James Baldwin's harsh critique in the *Partisan Review* in 1949, "Everybody's Protest Novel," which is addressed by R. C. De Prospo in the Afterword to this volume. In 1940, Richard Wright called his critique *Uncle Tom's Children,* and the phrase "Uncle Tom" has passed into our vocabulary as highly pejorative, the antithesis of "political correctness," endowed with a value very different from the interpretations Stowe intended. Critics obviously reflect and mirror cultural values, just as Stowe's novel itself is a product of cultural value systems. What provoked the critical response, and what issues, other than slavery itself, does this literary and cultural reception suggest? The essays that follow also consider contemporary theoretical problems, both cultural and literary. Although Stowe's book is a historical artifact of antebellum, antislavery discourse, it nonetheless provokes debate about contemporary issues—the roles of blacks and women in American society, and the cultural work that texts can do.

The essays in *The Stowe Debate* have been grouped in four sections, addressing the following areas of investigation:

1. Questions of language and discourse analysis

2. The prominent influence of domestic narratives and sentimentality as discourse strategies

3. The influence of the Bible on Stowe's construction of narrative, her development of character, and her sermonic style

4. Questions of race, gender, and slavery that are raised by Stowe's work (for example, how does Stowe's masterpiece represent slave characters, often stereotyping them, while effectively developing antislavery arguments that were also regularly heard from the pulpits "at the North" about the equality of all people and the national sin of slavery?)

Critical and theoretical concern with the cultural work that texts can do, such as the arguments advanced in Jane Tompkins's *Sensational Designs: The Cultural Work of American Fiction, 1790–1860*—a modern study that specifically addresses the rhetorical power of *Uncle Tom's Cabin*—offers a fresh perspective on the issues of rhetoric, race, and gender that have been points of critical discourse since the novel was first published.

The editors and authors have attempted to strike an effective balance between an in-depth analysis of specific problems and a wider examination of the various facets of the Stowe debate. The medium, of course, is language. But our understanding of the "rhetorics" employed in framing the issues of discourse depends on a keen sensitivity to the historical evolution of attitudes toward slavery and its consequences. Stowe was very aware of the national mood, and she was also a scholar of the Bible and its rhetorical strategies. The daughter of Lyman Beecher, one of the most powerful rhetoricians of the Second Great Awakening in New England; the wife of Calvin Stowe, another minister and professor of religion at Bowdoin College in Maine; and the sister of six ministers, Stowe understood the historical and moral force of her argument against slavery and was sensitive to the power of language to represent eternal values *and* to change human hearts. Hence, the grouping of the essays follows the topography set out by Stowe in organizing her masterpiece: (1) discourse strategies; (2) the rhetorics of domesticity and sentimentality in the home and marketplace; (3) the rhetorics of the sacred, or

5

discourse strategies of scripture and pulpit; and (4) the pervasive rhetoric of race—discourse strategies of popular and professional culture in antebellum America.

In part 1, Catharine O'Connell argues that both religious rhetoric and republican ideology in the novel are subordinated to the rhetorical principles of sentimentality. She suggests that the traditional moral authority of religion and republican ideals were no longer dependable, and that in their place Stowe inserted the moral power of sentimentality and domesticity: "For Stowe, the discourses of religion and republicanism had been hopelessly vexed and could no longer be relied upon to conclusively demonstrate the evil of slavery. . . . In the place of an authority that could be distorted by argument and interpretation, Stowe offers the authority of the individual heart and conscience, which she posits as immune to manipulation." Jonathan Edwards and his New Light Calvinists of the eighteenth century had suggested something similar when they broke with traditional religious authority and sought redemption through the transformation of individual souls.

O'Connell's critique is complemented by Jan Pilditch's essay on the role of satire as a rhetorical strategy, a study that connects Stowe's technique and voice to the rhetors of eighteenth-century England. Pilditch finds that satire and humor play significant roles in Stowe's strategy, as James Bense also argues in a later essay, and that Stowe frames ideology in traditional forms of language discourse. Melanie Kisthardt's essay investigates the theoretical premises of feminine discourse in Stowe's narrative, invoking more fully than any other essay in the volume the voices of contemporary theorists like Foucault, Bahktin, and Derrida.

In part 2, Susan Roberson, Bradley Shaw, and Isabelle White expand one component of O'Connell's opening argument by developing three separate treatments of Stowe's rhetoric of domesticity and sentimentality. From the very earliest midcentury responses to Stowe's work, the influence of sentimental writing, whether in contemporary fictional models or in the pervasive literature *for* women, has been cited as a crucial element in Stowe's methodology. These three essays examine the rhetorical traditions of sentimentality and the contemporary proliferation of literature for women, and they show how Stowe appropriates these materials for specific rhetorical purposes in the composition of her novel.

Part 3 reintroduces the importance of biblical rhetoric in Stowe's sermonic novel. Helen Westra introduces the reader to biblical millennialism as it was understood by Jonathan Edwards and his followers, while tracing patterns of millennial thinking from the 1730s into the Second Great Awakening of the nineteenth century. Mason Lowance expands Westra's approach by illustrating specifically how biblical typology was central to the development of character in *Uncle Tom's Cabin*. Both of these essays establish the significance of religious rhetoric as a means of communication in Stowe's midcentury universe, a universe that was well acquainted with the biblical and millennial patterns that permeate the novel from their pervasive employment in sermons, treatises, speeches, lectures, and essays. They were, of course, Emerson's techniques, and religious rhetorical strategies, particularly the figures and types of biblical discourse, were not "in the air" at the time Stowe composed her novel; rather, they were present in practically every piece of literature published or spoken.

Part 4 treats approaches to the novel that have foregrounded race and slavery as the central issue the work addresses. James Bense examines antebellum sermon writing for abolitionist depictions of slavery as an institution opposed to God's will, while Sarah Ducksworth examines *Uncle Tom's Cabin* itself as a social tract with stereotypical character types and the evolution of a black persona in American culture. Bense also addresses prominent issues of character formation, confronting the problem of stereotyping and the role of humor as a rhetorical technique. While Ducksworth explores the problems of stereotyping black figures, Susan Neuernberg examines particular concepts of race in antebellum American discourse, for example, the monogenetic and polygenetic arguments that invoked pseudoscience in support of pro- and antislavery positions. Michael Meyer critiques "refractive" and "reflective" images of black characters while assessing the pressures of racial ideology on a white writer, such as Stowe, and upon professional critics of literature and culture. The collection concludes with an afterword by Richard De Prospo, who examines these essays as contributions to the tradition of Stowe criticism, with particular emphasis on literary theory.

These essays clearly show that a significant contribution to the debate about slavery was the success of *Uncle Tom's Cabin* itself.

If Stowe's work can be directly linked to the commencement of hostilities through her stimulation of the national consciousness to action, then the cause of the Civil War must lie more in the moral indignation against slavery than in the attempt by the North to prevent the South from seceding from the Union. Of course these political matters were inextricably linked; public opinion was galvanized against the South *because of the moral indignation against slavery*, and because of the *perception* of slavery that was widely held by Northern sympathizers. This perception was communicated in antislavery sermonizing by abolitionist ministers like James Freeman Clarke; however, it was Harriet Beecher Stowe's work that reached an audience worldwide and helped to isolate the South in its insistence that slavery was either biblical in origin or benign in its treatment of those enslaved. *Uncle Tom's Cabin* offers the reader another perspective on the "peculiar institution," and the novel generated much stronger antislavery sentiment than some factual, real-life accounts had been able to do. As our essays demonstrate, the contrast between fictional and nonfictional representations of reality constitutes yet another dimension of the Stowe debate.

Stowe's work exerted considerable influence by crystallizing public reaction to the Compromise of 1850 and its Fugitive Slave Law. But many earlier accounts had also demonstrated the brutalities of slavery on the plantation, and none had the immediate power of Stowe's novel. If there was ever a direct connection between the power of language and rhetoric to inspire political and social action, Stowe's novel and the ensuing Civil War (of which her "Concluding Remarks" specifically warn) are where that connection is forged in America's history. For example, Stowe repeatedly cites Theodore Dwight Weld's *American Slavery As It Is* (1839), a detailed and factual account of the brutal treatment of Southern slaves; but it was her transformation of these episodes into dramatic fictional form that called much more attention to the problem. In 1853, Stowe also published *A Key to Uncle Tom's Cabin*, a work designed to verify the episodes and characters in the novel in the face of Southern challenges to slave narratives. Here she indicated that a parallel for Uncle Tom was the slave Josiah Henson, whose autobiographical narrative had been published in 1842 and whose story she claimed to represent in the fictional account of Uncle Tom. *A Key* provides a mother lode of information about Stowe's method of composition while it raises numerous questions about the effectiveness of fiction and drama contrasted with documents of fact.

The Stowe debate could indeed continue with an investigation of problems associated with this tension, which could in turn invoke data concerning the literary marketplace, publishing, and market considerations, as well as the internal issues of rhetorical strategies and artful representation. Stowe's work is a collage that draws together antecedent genres such as the American Indian captivity narrative, the slave narrative, the Puritan sermon and jeremiad, the sentimental novel, the epic poem, the heroic narrative, the spiritual autobiography, the saint's life, the melodrama, and many of the literary forms that appear in the Bible, including historical and prophetic narrative and apocalyptic and millennial writing. The connective tissue linking these episodes is the moral argument against slavery, and it is the art of Stowe's work that brings the elements together in a way that was at once rhetorically powerful and publicly perceived as truth.

The essays in this volume originated during the summer of 1992 at the Newberry Library in Chicago, site of a National Endowment for the Humanities (NEH) Summer Seminar for College Teachers, "*Uncle Tom's Cabin* and Antebellum American Culture." The seminar members worked well together as a group and had wonderfully stimulating discussions that summer, not always reaching consensus, as the essays clearly show. We wish to thank the Newberry Library staff, especially Ruth Hamilton, Fred Hoxie, and Richard Brown, who were gracious and attentive hosts to our seminar group. And we acknowledge the invaluable editorial expertise of the volume's external reader, Karen Oakes of the American Studies Program at the University of Hull, England. The combination of detailed and comprehensive observations and recommendations she provided is rare in our experience. We also wish to thank Jeff Chaffin, Director of Readers' Services, Washington College Library. Thanks also go to Bruce Wilcox, director of the University of Massachusetts Press, for encouragement, keen interest in our work, and a stabilizing influence as this volume moved from initial concept to a reality. Finally, we are each indebted to the NEH Summer Seminar and Fellowships program for bringing us together. At a time when some humanistic discourse seems divisive and uncertain of its objectives, our group members debated, stimulated each other, and discussed nineteenth-century American culture in ways that were fruitful, productive, enabling, and energizing. We were each pushed to reach beyond the formal structures of the seminar and to use the vast resources of the Newberry Library and Chicago to have an intellectual and cultural experience rarely found today in the academy. This book is the result of those preliminary investigations and a year of continued research into the intriguing Stowe debate.

> Mason I. Lowance, Jr., and Ellen E. Westbrook
> Amherst, Massachusetts, 1993

## N O T E S

1. Stowe was engaged in a lawsuit against a German publisher who printed her work in German without permissions or a royalty contract. She lost the suit, and the prevailing attitude of the Supreme Court at midcentury was that once a book was published, it entered the public arena if not the public domain, and the author lost control of it. The laws were substantially revised at the beginning of the 1900s. From the majority decision in *Stowe v. Thomas* (1853): "By the publication of her book the creations of the genius and imagination of the author have become as much public property as those of Homer or Cervantes. Uncle Tom and Topsy are as much *publici juris* as Don Quixote and Sancho Panza. All her conceptions and inventions may be used and abused by imitators, playrights [sic] and poetasters. They are no longer her own—those who have purchased her book, may clothe them in English doggerel, in German or Chinese prose. Her absolute dominion and property in the creations of her genius and imagination have been voluntarily relinquished; and all that now remains is the copyright of her book, the exclusive right to print, reprint, and vend it." See Meredith McGill, "Literary Property in Nineteenth-Century America," forthcoming.

# I
.

Language and Discourse in Stowe's Writing:
Approaches to *Uncle Tom's Cabin*

# 1

•

CATHARINE E. O'CONNELL

## "The Magic of the Real Presence of Distress": Sentimentality and Competing Rhetorics of Authority

The ongoing debate over the cultural meaning and value of Harriet Beecher Stowe's *Uncle Tom's Cabin* attests to the novel's rhetorical complexity; because Stowe engages and uses a wide range of contemporary arguments on questions of race and gender, it is possible to connect the novel to multiple and divergent political movements and rhetorical traditions. Through its polyvalent approach to the antebellum slavery debate, the novel provides a map of dominant rhetorics of the period and serves as a model of heteroglossia in American literature.[1] The convergence and competition of rhetorics within the novel reveals both the density of the historical debate over slavery and the generic ability of the novel to encompass multiple rhetorical positions.

In this essay I will examine in depth three rhetorical traditions that coexist and compete for narrative authority within *Uncle Tom's Cabin.* The first two rely on the authority of the church and state: the religious rhetoric of biblical and ministerial authority and the national rhetoric of republicanism. Against the authority of (male) sacred and secular institutions, Stowe invokes the rhetoric of sentimentality, the appeal to the authority of emotional experience. While I will argue that the novel ultimately privileges the rhetoric of sentimentality, the textual debate is crucial to the dynamic of the novel; by juxtaposing the public authority of God and country to the private authority of the heart, *Uncle Tom's Cabin* both joins and expands the parameters of antebellum discussions of slavery.

The rhetorical richness of *Uncle Tom's Cabin* results in part from its appearance at a moment of cultural and representational crisis. In *The New American Studies*, Philip Fisher observes that the period surrounding the Civil War provides fruitful material for the study of competing rhetorics: "To see the central episode of American history as the Civil War is to bring to the front the power of rhetorics, incomplete dominance of representation, and the borrowing or fusing of successful formulas of representation" (xv). Stowe's novel is a particularly strong example of the fusion Fisher ascribes to Civil War era texts. Not only does its overt theme address the most volatile political and social question of American history, but the novel's approach to the problem challenges assumptions about what constitutes "political" discourse and about the relationship between the "private" life of the emotions and public debate, assumptions heavily inflected with ideas about appropriate gender roles. A cross between the antislavery tract and the feminized sentimental novel, *Uncle Tom's Cabin* engages the rhetorical traditions associated with the two forms and at the same time blurs the distinctions between public and private, truth and fiction, reason and emotion, and male and female that were associated with these forms.

These distinctions have endured beyond Stowe's time; indeed there is still considerable critical debate over the political implications of sentimentality. Discussions of *Uncle Tom's Cabin*, whether friendly or hostile, tend to set up an opposition between the novel's sentimentality and its antislavery message. My contention here is that sentimentality functions as Stowe's best antislavery argument and that it is placed in counterdistinction to other modes of persuasion that are ultimately rejected. This is not to say that sentimentality is finally successful as a rhetorical strategy; one of the most interesting features of *Uncle Tom's Cabin* is the way it reveals the limitations of sentimental representation. However, the novel presents sentimentality as more powerful than other social languages, and understanding how and why it does so illuminates both the workings of the sentimental genre and the state of public debate over slavery in the early 1850s.

## *"You will feel for me": Stowe's Sentimental Paradigm*

Early in the novel, the fugitive Eliza arrives, terrified and exhausted, at the home of the middle-class, white Bird family. This scene enacts in the Bird family the transformation that the novel itself seeks from readers: witnessing the suffering of a slave with whom middle-class white readers can easily identify forces even disinterested Northerners to oppose the injustice of slavery. The model of sentimental response put forward in the Bird scene also brings into relief the impossible challenge of sentimental representation. The narrative asserts that it is the physical presence of the suffering slave that moves the Bird family so forcefully, and yet the appeal to the reader is premised on the ability of a written account of slave suffering to effect an equally intense emotional response. The confrontation between Eliza and the Birds acts out the representational goals of the work as a whole, while illuminating the obstacles to their achievement; it simultaneously insists on the primacy of the physical and the textual. The scene thus functions as a *mis-en-abyme*, reproducing and commenting on the structure and limitations of the novel's sentimental strategy. The novel's insistence on a textual effect as intense as physical presence results in an emphasis on the (white) reader's emotional history that frequently shifts the narrative focus from slavery to white family tragedies, and that ultimately makes opposition to slavery contingent on the power of the novel to make slavery emotionally comprehensible to white readers.

Before Eliza arrives on the scene, we are introduced to the Bird family in a way that establishes their role as ideal sentimental readers. They are relaxing in their parlor after a long day, and Eliza, like the novel itself, intrudes into this domestic time and space. Senator Bird is marked from the outset as the expert on extradomestic matters, and we are told that Mrs. Bird does not usually "trouble her head with what was going on in the house of the state, very wisely considering that she had enough to do to mind her own."[2] Her husband warns against relying on emotions to adjudicate difficult issues such as slavery: "[W]e mustn't suffer our feelings to run away with our judgment; you must consider it's a matter of private feeling,—there are great public interests involved" (144). From the moment of their introduction, Mary and John Bird personify the private/public, emo-

15

tion/reason opposition. The conversion of John constitutes a model of sentimental persuasion.

The entrance of Eliza disturbs the domestic tableau. When the Birds ask her to defend the decision to flee a kind master, she does not invoke theoretical arguments for her right to freedom but turns to Mrs. Bird with a powerful emotional appeal, asking, "Have you ever lost a child?" (149). When Mrs. Bird acknowledges that she has, Eliza confidently asserts: "[T]hen you will feel for me." The narrative does not rest with modeling a sympathetic response for readers but attempts to emotionally involve them in the scene; they must cry too for the sentimental message to be effectively transmitted. When Mary Bird goes into the room of her dead son, Henry, to find clothes for Eliza's son, Harry (the similarity in names further cements the emotional connection between the families), the narrator follows her into the enshrined room and turns on the reader. "And oh! mother that reads this, has there never been in your house a drawer, or a closet, the opening of which has been to you like the opening again of a little grave?" (153–54). Involving the reader in the pathos of the scene underscores the narrative centrality of the reader's emotional response.

While mothers like Mrs. Bird and readers who have lost children are presented as predisposed to respond emotionally, Senator Bird, with his public responsibilities and allegiance to an unemotional or even antiemotional epistemology, is an invaluable convert. If he can be made to respond emotionally, the power of a sentimental appeal is assured. The novel describes the successful transformation of John Bird from a political man to a man of the heart.

> How sublimely he had sat [in the Senate chamber] with his hands in his pockets, and scouted all sentimental weakness of those who would put the welfare of a few miserable fugitives before great state interests!
>
> He was as bold as a lion about it . . . but then his idea of a fugitive was only an idea of the letters that spell the word. . . . The magic of the real presence of distress,—the imploring human eye, the frail, trembling human hand, the despairing appeal of helpless agony,— these he had never tried. (155–56)

For Senator Bird, witnessing suffering has the magical effect of making impossible his detached indifference. Eliza's agony, the "real presence" of her distress, breaks down all of Bird's defenses. The religious overtones of calling this suffering a "real presence" imply that witnessing suffering has a mystical and transformative power. The inescapable irony, however, is that it is Eliza's literal, physical presence that moves John Bird, yet Stowe's model of sentimental representation depends on the premise that literal presence and narrative presence are indistinguishable in their effects.

Once Senator Bird has been transformed by witnessing Eliza's suffering, he is compelled to aid her. The novel does not posit the sentimental transformation as purely internal but argues instead that anyone who truly undergoes a change of heart will necessarily act on his or her beliefs. The novel finds Senator Bird in the comfort of his parlor but does not leave him there; we watch him pass an extremely unpleasant night transporting Eliza to safety. Stowe remarks that "if our good senator was a political sinner [for helping Eliza], he was in a fair way to expiate it by his night's penance" (156). The subsequent description of the terrible roads in Ohio and the discomfort of the carriage trip seem digressive, but the point is driven home that true sentimental sympathy consists not solely of weeping but of acting on the feelings for which those tears are the visible sign.

The compunction to act is an important component of Stowe's sentimental paradigm because it works against those interpretations of sentimental representation that deem it necessarily apolitical or antipolitical by foreclosing the possibility of action through its focus on emotions. Philip Fisher argues that it is the absence of the possibility of anything *but* an interior response that gives sentimental fiction its legitimacy: "That feeling and empathy are deepest where the capacity to act has been suspended . . . defines the limits of sentimental representation. . . . By limiting the goal of art to the revision of images rather than the incitement to action, sentimentality assumes a healthy and modest account of the limited and interior consequences of art" (*Hard Facts* 122). By taking as given the absolute division between action and emotion, such interpretations short-circuit discussion of sentimental literature by asserting its impotence as a generic attribute.

Critics who define sentimentality as divorced from politics tend to judge the genre as ineffective or even dishonest. Ann Douglas comments in *The Feminization of American Culture* that "sentimentalism might be defined as the political sense obfuscated or gone rancid" (254). Likewise Amy Schrager Lang posits a "gap between private feelings and public action on which sentimentalism insists" (34). Both critics go on to challenge the efficacy of any sentimental protest.

While Stowe's model of sentimental reader response does not define the change wrought by an appeal to emotions as primarily internal, the ability to respond is predicated on the internal authority of the reader's own heart and emotions. In this sense, the authority of emotions is qualitatively different from the other models of authority the novel engages. Indeed, it is this recourse to the reader's heart as final arbiter that frees sentimentality from the censure and sarcasm Stowe reserves for other models of authority. For Stowe, religious and political authority are subject to manipulation and perversion from which the individual heart is immune.

## *"Greek and All That": The Pitfalls of Religious Erudition*

There is no question that *Uncle Tom's Cabin* is a Christian novel, rooted in the Bible and Christian ethics. However, the presentation of Christianity in the novel is anything but straightforward. While the admirable characters and the narrator define themselves as Christians, so do many of the novel's most despicable characters. It is easy, of course, to tell one from the other, but the ubiquity of evil Christians makes the novel's relationship to Christianity unstable.

There are several historical reasons for this ambivalence. First, the late antebellum period was one of great division in Protestantism, with many denominations moving toward a more liberal, humanistic view of religion and away from the harsher, more theologically centered traditions.[3] Perhaps more important, however, was the division within the Christian churches over the question of slavery. Few commentators who identify Stowe through her Christian position on slavery examine the extent to which Christianity was used to defend slavery during the antebellum period. Staunch Christians were as likely to speak out in favor of slavery as against it, and it is within this context that Stowe suggests the limitations of religious authority in dealing with the slavery crisis.

The fundamental instability of the religious response to slavery is shown in *Uncle Tom's Cabin* through a debate between two ministers on board the ship transporting Tom and other slaves to New Orleans.

> "It's undoubtedly the intention of Providence that the African race should be servants . . . ," said a grave-looking gentleman in black, a clergyman. . . . " 'Cursed be Canaan; a servant of servants shall he be,' the scripture says. . . . It pleased Providence, for some inscrutable reason, to doom the race to bondage, ages ago; and we must not set up our opinion against that."
>
> . . . A tall, slender young man, with a face expressive of great feeling and intelligence, here broke in, and repeated the words, " 'All things whatsoever ye would that men should do unto you, do ye even so unto them.' I suppose," he added, "*that* is scripture, as much as 'Cursed be Canaan.' " (200–201)

This exchange articulates the nature of the conflict between different interpretations of Scripture, and it underscores the danger of proslavery interpretations.

Stowe's choice of biblical citation to put in the mouth of her proslavery minister engages Christian defenders of slavery at their most absurd. "Cursed be Canaan" (Gen. 9:18–27) was one of the favorite quotes of Southerners, yet it was one of the least logical biblical defenses of slavery. The connections between Noah's curse and the enslavement of African Americans was tenuous at best, although both sides of the debate considered it important; an antislavery biblical scholar put great effort into proving that the descendants of Ham could not be African: "That curse demonstrably no more applies to them than to us! . . . Canaan remained an Asiatic" (Cox 16). Supporters of slavery argued that the fulfillment of the curse of Canaan in America was miraculous evidence of the inevitable fulfillment of God's prophecies. The American system was "a standing proof that the word of God is true, and that slavery was entailed as a curse upon the Africans for the sin of their father Ham" (Hendrick 14). Frederick Douglass mocks this justification for slavery in his 1845 *Narrative*: "If the lineal descendants of Ham are alone to be scripturally enslaved, it is certain that slavery at the south must soon become unscriptural; for thousands are ushered into the world, annually, who, like myself, owe their existence to white fathers" (27).

This shipboard debate also underscores the importance of individual feeling and grants men and women the right to question the ways of God and to insist that God's ways be consistent with human standards of mercy and justice. The discredited minister argues that humans must not question the ways of God or expect to understand them. The minister Stowe endorses, and Stowe's own emphasis on the reliability of the heart, assumes that God's ways, if they are truly represented, *will* make sense to humans, *must*, in fact, because the only reliable way human beings have to judge truth from falsehood is the evidence of their own hearts.[4]

Stowe not only discredits proslavery ministers but asserts that they are dangerous to the faith of believers. Honest John, who harbors Eliza after Senator Bird helps her flee, states explicitly that proslavery ministers kept him from joining the church for a long time.

> I tell yer what, stranger, it was years and years before I'd jine the church, 'cause the ministers round in our parts used to preach that the Bible went in for these ere cuttings up,—and I couldn't be up to 'em with their Greek and Hebrew, and so I took up agin' 'em, Bible and all. I never jined the church till I found a minister that was up to 'em all in Greek and all that, and he said right the contrary; and then I took right hold, and jined the church,—I did now, fact. (160)

"Greek and all that," the marker of the difference between the educated minister and the common people, becomes the stumbling block for the wisehearted yet ignorant who know right from wrong even while they respect the authority of their ministers.

The argument that proslavery ministers drove good people from the church was used by other antislavery writers. William Wells Brown's 1853 antislavery novel, *Clotel, or The President's Daughter,* contains a proslavery minister whose antislavery daughter saves souls he cannot. The virtuous young woman, trying to convert an unbeliever, must respectfully ask her father to keep quiet about his views. "I think he is on the stool of repentance. . . . He, you know, was bordering upon infidelity, and if the Bible sanctions slavery, then he will naturally enough say that it is not from God" (121–22).

Antislavery tracts frequently accuse proslavery ministers of destroying souls entrusted to their care. In chiding a Northern minister who supported the Compromise of 1850, one writer asserts that, by taking such positions, the clergy has "shaken the faith of many weak Christians, and given a vast impulse to infidelity. There is, sir, great reason to fear that the blood of souls will be found in the skirts of some who have proclaimed themselves commissioned to sanctify the whip and the fetters of the slave, by first hanging them on the cross of the redeemer" (Jay 21). The moral authority of the clergy gave a particular significance to their pronouncements on slavery.

The argument that a certain position on slavery was dangerous to the Christian church was put forward not only by those on one side of the issue but, like virtually every other religious argument, could be turned either way. A large number of antiabolitionist ministers (whatever their position on slavery itself) argued that the agitation over slavery would tear churches apart, as indeed it did in the three national Protestant denominations that split into Southern and Northern churches over the question of slavery in the antebellum period: the Presbyterians into Old School and New School in 1837, the Methodists in 1844, and the Baptists in 1845 (Ahlstrom 101–15). An anonymous New Yorker in 1838 made a plea against abolitionists. "Witness the hostile array in which the professors of the same Christianity, and the members of the same denomination, are placed against each other. . . . [T]heir holy indignation would lead them, not only to curse the slaveholders, but to curse everybody who will not curse them also; or, at least say amen" ("An Appeal to the Reason" 13–14). Because the abolitionists took such an uncompromising position on slavery, national churches with large Southern constituencies often saw the abolitionists as a greater evil than slavery itself, particularly in the early years of abolitionist activism.

The debate over who was endangering the church was acrimonious, but the debate over who was misinterpreting the Bible and therefore blaspheming was conducted at an even higher pitch. Because of the unquestioned authority of the Bible, it became the favorite weapon of both pro- and antislavery forces. The abolitionists positioned themselves as driven by a Christian imperative to combat evil, and the South responded by "discovering" the biblical defense of slavery. A scholar of Southern evangelicals notes that "evangelicals viewed the scriptural argument as a discovery . . . because it was admirably suited to meet the specifically religious argument of the abolitionist. If, as evangelicals claimed, the Bible sanctioned slavery, then abolitionists . . . not only were wrong but were guilty of 'impiety' " (Loveland 200). Ironically, both sides believed that the Bible provided an absolute standard for settling debate, even when their own bitter disagreements showed that it could not possibly do so.

Proslavery Christians argued that the frequent mention of servants in both the Old and New Testaments, and the Bible's seeming acceptance of the perpetual class of people in bondage, establishes that slavery has a biblical foundation. A proslavery writer almost gleefully records the unscriptural response of an antislavery opponent when faced with this evidence.

> But the cap sheaf of all was the Rev. Dr. Bennett's set off to the tenth commandment. When I quoted this commandment, this reverend gentleman sneered a smile of contempt; and when he came to reply to me said—"But Mr. Jefferson has said that all men are born free, and are entitled to life, liberty, and the pursuit of happiness." Well, after this—I shall be surprised at nothing. . . . [T]o oppose a statesman to Jehovah, and the Declaration of Independence to the tenth commandment—was nothing short of blasphemy. (McCaine 19)

The political argument regarding slavery was also prominent, but for a minister to make the mistake of confusing the two, of seeming to place secular authority above sacred, was an error his proslavery interlocutor could hardly overlook.

Although many who put forward a biblical defense of slavery were arguing merely for an end to agitation about slavery and did not go so far as to posit slavery as good, some used the Bible to justify the most horrifying abuses of slavery. A South Carolina minister argued that the laws in Exodus (21:20–21) about the lenient punishment of a master who beats a servant so badly that the servant later dies prove that slaveholders have a divine right even to kill their slaves if they refuse to submit.

> Now, here are laws that authorize the holding of men and women in bondage, and chastising them with the rod, with a severity that terminates in death. And he who believes the Bible to be of divine authority, believes these laws were given by the Holy Ghost to Moses. I understand modern abolition sentiments to be sentiments of marked hatred against such laws; to be sentiments which would hold God himself in abhorrence, if he were to give such laws his sanction: but he has given them his sanction; therefore, they must be in harmony with his moral character. (Stringfellow 9)

This position is the logical extension of the proslavery biblical argument, but it led places many ministers would not have dared to go.

The response of those opposed to slavery privileged the New

Testament with its emphasis on loving one's neighbor and "doing unto others." Since these precepts are clearly incompatible with slavery and God would not contradict himself, the argument goes, slavery could not be endorsed anywhere else in the Bible.

> It is impossible for any person to practice human slavery an hour without violating the law of Love. . . . Now for us to pretend that the Almighty would give us this multitude of precepts as rules of our moral conduct, . . . and at the same time establish and sanction an institution in the same law containing the precepts, the necessary effect of which he foreknew would produce the necessary violation of them all, . . . is an absurdity too gross and too wicked for a moment's innocent toleration. ("A Condensed Anti-Slavery Bible Argument" 64–65)

The argument that the Bible could not cause anyone to do evil was a strong one, but it could not answer Southerners' literal interpretation of a number of Old Testament passages.

Stowe's intervention into this impossible debate was to go even farther than those who argued against slavery through the Bible and to put individual conscience at the center, even while positing the Bible as the source of moral authority. Throughout *Uncle Tom's Cabin*, proslavery interpretations of Scripture are countered not through argumentation but through an appeal to commonsense notions of right and wrong. Stowe's ultimate dismissal of biblical defenses of slavery occurs when Simon Legree, the epicenter of evil in the novel, quotes St. Paul's instructions to servants (Eph. 6:5–6), a favorite passage of slavery supporters. When Tom defies Legree's cruel orders to whip a helpless woman, Legree is infuriated: "Here, you rascal, you make believe to be so pious,—didn't you never hear, out of yer Bible, 'Servants obey your masters'? An't I yer master?" (508). Stowe does not join her contemporaries in debating what St. Paul really meant—Was he talking to free servants? Was his advice merely expedient?—but simply discredits the words by putting them in the mouth of Simon Legree. The true Christians in the novel are identified through what they feel and what they do, not through dogma or doctrine. Because the novel incorporates the pervasive and persuasive proslavery Christian arguments circulating in antebellum America, it moves away from an understanding of religion as grounded in the authority of ministers and their interpretation of the Bible.

23

## *"It's a Free Country": The Irony of Republicanism*

The rhetoric of republicanism is also central to Stowe's novel and presented as tainted in ways similar to the rhetoric of religious authority.[5] The commitment to individual rights put forward in the Declaration of Independence and the Constitution provided a potentially powerful indictment of slavery, and indeed much antislavery writing during the antebellum period relied heavily on the theory of republicanism. The problem for Stowe writing after the Compromise of 1850 was one of definition; if republicanism meant preserving the Union, then the greatest imperative was to appease, not rile, the South and thus to downplay the injustice of slavery. The second problem Stowe faced was more similar to the problem with religious discourse; it was possible to argue either that the republican ideology made slavery impossible, or that slavery had always been a constitutive part of that ideology because it was accommodated in the Constitution. This conundrum about how to read the Constitution was hardly unique to Stowe—disagreements over it were at least partially responsible for the major schism in the abolitionist movement—but the contradictions inherent in republicanism make it an unreliable source of authority in the novel.

The problem with republican arguments against slavery was that the Constitution, while never mentioning the word, assumes the existence of slavery in at least three places: the three-fifths compromise; the protection of the slave trade until 1808; and the fugitive clause. While the spirit of republicanism was undoubtedly inclusive, the letter of the law was exclusionary, and both sides of the slavery debate had to address this fundamental contradiction.[6]

The Constitution's tacit acceptance of slavery led radical abolitionists under the leadership of William Lloyd Garrison to call for the dissolution of the Union *by the North* and the rejection of the Constitution as proslavery. An 1845 publication of the American Anti-Slavery Society rejects any twisting of the Constitution to make its principles support a position that it was not originally intended to hold. "If it be objected, that though these provisions were meant to cover slavery, yet, as they can fairly be interpreted to mean something exactly the reverse, it is allowable to give them such an interpretation, *especially as the cause of freedom will thereby be promoted*—we reply, that this it to advocate fraud"

(6). This position makes virtually impossible an antislavery republican position that takes full account of the Constitution.

There were those who tried to force the Constitution to say
what it clearly did not, and it is perhaps arguments like the one
that follows that the Garrisonians believed constituted fraud.
One treatise tries to explain away the seeming approval of slavery
in the Constitution. The three-fifths compromise thus becomes
somewhat hypothetical. "The most it says is that *should* there be
any not included in the forgoing description, then only *three-
fifths* of *their* number should be estimated. But it does not pre-
tend that there are any such" (Tiffany 63). The clause mandating
the return of fugitives must undergo even greater contortions.
This clause, according to the argument, was always practically
meaningless. "When the enslaved is so fortunate as to escape the
jurisdiction of that power which enslaved him, in the eye of the
law he has gained his liberty—not by virtue of any law that sets
him free—but by the limits of that law by which he was enslaved. . . . And if, on examination [this provision] should be
found to be totally inefficient, so much the better" (Tiffany 79–
80). In other words, a clause of the Constitution cannot do anything at all, or rather the Constitution as a whole guarantees the
opposite of what the clause guarantees.

The central paradox inherent in the republican argument
against slavery is shown most dramatically in Stowe's novel
through the character of George Harris. Stowe's presentation of
George Harris illuminates the irony of applying the principles of
republicanism to a slave. Because he is willing to fight and die for
his freedom, George is a republican hero and is thus allied to a
tradition of American heroes. George is also the novel's most
dangerous slave because he recognizes that he has been deprived
of his rights and is courageous enough to fight for them; republicanism thus provides George Harris with the justification for
violent resistance. The logical necessity of George's violent resistance to slavery ultimately prevents him from being the novel's
central character and necessitates his removal out of the country
and eventually off the continent.

When George is first introduced, the reader learns of his immense ability and of the pettiness of a jealous master who takes
the talented inventor and puts him to work in the fields. George's
master defends his own right to be arbitrary and capricious by
referring to his Constitutional right to property: "It's a free coun-

try, sir; the man's *mine*, and I do what I please with him,—that's it!" (57). This statement by such a man about such a man is highly ironic, but the essence of the argument, that to interfere in the relationship between master and slave was to subvert the fundamental right to property, was made quite seriously in the antebellum era; in fact it was a central point in the Dred Scott decision. From the moment of his introduction, the character of George has a highly problematic relation to republicanism because it can reasonably be used to justify both his freedom and his enslavement.

The contradictions embodied in George are recognized by the character himself; Stowe makes George a particularly self-aware and articulate figure well worthy of the reader's respect. He simultaneously ridicules American ideals and calls for their realization. "Haven't I heard your Fourth-of-July speeches? Don't you tell us all, once a year, that governments derive their power from the consent of the governed?" (185). George's perception of the gap between principle and practice leads both to his assumption of the high moral ground by actually trying to live according to the values white Americans espouse, and his rejection of all laws pertaining to slaves because the slaves had no hand in their formation.

George's position shocks the benevolent but timid Mr. Wilson, who tries to dissuade him from running away. "Do you call these the laws of *my* country? Sir, I haven't any country. . . . I'll fight for my liberty to the last breath I breathe. You say your fathers did it; if it was right for them, it is right for me!" (187) George thus invokes the example of the most heroic figures of American mythology. George's assumption of the republican legacy is particularly appropriate and ironic since *his* fathers as well as Mr. Wilson's put forward such principles; George is half-white, and Stowe uses his white paternity to make his enslavement more ironic and his rebellion less surprising to white readers.

When faced with the prospect of having his family taken by slave catchers, George puts into practice his bold words. He vows to defend his family, and Stowe calls this stance his "declaration of independence" (298). This scene definitively establishes George's position as a republican hero and necessitates his disappearance from the center of the story. The irresolvable conflict between his natural rights as a man, and the property rights others have in him, comes to a crisis here through the slave catchers who cannot hear his appeal as a man, so fixated are they on his monetary value as a thing. As a true republican, George must fight for the rights tyrants will not recognize, and in the process he shoots Tom Loker. George thus becomes both George Washington and Nat Turner, and by bringing together these divergent cultural icons, Stowe implicitly recognizes that an enslaved George Washington must become a Nat Turner.

Stowe's intended audience for *Uncle Tom's Cabin* was the South as much as the North, which is easy to forget once one knows anything about the history of its reception. For instance a review of *Uncle Tom's Cabin* from the *Southern Literary Messenger* attacks Stowe for even daring to speak out on a public issue such as slavery and links her audacity to women's rights principles, which "[hand] over the State to the perilous protection of diaper diplomats and wet-nurse politicians. Mrs. Stowe . . . may assert her prerogative to teach us how wicked are we ourselves and the Constitution under which we live, but such a claim is in direct conflict with the letter of scripture" (Ammons, *Critical Essays* 8); this reviewer here invokes the authority of both the Constitution and the Bible to dismiss Stowe. Such responses can obscure Stowe's attempt to effect reconciliation and not exacerbate sectionalism (hence Simon Legree's Northern nativity and the humorous portrayal of the very Northern Miss Ophelia).

The logic of the argument that traps George in a position in which he must shoot Loker also traps Stowe; it ends in division and violence. George escapes being a murderer because some very good Quaker nurses take care of Loker, who actually benefits from the experience. Stowe escapes the implications of her argument through George by quickly sending him far away after the confrontation scene.

The threat of violence implicit in republican ideology surfaces in the novel again when Augustine St. Clare and his brother Alfred debate the problem. Alfred rejects the ideology of the fundamental equality of men, and his brother points out the dangers of whites rejecting this principle and slaves abiding by it.

> "Because," said Alfred, "we can see plainly enough that all men are *not* born free, nor born equal; they are born anything else. For my part, I think half of this republican talk sheer humbug. It is the educated, the intelligent, the wealthy, the refined, who ought to have equal rights and not the canaille."
>
> "If you can keep the canaille of that opinion," said Augustine. "They took *their* turn once, in France." (391)

The masses must be convinced that the republican ideology is truly "humbug," or those in power will be destroyed by the implications of their own words.

Later in the argument, Augustine introduces the specter of Haiti (392), thus alluding to the fear of slave rebellion that haunted the Southern mind. When Alfred tries to argue that there would have been no uprising if Anglo-Saxons, not Frenchmen, had ruled Haiti because of the "natural" superiority of the race, Augustine turns the argument on its head by pointing out how many "sons of white fathers, with all our haughty feelings burning in their veins" (392), exist in the ranks of the slaves. Stowe here both invokes and subverts the nascent "scientific" racism that began to appear in the 1850s and gained credence throughout the second half of the nineteenth century.[7] If indeed there was an innate aggression and dominance in those with white blood, mixed-race children would increasingly become "more white" in racial characteristics and less willing to serve as slaves. George is of course the perfect embodiment of this threat, and the conversation between the St. Clare brothers comes only five chapters after George has shot a white man. Toward the end of the novel, Stowe has George himself make the connection between his white patrimony and his fierce pride: "[F]ull half the blood in my veins is the hot and hasty Saxon" (611).

Stowe's subtle argument that the logic of republicanism leads to slave revolt, coupled with narrative endorsement of the ever-passive Tom over the proud George, plays on Southern fears and yet appears to assuage them. That George and Tom play opposing roles in the narrative has been pointed out by Richard Yarborough, who observes that the two slave characters "inhabit different worlds, parallel dimensions that never intersect. . . . One can imagine that, like matter and antimatter, if they were forced into contact, the result would be an explosion of immeasurable force that would leave only Tom, for he, not George, is Stowe's real hero" (53). While Stowe endorses Tom over George, the presence of George interjects the threat of violence into the novel.

The rhetoric of republicanism thus has a shifting place in *Uncle Tom's Cabin:* it reveals the hypocrisy inherent in American acceptance of slavery, it ennobles the slave willing to fight for his liberty, and it threatens slaveholders with the violent results of the philosophical contradictions inherent in their system. Although republican rhetoric is important to the novel, Stowe finally backs away from it once she comes inexorably to a moment of violence. George *must* shoot Tom Loker, but Tom Loker *must not* die; the logic of violence cannot come to dominate *Uncle Tom's Cabin.*

## *"Just Such Tears": The Sentimental Equation*

For Stowe, arguments against slavery from "the word" of the Bible or the Constitution finally falter on the vagaries of interpretation. What she offers as an alternative is the authority of the heart, which she posits as less susceptible to distortion than either Christianity or republican ideals. The "failure" of other discourses to provide an airtight argument against slavery helps to explain why Stowe privileges sentimentality.

*Uncle Tom's Cabin* is structured around the terms of the sentimental equation that first appear in the Bird scene. The novel first creates an equivalence between the emotional experiences of slaves and white readers, particularly the intense emotional trauma of losing a beloved child. The second half of the novel attempts to reproduce those feelings as intensely as possible through the medium of a white child who is presented as appealingly as possible and is then closely linked to a slave figure. The death of one prefigures the death of the other and (ideally) reenacts in readers the intense emotions associated with losing a child. Little Eva thus becomes the sentimental linchpin; she can induce feelings in readers that can then be transferred onto Tom. The Eva and Tom dyad is the second part of the sentimental appeal; committed to the power of emotions, the novel does not merely assert the emotional connections between white readers and slaves, it forces its readers to *feel* the connection.

Stowe's choice of a child's death as the central sentimental metaphor for the novel resonated in significant ways with both the literary and social conventions of the antebellum period. The death of a child was an extremely common trope in nineteenth-century sentimental novels; indeed such a figure was ubiquitous.[8] Perhaps even more important was the meaning of a child's death in American culture at large. The valuation of domesticity over the course of the first half of the nineteenth century was accompanied by an increased emphasis on the beauty and innocence of childhood. Indeed the cult of domesticity could as easily

29

be called the cult of the child.[9] The beatification of childhood, coupled with women's increasing self-definition as nurturing mothers, gave the death of children intense social meaning, both painful and poignant. This attention to the death of children evolved into what Karen Halttunen calls a "cult of mourning," which involved elaborate rituals for dealing with death and making it meaningful as a familial and communal experience. For antebellum Americans, bereavement was not outside the bounds of public discourse but was very much part of it, and thus available to Stowe as a way of talking about and eliciting strong emotions.

Stowe first employs the image of the death of a child as a metaphor for the suffering of slaves when Tom must part from his three small children. His pain is described both *as* a parent's agony and *like* a parent's agony; if readers have trouble seeing in the slave Tom a loving parent, the explicit analogy will presumably help them along.

> [H]e turned to the rough trundle bed full of little woolly heads, and broke fairly down. He leaned over the back of the chair, and covered his face with his large hands. Sobs, heavy, hoarse and loud, shook the chair, and great tears fell through his fingers on the floor; just such tears, sir, as you dropped into the coffin where lay your first-born son; such tears, woman, as you shed when you heard the cries of your dying babe. (90–91)

Stowe insists that if readers have experienced this terrible loss, they must understand and appreciate Tom's suffering when facing permanent separation from his children. If they understand Tom's pain as the same as their own, presumably they will be incapable of supporting an institution that imposes a separation as merciless as the grave's.

Stowe uses negative examples of characters who cannot or will not feel for the slave to further underscore the importance of emotional identification. In the same chapter in which a slave mother drowns herself after being separated from her child, we see a woman indifferent to the suffering of slaves. A more sympathetic woman asks: "Suppose, ma'am, your two children, there, should be taken from you, and sold?" (200). The wording of the answer is revealing: "We can't *reason* from our feelings to those of this class of persons" (emphasis added). Reason does not belong in the equation at all; one must feel the suffering of slaves and reject the distancing discourse of reason.

The character who is presented to the reader with the most sentimental fanfare and with the greatest expectation of reader emotional investment is not a slave, but a little white girl, Eva St. Clare. The sentimentalization of Eva and her role in the anti-slavery appeal have long been considered problematic by critics of the novel. Ann Douglas, for instance, considers Eva extra-neous, at best: "Her only real demand on her readers is for self-indulgence" (*Feminization* 4). In my assessment of the novel's sentimental strategy, Eva is essential to the process of making the reader feel the suffering of the slaves. From the moment Eva is introduced, it is clear that she is exceptional and that she is to be viewed in sentimental terms. We are told not to read her as just a little girl: "There was about [her] an undulating and aerial grace, such as one might dream of for some mythic and allegorical be-ing" (230). We watch her charm Tom and everyone else on board the ship, and we are clearly supposed to be charmed also.

After Eva has had about a hundred pages to ingratiate her-self into our affections, we discover that we are once again up against the recurring motif of the death of a beloved child. Eva is doomed, and we are doomed to watch and weep over her demise. Once Eva's decline has begun, Stowe connects her to all those dead children endlessly and lovingly eulogized by bereaved par-ents. "Has there ever been a child like Eva? Yes, there have been; but their names are always on grave-stones. . . . In how many families do you hear the legend that all the goodness and graces of the living are nothing to the peculiar charms of one who *is not*" (383). Such a description of children who die young is likely to awaken the emotions of parents who have had the misfortune to lose a child; Stowe once again draws on the trauma of parents to excite emotional involvement in her story.

The description of Eva's death itself is protracted and puts the reader through the emotions of those surrounding the child's bedside. As Richard Brodhead observes, "Little Eva does not merely die but makes a scene of her death. Through this repre-sentational labor she opens up a space that both enables and actively solicits deep emotional participation" (91). The scene in which Eva distributes her curls to all the household servants provides the opportunity for Eva to show her perfect love for the slaves, thus modeling behavior for the reader. The staging of this scene also allows Stowe to create an appreciative fictional au-dience for the emotional performance that is actually put on for the reader's benefit; the reader should take a hint from the weeping slaves about how to respond to Eva's death.

The description of Augustine St. Clare's agony as he stands over the deathbed of his child calls attention to the momentous importance of the scene. Stowe again alludes to the reader's own experiences in similar situations. "What was it he saw that made his heart stand still? . . . Thou canst say, who hast seen that same expression on the face dearest to thee,—that look indescribable, hopeless, unmistakable, that says to thee that thy beloved is no longer thine" (426). The register of language in this passage undergoes a considerable shift from the usual narrative voice; Stowe uses the archaic "thee" and "thou" forms that usually appear only in direct quotations (from the Bible or the speech of Quakers). This shift has the paradoxical effect of making the passage more formal and more intimate. This language is usually associated with the Bible, so there are sacred associations, but "thee" and "thou" are also the English equivalents of the familiar forms in French and other languages. The tone of this passage thus sanctifies Eva's death, while insinuating that readers have an investment in it through their own terrible experiences.

The description of Eva's death is the most extended instance of sentimental narration in the novel, and critics who disparage the novel's sentimentality find Eva's death the most objectionable part of the novel. In *Love and Death in the American Novel*, Leslie Fiedler reports "an especially queasy voyeurism in this insistence on entering the boudoirs of immature girls" (256). A critic writing more recently asserts that "the scene's luxury characterizes the most familiar and least desirable feature of nineteenth-century sentimental fiction, the excess of conventional props (funereal and linguistic) to stimulate an excess of feeling" (Joswick 254). To say that the scene stimulates an excess of feeling implies that there is a certain amount of feeling that is acceptable or appropriate and that Stow goes too far. But the questions must be asked: The emotion is excessive or appropriate for what purpose? What does all this emotion do?

To assess what the emotion surrounding little Eva's death does, we need to first establish what her death *does not* do; it does not free the slaves, not even or especially not Tom. This "failure" has been the basis of much criticism of the novel; Ann Douglas uses it as evidence of the impotence of the sentimental novel: "Little Eva's beautiful death, which Stowe presents as part of a protest against slavery, in no way hinders the working of that system" (*Feminization* 12). While this argument assumes that Eva's death must "do something" on the level of plot, critics who defend the novel argue that Eva's death signals the insignificance of "the world" compared to the spiritual realm that Eva's holy death invokes. Eva's death thus becomes a spiritual victory not only divorced from but antithetical to material politics. Jane Tompkins asserts that for Stowe, "death is the equivalent not of defeat but of victory; it brings an access of power, not a loss of it" (*Sensational Designs* 127). The importance I perceive in Eva's death does not occur on the level of plot or theology; the extremely sentimental depiction of Eva's death teaches the reader how to respond correctly to the untimely death of one of the novel's major figures. The eventual effect of this "lesson" is to force the reader to pay attention to *Tom's* death.

Eva's death cannot be satisfying in and of itself. The angelic child accepts her death in large part because she believes it can help free the slaves. She says to Tom: "I would be glad to die, if my dying could stop all this misery. *I would* die for them, Tom, if I could" (401). She later makes her father promise to free Tom as soon as she is dead (404). Instead of achieving his freedom, Tom is plunged into the darkest possible slavery after Eva's death. Eva's only deathbed request goes unanswered because her death is not, finally, the point, and the reader is dissuaded from getting "stuck" emotionally on its poignancy. The reader must immediately follow Tom to Legree's Red River plantation and experience the cycle of sacrificial death all over again.

Eva's death models a response to Tom's, which it anticipates and rehearses. The sentimental presentation of Tom's tragic death is similar to the presentation of Eva's despite the many obvious differences in circumstances. The connections the novel posits between Eva and Tom have been pointed out by a number of critics, most notably Elizabeth Ammons and Jane Tompkins, both of whom focus in particular on the Christlike and "feminine" natures of both characters. Eva and Tom both are willing to sacrifice themselves for others, both have an almost instinctive understanding of Christianity, and both influence others more through virtuous example than by direct action. Ammons observes that "Stowe makes the living double and soul mate of ethereal motherly Eva the black man Tom. . . . Tom's passivity, his piety, his gentleness, his inexhaustible generosity of spirit, his nonviolence, his commitment to self-sacrifice: . . . these are the virtues of Christ, which are in Stowe's theology maternal" ("Stowe's Dream" 166–67). By giving both Eva and Tom characteristics readily identifiable to mid-nineteenth-century readers as Christian and womanly, the novel persuades us to see them as the same in their symbolic function, if not their physical attributes. This emphasis on sameness diminishes the physical differences between them and the great cultural meaning those differences in gender, class, caste, age, and appearance possessed in antebellum American culture.

By linking Eva and Tom, the novel establishes Tom's right to the attention and affection accorded Eva. The piquant and innocent charm that marks Eva as the quintessential sentimental child refracts onto Tom the attributes of sentimental virtue. Philip Fisher observes this function of Eva, noting that Stowe "wisely interposes between the reader and the slave, a child. By doing this she is able to borrow from the nearly completed historical sentimentalization of the child, the energy to begin the more difficult and historically risky sentimentalization of the slave" (*Hard Facts* 99). Eva serves as the conduit through which Tom's suffering and experience is rendered accessible and authentic to a readership familiar with the conventions and values of domesticity and Christianity. Eva's role in Stowe's sentimental appeal is to elicit tender feelings from a white audience, ground those feelings in the authority of Christlike love and womanly virtue, and transfer those feelings onto the slave Tom.

By the time Legree beats Tom to death, readers have been well prepared for Tom's death, well prepared to respond emotionally because they have learned to associate the death of the slave with the tragic loss of white children. Tom's death is effective precisely because it is a retelling of Eva's, and herein lies the fundamental contradiction of Stowe's sentimental strategy: the white reader can feel the suffering of an/Other only when the Other has become them. The reality of slave suffering is contingent on the ability of white readers to construct an emotional analogy. Any elements of slave experience that are inaccessible to white readers are therefore elided.

This emphasis on sameness and accessibility makes the sentimental appeal problematic. In discussing white women's abolitionist writing, Karen Sanchez-Eppler has observed that "the problem of antislavery fiction is that the very effort to depict goodness in black involves the obliteration of blackness" (39). In Tom's case, of course, it also involves the obliteration of his masculinity, which suggests James Baldwin's famous condemnation of Tom "robbed of his humanity and divested of his sex" (*Notes of a Native Son* 13). The narrative feminization and whitewashing of slave characters is organically connected to the novel's reliance on the power of empathy and emotional identification. Therefore the success of the sentimental appeal is predicated on its limitations; the constructed connections between white (female) readers and slaves form the basis of the antislavery argument, yet these connections mitigate against a recognition of innate human rights, substituting instead a standard of recognition of essential sameness. Both the power and limitations of this "we are the world" sensibility inhere in Stowe's sentimental strategy.

The assumptions undergirding Stowe's sentimental appeal limit the rhetorical power of *Uncle Tom's Cabin;* however, the novel's engagement with and challenge to other rhetorical approaches indicate the extent to which division over the slavery question compromised social languages ranging from the patriotic to the pious. Rather than representing a retreat from public political discourse, as some critics have suggested,[10] the endorsement of the authority and authenticity of emotional experience in *Uncle Tom's Cabin* offers an alternative way *into* the public debate over slavery, a debate that by 1851 had become hopelessly vexed.

## NOTES

1. Mikhail Bakhtin's theoretical apparatus in *The Dialogic Imagination* is particularly useful in discussing *Uncle Tom's Cabin* because the novel contains so many social languages in competition or dialogue with each other. In Bakhtin's formulation, novelistic language is and always must be "contested, contestable, and contesting—for this discourse cannot forget or ignore, either through naivete or by design, the heteroglossia that surrounds it" (332). Thus Stowe's incorporation of a range of positions on the slavery debate implies not a departure from some ideal of novelistic unity, but a multivocal approach that is not only appropriate to but constitutive of the novel as a genre.

2. Stowe, *Uncle Tom's Cabin* (1981), 142. All subsequent quotations from the novel are from this edition, cited by page number in the text.

3. The competition in antebellum American culture between the Calvinist tradition and sentimental Christianity has been discussed by Ann Douglas, Barbara Welter, and James Turner, among others.

4. For the connection between theological reliance on individual conscience and women's sentimental fiction, particularly Stowe's, see Camfield.

5. In this essay, *republican* and *republicanism* refer not to a specific trend within early American politics but to the founding national ideology. This broad definition was the one used by the writers I discuss; indeed the lack of precision in the use of the terms was one reason for the acrimonious debate over their "true" meaning.

6. The paradox in the Constitutional accommodation of slavery is the obvious effort made to avoid actually using the words *slave* or *slavery*. The three-fifths clause states that, for purposes of taxation and representation, slaves or "all other persons" count as three-fifths of citizens (art. 1, sec. 2). Restrictions on the slave trade, or "the migration or importation of such persons as any of the States now existing shall think proper to admit," were prohibited until 1808 (art. 1, sec. 9). And fugitives "held to service or labor in one State" were to be returned to "the party to whom such service or labor be due" (art. 4, sec. 2).

7. Fredrickson discusses the emergence of "scientific" racism in his third chapter, "Science, Polygenesis, and the Proslavery Argument." Nuernberg also addresses the issue later in this volume.

8. For a detailed discussion of the conventions of the early American sentimental novel, see Herbert Ross Brown. Also see White in this volume.

9. For information on the cult of domesticity and attendant attitudes toward children, see Nancy Cott, Barbara Welter, and Mary Ryan. See also Shaw and Roberson in this volume.

10. Versions of these arguments are put forward by Mary Kelley and Lauren Berlant. Kelley reads the sentimental emphasis of antebellum women's writing as evidence of the constraining nature of domesticity: "The heart was the symbol of woman, of woman's involuntary life. . . . The heart's record was the woman's revealed record of her life of domesticity, the only life she could have" (221). Berlant holds that because they provide a "domestic antidote" (246) to social injustice, sentimental novels such as Stowe's create "a space for female dissonance while maintaining the economy of exclusion that otherwise marks the domestic sphere" (246).

# 2.

## Flirting with Patriarchy: Feminist Dialogics

I write and you are not dead.
The other is safe if I write.

—Hélène Cixous

"Mr. Haley and Tom jogged onward in their wagon, each, for a time, absorbed in his own reflections. Now, the reflections of two men sitting side by side are a curious thing, —seated on the same seat, having the same eyes, ears, hands, and organs of all sorts, and having pass before their eyes the same objects, —it is wonderful what variety we shall find in these reflections!"[1] This scene captures the rhetorical framework of *Uncle Tom's Cabin*, in which the dominant culture, represented by Haley, and the Other, characterized by Tom, survey the outward landscape while their thoughts make visible private meaning. For Haley, the journey means the end of conflict on the Shelby farm and the possibility of economic gain. In contrast, the journey for Tom marks the beginning of conflict, of loss, of loved ones, with little possibility for their reunion. Haley interprets as good nature Tom's stoic acceptance of events beyond his control. As an object in a market economy, Tom is not supposed to have "reflections," yet Stowe uncovers these to contrast with Haley's. In this way, she gives voice to the Other; though silent, Tom's thoughts shout from the page (193). *Uncle Tom's Cabin* is structured on such "variety" of "reflections," the dominant juxtaposed to the marginalized Other to create a polyvocal and dialogically open-ended text.

Examining Harriet Beecher Stowe's rhetorical grounding of the Other (Beauvoir xvi–xxvi) provides a key to the novel that opens rather than closes dialogue. Writing the Other makes visible the invisible, gives speech to the muted, and brings the marginalized into the social context while valorizing the attributes of Otherness. The novel is accessible and didactic precisely in relation to the audience's familiarity with and acceptance of the normative and prescriptive aspects of sentimental and sermon traditions. Thematically, all conflicts are resolved, all villains punished, all protagonists rewarded—if not on earth, in heaven. However, Stowe's final millennial warning and the unresolved quality of dialogue initiated by the characters signify not resolution but potential—possibility for reenactment, for future moments when the Other's voice will be raised. Structured on this process, Stowe's novel exposes the various poses and masks the Other assumes in order to be heard, to deflate monolithic identity, and to reveal the hypocrisy inherent between the lines that define and delimit interaction. *Uncle Tom's Cabin* as tour de force weaves rhetoric that would be palatable to the reader even as its structure promises a platform for dissenting voices. Stowe appropriates the language of power to speak the unspeakable, to place her outsiders within dominant discourse while maintaining Otherness.

This she accomplishes by "layering meaning upon meaning, voice upon voice upon voice," creating, in Bakhtinian terms, "a corridor of voices" that not only "augment understanding" ("The Problem of the Text" 121) but also scrutinize the source of oppression. Where and when the Other enters the dialogue with dominant culture often represents divergence from, and critique of, the ostensibly rational language of the fathers. In this essay I will examine the points at which Others (women and slaves) enter the dialogue and how their compliance with or reversal of dominant rhetoric reveals the tenuous nature of its "logic."

Luce Irigaray's *mimétisme* is useful here and correlates well with the concept of polyvocality in dialogics and resistance to hegemonic relations (*This Sex* 76, 220). *Uncle Tom's Cabin* privileges many characters' voices as well as voices within individual characters. In this effort can be read Stowe's effort to "assume the feminine [Other] role deliberately," which, according to Irigaray, is to "convert a form of subordination into an affirmation, and thus begin to thwart it" (76). To "play with mimesis" is

> to try to recover the place of . . . exploitation by discourse, without . . . [being] simply reduced to it. It means to resubmit [oneself] . . . to 'ideas' . . . that are elaborated in/by a masculine logic, but also to make 'visible,' by an effect of playful repetition, what was supposed to remain invisible: the cover-up of a possible operation of the feminine in language. It also means 'to unveil' the fact that, if women are such good mimics, it is because they are not simply reabsorbed in this function. *They also remain elsewhere.* (76)

This metaphor captures the subtle subversiveness of Stowe's appropriating patriarchal language in order to move beyond it and to create a place for her characters' voices. Flirtation and miming reveal the characters' knowledge of dominant culture and the source of their alienation from culture. However, the very process of weaving should be considered neither absolute compliance with dominant culture nor the counterimposition of a different hegemony. As a Beecher, Stowe held a secure position in dominant society; as a woman in the nineteenth century, she was also aware of her marginalized position. This double consciousness informs her work by exposing private and public voices. A dialogic approach reveals polyvocality, the playful movement in and beyond dominant culture to emphasize the open-endedness of the *process* of engagement, rather than its definitive outcome.

Chapter 1 of *Uncle Tom's Cabin* establishes a critique of patriarchal discourse, which becomes the rhetorical authoritative tenor throughout. The narrative voice, in effect, "mimes" the genteel labeling of a patriarchal elite that perpetuates the objectification of the Other. Mr. Shelby and Haley are referred to as "*gentlemen*" for "convenience sake" only (41). Haley, a "coarse, commonplace," pretentious man whose outward appearance is a profane exaggeration of capitalist excess and whose language is alternately obscene and illiterate, is rhetorically linked to Shelby, who has the "appearance of a gentleman" (42), but whose actions belie the nature of a gentle-man. Shelby's paternalism toward the child slave Harry, whom he calls "Jim Crow" while "whistling, and snapping a bunch of raisins toward him" (44), and his laughter at Haley's "elucidations of humanity" (48) create a bond between the coarse and refined "gentlemen" from which Shelby cannot be extricated. The irony of the scene is heightened by the gentlemen's "earnest conversation" (42), the tenor of which is Other as commodity. That ubiquitous signifier of patriarchal language, the *"law"* (51), is rhetorically challenged by paratactic repetition of "so long," which suggests a critique and defiance of such commodification. Likewise, the introductory chapter establishes the aversion of patriarchy to engagement with Others' voices. Shelby contemplates "some fuss with [his] wife" as he concludes business with Haley (50). For all of Shelby's "good nature and kind[ness]" (51), the "heaviest load on his mind" lay not in thoughts for Harry, his mother Eliza, and Tom, but in "the foreseen necessity of breaking to his wife the arrangement contemplated,—meeting the importunities and opposition which he knew he should have reason to encounter" (53). The stage is thus set for encounters with the Other, which in *Uncle Tom's Cabin* will be oppositional. How and when does the Other enter the dialogue? As the chapter ends, we discover that engagement is delayed when one is blinded by outward appearance or preoccupied with social obligations, often both. Although forewarned about the impending sale, Mrs. Shelby "dismiss[es] the matter from her mind . . . entirely" (53) because, as herself an object in a phallocentric economy, she is unaware of financial burdens and has complete faith in the social roles that she and her husband play and in their mutual "humanity."

Finally, chapter 1 introduces a paradigm for marginalized characters' survival in a phallocentric culture that implies both subservience toward and disparagement of the masters. When Harry performs to please Shelby and his "guest," attention shifts from the boy's agility and flair for caricature to his audience's response. As they fling fruit to the boy and laugh "uproariously" (44), their humanity is subsumed in their respective patronizing and materialist views of the scene. Through miming, the Other manipulates the source of his oppression by appearing to act within the normative cultural pattern, all the while unmasking and, often, subverting it. The introductory chapters describing life on the Shelby farm provide a model for reading how Others' voices enter the dialogue as miming, from the most abject Harry to the most apparently privileged Mrs. Shelby—a woman who enjoys the roles assigned to her by patriarchy—who mimes "every female artifice" (113) to thwart her husband's plan. The slaves Sam and Andy continue the subversion to delay Haley's reaching Eliza by posing as stupid and mendacious, two traits they know patriarchy expects of them. They also play off two "generic view[s]"—that slaves are "cussed liars" and that "[g]als is nat'lly made contrary" (114–15)—to trick Haley into taking an abandoned, dead-end road and generally keep him in "a state of constant commotion" (116). Thus, the criteria used by the dominant culture to define blacks, children, and women are used to reveal their inner voice—their "elsewhere."

When they recognize their mutual Otherness, these characters tacitly create communities that enter the culture to oppose it and to assert their voices. Andy senses this affinity among Others and tells Sam, "[I]t's allers best to stand Missis' side the fence" (97). His capacity for "bobservation" is indeed "a very "portent habit" worth "cultivatin'" (103), since the ability to "read" others is essential for survival. Stowe valorizes such confederacy of Others, likening Sam to a "patriot in Washington" (96) and Andy to a "philosopher" (101). The subversive pantomime begun by Sam and Andy to "help" Haley prepare his horse (97–102) is joined by Mrs. Shelby. With the help of Tom's wife, Chloe, she too graciously plays her part as hostess to prolong the domestic subterfuge and thus the delay. The miming begun by Harry becomes a strategy for lending one's voice to the culture without submitting to it. Unlike the historical Christmas debauches proffered and encouraged by slave masters as prelude to a New Year's sale, the suspension of normative roles on the Shelby farm thwarts authority but does not end in silence. Rather, it sets in motion the possibility of still other voices joining the dialogue. The combined effort to erect obstacles for Haley facilitates Eliza's escape, thus establishing space for the Quaker voices and George Harris's voice of violent revolt to join the polyphony. Of course, the designs of the dominant culture are carried out—but not fully. Tom is sold, but through this his voice is carried south, just as Eliza's reciprocally carries throughout the North. In effect, the voices multiply and expand their spheres of influence, rather than being diminished, silenced, or trivialized.

Articulating the private reveals the weakness of supposedly rational, logical, public discourse. Mrs. Bird is characterized as one who does not "trouble her head" (142) with public issues, like Mrs. Shelby, who assumed she could "gild over" (84) public oppression. However, when the consequences touch both women personally, inescapably on their "moral and religious sensibility," they shift the private into the public (52). Mrs. Bird's miming is more confrontational than Mrs. Shelby's, even though, ironically, she epitomizes the conventional sentimental heroine. Amid all the sentimental rhetoric—a petite, "blushing," easily frightened woman with a "peach-blow complexion, and the gentlest, sweetest voice" (142–43)—Stowe inserts images of warfare as Mrs. Bird raises her private voice to encourage public action. The demure wife interrupts her husband's "clear argument" about law with private feelings for the public good and presses her "assault" with no pity for "the defenceless condition of the enemy's territory" (144–45). Only when she is "pretty well aware" that her husband is contemplating an un-reasonable act against the very law he helped pass does Mrs. Bird resume the pose of quiet docility associated with sentimental heroines. But her retreat is tactical; the private "domestic" voice has won the day, and thus she "prudently forbore to meddle," ostensibly the dutiful wife "ready to hear her liege lord's intentions, when he should think proper to utter them" (152). The narrator consolidates her victory when the oppressed is transformed from an abstract idea into the "magic of the real presence of distress" (155–56). When Eliza and Harry arrive, Mrs. Bird can afford to relent in her "attack" because the fugitives' presence is tangible proof of her argument, and the whole of patriarchal logic that allows such oxymoronic utterances as "It's a free country. . . . the man's *mine*" (57) is more than called into question; it dissolves under the gaze of an "imploring human eye" (156).

Throughout the novel, the validity of patriarchal authority is deconstructed at its source—the logic that ostensibly invalidates attacks on authority. The "dangerous game" that the militant slave George Harris "play[s]" (182) is mirrored by Stowe's rhetoric, which deflates logic and foregrounds Others' voices even as it mimes patriarchal rhetoric. While his "game" may be more obvious than Stowe's, hers is equally "dangerous," as her inclusion of a character who rhetorically threatens both the specious security of patriarchal logic and the peaceful domestic sphere testifies. No sentimental domestic warrior, George looms as a warning to patriarchy of the severe alternative to ignoring Others' voices. The irony of the chapter, titled "In Which Property Gets into an Improper State of Mind," lies in the capacity of "property" to articulate a point of view that dismantles the logic of patriarchal text—its laws and theology.

The speaker for patriarchy, "good-natured" Mr. Wilson, is

described as one whose mind "may not inaptly be represented by a bale of cotton—downy, soft, benevolently fuzzy and confused" (185). "Not inaptly," the double negative, signifies the genteel narrative voice, reluctant directly to condemn this character who is not malevolent but who can be misled by the hypnotic effects of patriarchal reasoning. Stowe's use of Mr. Wilson to propagate the logical rebuttals to George's flight highlights the invidious aspect of patriarchal logic, which is not only appropriated by the deliberate oppressor but can beguile the well-meaning man, as well. Again, a paratactic style exposes the weakness of Mr. Wilson's "confused notion of maintaining law and order" (183) and of his quoting Scripture. Frequent dashes mark the hesitations of a man whose words seem ever more ironic set against George's frenetic expostulations. Since George paces about the room like a caged animal, flailing the air and glaring like a man on the verge of a breakdown, one would expect his speech to be irrational, yet the scene stages just the opposite. Wilson's security in the text that he quotes, advising that all must "submit to the indications of Providence" (184), proves to be irrational in context of George's rebuttal, which personalizes the Scripture for Wilson. Confronted with the hypothetical case of his inaction if his family were held captive by Indians, the "little old gentleman stared with both eyes," expressing horror, disbelief, and the stark realization that, in such dire circumstances, swift and deliberate action—not submission—will serve any "rational" man. Although George's "bitter smile" (184)—following a "flashing eye" (183)—suggests a loss of control, his "rational" reply leaves Wilson stupefied.

Wilson's position is ultimately untenable because the rhetoric of freedom, devotion, and piety either applies to all or to none. And therein lies the crux of the issue. When George demands, "Can't a fellow *think?*" the obvious response in a culture that values George only as barter is that a fellow may, but a slave may not (185). That is the only "logical" conclusion, which is belied by the rhetoric, the tenor of George's responses, and the "logic" with which Wilson hopes to change George's mind. As the chapter ends, George assures Wilson that he will *"think of that"* (191)—that is, of God—which echoes the chapter title and ironically reenforces on two levels the arbitrary nature of patriarchal rhetoric: first, as an "object" a slave is supposed not inherently capable of thought; second, the dominant culture needs to control and channel the slave's thoughts to maintain the phallo-centric economy and silent resistance/Otherness.

In the next chapter, Stowe elaborates on the fallacious logic of religion that defends slavery through texts. Two clergymen offer divergent Scriptural passages, which John the drover "inter-prets" for the assembled group. From one minister's espousal of "Cursed be Canaan" (200) to justify slavery, John extrapolates the "logical" conclusion that "we must all be resigned to the decrees of Providence" (201). Assuming a rube persona, John prods Haley with the simplistic beauty of embracing this text to assuage personal responsibility for oppression. Haley admits never having considered this "refreshing" view because his mo-tives had always been economic. In this exchange, Stowe sug-gests that Haley's assessment of professional motive is more honest than the minister's obfuscation of individual choice and responsibility. John's "curious smile" implies that he enters the dialogue in a sardonically playful manner to deflate the text's power. While John addresses the "differences in parsons" and suggests that the "Cursed be Canaan" text "won't go down with the Lord" (202), the narrative voice suggests that all texts—and, by extension, perhaps all language, as well—are inappropriate to signify the living reality of the oppressed. As the scene closes, a slave, "John, aged thirty," is led from the ship and met by his inconsolable wife. John the drover, who exposed the arbitrary nature of texts, and John the slave, who has no text of his own, whose existence is merely written as a ledger account, are rhetor-ically linked. Witnessing such horrors—daily rituals of the insid-ious economy—requires no "text" because "every day is telling it" (202).

Nevertheless, Stowe's "text" retells the story that "needs not be told" and thus reveals a tale that contrasts with the idyllic ro-mance promulgated by slavery's advocates. Stowe's "alternate text" gains power by suggestion and repetition of paradigms and symbols of the Other. The Quaker settlement depicts the capac-ity of the marginalized to carry out "practical results" (52) by *avoiding* dialogue with this dominant culture. The Quakers' is the silent harmony of life defined by feeling rather than by reason. Beyond the dominant culture, this alternative interpre-tive community represents the antithesis of "reason." That this community exists marginal to the dominant society and lives according to intuitive acceptance of humanity (in and for all of its diversity) concretely illustrates "elsewhere." The harmony, "good fellowship," and "confidence" of these scenes contrast markedly with the ironies and oppositions inherent in encounters between the Other and the dominant culture. Simeon's "anti-patriarchal operation of shaving" (223) further implies that the gap in understanding is not gender specific. Rather, the chasm is created by the discrepancy between rational discourse and a "living Gospel, breathed in living faces" (224). Like the individual character Mrs. Shelby and the comic duo Sam and Andy, such larger "communities" achieve "practical results" through "a thousand unconscious acts of love and good will" (224), unlike the conscious debate over oppression in theoretical and religious terms that ultimately achieves nothing. Similar communities formed on the margins of society reappear throughout the novel (Tom/Eva, Cassy/Emmeline) and provide an interpretive framework that contradicts—even when it does not enter into—phallocentric discourse. The Quakers are emblematic of the space that opens to accommodate all voices. Totally nonpatriarchal, they neither aid nor identify themselves by or with hegemony.

Tom, in contrast, is "a sort of patriarch," and "a sort of minister" whose simplicity and "earnestness" (79) are valorized in proportion to their lack in the fully patriarchal leaders of the dominant culture. Tom exemplifies Stowe's alternate text of feeling in his prayers, which are "enriched with the language of Scripture" but are not grounded in it. The narrator's use of the word "unconsciously" (79) again foregrounds feeling over exegesis. Tom has not "learned to generalize, and to take enlarged views," nor has he "been instructed by certain ministers of Christianity" (209). In contrast to the intellectuals and logicians who must analyze and critique the "authenticity of manuscript, and correctness of translation," Tom's "reading" has "no annotations and helps in the margin from learned commentators"; rather, it is "embellished with "guideboards of [his] own invention," which reveal "more than the most learned expositions" (229).

That Tom is a "slow reader" (229) also points to the advantage of not being schooled in the language of the fathers enough to internalize it. Nascent literacy later provides a bond between Tom and Eva and suggests the communal effort of Others to write their history. When they collaborate to compose a letter to Chloe, Stowe describes the effort as begun with "a grave and anxious discussion, each one equally earnest, and about equally ignorant; and, with a deal of consulting and advising over every word, the composition began, as they both felt very sanguine, to look quite like writing" (348–49). Struggling with a language not one's own to express ideas for which the language has no words requires invention, such as Tom's marginalia, that to the dominant culture would be meaningless.

Stowe, however, knows the language of the fathers; she was weaned on it, and in *Uncle Tom's Cabin* the central debate on slavery is voiced through Stowe's miming of it. In 1850, Stowe anxiously hoped that her father, Lyman Beecher, would "preach on the Fugitive Slave Law, as he once preached on the slave-trade"; the style Stowe advocates in reference to her father's Litchfield sermon is free of "hair-splitting distinctions and dialectic subtleties" and emphasizes "direct, simple and tender language" (Stowe, *Life and Letters* 131, 50). As Stowe weaves the various rhetorics of the slavery debate, she mimes both the abolition and pro-slavery sides through a combination of her father's preaching styles.

Nowhere in *Uncle Tom's Cabin* is Stowe's capacity for miming patriarchal discourse more evident than in the debates between St. Clare and Ophelia, which highlight the ambiguity of logical discourse. The reader's sympathies alternate between the slaveholder who hates slavery, and the Northerner who is repulsed by it but also by the slaves themselves. When St. Clare sums up Ophelia's scorn for slavery's immorality as mere "sectional prejudices" (319), he deflates her (abolitionist?) zeal. In effect, her loathing of physical contact with slaves (255, 273) underscores the North's hypocrisy, its engagement with slavery on a theoretical level only. Stowe devotes a significant portion of the novel to Ophelia's and St. Clare's "debates," and the effect culminates in ambiguity, not clarity, which reflects how complex is the discourse of oppression. Stowe efficiently deflates Ophelia's Northern indignation and assumption of a moral high ground based solely on her lack of direct participation. She does so by giving full rein to St. Clare's theory of a correlation between morality and climate (330). St. Clare challenges Ophelia's contempt for slavery's abuses by exposing and deconstructing every "warp and bend" of the "language and ethics" used by politicians and clergy to justify oppression (331). Ophelia's mistake—and perhaps the reader's as well—is assuming that those who create the language of oppression actually believe in their chimera. St. Clare exposes her error; complicity derives only from the convenience of using others, not from fervent belief in the right to do so. With an "unconscious eagerness," St. Clare postulates the absurdity of the abolitionist argument against the "*abuses* of slavery," since the "*thing itself* is the essence of all abuse" (332). Throughout St. Clare's monologue, Ophelia is interrupted when she tries to comment, which she does only twice (333, 338). The "cold-blooded" (333) Northerner is at a rhetorical disadvantage; when St. Clare's exhortations end, Ophelia can only concede: "I never thought of the matter in this light" (341). These passages foreground the complexity of the slavery debate, adding to the myriad voices those of the Northerner who "wouldn't have" the "awful responsibility of slavery for a thousand worlds" (271) and the slaveholder who "hate[s] . . . the THING" (342). Through miming the arguments for and against slavery and even reversing their typical spokespersons—St. Clare hates but defends slavery, while by the end of the scene Ophelia seems to have capitulated—Stowe creates a rhetorical impasse, the result of "hairsplitting distinctions."

This section also reveals a problematic element of rhetoric, for Stowe creates a character motivated by feeling, while at the same time deconstructing the sentimental idea that feeling alone is somehow conclusive and rhetorically omnipotent. Therefore, in the conjunction of St. Clare and a "womanish sentimentalist" (342), one may detect Stowe's deflation of the most extreme claims made for sentiment. But neither is any extreme claim implied for St. Clare's shrewd rhetorical evasiveness. His reluctance "to define [his] position" on slavery does acquire power, especially in the context of his later exegesis on the corrupted language systems politicians and clergy formulate (331). However, his indeterminacy is grounded in cowardice; while he avowedly "lives by throwing stones at other people's glass houses," he adamantly refuses "to put up one for them to stone" (280). As earlier scenes that deflate logic through irony attest, the novel's rhetoric implies suspicion of all discourse, since, whether constructed for good or ill, discourse inherently poses the threat of objectification of the Other. In addition, St. Clare's "sarcastic curl of the lip" (262) recalls George's "bitter smile" (184), indicating that an ironic stance may be the rhetorical norm for confronting (absurdly) logical discourse. However, the two men differ significantly in their responses, for while St. Clare feels himself a victim of slavery, the only stance he can afford is a distanced and playful one because, as a member of the dominant culture, he is in a position to choose. His aesthetic distance form slavery's ugly abuses is glaringly exposed as the opposite (and equally pernicious) extreme of abuses—an immersion in paternal indulgence revealed in Adolph's pretenses (254, 256, 270, 321) and in Dinah's lack of personal responsibility and order within the kitchen (309–18). By exercising his freedom within a system that keeps others in a "dependent, semi-childish state" (318), St. Clare, in effect, silences their voices as effectively as does the viciously abusive slaveowner who destroys his "chattel" Prue.

But what of one's own inner voice? To the dialogue of marginalized and phallocentric voices, Stowe integrates the private voice of the masters to reveal yet another level to the complex social intercourse. Patriarchy's glimpses into the private voice are, however, often cursory or obscured through various types of self-deception. For example, St. Clare perpetuates the very fraud he sees through, even though he does not "defend" the institution, which he feels is not "quite right" (329). George Harris's "narrow-minded, tyrannical master" assuages an "uneasy consciousness of inferiority" (55) by restricting George's freedom. Once George is reduced to an object, the master can assume superiority and silence his inner voice. Mr. Shelby, like St. Clare, privately hates the ugliness of slavery, but Eliza's and Harry's escape casts aspersions on his "honor" (93). Further, he publicly chastises Sam for thwarting Haley's efforts to recapture his "property," even though Shelby "instinctively see[s] the true state of the case, through all attempts to affect the contrary" (135). Through such dissembling one avoids confrontation with the private voice, which is a form of encounter with the Other, and which accordingly threatens not only the institutions of society but the conventional definitions of self.

By far the dominant method for avoiding confrontation with private or Others' voices is immersion in language of the father. Shelby, Bird, and St. Clare all opt to "busy" themselves with newspapers—material documents of phallocentric reasoning—to evade or at least postpone confrontation (82, 145–46, 328). Mr. Bird's "whimsical mixture of amusement and vexation" (146) sums up the attitude of all these men who, as heirs to power, can afford to be amused and yet, as basically good-natured men, cannot fully reconcile the vexing contradictions of their positions. That newspapers will prove ultimately to be only desperate and ineffectual distractions from the private voices is exposed in Mr. Shelby's holding his paper "bottom upwards" (82). Haley brings to this preoccupation a more blatant but equally obsessive shift from the public rhetoric of newspapers to the private accounts wrought from the sacrifice of human beings. Following his unsettling encounter with John the drover, Haley takes refuge in "adding over his accounts,—a process which many gentlemen . . . have found a specific for an uneasy conscience" (202–3).

Silencing the Other is easier than quieting conscience, and often aids in the latter effort. By objectifying the Other, patriarchy can limit dialogic intercourse, "appropriating" the Other to patriarchy's "use and improvement" (341). Therefore, women are relegated to a utilitarian position as intercessors between men and God. Stowe's description of Mr. Shelby reveals the patriarchal delusion of redemption without participation. Shelby "seemed somehow or other to fancy that his wife had piety and benevolence enough for two—to indulge in a shadowy expectation of getting into heaven through her superabundance of qualities to which he made no particular pretension" (53). This vague, fanciful notion is echoed by St. Clare, who sends his womenfolk off to church with the hope that female "piety sheds respectability" on patriarchy (277). Even George Harris, himself objectified by patriarchy, assumes that Eliza's intercession through prayer will protect him from evil. Eliza's rebuttal—"O, pray yourself" (65)—is unanswered but reenforced in Stowe's final millennial warning to her audience.

Eliza's admonition foregrounds individual responsibility and dialogic participation with the Other. This admonition, however, falls on deaf ears as patriarchy forfeits the moral strength upon which its position should depend by constructing walls of "reason" or objectifying Others, often both. Throughout the novel, Stowe creates what Frances B. Cogan calls "weak fathers" ("Weak Fathers" 8) whose struggle with private/public voice renders them impotent and whose dependency on a phallocentric economy makes them incapable of change. Shelby's cry— "I can't help myself" (83)—foreshadows St. Clare's "habit" (329). Whatever the rationale—external circumstances or ennui—the result is the same: avoiding confrontation with the

Other. Confronted by his wife, Mr. Shelby can muster only "half-slumbering regrets"; he feels only "unpleasantness" in light of Tom's stoic bravery. It rests with Mrs. Shelby to face the pain her husband causes when, "pale and anxious" (167), she enters Tom's cabin and promises to keep "trace" of him, and when she speaks to Haley "in an earnest manner" about his treatment of Tom (168). Shelby, in contrast, flees from the outcome of the process he initiated to avoid the "unpleasant scenes of the consummation" (169). His inability even to bear witness to the real consequences of his actions heightens the irony of Shelby's impotence.

St. Clare carries the penchant for avoiding the Other to an extreme grounded in his failure to overcome romantic idealism (objectification) in relation with the women in his life. He marries not a woman but "a fine figure, a pair of bright dark eyes, and a hundred thousand dollars" (240), from which he retreats claiming "sick-headache as the cause of his distress" (242). Once his wife Marie delivers a new recipient for his affections, however, St. Clare's tendency for "sick-headaches" becomes Marie's passive-aggressive "principal forte" (243). The repetition of this significant complaint rhetorically connects St. Clare with the female characters even as it exposes more of the myriad devices that inhibit dialogue. It also sharply divides the characters who have the luxury of "romance and ideal" (241) in their lives (a solipsistic indulgence that undercuts dialogic interaction) from those for whom "the *real* remain[s]" (241) and who view reality in the particular, not in the abstract. The headache absolves those with power from responsibility for their actions; the slave with a headache, however, is viewed as nothing less than a fake, as was Mammy (263).

St. Clare's predilection for "the ideal and the aesthetic" (239) is intimately connected to his mother, while his ennui results from unresolved private/public conflict over her premature death. His rhapsodic memories of her emphasize the ideal even as they reveal the tension that estranges him from his mother as "living fact, to be accounted for." His reflections strengthen the ideal— "[S]he was *divine!* (333)—which objectifies her, thus barring dialogue. He segues from his mother's lesson on interaction with Others to a vitriolic harangue against virtue as "poor, mean trash" (338). These scenes deconstruct the value of romantic idealism. He does not "remember" the lesson; rather, he blames his mother for leaving him when "she might have stimulated [him] to . . . enthusiasm," might have inspired him to be a "saint, reformer, martyr" (338). This suggests Stowe's deflation of the maternal influence paradigm and implies a challenge to separate sphere ideology. St. Clare laments the loss of his mother for the influence she *might* have exerted over him, yet he is completely unmindful of the influence she *did* exert.

Rejecting his mother, St. Clare re-creates her in Eva. St. Clare's "absorbing devotion" to the daughter who bears his mother's name in the hope it "would prove a reproduction of [his mother's] image" (243) proves his attachment to the ideal. Descriptions of the mother and the child rhetorically strengthen this association. The mother was more "angel than mortal" (334); the child is "an evangel" (278) to St. Clare. The mother's "pale cheeks" and "white dress" link her to "the saints" in Revelation (334) and, ultimately, to Eva, who carries an aura of "glory" from the sun reflecting off her "white dress" and "golden hair" (401). Eva's appearance strikes St. Clare "suddenly and painfully," her "beauty so intense, yet so fragile, that we cannot bear to look at it" (401). The plural pronoun, of course, includes the reader in an awed response to the ethereal quality of the romantic ideal. "We" also includes the reader in the capacity to "think *much*, very much, in a moment" (404), prerequisite, Stowe suggests, to interaction. Earlier, Eva had pleaded with her father to "go all round and try to persuade people to do right" about slavery (403), just as the mother drew her son's attention to the painting of Jesus healing the blind man (338). However, an "evangel" apparently must rush in where men fear to tread, because upon the loss a second time of his romanticized ideal, St. Clare forfeits his promise to Eva by delaying his servants' emancipation.

While St. Clare's romantic code hinders his response to Others' voices, Simon Legree's rejection of the ideal demonstrates the violence of men who feel the threat of Others exposing their private voices. Legree rejects dialogue with the Other when he psychologically obliterates the mother. Legree's "day of grace," the moment when his mother's entreaties "almost persuaded" him to repent, is marked by "conflict" between public and private voices and ends with his "set[ting] all the forces of his rough nature against the conviction of his conscience" (528). Such rejection creates the hellish atmosphere in which interaction exists on a brute level only. The polyphony of diverse voices in dialogue becomes a cacophony of barking, "ferocious-looking dogs" (492) and drunken "singing, whooping" (531). Legree's attempt to "drink, and revel, and swear away" the mother's "memory" (529) is a futile effort to silence the Other.

Equally futile is his attempt to diminish the Other by assigning derogatory labels—"she-devil," "minx," and "hag" (522, 566, 570)—and by erecting constructions of insanity around the Other. Stowe deflates these constructs in the narrative assessment that they are valid only to "coarse and uninstructed minds" (526). More subtle is their subversion in Legree's own unselfconscious attachment to his slave mistress Cassy, the "substitute" for the mother he has "killed" (Irigaray, "Women-Mothers" 49). As a result, he is "uneasy" about Cassy's "influence," from which he could not "free himself" (526) as he had from his mother's influence, because in the process of making Cassy an "object," he ignored the "subject," who learned and used against him the vulnerable "string[s]" that she could "vibrate" (537). Through her reading and manipulating one of these strings, Legree's superstition, Cassy executes her "*coup d'etat*" (571), slowly driving him insane with carefully planted suggestions of the garret's being haunted by a slave woman who was tortured to death there (564–71). Cassy taps the source of her oppression, manipulating Legree's "superstitious excitability" to secure her "liberation" (565). Therefore, although "all her words and language" possess a "strange, weird, unsettled cast," she becomes "in a measure his mistress" (567). Cassy speaks to Legree with an "imperative tone" (494), "scorn," "bitterest contempt" (526), "hissing" whispers (525), but that which remains unspoken poses the greatest threat. The bitter pain beyond language—the "word of choking feelings in her heart"—keeps her "silent" (526). Suggestion and pantomime with the "mother's shroud" gain Cassy her freedom and destroy Legree, whose own private horrors related to his mother will not be silenced, despite his precautions, so the mere sight of "ghostly garments" and the touch of a "cold hand" prostrate him, ironically, in the conventional heroine's posture— "a swoon" (596).

Cassy deliberately crosses over into silence, the condition to which dominant discourse wants to relegate the Other, to mime Legree's superstitions and to silence him. Throughout the novel, Others' silences represent genuine voices that harbor undercurrents of rebellion. For example, when Legree tells Tom, "*I'm* your church now! . . . you've got to be as *I* say," Stowe creates an "invisible voice," "something within" Tom that answered "No" (482). In characters' silences we find brooding, nascent thoughts, preludes to action, and signifiers of rebellious voices, as with George Harris (56), with Cassy (526), and even with Chloe (93).

The final battle between Legree and Tom most dramatically illustrates this power. The battle is waged over language—specifically, the power over what can be spoken, and when. Legree, who was quick enough to demand Tom's silence when the latter sang a hymn (489), now demands Tom's speech to betray Cassy and Emmeline (582). Stowe elevates Tom and his silence, reducing the controller of language to "an incensed lion" (582), "foaming with rage" (583). Although Legree carries out his threat to "count every drop of [Tom's] blood" (582), he is thwarted in his victory by the narrator's allusions to Christ's "torture, degradation and shame" (582), which clearly valorize Tom while degrading Legree to the level of a truly "miserable critter" whom Tom "forgive[s] . . . with all [his] soul" (584). For Legree, this is the final blow, slave forgiving master, just as Legree's mother, at her death, forgave him (529). And as he tried to silence her, so he delivers a fatal blow to Tom. The structural reversal of beast/human clearly shows the power of silence. Before the scene's end, yet another reversal foregrounds Tom's assertion of choice; when Legree claims victory over silencing Tom, the victory is cut short by Tom being "roused" enough by Sambo's and Quimbo's sympathy to "pour forth a few energetic sentences" on redemption (584, 585).

While all Others' voices are silenced by the end of the novel, it is important here to distinguish a *chosen* silence from that imposed by the dominant culture. If to live is to be denied self, to be continually objectified, to be stripped of free will (as is Tom's case), then choosing resistance is to assert self through silence/death, to assume a measure of control, to deny compromise with the oppressor. More important, though Tom and Eva are silent, accepting death does not end dialogue; rather, death may be seen as a narrative strategy that "force[s] others to read one's death" (Higonnet 68). This is borne out by the powerful "Tokens"—the "long, shining curl of fair hair" and the "silver dollar" (527)—symbols of Legree's past and present that initiate a chain of events that render Legree quite mad. The "golden tress," the narrator warns Legree, "was charmed," possessing "a

spell of terror and remorse" to "bind [his] cruel hands from inflicting uttermost evil on the helpless" (531). In addition, George
Shelby's preservation of "UNCLE TOM'S CABIN" continues dialogue
with the Other, as he instructs all those who view the "memorial"
to be reminded "to follow in his steps" (617). "All silence,"
according to Adrienne Rich, "has meaning" (308), and in the
novel, dialogic interaction begins with the ability to read silences
and to interpret Others' language.

Progressing beyond mere words is the key to understanding
the silent language of "elsewhere." Tacit understanding leads to
the formation of impromptu "communities" that share—if only
for a time—Otherness. Such unions—Sam, Andy, and Mrs.
Shelby; Cassy and Emmeline; Ophelia and Topsy—like Topsy,
just "grow'd" (356), contrasting sharply to patriarchal networks
that construct often elaborate and rigid codes to define existence
and exclude Others. While Eva and Tom draw Others to them by
preaching, the initial and lasting impact lies on the symbolic
level. Although Eva is conjoined with "an especial band of angels" who "sojourn for a season" on earth (383), Tom is very
much of the earth, "large, broad-chested, powerfully made" but
"self-respecting and dignified" (68). Stowe describes Eva as a
"sunbeam or summer breeze," a "mythic and allegorical being"
(230), who "glide[s]," "flies," "like a shadow" with "fairy footsteps" and a "cloud-like tread" (231). Tom, on the other hand,
treads among the "sullen, scowling, imbruted men, and feeble,
discouraged women," rests on a "heap of straw, foul with dirt,"
and endures the lashes and overwork comparable to "the worst
torture of the inquisition" (494–95, 539–40). To both, however,
come master and slave, virtuous and corrupt, naive and cynical—all equal in their presence. Their deaths mark the unresolved quality of dialogue, since the survivors carry their message
into the larger world. Stowe attributes to Eva's death "the victory
without the battle, —the crown without the conflict" (429). But
Tom's saga continues to dramatize the "conflict"; just as after his
death Others continue the struggle, spurred on by his memory.
The "victory," therefore, does not signify closure because the
interplay of myriad voices is ongoing.

Thematically the novel is closed, as all surviving characters
reunite fortuitously. George Shelby intercedes (and thus rejects
his father's inheritance) to initiate the reunion of characters
uprooted by patriarchy's actions (603). Although Topsy and the

Harrises are expatriated, dialogue is not aborted. Stowe has not raised myriad voices only to return to silence. The suggestion of continued dialogue beyond the text lies in her emphasis on the characters' free choice to determine the course of their lives (610, 612). Thematically, they are silenced, but the possibility of "the world yet hear[ing] from" (612) George Harris—the only character who espoused violence—remains and projects his voice beyond America's shores.

The Shelbys frame the novel and dramatize both the erection and the deconstruction of barriers to dialogic interaction. If the novel ended with George Shelby doing "what one man can" to end oppression, the resolution of motherly influence on sons would be intact; George would have the final word. That he does not, however, strengthens the impression that dialogue continues and adds a final, authoritative voice to the chorus of Others'. The section "Concluding Remarks" continues the "sympathetic influence" (624), while the rhetoric conjoins sentiment with threats. Stowe mimes the jeremiad rhetoric of the fathers (Tompkins, *Sensational Designs* 139–41; Bercovich 9), taking as her "text" examples of the "living dramatic reality" (622) and converting the "application" to sentimental feeling (624). While she does exhort the "mothers of America" to inculcate proper feeling in their sons (623, 624), it is to all Americans—North and South, male and female, privileged and underprivileged—that Stowe directs her warnings against the "sophistries of worldly policy" (624). In the jeremiad tradition, Stowe conjures images of "a mournful spectacle" at which "the country will have reason to tremble" (625). Stowe depicts the millennial *"dies irae"* that St. Clare foretold (344) as imminent fact, evinced by all nations "trembling and convulsed," not just America but the whole world "surging and heaving . . . , as with an earthquake" under a "mighty influence" (629). Should her audience delay "repentance, justice and mercy," as surely as "the millstone sinks in the ocean," all nations shall experience "the wrath of Almighty God" (629). Stowe assumes the authority of patriarchal ministers in her mastery of the rhetoric, even as her inclusion of sentimental rhetoric adds an Other voice.

This section's authority derives from Stowe's emphasis on documented evidence to support her appeal for emancipation (627–28). Her evidence is grounded in the everyday world, with which she was familiar, whether directly or indirectly. Stowe's quoting here letters she had actually received is balanced with biblical citation. The secular "text" precedes the scriptural, which illustrates the dangers of not heeding the former. As evidence of African Americans' capabilities, "even without any particular assistance or encouragement" (627), the letters assuage readers' fears of emancipation. The biblical citation clearly shows that failure to emancipate is the true source of fear, because God will "appear as swift witness against those that . . . *turn aside the stranger*" (629). Combining real documents with sentimental rhetoric in the sermon, Stowe weaves texts, an act that—as in the blending of voices—resists the word of the fathers and its attendant objectification of the Other. Including the very secular voices of the "stranger[s]" with the voice of God, Stowe ends where she began—with the polyphony of voices, making a space for the inclusion of the Other in the dialogue.

## N O T E S

The epigraph is from *"Coming to Writing"* 4.

1. Stowe, *Uncle Tom's Cabin* (1986) 192. All subsequent quotations from the novel are from this edition, cited by page number in the text.

# 3

.

JAN PILDITCH

# Rhetoric and Satire

The abolitionist literature of the nineteenth century was intended to persuade readers against the institution of slavery, and *Uncle Tom's Cabin* was no exception. Harriet Beecher Stowe was the "little woman" who started a war, or, as Ann Douglas remarks in her introduction to the novel: "No woman before or since Stowe has so successfully written a novel designed to stir up the nation in the cause of the major issue of the day."[1] The providential plot of *Uncle Tom's Cabin,* the sermonizing, the sentimental strategies at work within the text all function to serve this end. A focus on the rhetorical strategy of the work, however, can discover another aspect of the language's persuasiveness. Such a focus reveals that in addition to Stowe's sermonizing and sentiment a sustained satiric activity is at work within the text. This has received relatively little attention from critics, eager to validate the more "female" sentimental texture of the novel. For instance, Jane Tomkins ("Sentimental Power" 104) argues for a reassessment of the sentiment in *Uncle Tom's Cabin* and suggests that Stowe in this novel reconceives the role of men in human history by relocating the center of power in American life from government to kitchen. Preaching and satire were forms suited to the reputable "male" genres of the nineteenth century dealing with abstract, political, and social truths. Satire, especially, was a difficult literary mode for a nineteenth-century woman beset with notions of gentility to embrace.

Tidy linguistic sexual polarities, however, are not always confirmed by practice, and the language of the sexes cannot be categorized in any simple schematic way. The wit, humor, and logic with which Stowe conducted her attack on slavery belies the widespread general impression of her as intuitively a protofeminist or sentimental lady novelist. The strength of feeling she was able to evoke in relation to the slave system is undeniable, but modes of discourse are often learned, and disclosing the strategy of any text requires attention to traditional models. A focus on the wit, humor, and logic of *Uncle Tom's Cabin* yields some significant feminist value. It suggests that Stowe appropriated sermonic and satiric modes in ways that broke down the traditional polarity between man as speaker and woman as mute.

Stowe's home life was, of course, imbued with the rhetoric of preaching, and the broader intellectual culture in which she lived was steeped in the rhetoric of the great Augustan satirists who had formed the contemporary model for many earlier American writers. Nor was the association of satire and preaching in American literature uncommon. The American Puritans, like their British counterparts, had rendered their satires acceptable to their religion by taking to heart John Milton's notion that laughter "hath oft-times a strong and sinewy force in teaching and confuting" (Weber 1). They wrote their satires not merely to entertain, but, in the service of their God, to bring an erring flock back into his fold.[2] In America this often entailed subverting the structure and language of the Puritan jeremiad to satiric purposes. The traditional naive narrator of European satires was inclined, in American satires, to take on many of the hallmarks of a visible saint. During the course of the Revolutionary War, and certainly by the latter part of the eighteenth century, the preacherly aspects of Puritan satire had grown to incorporate service to the new Republic. For example, Francis Hopkinson wrote to Franklin in 1778, during the War of Independence, that he wanted to do "all the Service [he] could with [his] pen— throwing in [his] Mite at Times in Prose and Verse, serious and satirical essays, etc." (Pickering, 167–69). Satire was used as another means of keeping America free from Old World corruption, and in *The Power of Sympathy* (William Brown, 1789) the character Reverend Worthy remarks that satire is one way of preaching. It is, he says, "the correction of the vices and follies of the human heart. A woman may, therefore, read it to advantage" (Hart 23). The American satirists of the early Republic made a tacit equation between their duties and those of the preacher, similarly urging their readers toward spiritual perfection (Roth), although women were more often the passive recipients, the subjects and objects of the sermons and satires, than their creators, as the Reverend Worthy's remarks testify.

Yet in terms of Stowe's motivation for the writing of *Uncle Tom's Cabin*, ideas similar to those of earlier American satirists, of the service and utility of art, can be detected. The letter, for instance, that Stowe received from her sister-in-law after the passage of the Fugitive Slave Law in 1850 urges her to write because: "Hattie, . . . if I could use a pen as you can, I would write something that will make this whole nation feel what an accursed thing slavery is" (Forrest 252). Stowe's decision to take up her pen in the cause of slavery, her entry into didactic and satiric modes of discourse, ran counter to the overtly feminized and, in the nineteenth century, underrated personal and "subjective" genres of her contemporaries. It moved her toward those "objective" genres of the nineteenth century that dealt with political, social, and abstract truths.

That Stowe appropriated either didactic or satiric forms of literary authority, however, cannot be taken for granted. Her famous claim that the plot for *Uncle Tom's Cabin* came to her in a vision, and that she began to write under "God's influence" (Douglas, "Introduction" 8), exploits the most pervasive argument offered by women in the nineteenth century who wanted to preach: they had received a call from the Lord, and their authority was, therefore, not their own, but Holy Spirit's.[3] Such claims neatly relegated responsibility, while simultaneously challenging male authority by their appeal to a higher one. As a Christian woman, and in common with many others, Stowe determined to speak against slavery; but as a nineteenth-century American woman, she did not easily assume the authority to do so. For a woman, to preach or even to comment publicly on any matter was to court social ostracism. For a woman to satirize was even more hazardous. Humor is aggressive, and satire especially so. It requires from its purveyors a position of superiority that is acquired only with difficulty by women accustomed to positions of inferiority. It is also rude to make fun of people, and Stowe herself cautions against the potential unladylike unmannerliness of the form. She comments on this in an early letter of 1832 when referring to a piece, written in the style of Dr. Johnson, that she was about to present at a local literary society: "I have been stilting about in his style so long that it is a relief to me to come down to the joy of common English" (*Life and Letters* 181).

Thus, in common with many earlier American writers, Stowe seems to have experimented with the satiric mode. (One thinks of Franklin teaching himself to emulate the style of Addison, the Revolutionary writers appropriating the style of Swift and Pope, of Irving writing in the manner of Sterne.) Unlike her male predecessors and colleagues, however, Stowe appears to feel that the mode may be unseemly for a woman. "My second [piece was] a satirical essay on the modern uses of language . . . some of the gentlemen requested leave to put it in the 'Western Magazine' and so it is in print. It is ascribed to Catherine or I don't know that I should have let it go. I have no notion of appearing in propria persona . . . I try not to be personal, and to be courteous even in satire" (*Life and Letters* 83). The use of a satiric mask or persona is of course a common device of the satirist, and Stowe's wish "not to be personal" can be said to be in accord with Dryden's traditional advice to "lash the vice but spare the man."

What, however, of the wish to be "courteous even in satire"? Stowe had in fact written a satire on certain members of the club who had fallen into the habit of joking about "the worn out subjects of matrimony and old maid and old bachelorism" (*Life and Letters* 83). She had avoided particularity by generalizing the vice and writing her satire as a set of rules, as if from the ladies of the society, that forbade all such allusions in future. The fear of discourtesy voiced in her letter suggests that she was constrained in this literary endeavor by nineteenth-century notions of gentility. Stowe's letter goes on to discuss the possibility of writing a set of letters using a satiric persona, but the project is abandoned. Her cousin Elizabeth felt it would be criticized unmercifully. "I am unused to being criticised," Stowe writes, "and don't know how I shall bear it" (*Life and Letters* 83).

The gentlewoman's sensitivity to the giving and receiving of offense surfaces again following the publication of *Uncle Tom's Cabin* in a letter from Stowe to Lord Shaftesbury, the British philanthropist and activist on behalf of Britain's poor. "It was my hope," she writes, "that a book so kindly intended . . . might be permitted free circulation among the [Southerners] . . . that the gentle voice of Eva . . . might be allowed to say those things of the system which would be invidious in any other form" (Wagenknecht 181). In this letter, however, one senses some shift in tone from that of the young girl of twenty-one who was prepared to abandon a literary mode she found attractive in order to avoid criticism. The honest uncertainty of the earlier letter is replaced in this one by a note of reprimand for the book's critics: kind intentions have been spurned and reasonable hopes dashed. There is also, in this later letter, a less-than-honest emphasis given to the critics' rejection of the "gentle voice of Eva." *Uncle Tom's Cabin* does, after all, contain a considerable amount of preaching, which goes unmentioned in her letter; and the sustained satiric attack at work within the text, which occurs at the expense of ministers, senators, slave owners, and slave dealers, among others, is hardly conducted in the "gentle voice of Eva."

Even the qualified modesty of Stowe's posture toward Shaftesbury is undermined by her own demonstrable capacity to think strategically on the subject of rhetorical attack, satiric or otherwise. In *Uncle Sam's Emancipation*, published in 1853, she wrote: "The great error of controversy is, that it is ever ready to assail persons rather than principles. . . . If the system alone is attacked, such minds [enlightened, generous, and amenable to reason] will be the first to perceive its evils, and to turn against it" (182). If the system is attacked through individuals, Stowe goes on, "a thousand natural feelings, will be at once enlisted for its preservation." Stowe was quite tactical about method of attack and particularly aware of the point at which certain rhetorical strategies can become counterproductive. Given, then, that satire and sentiment occurring within the same novel is hardly unusual in the nineteenth century, as even a cursory reading of Dickens can testify, Stowe's reliance on the "gentle voice of Eva" in her letter to Lord Shaftesbury would seem to signify not so much a genuine intent as an anxious unspoken recognition of trespass on a male preserve.

Satire, like the sermon, is a literature of authority, and nineteenth-century American women did not have easy access to such authority. For the preacher, the often cited Protestant Doctrine of Accommodation "implied that the Divine Author was employing the writer in His service" and empowered him in the role of a hyperprivileged, Christlike mediator between God and his congregation.[4] His authority, like Christ's, was divine and male. Numerous theological and social arguments were put forward in the nineteenth century to ensure that this remained so. The satirist, writing in the secular sphere, mediates between the real and the ideal. In place of the preacher's divine inspiration the satirist must exhibit a "monolithic certainty" to create, via rhetoric, an appearance of authority.[5] Ultimately, authority is endowed by society's tacit acceptance of the values promoted. Thus satire even more than other genres is heavily dependent for its success on reference to, and interaction with, contemporary life, with which the satirist is usually at odds.

Satire exposes hypocrisy by pointing to society's failure to live up to its own publicly espoused values. For a woman to adopt this authoritative stance means that she must, as Nancy Walker has suggested, "break out of the passive, subordinate position mandated for [her] by centuries of patriarchal tradition and take on the power accruing to those who reveal the shams, hypocrisies, and incongruities of the dominant culture" (9). As Stowe had realized as early as 1832, entry into this mode of discourse rendered one eligible for, and vulnerable to, the counterattack. Her rhetorical strategy in *Uncle Tom's Cabin* is, therefore, complex and ranging in tone, intensity, and posture.

Stowe is, for instance, demonstrably ambivalent toward the superiority associated with the classical persona of the "man of letters" adopted by the Augustan satirists. In chapter 11 of the novel she conducts a mild Horatian attack on the Kentuckians who sit with their muddy shoes on the mantelpiece of a tavern, "a position decidedly favourable to the turn of reflection incident to western taverns, where travellers exhibit a decided preference for this particular mode of elevating their understandings" (175). At this point Stowe aligns her authorial stance, as did many Augustan satirists, with that of the "men of letters." Via the authority of her superior knowledge she satirizes the men of no letters. The subsequent exposition of Kentuckian character, as evinced by the wearing of their hats, concludes with the ironic observation that the hats were in fact "quite a Shakespearean study." The persona sits uneasily, however. Stowe, after all, was not writing against mere ignorance and provincialism, but against slavery, and was doing so in a democracy where an elitist stance, like the giving of offense, could be less than persuasive. Further, to align her satiric persona with "the men of letters" would have been to align it with the very power structure under attack.

More commonly, then, in *Uncle Tom's Cabin*, it is the "men of letters" who are themselves satirized, usually for a failure to act, or to simply believe. Even if Cicero, as an erudite Roman "man of letters," had had the Bible, "he must first fill his head with a thousand questions of authenticity of manuscript, and correctness of translation" (229). With this stance Stowe taps into the true root of American satire and her own cultural milieu. Here the authorial stance is anti-elitist and asserts a value, an act of simple faith, to which the least educated of readers might aspire. That the "men of letters" and those like them within the text, most notably the aristocratic Southerner St. Clare, are demonstrably incapable of such simplicity becomes the subject of derision and censure. It is a stance befitting a nineteenth-century democratic and Christian America, and its anti-elitism is not uncommon, but whereas male-perpetrated American satire of this type is replete with braggarts, Stowe quietly uses the superior position of the satirist to champion the victims of cultural expectations and does so by reference to a religious normative value. Despite her Christian ideals, however, Stowe could not simply emulate the Augustan satires of an Alexander Pope in order to attack the institution of slavery.

The conceptual conventions of a given society are, as Northrop Frye says, "largely invented by dead cranks" (226). For Pope, regardless of earthly circumstance, "to reason right [was] to submit" (1.157–64). This meant, of course, submission to an absolute God whose absolute virtues become, in Pope's work, the measure of humanity's feeble reasoning and pride. The normative value of his satires is both greater than and external to the self, so that submission becomes not only desirable but, given the infinite power of God, also inevitable. Life, unless it be eternal life, is not an issue. Stowe was confronting the evils of slavery in a society where, on the contrary, life, liberty, and the pursuit of happiness were considered by most to be inalienable rights. In her text any belief in submission to a divine and absolute plan is constantly undercut by the vividly depicted realities of the slave system. The specter of Nat Turner haunts her text; in the figure of George, in the stories of women who will die rather than live without their children, and in Tom's advice to Cassy, who has already murdered one child rather than let it fall into slavery: "It's different with you; it's a snare to you,—it's more'n you can stand,—and you'd better go, if you can" (562).

Further, Stowe and her society were steeped in nineteenth-century postmillennialist thought. It was the saving of souls, voluntarism, and the use of "means," it was thought, that would usher in the bright new Jerusalem. An end to the "peculiar institution" of slavery required action, not submission, and yet, it must be said, at the center of Stowe's text lies a submissiveness embodied in the character of Uncle Tom to which Pope himself would have subscribed. This has created considerable debate, and Tom's submissiveness has seemed to many incongruous and even objectionable, particularly when measured against the tenets of realism, political or social, rather than in terms of a Christian ideal. To perceive the character of Tom in terms of the satiric impulse of the text, however, is to view his submissiveness in terms of that ideal, and his humanity in terms of an accommodation. Seen in this way, his character becomes a Christlike mediation between real and ideal and can be recognized as an important part of Stowe's rhetorical strategy and of her appropriation of literary authority.

Ann Douglas, among others, has remarked, in defense of Stowe's portrayal of Tom: "If 'Uncle' Tom is asexual, he is so only in the way St. Paul chose to be and urged others to be" ("Introduction" 27). That is to say that Stowe separates him from his family at the beginning of the text to ensure that his first concern is always for God and salvation. Stowe nevertheless emphasizes Tom's humanity. He is described as a "large broad-chested, powerfully-made man" and is not incapable of action, as his later rescue of little Eva demonstrates. Yet when he is introduced as our hero early in the text, he is described in neither heroic nor romantic terms but in terms of morality and religion. "His truly African features were characterized by an expression of grave and steady good sense, united with much kindness and benevolence . . . his whole air was self-respecting and dignified, yet united with a confiding and humble simplicity" (68). This carefully balanced description serves to introduce the reader to the true "man of humanity" who was promised but not delivered by the ironic title to chapter 1. Tom is not merely human, however. He is marked early in the text as a type of visible saint, after the manner of the New England Puritans. In addition to his good character he is, for his community, "a sort of patriarch in religious matters . . . looked up to with great respect as a sort of minister" with a special excellence in prayer.

Indeed, so clearly did Stowe designate Tom as an exemplar or type that one dumbfounded contemporary reviewer was driven to remark in the London *Times* of September 3, 1852: "If Mrs Stowe's portraiture is correct, and if Uncle Tom is a type of a class, we deliberately assert that we have nothing more to communicate to the negro, but everything to learn from his profession and practice" (5). Stowe's signification of Tom as "a type of a class" of human ideal was not only revolutionary thinking for the nineteenth century in terms of race but placed within the text a referent necessary for satire. Tom's human aspects accommodate Pope's absolute terms, and in marking Tom a visible saint Stowe creates the satiric normative value. It is one her society would recognize as a divine ideal, and one to which, as American Christians, they must assent.

The structural function of Tom's character as a referent for satire is made apparent at the prayer meeting held in his simple log cabin. The very premise is evocative of America's founders, and Tom's prayer, "enriched with the language of Scripture, which seemed so entirely to have wrought itself into his being as to become part of himself, and to drop from his lips unconsciously" (79), is in marked contrast to the prayers of the actual ministers depicted in the text. Their prayers are compared not with Tom's, but with George's reading of Revelation. (George, who was a bright boy, "finding himself the object of general admiration, threw in expositions of his own from time to time" (79) to the general admiration of his unlettered congregation.) "It was agreed on all hands that a minister couldn't lay it off better than he did"; that it was "reely 'mazin'!" (79). The comparison is of course hardly complimentary and satirically might justly be said to fall into the category of what Dryden would have called a "transitory lashing." That feeling of unease associated with all satire is created by the comparison the reader is driven to make between the true preacher, Tom, and those ministers who would gain their authority by mystifying exegesis of the Scriptures. They are shown to be ingenuous and implicitly vainglorious by a woman writer claiming the autonomy and power of the satirist. In this way Stowe risked alienating the patriarchal power base of her society, and those upon whom women and slaves alike were dependent for their freedom.

Stowe's appropriation of satiric authority is, therefore, covert. Tom is created as a kind of quasi-seculiar, neo-Puritan "type," and the use of "types" in Puritan literature was a commonplace. It was essential to the Doctrine of Accommodation. Puritan narratives were developed as statements about the elect Christian's journey through earthly life: "Abraham became more than an Old Testament hero; he is a type of Christian pilgrim, an individual selected by God for the fulfillment of a predetermined Divine purpose" (Lowance, "Religion" 39). Tom is signified to be just such an individual. When the scene shifts from that of Tom's visible sainthood to the material matter of his sale, it is, says Mrs. Shelby, "God's curse on slavery" (84). These words set in motion a Providential plot line whereby Tom is marked as God's own, and all human efforts to save him are doomed to failure. Mr. Shelby will not listen to his wife and never earns enough money to buy Tom back; the best womanly efforts of Chloe and Mrs. Shelby fail; even the life and death of Eva fail to secure his deliverance. St. Clare intends to set Tom free but is undone by his own philosophically indecisive nature and is murdered without having done so. Ultimately the curse is visited on the children, as the now grown Master George arrives too late. The systematic debasement of Tom, as one of the elect, by his owner, in the final chapters, and its clear signification that God's curse had been cast on an unredeemed America, ensured that Christian readers could never "feel right" about the "peculiar institution" of slavery.

It is in the creation of this kind of unease that the curse has been associated with satire.[6] That is, it is the use of the power of the word to initiate action in the real world. In *Uncle Tom's Cabin* Stowe's revelation of God's curse becomes associated with her satire, and, if God has cursed, can it behoove a Christian woman to do less? By taking her argument from the secular and political sphere and into the realm of the spiritual Stowe effectively grounds the authority for her satire, like that of the women preachers of her day, in the work of the Holy Spirit.

Stowe reinforces the Divine authority for her satire throughout *Uncle Tom's Cabin*. Mrs. Shelby establishes, early in the text, that slavery is "a deadly evil. It is a sin to hold a slave under laws like ours" (84). The eschatological view of American history is constantly emphasized in the text via a vast array of scriptural imagery, parallels, quotations, sermons, and preaching. Eliza's river crossing is both actual and symbolic, and Eva and Tom, sharing a simplicity of faith, feel just alike about the Scriptures.

All they knew was, that they [Revelation and prophesies] spoke of a glory to be revealed, —a wonderous something yet to come, wherein their soul rejoiced, yet knew not why; and though it be not so in the physical, yet in moral science that which cannot be understood is not always profitless. For the soul awakes between two dim eternities, — the eternal past, the eternal future. (380)

The reader is always aware of what is at stake. It is America's special status as the nation marked for the coming millennium. It is eternal life and the death not only of bodies, but of souls. In these terms those who would support the institution of slavery become both sinful and stupid—fit targets for satire. Thus Stowe can add to her imprecatory inveighing against the wicked soullessness of slavery countless satiric thrusts at its obtuse materialism: " 'Now' said the young man, stooping gravely over his book of bills, 'If you can assure me that I really can buy this kind of pious, and that it will be set down to my account in the book up above, as something belonging to me. I wouldn't care if I did go a little extra for it' " (237). The conversation is ridiculous. The trader's hypocrisy is further highlighted by constant appeals to Tom's good conscience. After one such exhortation Stowe underlines the irony: "Tom assured Haley that he had no present intention of running off. In fact the exhortation seemed rather a superfluous one to a man with a great pair of iron fetters on his feet" (174).

The business of chattel slavery, which bought and sold humanity like animals, demanded a world without God or conscience. Haley, however, could do without neither. Nor can the reader, for the issues are clear-cut. To fail to align oneself with the Christian ideal of the satirist is to align oneself with the illogical folly and evil of a slave trader who is putting at risk his temporal dignity and his eternal life.

Stowe's capacity to evoke the Christian ideal is such that the language of the text acquires polyvalency in which the real and the ideal images of America are often conflated. In this way the language of the text can be charged, at any moment, to create an unavoidable feeling of unease. In one of the most powerful satiric attacks in the book Stowe depicts a materialism so gross as to render value all but defunct, and yet she ensures that its opposite is simultaneously present. In this attack on slave traders and catchers, satiric inversion is recognizable in the opening remarks: " 'By the land! if this yer an't the nearest, now to what

I've heard folks call Providence,' said Haley. 'I do b'lieve that ar's Tom Loker' " (122).

In slave trader Tom Loker, however, "brutal and unhesitating violence was in a state of the highest possible development." In true satiric form the metaphors and images of the episodes are drawn from the lowest possible sources. The slave traders are "cat-like," with a "peering mousing expression." Marks has a hand "like a raven's claw," and Tom Loker's status as a satanic type is confirmed for readers familiar with the Book of Revelation by a look "as affable as was consistent, as John Bunyan says, 'with his doggish nature.'" In keeping with the plot of satire, whose effect is to widen the gap between perceived and actual achievement (Kernan), the reader is pressed on every side by the brutal and animalistic, and the movement of the section is relentlessly downward. There is a parodic sermon preached on the text "This yer young-un business makes lots of trouble in the trade." Haley and Marks provide the examples, but it is left to Tom Loker to expound on what is to be done.

> "Help it? why, I buys a gal, and if she's got a young un to be sold, I jest walks up and puts my fist to her face, and says, "Look here, now, if you give me one word out of your head, I'll smash yer face in. . . ."
> Mr. Loker brought down his fist with a thump that fully explained the hiatus.
> "That ar's what ye may call emphasis," said Marks, poking Haley in the side and going into another small giggle. (125)

When it is remarked that if Tom Loker "ain't the devil" he is his twin brother, the reader is both enlightened and repelled. The later discussion of redemption and Haley's testimony—"I believe in religion"—become obscenities, and Stowe's prophecy of an unredeemed America continues to appall as she retains her satiric authority addressing the reader, now in what seems a travesty of the usual sentimental lady novelist's aside. In direct reference to the Fugitive Slave Law that stimulated the production of her novel at least as much as God did, she begs the

> refined and Christian readers . . . to begin to conquer their prejudices in time . . . the catching business . . . is rising to the dignity of a lawful and patriotic profession. If all the broad land between the Mississippi and the Pacific becomes one great market for bodies and souls, and human property retains the locomotive tendencies of this nineteenth century, the trader and the catcher may yet be found among our aristocracy. (132)

The subversion of religious language to the purposes of satire is not unusual in American literature, but it is seldom—and seldom more unexpectedly—accomplished so deftly.[7]

The rhetorical strategy of *Uncle Tom's Cabin*, then, would appear to consist of two complementary thrusts, both akin to those of the Doctrine of Accommodation, "the one bringing truth down to earth, and the other gradually raising the earthly mind to heaven" (Lowance, "Religion" 41). Stowe's satire, conducted by a woman, targets for the most part the white male patriarchal power base of her society. As with most satire, its effect is reductive. It·diminishes those with power in society to the status of immature boys and animals, truly bringing the truth down to earth. Thus Mr. Shelby appears petulant in the face of his wife's logic. "I don't know why I am to be rated, as if I were a monster, for doing what everyone does every day" (82). That everyone is doing it is a feeble excuse for any action, and senators, entrusted with state legislation, are shown to be little better. Sam is able to discuss the matter of Eliza's escape "profoundly in all its phrases and bearing, with a comprehensiveness of vision and a strict lookout to his own personal well-being that would have done credit to any white patriot in Washington" (96), while Mr. Bird,

> [h]ow sublimely he had sat with his hands in his pockets, and scouted all sentimental weakness of those who would put the welfare of a few miserable fugitives before the great state interests. He was as bold as a lion about it, and "mightily convinced" not only himself, but everybody that heard him:—but then his idea of a fugitive was only an idea of the letters that spell the word. (155)

The senator is that worst of fools, the self-deceiver, and dangerous in that his empty rhetoric has the capacity to convince others. Then, as Bakhtin has demonstrated, if the king can be shown to be a fool, a possibility is opened that the fool could be a king. By reducing those with power in her society to the level of fools and worse, Stowe's satire simultaneously privileges the sentimental discourse of the text, the thrust of which is upward, toward heaven. In this way those afflicted with "sentimental weakness"—the women and children of the text, but in particular Uncle Tom—appear not only more moral, tender, and humane, but more intelligent. Their discourse is privileged by knowledge and experience. The senators, who, unlike the women and slaves, have both political voice and the power to act

69

in society, sit with their hands in their pockets, another immature attitude, sublimely mouthing platitudes on subjects about which they know nothing.

Reducing those with power in nineteenth-century society to the status of small boys rendered them more susceptible to the influence of women, so that Stowe's appropriation of the predominantly male authority of the satirist serves a recognizable feminist end. She does not, within the text, appear to envisage women acting entirely on their own behalf, but by attacking the power base of her society, she had stepped well and truly beyond her proper sphere. The counterattack, conducted largely on the basis of her unladylike conduct, serves only to confirm her success. George F. Holmes was right in his 1852 review to associate her with Thalestris of Billingsgate, "hurling unwomanly oaths and unwomanly blows at whom she chooses to assail," and if his metaphor of the "critical lash" proves rather less "interesting" (cited on 14) when removed from the discourse of feminist criticism and put into the discourse of satire where it is commonplace, this is no real loss. To restore *Uncle Tom's Cabin* to its true vitality and vigor we might proceed from a nonessentialist base and agree with Holmes. There is something decidedly unladylike about conducting a satiric attack from behind the petticoats of a sentimental novelist.

## N O T E S

1. Stowe, *Uncle Tom's Cabin* (1981), 13. All subsequent quotations from the novel are from this edition, cited by page number in the text.

2. For a full discussion of Puritan satire, see Aldern.

3. For a full discussion of women and preaching in America, see Ruether and Keller.

4. I am indebted for my discussion of the Puritan Doctrine of Accommodation to Mason I. Lowance, Jr. See Lowance, "Religion."

5. For this, and for a wider discussion of satiric theory, see Kernan.

6. Satire has long been associated with rhetorical and literary device but is not necessarily a literary form exclusive to sophisticated societies. For a full discussion of satire's association with cursing see Robert C. Elliot, who has used folklore, myth, and anthropology to show that a type of satire flourished even in primitive societies.

7. This aspect of American satire has been noted in texts from Puritan times to the present. For a discussion of the origins of this subversion, see Arnon.

# II

•

Domesticity and Sentimentality as Discourse
Strategies in *Uncle Tom's Cabin*

# 4

.

S. BRADLEY SHAW

## The Pliable Rhetoric of Domesticity

We can say two things with relative certainty about Harriet Beecher Stowe's *Uncle Tom's Cabin:* it was a popular book and it was
written and received as a "gendered" text. But these two simple
assertions are also at the center of critical debate about the novel.
For most of the twentieth century, our modern critical aesthetic
has dismissed Stowe's book, suspicious of its popular melodrama
and its excessive feminine sentimentality. In the last two decades,
contemporary scholars (particularly feminist revisionists) have
addressed these suspicions by turning them upside down and
asking us to see *Uncle Tom's Cabin* as a complicated and powerful literary work because of its effective manipulation of the
latent cultural and political power of domestic sentimentalism.[1]

While this sympathetic reevaluation of Stowe's novel as part of
the sentimental tradition has raised *Uncle Tom's Cabin*'s critical
stock by connecting the book with sophisticated rereadings of the
nineteenth-century woman's creed of hearth and home, contemporary critics are still debating how to describe the relationship
between the novel and this cult of domesticity. Ann Douglas
argues that "*Uncle Tom's Cabin* in its inception, style, and substance, is a powerfully feminist book" that merely manipulates a
"superficial" subscription to "feminine sentimentalism" ("Introduction" 13–19). Jean Fagan Yellin takes Douglas to task for "in-
explicably" ignoring "crucial" distinctions between the radical
feminism of abolitionists like Angelina and Sarah Grimké and
the "domestic feminism" of Stowe's sister, Catharine Beecher

73

(104). Yellin presents *Uncle Tom's Cabin* as an ideological battle between those two positions and ultimately places Stowe in her sister's more conservative camp. And while Yellin concedes that "within the process of defending Christian domestic values" Stowe does at times endorse a reformist critique of nineteenth-century America, it is Jane Tompkins who fully explicates the inherent radicalness of *Uncle Tom's Cabin* as the representative "*summa theologica* of nineteenth-century America's religion of domesticity," the highest expression of "a monumental effort to reorganize culture from the woman's point of view" (*Sensational Designs* 124–25). Along with Tompkins, Elizabeth Ammons also argues that *Uncle Tom's Cabin* should be read as a matrifocal document that "placed woman at the center of a radical script for social change." But Ammons offers a slightly different relation between Stowe's novel and matrifocal ideology. While Tompkins views it as the apex of the ideology, Ammons concludes that Stowe's argument "grew out of and exploited the new but widely shared idealization of motherhood as a powerful moral force within the body politic" ("Stowe's Dream" 159–60).

The tension between these readings of *Uncle Tom's Cabin* as reactionary, powerfully feminist, subversively conformist, and radically conservative does not result from a needlessly contentious scholarship but grows naturally out of thoughtful historical readings of a powerful rhetoric that had a wide range of practitioners and offered a multiplicity of cultural constructions. *Uncle Tom's Cabin* needs to be understood within the wider rhetorical complexity of Stowe's engagement and employment of domestic ideology. In this essay I present various deployments of this rhetoric to demonstrate its pervasiveness as well as the elasticity and multiplicity of this ideological language in radically different contexts. In the first section I examine the domestic rhetoric of several antebellum periodicals to establish continuities and contradictions inherent in both the reception and contemporary context of Stowe's novel. In the second section I offer a reading of three rival analogues to *Uncle Tom's Cabin* to illustrate the pliable persistence of the tropes and rhetoric of domestic ideology as it addressed the issue of American slavery.

## Domestic Rhetoric and Antebellum Periodicals

Nineteenth-century family and women's periodicals provide an important part of the historical context for Stowe's novel. Re-

cent feminist scholarship has challenged preconceptions about
the antifeminist and antiliterary nature of these periodicals and
has revised the view of how the public feminine discourse of
these popular magazines shaped the aesthetics of women's engagement with literature and culture as both readers and writers
(see Humphreys and Zuckerman). Although the audience for
these antebellum women's journals consisted of primarily upper-
middle-class women who had both the time and money to read
them, Mary Ellen Zuckerman argues that these antebellum periodicals "played an important role in developing an audience
for women's journals, inculcating the reading habit in women, as
well as offering opportunities for female writers and editors" (x–
xi). While none of these journals ever approached the mass
circulation of late-nineteenth-century monthlies like the *Ladies
Home Journal*, the sheer number of individual periodical ven-
tures argues for their importance in shaping the culture of antebellum women. Even with the limited regional distributions and
short publishing histories of some magazines, the approximately
eighty periodicals created for American women between 1800
and 1865 were clearly part of a widespread and persistent effort
to define women's cultural status.[2]

The success of *Uncle Tom's Cabin*'s appeal to the rhetoric of
domesticity depended on having a mass audience familiar with
its conventions. Nineteenth-century women's periodicals helped
to educate this audience in these conventions by helping to
develop, articulate, and disseminate the cultural creed of "woman's sphere." According to this dominant antebellum ideology,
gender clearly distinguished the worlds of home and public
work. While men engaged the physical, moral, and competitive
dangers in the public realm, wives and mothers remained within
the home to cultivate a redemptive sanctuary. This domestic or
woman's sphere provided males with relief from the trials of the
public sphere and even more importantly offered feminine influence as the morally civilizing catalyst that would ultimately redeem the whole of culture.[3] Rev. W. R. Williams's 1851 essay the
"True Sphere of Woman" from the *Mother's Journal and Family
Visitant* offers a typical recitation of the creed:

> Much has been said in our day of the exaltation of the female sex.
> Woman's highest glory is, after all, not in the thronged arena, and
> jostling crowds of public life; but in those scenes where she shines
> unrivalled and indispensable, as the sister, the daughter, the wife,
> and the mother; the guardian of weakness, the attendant of sickness,

and the instructor of childhood. And that same law of heaven, irrepealable by all the vaunting philosophy of the times, that made her the *mother*, made her influence on the outer fields and walks of society the *most powerful* when it was the *least direct.* (303)

Implicit in Williams's essay is the need to define woman's sphere as part of the contemporary debate about women's social role, and his italics emphasize the idea of "mother" as the central notion of this ideology of women's sphere. Social historians have suggested that a unique idealization of motherhood resulted from the cultural transformation wrought by the industrial revolution. The agrarian model in which both men and women worked in the home and functioned as parents was displaced by a theory of feminized parenthood, or "motherhood," as men's work became more directly identified with the public sphere of office and factory (see Bloch). The argument is not that motherhood is a totally new invention, but that in the late eighteenth century and first half of the nineteenth century this biological status is thoroughly invested with a new ideological function—mother and her domestic territory become the moral center of culture.

Abundant evidence for this ideological transformation is readily available in these antebellum periodicals. The magazines seem obsessed by the need to define and reify this maternal ideal. If Reverend Williams's essay had not been published in the *Mothers' Journal and Family Visitant*,[4] it could have easily found a place in any of the following periodicals: *Mother's Magazine; Mother's Magazine and Family Monitor; Home, A Fireside Monthly Companion and Guide for the Wife, the Mother, the Sister and the Daughter; Mother at Home and Household Magazine; Mother's Assistant; Mother's Monthly Journal;* or *Mrs. Whittelsey's Magazine for Mothers and Daughters.* In these periodicals, Williams's definition of the true sphere of woman might have been printed alongside other essays, fiction, or poetry with titles such as "A Pious Mother's Grave," "The Power of Maternal Love," "An Indian Mother's Love," "A Mother's Love," "Mother, Home, and Heaven," "A Mother's Tears," "A Mother's Influence," "Efficacy of a Mother's Tears," "A Mother's Thoughts on the Loss of a Beloved Boy," "A Dying Mother's Reproof," "My Mother's Death," "Mother's Duty and Reward," "The Impenitent Mother," "A Western Mother's Question Answered," "The Bereaved Mother," "Maternal Associations," or

"Maternal Association among the Cherokees." Of course, explication of this maternal ideal was not limited to periodicals and articles with the word *mother* in their titles, but these titles clearly point to the matrifocal character of these antebellum women's magazines.

*Uncle Tom's Cabin* grows out of this matrifocal emphasis of domestic ideology. In 1851 when women subscribed to the *Mother's Magazine,* they received as a premium *The Mother's Hymn Book.* Along with an assortment of hymns for family worship, this volume offered an appendix with a "Constitution for Maternal Associations, and One Hundred and Fifty-four Questions for Discussion at Maternal Meetings." If a maternal association exhausted this discussion material, the 1851 serial publication of *Uncle Tom's Cabin* in the *National Era* must have given them something to talk about. Stowe's opening chapter introduces us to Mrs. Shelby, a mother whose "high moral and religious sensibility and principle" suggest she is an orthodox member of the cult of domesticity:

> Her husband, who made no professions to any particular religious character, nevertheless reverenced and respected the consistency of hers, and stood, perhaps, a little in awe of her opinion. Certain it was that he gave her unlimited scope in all her benevolent efforts for the comfort, instruction, and improvement of her servants, though he never took any decided part in them himself. In fact, if not exactly a believer in the doctrine of efficiency of the extra good works of saints, he really seemed somehow or other to fancy that his wife had piety and benevolence enough for two—to indulge a shadowy expectation of getting into heaven through her superabundance of qualities to which he made no particular pretension.[5]

Although the satiric humor directed at Mr. Shelby calls into question the immediate effectiveness of womanly influence, Stowe clearly invokes the cultural paradigm of "separate spheres." Senator and Mrs. Bird's household and the Halliday's Quaker kitchen present variations of the same paradigm, and in a novel of fragmented families and a fractured and diseased culture these locations offer the clearest descriptions of social and domestic harmony.

Along with Stowe's recitation of the creed of domestic influence, her readers encounter a plot that could be summarized with two words—motherly problems. Chapter 2's title, "The Mother," announces this maternal focus, and slavery's threat to break up Eliza's family carries the action through the first quarter of the narrative. On Tom's trip south, the "peculiar institution" of slavery continues its various assaults on the sacred office of mother as slave children are continually separated from slave mothers. The two principal antagonists of the Southern plot also fall under this label of motherly problems: Marie St. Clare's vain self-centeredness offers a clear portrait of antimother, and Simon Legree's hellish Red River plantation is haunted by his problematic relationship to his dead mother. From the early description of the strength of Eliza's "maternal love" (104) to Stowe's final appeal to the "mothers of America," the author engages and deploys the matrifocal language of domestic rhetoric.

*Uncle Tom's Cabin*'s appeal to the rhetoric of domesticity seems obviously dependent upon the education of a mass audience by these women's periodicals. But the more difficult question of whether Stowe's novel blindly participates in a reactionary compensation myth, or hides behind this domestic rhetoric in a subversive attack on the patriarchy, or openly employs the language of female power to reorder culture from a womanly perspective might be more effectively addressed by looking at a wider range of the rhetoric's use.

The complex relationship between the assertions about *Uncle Tom's Cabin*'s popularity and its production and reception as a "gendered" text is not merely a creation of contemporary feminist revisionism but is embedded in the nineteenth-century response to the novel as well. About seven months after J. P. Jewett and Company first published *Uncle Tom's Cabin, or Life among the Lowly* in two volumes, the October 2, 1852, issue of the *Eclectic* (a Portland, Maine, "Weekly Paper, Devoted to Literature") offers the following lament to the editor. This "Voice from a Sufferer" cries out:

> Mr. Editor: I am a victim to the popular excitement about Uncle Tom's Cabin. Mrs. Tyke read it in chapters in the New Era long ago,—and she, as well as the little Tykes, has been reading it in two volumes ever since. Never was mortal so hunted down by a book before. I have no peace—morning, noon or night. Indian cake at breakfast suggests sympathetic allusions to the thousands of poor Uncle Toms at the South, who must eat hoe cake or die; dinner is enlivened by conversation upon the incidents of the work; and I am pestered every evening after tea, by my eldest daughter's imploring me to hear "the last sweet song about little Eva."

The young ladies are working fancy sketches of Uncle Tom's physiognomy in black worsted; the baby has a woolly headed doll *whom* she tries to call Topsy; and my house is lumbered up with fresh editions of "Uncle Tom's Cabin," and "Aunt Phillis's Cabin," and "Southern Life as it is," and "Southern Life as it isn't," and goodness knows what else beside. Our youngest has fortunately been christened—but Mrs. Tyke gives dark and mysterious hints about naming somebody else Eva one of these days, if circumstances permit. I am almost driven to say that I hope circumstances never will permit.

I haven't read the book. I won't read it. People say it is a remarkable work. I do not doubt it. If it wasn't, it never would set all creation so agog.—Young ladies are astounded that I am ignorant of its contents, and throw up their hands, exclaiming—*"Haven't* read Uncle Tom's Cabin?" whereupon a chorus of astonished bystanders chime in, "Well, I *am* surprised!"

Will not somebody write something or do something to change this wearisome subject? I think of it all day, and dream of it all night. It will be the death of me. But as I say to Mrs. Tyke every morning, as sure as my name is John Tyke, I will *not* read the book. No! not even if people point at me in the street as

THE MAN WHO NEVER READ UNCLE TOM'S CABIN. (5)

Mr. Tyke's lament obviously points to Stowe's book as a phenomenon of popular culture. Along with the novel's immediate publishing success (50,000 copies were sold in eight weeks, 300,000 within a year, and 1,000,000 by early 1853), Tom, Topsy, and little Eva would maintain a life of their own outside the novel until the end of the century. That the novel and its contemporary spin-offs became the fodder for journalistic humorists like Mr. Tyke also testifies to the scope of its appeal; although he claims a prideful ignorance for never having read Stowe's book, the humor of his piece depends on his audience's (and his own) familiarity with the novel's characters and plot. Aside from corroborating *Uncle Tom's Cabin*'s incredible popularity, Tyke's suffering cry also clearly identifies *Uncle Tom's Cabin* as a gendered text. The novel has so moved the immediate and extended community of women around him that he perceives himself as both trapped in the prison of female influence and endlessly hounded by assertions of womanly power. As Mr. Tyke first pleads for a new popular subject and then retreats into his defiant and everlasting "no" to escape the "hunt" of Uncle Tom, Topsy, and little Eva, his lament simultaneously offers a parodic testimony to the power of domestic ideology and critiques its methods and effectiveness.

While the *Eclectic* has room for this humorous criticism of the novel's powerful feminine influence, Mr. Tyke ultimately might be appealing for sympathy from the wrong editor. In a sense, this weekly family magazine has itself been set "agog" by the "popular excitement about Uncle Tom's Cabin." For example, later editions of the *Eclectic* dutifully report on Calvin and Harriet Beecher Stowe's triumphal European tour and announce a new edition of *The Homes of American Authors* that will include an engraving of "Little Eva's Birthplace." The *Eclectic* offers a favorable review of *A Key to Uncle Tom's Cabin* and opens the same issue with an "original" poem "To Mrs. H. B. Stowe" that celebrates "the announcement of [Stowe's] first receipt of ten thousand dollars from the Publishers of Uncle Tom's Cabin."

But the *Eclectic*'s praise of Stowe and its various adaptations of the tropes of domestic ideology do not place the periodical squarely in the camp of *Uncle Tom's Cabin*. This "Home Circle" weekly can also offer a favorable review of Mary Eastman's "anti-Tom" novel, *Aunt Phillis's Cabin, or Southern Life As It Is*. The editors even reprint one of its chapters, "A Negro's Passion for a Ruffled Shirt," because they were amused by some of its humorous "descriptions of negro life" (Eastman 68). Eastman's own use of domestic ideology makes clear that the antislavery argument of *Uncle Tom's Cabin* and its ideological rhetoric are not one and the same.

The flexible uses of domestic rhetoric in the aptly named *Eclectic* point to a similar pliability readily apparent in many of the negative reviews of Stowe's novel in Southern periodicals. Remarkably, the rhetoric of domesticity was available to excoriate the very book that is now often held up as the sacred text of this ideology. For example, comments on Stowe's work and the "problem" of *Uncle Tom's Cabin* in the *Southern Literary Messenger* return again and again to domestic rhetoric's notion of separate spheres. This domestic language is prominent in the *Messenger*'s initial October 1852 review of *Uncle Tom's Cabin* by George F. Holmes, which opens by treating the novel as a problem of socialized gender roles. For Holmes there is a difference between "*lady*" writers and "*female*" writers: "[W]here a writer of the softer sex manifests, in her productions, a shameless disregard of truth and of those amenities which so peculiarly belong to her sphere of life, we hold that she has forfeited the claim to be considered a lady, and with that claim all exemption from the utmost stringency of critical punishment" (630). Holmes then accuses Stowe of adopting the "novel doctrine" of woman's political equality and looking "beyond the office for which she was created—the high and holy office of maternity." According to Holmes, she would hand "over the State to the perilous protection of diaper diplomatists and wet-nurse politicians" of the school of woman's rights (631). In a later *Messenger* issue, John R. Thompson offers a lament and description of the novel also decidedly gendered by the ideology of separate spheres: "If she deliberately steps beyond the hallowed precincts—the enchanted circle—which encompass her as with the halo of divinity, she has wantonly forfeited her privilege of immunity. . . . We cannot accord to the termagant virago or the foul-mouth hag the same deference that is rightfully due to the maiden purity of untainted innocence" (722). With this asserted, Thompson suggests he will still stand by the notion of separate spheres and gentlemanly restrain his "critical lash." Ann Douglas has already noted the irony of Thompson's revealingly troublesome metaphor for approaching Stowe's work ("Introduction" 14), but what interests me more are the rhetorical and ideological continuities among Holmes, Thompson, and Stowe. Implicit in their tacit assumptions about "the enchanted circle" of a "hallowed" woman's sphere and the "high and holy office of maternity" are the very grounds for Stowe's appeal in *Uncle Tom's Cabin* to the "mothers of America" and their "sacred love" (623).

One explanation for the use of this domestic rhetoric to condemn what has been identified by late-twentieth-century readers as domesticity's high-water mark would simply be to say that Holmes and Thompson reveal the "dark side" of domestic ideology—that is, the ideology itself is a compensation myth designed to reinforce female subordination. Thus, when Holmes and Thompson invoke the language of separate spheres to chastise Stowe and *Uncle Tom's Cabin*, they are merely appealing to a de facto patriarchal language to assert their authority.

But while this simple explanation works for Holmes's and Thompson's use of this rhetoric, it does not completely explain a more complex juxtaposition of this language of domesticity in a later issue of the *Southern Literary Messenger*. For the nineteenth-century editors of the *Messenger* this language was so

81

pliable that they saw nothing incongruent when they placed an essay that offers caustic abuse of Stowe's novel next to a poem that could be viewed as a representative production of the sentimental literary tradition of *Uncle Tom's Cabin*. The immediate subject of the essay "Woman's True Mission" is a response to an appeal by "noble ladies of England" to their American sisters on behalf of African slaves.[6] As they bring "Uncle Thomas" into their "luxurious boudoirs," these English noblewomen ignore the cries of their own native poor and proceed in a "strange wandering from woman's sphere." The essay invokes the traditional language of the cult of domesticity to question these women's response to Stowe's novel: "Honored be a woman in all the beautiful phases of mother, wife, daughter and sister" whose humble and "sacred" duty guides and redeems society. But "the noble ladies of England" have stepped into "man's domains" and left "their lords" to "sing in fatherly tones soft 'cradle songs,' whilst they sent loud wailings over the broad Atlantic" (303–4). Stowe herself has aberrantly departed from the bounds of her sphere and American womanhood:

> Fortunate is it for America, that she has succeeded so much better than the mother country in not only enlightening her daughters regarding her institutions, but in teaching them so successfully woman's mission. . . . though there is an American who, "unsexed," has placed herself at the helm of that piratical ship, from whose mast floats the black flag of anarchy, thanks be to the wisdom-imbued mothers of America, that reprobate woman stands almost alone. . . . And though she may be a fitting recipient for the caresses of English women, the daughters of America feel that she has been carried far beyond the gates of the city; far from their sympathies and their respect. Let her gloat over the golden heap conjured into being by the wand of her falsehood . . . but in the midst of her triumphs let her remember that forever more she is an American woman whose name the pure-minded women of her own country hold in pitying contempt. (305–6)

Beyond the pale of American womanhood, the piratical Stowe is also a monstrous author who is guilty of corrupting these women of England with Gothic horrors. The essayist's images are ravenous: they have "supped full of horrors" and "feasted on the pages of a book" worse than "nerve-shaking, shudder-creating, *Mysteries of Udolpho*" (304). That such criticism of Stowe and her readers begins with the rhetoric of separate spheres once again demonstrates the lack of restriction on the employment of the cult of domesticity's discourse.

The poem that follows this invective against Stowe is a representative example of the sentimental literary tradition of *Uncle Tom's Cabin.* "The Mother's Vision: The Birth-Day in Heaven of Mary Ann. Her Second Year among the Angels" records a consoling "vision" for a mother whose "bright-eyed" "young gazelle" was overcome by the "pale and marbled brow"—"the signet-mark of Death" (306). The grieving mother is given a comforting glimpse of an "angel mother" who now cares for her departed. "Cherub" children sing to her a song of consolation:

> Mother! dear Mother!
>   Dry up thy tears,
> Forget thy sorrows,
>   Dismiss thy fears;
> For we all are happy
>   With God above,
> Enfolded and gladdened
>   In endless love. (307)

The song concludes by asking the "sweet Mother" to "hasten" to this heavenly home; and the mother returns from her vision with "Her spirit bowed in sweet consent / Beneath her father's will" (307). The poem offers all the gendered complications of the sentimental tradition and its matrifocal religion. While on one level it seems to be part of a compensation myth with a male deity reigning over the sacrificing mother, the poem does offer a clearly feminized heaven in which the one "father" of the poem has difficulty competing with a heavenly host of capitalized "Mothers." The values of this feminized religious world, with its focus on the emotive power of a mother's love and grief, are part of the rhetorical foundations for *Uncle Tom's Cabin.*

This juxtaposition of motherly poetry and diatribe against Stowe might seem strange to cultural historians: How would an audience that obviously knows *Uncle Tom's Cabin* and its story of motherly trials, childhood death, and family separation read the irony of this juxtaposition? But for the editors and readers of the *Southern Literary Messenger,* this incongruity was probably less problematic. First of all, the popularity of poems like "The Mother's Vision" may have made the poems somewhat invisible; as part of the massive cultural effort to define women's place in antebellum America, at some point the ideological content of such poems became transparently commonplace. This is not to argue that the rhetoric of domesticity was reduced to meaningless cliché; rather, the language of sentimentality became part of the expected fabric of cultural discourse. Secondly, this pervasiveness allows the *Messenger*'s caustic critic access to the domestic rhetoric of separate spheres without being worried about the logical complications of using it against the author of *Uncle Tom's Cabin*. Rather than simply viewing this odd juxtaposition of different facets of domestic rhetoric as an example of editorial blindness or as evidence for the ultimately patriarchal roots of a restrictive ideology, the adjacent poem and criticism represent the vast range of the language of domesticity and the variable missions it serves.

An 1855 essay by Rev. C. B. Parsons, "Woman's Power and Influence," also illustrates the persistent range and rhetorical power of domestic ideology. Although Parsons employs the rhetoric as a male cleric, his own rather conservative argument about woman's moral influence is overwhelmed by the scope of this discourse. Ultimately, his vision of woman's "regenerative" power moves Parsons beyond the limited notion of women as domestic moral guides and authorizes their role as midwives for a democratic millennium for America. Published in *Home Circle*, the women's journal of the Methodist Episcopal Church, South, Parsons's essay begins with a familiar rendition of the formula of separate spheres: morality and religion are "under the direction and control of the female mind, more than the male." While his immediate purpose is to encourage temperance, decrease the use of tobacco, and get more men into church, Parsons proclaims that no "evil propensity" in man "lies beyond the reach and control of woman's influence" (352–53).

Parsons's notion of women's "boundless sway" over men ultimately gives "female influence" and "woman's power" eschatological authority in America's democratic millennium. Because females possess more "piety and patriotism" than males, "no one can so well be the instrument of this heavenly work as woman—intelligent and Christian woman—whether in her capacity of mother, sister, lover, or wife" (354). This "sovereign power" of maternal authority when "politically considered" is of "vast consequence" with its "stupendous power" working on the "hearts of men." While the patriarchal limitations of the motherly compensation myth are clearly present in Parsons's recitation of the rhetoric, his immediate agenda of temperance and higher male church attendance is also clearly dwarfed by the "Amazonian spirit" his rhetoric engenders: "If the women of the world would combine for its moral renovation, they would achieve it, for they have the power to do it. Wars would cease—the Church would come up from the wilderness—order and peace would be restored—and the Millennium would commence. Where shall the first society be formed?" (355–56). Parsons's question seems to suggest that he is unaware of the discourse community that has already codified his rhetoric. His reading audience of antebellum women would have probably known that such organizations had been assembling for about twenty-five years. These women might have even subscribed to the *Mothers' Journal* or *Mother's Magazine* in order to understand how to form and administer such an organization. They might easily have owned a copy of *The Mother's Hymn Book* complete with maternal catechism and a ready-made "Constitution for a Maternal Association" in the appendix. If Parsons was unaware of such societies yet fully enveloped in the powerful rhetoric they produced, his essay offers a forceful argument for the persistent pervasiveness of this discourse. While Parsons's notions of motherly power can on one level be dismissed as part of a conservative patriarchal conspiracy to subjugate women, the rhetorical force of the discourse presents clear testimony to the radical empowerment that domestic ideology offered to women. Although Parsons's own goals are limited to putting a tighter lid on the tobacco tin, the rhetoric that shapes and ultimately overwhelms his immediate agenda opens a Pandora's box of womanly power.

## Domestic Rhetoric and the "Peculiar Institution"

The difficulty in finally labeling Reverend Parsons's essay as conservative or radical suggests something of the rhetorical complexity of *Uncle Tom's Cabin*. This complexity is not limited to the popular periodicals of antebellum America; this same pliable persistence of the tropes and rhetoric of domestic ideology is also readily apparent in what might be called three rival analogues of Stowe's text: Catharine Beecher's 1837 *Essay on Slavery and Abolitionism, with Reference to the Duty of American Females,* Sarah Josepha Hale's 1852 revision of her 1827 novel *Northwood, or Life North and South: Showing the True Character of*

*Both,* and an obscure 1855 novel by an equally obscure Elizabeth D. Livermore, *Zoë, or The Quadroon's Triumph: A Tale
for the Times.* All three texts are wrapped up with *Uncle Tom's
Cabin* in one of the central dramas of domestic ideology. Beecher, Hale, and Livermore, like Reverend Parsons, argue that
women through their innate moral and spiritual superiority will
help coauthor with God an eschatological history that places
American democracy at the epicenter of Christ's millennial
kingdom. But whereas Parsons connected this feminized millennium with a limited concern for tobacco smoke and poor church
attendance, these three women follow the power of their domestic rhetoric to an inevitable engagement with the critical issue of
antebellum culture—the "peculiar institution" of chattel slavery.

Catharine Beecher's 1837 enactment of this central drama in
*An Essay on Slavery and Abolitionism* offers her sister's novel
both a model for an antislavery hero and an inversion of the
eschatological map that Stowe would use fourteen years later.
Beecher wrote her *Essay* in response to a letter of appeal from her
former student Angelina Grimké, asking her to use her influence
to develop a female abolitionist movement. Beecher rebukes the
request with a standard formulation of the separate spheres
doctrine that prohibits (or protects) women from being sullied by
debates about controversial issues in a public forum. According
to Beecher, woman's "subordinate relation in society to the other
sex" does not leave her without power. In fact, her "influence" is
equally "important [and] all-pervading." But female access to
power is dramatically different from men's:

> Woman is to win every thing by peace and love; by making herself
> so much respected, esteemed and loved, that to yield to her opinions
> and to gratify her wishes, will be the free-will offering of the heart.
> But this is to be all accomplished in the domestic and social circle. . . .
> A woman may seek the aid of co-operation and combination among
> her own sex, to assist her in her appropriate offices of piety, charity,
> maternal and domestic duty; but whatever, in any measure, throws a
> woman into the attitude of a combatant, either for herself or oth-
> ers—whatever binds her in a party conflict—whatever obliges her in
> any way to exert coercive influences, throws her out of her appropri-
> ate sphere. (99–102)

The irony of Beecher's very public rebuke of Grimké points again
to the complications of domestic ideology, and the alliances and
inversions between Beecher's essay and her sister's novel are

complicated as well. While both employ language that seems conventional to domestic ideology, they use it to ask their readers for decidedly different actions in response to American slavery.[7]

The older sister's extended description of the ideal antislavery advocate offers a paradigm for Stowe's hero. If according to this domestic ideology women cannot enter the battleground of politics, what is a woman to do when faced with the "national sin of slavery" (109)? For Beecher, this woman must influence those around her toward a less incendiary debate that will ultimately result in the South relinquishing slavery because it is not in "her highest *interest.*" This "conviction" will be the result of "*calm, rational Christian* discussion" led by those Beecher calls "*reprovers.*" These "reprovers" assume this Christian office with "peculiar qualifications" (136–50). Ultimately, Beecher connects the "difficult and self-denying duties" of these reprovers to the "Redeemer of mankind" who with "so much gentleness, patience, and pitying love, encountered the weakness, the rashness, the selfishness, the worldliness of men" (150–51). Others have suggested that before one dismisses Uncle Tom as just the emasculated product of a fearfully racist antebellum culture, one must also recognize him as a radical new Christ figure of matrifocal religion. But viewed in the light of Beecher's essay, perhaps in the process of this transfiguration into a feminized Christ, Uncle Tom also functions as a black version of reprovers like William Wilberforce and Thomas Clarkson. Beecher uses portraits of these English antislavery advocates to serve as models for political action: Wilberforce's "benignity" and "kindheartedness" "disarmed the bitterest foes" (18–19), and Clarkson's patient and persistent labor and suffering helped to stop the slave trade by "eminently judicious influences" (86). Beecher criticizes abolitionists for not adhering to these biographical exempla: not even William Lloyd Garrison's "warmest admirers will maintain" that he possesses these "peculiar traits" (21). While Stowe's antislavery novel is perhaps more rambunctious than it is "eminently judicious," in a sense she offers in the character of Tom an antislavery advocate who possesses all of Beecher's ideal characteristics of effective "reprover": he has "clean hands," maintains his "humility and meekness," and seems to have an innate sense of "tact" and "discretion" (Beecher 146–51). Tom can only be considered a version of Beecher's antislavery advocate in a limited sense; as Jean Fagan Yellin points out, in "*Uncle Tom's*

*Cabin,* none of the characters—black, mulatto or white, male or female—becomes involved in the public struggle against slavery" (100). But as a means of answering the problem of how a woman can raise her voice on the controversy of slavery, the character of Uncle Tom functions like Beecher's reproving advocate.

A part of both sisters' engagement of domestic ideology with the problem of slavery is an appeal to eschatological language, but Beecher's and Stowe's national wake-up calls ask their readers for decidedly different actions. Beecher's appeal is for American women to soothe heated political debate through maternal influence before it gets out of control, whereas Stowe seeks to disturb a complacent Christian church. In her jeremiad, Stowe's "signs of the time" invert the plotting of God's "*day of vengeance*" offered by Beecher fourteen years earlier. Beecher's prophecy follows this plot: the healthy debate in the South about eliminating slavery disappeared with the disruptive arrival of the abolitionists (89); further abolitionist activity will force "an exasperated majority" of slaveholders into instituting such harsh slave laws that it will ultimately lead to an American apocalypse. As good slaveholders and Christian Southerners lose the possibility of effective influence, "the cruelty and unrestrained wickedness" of the slave system will escalate "till a period will come when the physical power will be so much with the blacks, their sense of suffering so increased, that the volcano will burst,— insurrection and servile wars will begin. Oh, the countless horrors of such a day!" In this "burning hour" when the South "sends forth the wailing of her agonies," the North and the West hear and "lift up together the voice of wo[e]." If Nat Turner's 1831 slave rebellion still indirectly haunts Stowe's narrative through the emasculation of Uncle Tom and the exile of George Harris to Liberia, Turner's insurrection kindles a much more explicit nightmare for Beecher writing just six years after his rebellion. Beecher merges her apocalyptic language with sentimental rhetoric: if this "most horrible of all scourges" results in "the slaughter of fathers, sons, infants, and of aged," and if it brings forth "the cries of wives, daughters, sisters, and kindred, suffering barbarities worse than death," will it "bring no fathers, brothers, and friends to their aid, from the North and West?" (95). After painting a graphic picture of the young Republic in terror and chaos, Beecher offers her version of domestic feminism as a means to put off the national apocalypse and help God authorize a matriarchal eschatology: "[W]ithout the influence of these principles of charity and peace, [this conflict] will shake this nation like an earthquake, and pour over us the volcanic waves of every terrific passion. The trembling earth, the low murmuring thunders, already admonish us of our danger; and if females can exert any saving influence in this emergency, it is time for them to awake" (137). Stowe's jeremiad seeks to put off the *"day of vengeance"* through a national "repentance":

> This is an age of the world when nations are trembling and convulsed. A mighty influence is abroad, surging and heaving the world, as with an earthquake. And is America safe? Every nation that carries in its bosom great and unredressed injustice has in it the elements of this last convulsion.
>
> For what is this mighty influence thus rousing in all nations and languages those groanings that cannot be uttered, for man's freedom and equality?
>
> O, Church of Christ, read the signs of the times! Is not this power the spirit of HIM whose kingdom is yet to come, and whose will to be done on earth as it is in heaven? (629)

The "day of grace" that Stowe holds before her readers is not an ameliorating compromise to save the union through gradual reform, but a call for action to right the injustices produced by a slave system that she has presented as a threat to the cultural icons of mother love, home, and family.

If Catharine Beecher's *Essay on Slavery and Abolitionism* has a novelistic counterpart, Sarah Josepha Hale's *Northwood: A Tale of North and South* would seem to be a much more likely candidate than *Uncle Tom's Cabin*. Hale's use of domestic ideology to engage the issue of slavery is clearly apparent in *Northwood*'s 1852 preface. There Hale cites the original 1827 publication of the novel (then subtitled *A Tale of New England*) as the commencement of her "literary life," which would directly lead to the editorship of the *Ladies' Magazine* and *Godey's Lady's Book*. She tells us that the novel was "written literally with [her] baby in [her] arms" as she struggled to "perform [the] sacred duties" of a mother. With these links between motherhood and authorship firmly established, Hale introduces the larger political context of her novel. Although she does not describe her 1852 revision as a direct response to *Uncle Tom's Cabin*, she does present the re-publication of *Northwood* as an answer to

"Abolitionism" and its disturbance of "the harmony between the South and the North." Hale's 1852 revision of her conventional novel about the trials and triumphs of economic reversal and decorous courtship adds two chapters that "show more plainly" how this troubling national problem should be addressed through civilized discussion (iii–iv).

Like Beecher and Stowe, Hale addresses the problem of slavery with a domestic rhetoric of female influence that also appeals to an eschatological vision for America's future. The moral center of the novel is the gentle patriarch of the New Hampshire village of Northwood, Squire Romilly. Although his eldest son has been raised as the heir of his slaveholding Charleston brother-in-law, Romilly is a quiet and slow emancipationist. In the 1852 edition, he is allowed to share with a visiting Englishman his conviction about the rising "destiny of America" "to instruct the world." According to Squire Romilly, "the greatest mission of our Republic [is] to train here the black man for his duties as a Christian, then free him and send him to Africa, there to plant Free States and organize Christian civilization" (166–67). But Romilly's (and Hale's) position on gradual emancipation and colonization raises complications for domestic ideology's faith in the ideal American democracy.[8] When the youngest Romilly boy enters the adult's discussion with his innocent assertion that slaves too "have equal right to life, liberty, and the pursuit of happiness," he immediately becomes perplexed when he tries to balance this American notion with the fact that his eldest brother is a "slaveholder." The questions raised are plain and troubling not just for the young Romilly boy but for an optimistic young nation: How can chattel slavery coexist with the radical freedoms claimed by American democracy? Significantly, Hale sends in Mrs. Romilly to rescue the boy and the novel from these troublesome questions: "Before he had settled his doubts, his mother changed the subject" by prodding her husband to begin family devotions. This matriarchal influence around the Romilly family hearth leads to an assertion of the millennial solution of domestic ideology. Squire Romilly's devotional text is the twentieth chapter of Revelation in which Satan is bound in a bottomless pit for a thousand years. The Englishman is taken aback by the family reading scene. He hears the "strange passages" as if "for the first time." Until these family devotions, "he had considered the whole as a myth—but it appeared that this family believed in the actual coming of the events foretold." Faced with the forthright faith of this domestic circle, the Englishman asks himself if the apocalyptic prophecies will "come" as reality (169). Squire Romilly (and apparently Hale as well) firmly believes in "two great elements of human progress which the millennium will introduce": in that "good time coming," God will "change man's heart" and "chain the devil" (171). Thus, American slavery "will cease" along with all other oppression when humankind can see the "truth" plainly.

With America already firmly on the path of that millennial hope, Hale maps out the "*right* way—the Christian way is good and peaceable—of converting slaves into free men" (172) in Romilly's posthumously revealed journal, which Hale adds as part of the new final chapter for the 1852 edition. The protagonist of the novel, the transplanted slaveholding Romilly, quotes his dead father's wisdom extensively in a series of letters to his new bride. These letters discuss how they will deal with their status as Southern slaveholders: Although abolitionists are troublemakers and slavery is not forbidden as sin, it is ultimately the duty of Christians to "break every bond." Both old and young Romilly argue that American bondage will most effectively be broken with the education of slaves by "pious" and self-sacrificing American women. This new wife is to come to Charleston to educate slaves in Christian virtue in order to prepare them for freedom. The young Romilly's letters appeal to the second sacred book of America, *Pilgrim's Progress:* Whereas Bunyan's Christian made his way alone, "when the *woman,* Christiana went, *she took the children with her.* She drew nearly all she met to join her, and angels led them on through pleasant ways to heaven and eternal life" (389–402).

Along with Beecher, Hale strived to avoid the "partizan" political conflict as part of an ideological commitment to separate spheres:

> "Constitutions" and "compromises" are the appropriate work of men: women are conservators of moral power, which, eventually, as it is directed, preserves or destroys the work of the warrior, the statesman, and the patriot.
>
> Let us trust that the pen and not the sword will decide the controversy now going on in our land; and that any part women may take in the former mode will be promotive of peace, and not suggestive of discord. (407)

While Stowe would have resonated with the rhetoric of maternal influence and recognized the eschatological vision of domesticity that both Beecher and Hale employ, ultimately Stowe's "pen" can not be seen as entrenched in this conservative political camp because *Uncle Tom's Cabin* is at the very least "suggestive of discord."

But if Beecher's and Hale's works represent a more conservative use of domestic ideology when faced with the problem of American chattel slavery, Stowe's novel is hardly the most radical appropriation of domesticity's rhetoric. Elizabeth Livermore's *Zoë, or The Quadroon's Triumph: A Tale for the Times* (1855) is more than "suggestive of discord" in its attack on the evils of American slavery and limited role of women in political and religious debate. Yet while *Zoë* relishes a good fight on these issues, Livermore is also perfectly at home with the rhetoric and tropes of domestic sentimentalism present in these other antebellum women's texts. Like Beecher and Hale, Livermore appeals to the conventional concept of woman's influence as it engages the problem of American slavery in the context of the nation's eschatological future.

Livermore embeds her radical antislavery and female empowerment argument within the dominant and pervasive plot of antebellum woman's fiction—*Zoë* is the story of a young girl (in this case an emancipated Santa Cruz slave) forced to make her own way in the world.[9] In the course of telling this conventional story, Livermore appropriates domesticity's rhetoric for a radical analysis of women's place in American culture. The second volume of the novel engages these larger issues during Zoë's steamship passage home after a European education, as the ship stops for passengers on the eastern seaboard and gulf coast of the United States. While Stowe achieves her geographic breadth by having Eliza escape north and Tom be sold south, Livermore has regional representatives board Zoë's steamship; the perspectives of Boston, Cincinnati, New Orleans, Iowa, and the Rockies are encompassed on the deck and cabins of the ship. This broadness of geographic scope is echoed by the sundry voices the narrator allows to take over this second volume. One of these voices dominates so that it inhabits the ideological center of the novel. During the course of the steamship journey, Mr. Lindsay, a Unitarian minister from the Queen City of Cincinnati, is the novel's voice of reason that brings together several disparate

92

parties—a Santa Cruz quadroon, a colonial Dane, three Boston Brahmins, and a brash "Young American" from the West. Lindsay accomplishes this partly through a politic politeness, but also through an infectious optimism about the nature of humankind and the rising glory of America. But several other voices filtering through Mr. Lindsay complicate his optimistic centrality and offer a radical feminine critique of American culture.

Mr. Lindsay introduces the first of these layered voices by reading a letter from his wife in Cincinnati. With earnestness and wit Mrs. Lindsay reports to her husband that recent women's meetings have resulted in "an army of Amazons" planning to right the physical, economic, and moral corruptions of Cincinnati (2:134). After this initial encounter with Mrs. Lindsay's words, Zoë "plainly sees" that "America is the *future* of this world for the next age," and she continues to pump Mr. Lindsay for news from his wife and her "signs of the times" (2:174). Lindsay obliges (and the narrator as well) by devoting an entire chapter to Mrs. Lindsay's report of the initial literary endeavor of a "Mrs. Pumpkin." Written in the style of Fanny Fern—brash and satiric—Mrs. Pumpkin's chapter, entitled "Too Much Man," narrates her anticipated construction of a female manifesto.

Without an illustration for a frontispiece, Mrs. Pumpkin must first sketch herself for her reader: She is of "the good old stock of the Puritans," which makes her a friend of "liberty"; she is Unitarian in religion, "which makes me a believer in all the faiths which ever were preached"; "I have no children, so, having all creation to select from, I have a very large family"; "I have no accomplishments, so I am quite an artist. I always like to read prose better than rhyme, therefore, I am a poetess" (2:178). Does Mrs. Pumpkin contradict herself? If so, she is large, she contains multitudes. Or as she says of herself: "So they try to manage me, but they don't find it so easy. No, no, Mrs. Pumpkin is not a ripe, round pumpkin for nothing. She is going to have her say and tell it in her own globular way, and not feel when her work is done as a watchmaker would if he had left the main-spring out" (2:185). The "main-spring" of this particular composition is found in the refrain of her title, "Too Much Man." The phrase originates in her own response to what she labels a typical flippant male dismissal of a sentimental tale of family woe. After hearing that a "drunkard's wife and children lead a life of misery," the male will say " 'Very sad, very bad' . . . and then sips his tea and laughs and chats as if nothing had happened." Mrs. Pumpkin's judgment is that this is *"Too much man*, altogether! *too much man!"* (2:176). She then uses variations of this refrain to link what she considers the cowardices and injustices of American male culture, and the principal wrong she addresses is American chattel slavery.

To answer these failures of male-dominated culture, Mrs. Pumpkin offers a prophecy for a new world that grows directly out of the domestic ideology of separate spheres. According to her version of the doctrine, there are two principal divisions within the human family: (1) "the *Feminines*, which include the very choicest portion of both sexes of all races, conditions, classes and color"; and (2) the *"Ani-*MALS, or animated *evils*," which stand in opposition to the *Feminines* (2:177). As Mrs. Pumpkin reads her signs of the time, the female nature is moving into ascendancy. In this new feminized age, old male occupations will be curtailed: "There are to be no more wars," and [p]olitics and law" will be gone with their "logrolling, and litigation." This millennial future is the natural result of the fact that "America is a woman," along with religion, the arts and sciences, literature, farming, and horticulture: "Justice and Truth are going to carry the day, and they are women, so if [men] don't consent to be *Feminines*, they are in danger of being nowhere and nothing at all in the new times coming. But the trouble is they won't believe in the advent of the new era. They are too proud to look at the signs of the times, and be strong in faith. They had rather reason and argue of the future from the past. *Too much man! too much man!"* (2:179–80).

For Mrs. Pumpkin, the essential blindness of American male culture is revealed in its response to the rising status of women and the issue of slavery. In her "new times coming," the "pipe-laying, and lobbying and caucusing" of male politics will be re-vealed as acts of "cowardice" that cannot abide "a word" spoken "about the women or the negroes." According to Mrs. Pumpkin, if slavery is spoken of in any public forum—in conversation, from the pulpit, in print, or in political debate—men are "half frightened out of their wits":

> They are *afraid* the negroes will rise and kill them, though they have had proof upon proof that they never do so when their freedom is given them; so out of *fear* they keep them in bondage. They are *afraid* they shall come to poverty, or shan't be thought so grand if they do them the simple justice to free them, so they tighten their

chains. They are *afraid* the Union will split to pieces if they even talk upon the subject, and try to devise methods to set this matter right. . . . There is one thing I wish they had more wholesome fear of, and that is *breaking the commandments of God* and of not *doing their duty to Him, to their fellow men, and their own souls. A thousand times too much man!* (2:183–84)

In this harangue against male political cowardice, Mrs. Pumpkin delights in parodying the motherly role that she refuses to play in this particular context: "Do they want to be petted like a little baby, thus? 'They shan't be hurt, no, they shan't! The niggers shan't kill them, no, no; the women shan't hurt them, indeed they shan't! Hush, hush!' Why can't they be courageous, like a woman. She sees no bugbears in the way. Slavery is too delicate a subject to think of, much less to speak of plainly, is it?" (2:186). As a woman Mrs. Pumpkin claims the freedom to talk about such issues without fearing the "crack of doom" or "the Union falling to pieces." She claims women's apolitical power is the only answer to these plaguing problems of male politics and government.

Mrs. Pumpkin's vision of "*Too much man, man, man!*" drives her to a conflation of white women and black slaves that rivals the feminized Christ of Stowe's Uncle Tom. The relationship she establishes is much more outrageously direct than the symbolic transfiguration of Uncle Tom. She claims that her husband is "a great trial to some people for being a friend to niggers and women," but he can take no other position since his wife is "a woman and a nigger too"—a "white nigger." Mr. Pumpkin has "given one woman her freedom . . . and there is no knowing what may come of it! If she should take a fancy to dye her face black and crisp her hair to rectify a mistake of nature, seeing she is a nigger, he would only say: 'Is that judicious, my dear? However, I wish you to act out your own genius'" (2:187). As a "white nigger," Mrs. Pumpkin asserts that she knows the slave's "character and peculiar wants," and from this perspective of "nigger" and "woman," she can only arrive at this version of her refrain: "*Too much men,* five million times *too much men!*" (2:188).

Mrs. Pumpkin concludes by contemplating the outrageous sales of her book. Although it is difficult to say if Elizabeth Livermore had the same brash hope for the success of *Zoë*, it is clear from her novel's preface that she adheres to Mrs. Pumpkin's politics and vision. Livermore argues that the earth is progressively moving toward its "thorough completion" through humans "becoming co-workers with God." As we approach "the glorious appointment which God has in store," there

> come up to the surface of society, those who have been regarded as inferior elements in its construction, even those *little ones in Christ's kingdom*, in whom the feminine, the graceful and tender, the imaginative and artistic qualities are largely mingled. Then, woman will be freed from the chains which enthrall her, and will step forth as she is, the subtle, spiritual genius, to impel to high deed the "lord of creation." Then the African, child of the sunshine, in whom is wrapped up what we, in our country, have as yet vainly looked for—poetry, music, high art, and full reflection of God's love as revealed through our Savior, will take his true and blissful position. (1:iv–v)

If this version of the feminized millennialism of domestic ideology can preface a novel that encompasses both the conventional plot of Zoë's arduous self-development and self-sacrifice *and* Mrs. Pumpkin's panegyric, it once again illustrates the difficulties of trying to label Stowe's use of domestic rhetoric as conservative, radical, or subversive. This rhetoric of separate spheres, female influence and eschatological vision seems pliant enough to be employed in all these ways—even in the same text.

At several points in *Uncle Tom's Cabin* Stowe takes to task male preachers for their narrow misuse of Scripture and the pulpit in defense of slavery (200–202; 278–81). If we consider Stowe's novel her own pulpit for a feminized sermon against slavery, she claims for herself much wider "proof-texts" and a more pliable homiletic voice. Although Stowe's narrator clearly condemns Augustine St. Clare for his troublesome passivity, she takes the risky narrative strategy of letting him function as her ideological mouthpiece through the middle third of *Uncle Tom's Cabin.* And as St. Clare's own rhetoric runs the gamut from sardonic to sentimental, it again suggests the inclusive power of Stowe's domesticity. Like Livermore's "African" in whom is wrapped up "poetry, music, high art, and full reflection of God's love as revealed through our Savior," St. Clare's first description of Tom presents the slave as "all the moral and Christian virtues bound in black morocco, complete!" (234–35). Although buried in St. Clare's urbane cynicism, this description of Tom immediately follows his "saving" of little Eva and effectively articulates the beginning of his transformation into a self-sacrificing Christ figure. Tom is not just a believer of the Book, he *is* the

Book—the Word once again made flesh. But significantly, St. Clare offers more than one biblical incarnation:

> "My Mother," said St. Clare, getting up and walking to a picture at the end of the room, and gazing upward with a face fervent with veneration, "*she* was *divine!* Don't look at me so!—you know what I mean! She probably was of mortal birth; but, as far as ever I could observe, there was no trace of any human weakness or error about her. . . . Why, cousin, that mother has been all that has stood between me and utter unbelief for years. She was a direct embodiment and personification of the New Testament,—a living fact, to be accounted for, and to be accounted for in no other way than by its truth. O mother! mother!" said St. Clare, clasping his hands, in a sort of transport. (333)

At this moment, St. Clare's sophisticated wit is displaced by the rhetoric and ideology of domesticity, and the Christlikeness of Tom in this novel is difficult to separate from the Christlikeness of good mothers. Characters like Tom and St. Clare's mother, who embody all of the moral values and underpinnings of her novel, function as Stowe's "proof-texts," and employing a range of voices and tones to find access to this domestic ideology points not only to Stowe's own remarkable rhetorical skill but also to the pliable nature of antebellum America's domestic rhetoric.

## NOTES

1. For a brief history of this critical response see Sundquist, Introduction 1–7.

2. See Humphreys and Zuckerman. Frank Luther Mott argues that national mass-circulation ten-cent monthlies like the *Ladies' Home Journal* were made possible because of developments in technology and distribution at the end of the nineteenth century. These inexpensive monthlies "recruited" about five million new readers between 1885 and 1905 (8).

3. For the social history that gave rise to this doctrine of separate spheres, see Cott. For competing versions about the impact of this ideology on American women, see Welter, "The Cult of True Womanhood" and Smith-Rosenberg.

4. Although most of the contributors to this Philadelphia periodical were male doctors of divinity like Williams, the magazine was edited by a woman, Mary G. Clark.

5. Stowe, *Uncle Tom's Cabin* (1981), 52–53. All subsequent quota-

tions from the novel are from this edition, cited by page number in the text.

6. This Stafford House Appeal was signed at the meeting by a number of prominent women of the British social world and then circulated for the signatures of 562,448 other women of the British realm (see Fladeland 351–53).

7. In "Doing It Herself," Jean Fagan Yellin also notes this irony, but she sees Beecher's *Essay* as an ideological prooftext for *Uncle Tom's Cabin.* Yellin's argument is helpful both in establishing points of continuity between Beecher and the Grimké sisters and highlighting their central dispute on "how and where women should act" in an American democracy.

8. Hale fully develops this position in her 1853 novel, *Liberia, or Mr. Peyton's Experiment.*

9. As the daughter of emancipated Santa Cruz slaves, Zoë is separated from her family for a European education that should help her social status. The first volume of the novel recounts Zoë's difficulties in Europe; there she endures social ostracism and harsh teachers as a refining fire for her already sensitive moral nature. The second volume narrates her return via steamship to her island home where her father has suffered financial reversal. Zoë faces the humiliation of manual labor with dignity and defends her virtue from lecherous suitors with fortitude. But apparently Livermore can find no place for her heroine within a balanced social harmony, and Zoë, too good for this world, redeems others through her selfless and beautiful death. See Baym, *Woman's Fiction,* for a discussion of the over-story that informs *Zoë.* Zanger's "The 'Tragic Octoroon'" and Bond's "Disorder and the Sentimental Model" offer helpful descriptions of a related conventional plot—that of the "tragic Octoroon." Since a central concern of the novel is with race, *Zoë* has some affinities with this subgenre: She is "raised and educated as a white child," and her condition is "radically changed" through financial reversal (Zanger 63). But because Zoë is the acknowledged child of two former slaves, she has no "white" father to lose, nor is sexual vulnerability or victimization at the heart of the plot. Neither Zanger nor Bond identify *Zoë* as a work in this subgenre.

# 5

.

ISABELLE WHITE

# Sentimentality and the Uses of Death

Death scenes sold novels in mid-nineteenth-century America. A publisher's blurb in Susan Warner's *Hills of Shatemuc* (1856) advertised "inimitable" death scenes, and Sarah Evans's *Resignation* (1855) promised fifty-seven death scenes—one every ten pages (Herbert Brown 343). This obsession with fictional death has frequently been deplored as revealing unhealthy attitudes and then dismissed, or it has been linked (for instance by Ann Douglas's much-discussed *Feminization of American Culture*) with sentimentality and with a general decline in American culture.[1] But sentimental rhetoric itself deserves more complex analysis; and the popular death scene, represented in *Uncle Tom's Cabin* by the deaths of Eva and Tom, the most memorable characters in Harriet Beecher Stowe's book, is at least in this instance used for positive and significant cultural purposes. Still, Stowe's treatment of death involves her in inevitable contradictions. Her gender places her in a decentered position in her culture, but she of course occupies a privileged position in terms of her class and her race. She is thus positioned to both articulate and challenge the dominant ideology (Kaplan 3), and the individualistic ethic of nineteenth-century America is frequently in tension with Stowe's communal impulses. Still, the nonrealistic death scenes provide Stowe and her readers the occasion for shared public mourning and thus attempt to repair one of Victorian culture's major ruptures, the split between the communal

99

self-sacrificing values that had come to be considered feminine and the individualistic values that emphasized property rights and competitive self-interest, values that were associated with the public world of privileged white men and that were used to defend slavery.

*Uncle Tom's Cabin* protests slavery by protesting this individualistic value system. Stowe's novel thus becomes a criticism of her culture at large, with slavery functioning as a powerful symbol of the materialistic values on which capitalism is based and that are in turn perpetuated by capitalism. Slavery is not for Stowe, as it apparently was for many (Foner 9), a symbol of the profound differences between North and South. Rather it is a symbol of a system of values that places financial gain above all else, a system that, as her subtitle suggests, reduces a human being to a thing. Stowe compares slaves to capitalism's laborers not, as St. Clare's brother does, to defend slavery, but rather to condemn any system that is based on "appropriating one set of human beings to the use and improvement of another without any regard to their own."[2] St. Clare explains to Ophelia that the laborer is "as much at the will of his employer as if he were sold to him" (340). The difference between the two systems, he says, is that slavery is a "more bold and palpable infringement of human rights"; it "sets the thing before the eyes of the civilized world in a more tangible form, though the thing done be after all, in its nature, the same" (341). St. Clare is correct in connecting slavery with capitalism, a point that Stowe reinforces by her portrayal of Legree's plantation. As William Taylor first noted in *Cavalier and Yankee*, life on Legree's plantation, the nadir of experience in the novel, is life in a factory rather than in a home (310). Workers are machines to Legree; having once tried caring for his slaves, he has decided that it is more profitable to use them up and replace them.

Stowe's argument against individualistic and materialistic values goes beyond her culture's economic structure to the related issues of its restrictive gender roles and its increasingly secular view of life. As Barbara Bardes and Suzanne Gossett point out, the discourse of the midcentury debate regarding slavery had focused on political, constitutional, and legal issues and had thus effectively excluded women (43). While women speaking in public violated social norms, privileged women had available to them the discourse of imaginative writing, and Stowe took full advantage of her opportunity. Stowe's book thus expands the terms of the slavery debate by framing it as a conflict between competing sets of values and by making those values gender specific to a significant extent. Gender identity intersects with class and race (Kaplan 3), and attitudes typical of gender catego- ries in *Uncle Tom's Cabin* are not entirely consistent. Still, most of the white men in *Uncle Tom's Cabin* speak on behalf of the values Stowe rejects; her women generally oppose them. Eco- nomic and legal arguments were used to support slavery; and money and law, primarily male concerns, were subject to reason. Against these defenses of slavery, Stowe presents the primarily emotional claims of family and of Christianity, which had by midcentury been to a large extent abandoned to women and others whose status in the culture was at best ambiguous (Doug- las, *Feminization*).

Two of the novel's married couples, the Shelbys and the Birds, embody this split. Mr. Shelby is, by his culture's definition, a good man; as such his priorities are financial. He has concluded that if he does not raise money by the sacrifice of some slaves, all will be lost. His decision to sell Eliza's son and Tom is thus a reasonable one. But it is not the decision his wife would have made. She understands Tom's relation to his family as well as to hers, and she especially understands Eliza's relation to her child. Mrs. Shelby is unable to "reason away" her emotions as her husband can his. Committed to business, Mr. Shelby leaves religion to his wife; he believes that she has "piety and benev- olence enough for two" (53).

If Mr. Shelby's priorities are financial, Senator Bird's public priorities are political; and both territories help Stowe map her gendered indictment of slavery. Having voted for and argued for a state Fugitive Slave Law, Senator Bird believes that preserving the relationship between states takes priority over helping fugi- tives, that "public interests" require putting aside "private feel- ings." But Mrs. Bird knows that her husband's public action does not reflect his true nature. When Eliza and Harry appear at their house, Mrs. Bird discreetly waits for her husband to be con- fronted by "the magic of the real presence of distress" (156) and to realize that he must contradict his public persona by person- ally taking the fugitives to their next stop.

In addition to dramatizing conflicting systems of value, Stowe offers, by implication, alternatives to the dominant values she rejects. The world of women offers for Stowe viable alternatives to the marketplace, which is male. The women, who follow their emotions and assert the value of family and religion, are right as Stowe sees it; and at least sometimes they put their impulses into action through their influence on others. The gentle Quaker Aunt Dorcas, another example of female influence, nurses slave dealer Tom Loker back to health after he has been shot, and she persuades the evil man to spend his time trapping bears and wolves rather than chasing fugitive slaves. A woman's means of asserting the values of home and religion is her power to appeal to the emotions and thereby access the authority of home and religion. This is of course Stowe's method in the novel; she addresses mothers repeatedly, whom she expects in turn to influence others.

Cora Kaplan says that women's texts "often move through the rhetoric of radical individualism towards a critique of both patriarchal and capitalist relations." Clearly, Stowe's rhetoric does this. Kaplan continues that the texts remain "painfully classbound and often implicitly or explicitly racist, displacing on to women in subordinate groups the 'bad' elements of female subjectivity so that a reformed and rational feminine may survive" (3). Stowe does of course participate in some of the racial stereotyping of the nineteenth century, though as both Elizabeth Janeway (214) and William Chafe (66–70) point out, the stereotypes are typical of those ascribed to marginalized groups generally. But she does not displace onto subordinate women (female slaves would be the obvious choice) negative elements. Stowe instead concentrates negative feminine characteristics in Marie St. Clare, a woman of wealth and status. Marie is totally self-absorbed, thereby providing the reverse image of Stowe's ideal woman. Stowe also calls into question conventional ideas about class in her treatment of Mrs. Shelby, a woman of privilege though of restricted power. Stowe endorses the concept of class but interprets status in nonconventional terms, calling Mrs. Shelby a "woman of high class, both intellectually and morally" (52).

Stowe's use of death scenes is a powerful means of reducing the isolation fostered by the growth of capitalist individualism and of intensifying the communalism inherent in her affirmation of femaleness. While the focus on competitive individual achievement involves at least a degree of withdrawal from others, Stowe's death scenes dramatize her insistence that readers not withdraw, that they feel their connection with others. In mid-nineteenth-century America, a family member's death was expected to unite the family; and the family was frequently evoked as a model for the nation. Catharine Beecher, for instance, presented the self-sacrificing family as a model for the country; and her sister agreed. The popular mourning literature of 1830–70 responded to and attempted to counteract the diminishing communal significance of death, advising the bereaved on how to behave under these new circumstances, responding to the severing of connections, and implying that an appropriate natural response cannot always be expected. According to the manuals, the mourner whose heart is softened feels benevolence toward all; and weeping over the dead can serve as preparation for a vital religious experience. Grieving, then, teaches people to love one another, thus making this world more like the domestic heaven depicted by the cult of mourning (Halttunen 130–31). Creating social harmony in a world in which connections were being broken by the increasing individualism and increasing mobility basic to capitalism was Stowe's purpose, and eliciting shared grieving was her method. Eva's death is thus not, as Ann Douglas says, "essentially decorative" (*Feminization* 4); her death (and Tom's as well) is central to Stowe's project of undermining support of slavery by discouraging withdrawal from the human community and by incorporating slaves into that community. Jane P. Tompkins takes issue with Douglas's "trivializing view" of Eva's death and argues, as I do, that death is victory and brings an access to power (*Sentimental Power*).

As slavery is a powerful symbol for the dehumanizing tendencies of the materialism and individualism of Stowe's culture, death is a powerful and complex symbol for a passive but at least sometimes effective response to these tendencies. The deaths of Eva and Tom assert feminine values and elicit the perspective of and response from emotion that is suppressed in many of Stowe's men. They thus reveal that a traditionally powerless person can become powerful by selflessly dying for others. To put it another way, death can be a means of breaking through ordinary human limitations, or in the cases of a child and a slave, extraordinary human limitations. Dying, the only complete release from the self-concern of extreme individualism, provides the occasion for a dramatic condemnation of an unsatisfying world. Paradoxically, the individual must leave the community to affect the community, and the death of a member of the community strengthens the community's bonds.

Eva, whose death is the focus of much of the novel's emotional appeal, belongs to a class of children familiar to nineteenth-century readers. (Barbara Welter says that mothers, having been warned that especially advanced mental or religious powers were a sign of consumptive tendencies, watched fearfully for signs of precocity in their children and often interpreted children's deaths as signs that they were too good for the world [*Dimity Convictions* 11].) Stowe writes of these children: "When you see that deep spiritual light in the eye—when the little soul reveals itself in words sweeter and wiser than the ordinary words of children, hope not to retain that child; for the seal of heaven is on it, and the light of immortality looks out from its eyes" (383). Eva's death emphasizes her spirituality and allows her to exert influence far beyond that of an ordinary child. St. Clare sees his daughter as a messenger—"O, Evangeline! rightly named . . . hath not God made thee an evangel to me?" (278)—though her message has not penetrated his spiritual malaise. As the time of her death approaches, however, Eva becomes more effective. Having earlier said that she could understand why Christ died for us and that she herself would die for the slaves if she could, Eva commissions her cynical father to persuade people that slavery is wrong: "When I am dead, papa, then you will think of me, and do it for my sake. I would do it if I could" (403). Though St. Clare replies that he will do anything she asks, he continues after her death in ideological limbo; and his procrastination means that Eva's wishes are not carried out. The child's power here is limited by requirements of plot, if nothing else; if Stowe is to show slavery at its worst and to dramatize the danger of St. Clare's spiritual position, Tom must be sold again.

In other cases, however, Eva's death and the love upon which it is based effect real change. Her love converts the previously unmanageable Topsy to an orderly, Christian life, thus transposing a victim of the individualistic profit motive into a communal world of domesticity. Eva says to the slave child, "I love you and I want you to be good. I am very unwell, Topsy, and I think I shan't live a great while; . . . I wish you would try to be good, for my sake; —it's only a little while I shall be with you" (409). Eva's appeal based on a love and acceptance that is contrary to isolating individualism touches Topsy; and more important, it changes her. Grieving for the dead child, Ophelia learns to follow Eva's example and to love and accept Topsy. Eva understands well how to exercise the power of the powerless, and her ability to persuade others to adopt her anti-individualistic, antimaterialistic values is enhanced as her death approaches.

In another instance, Eva's power after death combines with the power of other mistreated or ignored women to haunt Simon Legree, whose evil is the result of his dedication to the profit motive that requires him to resist and finally suppress the emotions elicited by his mother's piety. The women's power in this case is transmitted through a lock of hair Eva had given Tom when she was near death. Given to Legree by the overseers who find it around Tom's neck, the hair becomes an instrument of torture. The "witch thing" twines around his fingers as if alive (527), and he pulls at the hair as if it has burned him. The reason for his extreme reaction, the reader later learns, is that the hair reminds Legree of another lock of hair, this one from the letter that informed him of the death of his mother, who on her deathbed forgave his curses and his rejection of her. Stowe attributes supernatural power to the strand of hair: "Ah, Legree! that golden tress was charmed; each hair had in it a spell of terror and remorse for thee, and was used by a mightier power to bind thy cruel hands from inflicting uttermost evil on the helpless" (531).

Simon Legree is the epitome of the evil Stowe perceives in her culture; and the powers of three females—the mother whose values he rejected, the woman he owned and used sexually, and the child who was willing to die to free the slaves—join to destroy him. As Legree becomes a haunted man, his fears work to the advantage of Cassy, a slave concubine who, at the expense of her sanity, has gained some power over her master. Hiding in the attic awaiting an appropriate time to escape, Cassy's young friend Emmaline sings of judgment and of parents and children, as Legree sits below fearing that his dead mother will appear. Later, as the man dreams of Cassy holding his mother's shroud, the slave reaches out in the night and touches his hand, saying "Come, come, come" (596). Cassy and Emmaline escape; Legree drinks more and more and is left sick and dying. Legree is more out of touch with the values that had come to be identified with mid-nineteenth-century women than is any other man in the novel. He has rejected his mother and broken her heart, sexually abused Cassy, and created in his plantation an isolated, hierarchical world totally antithetical to the warm, communal one Eva wants to give the slaves. But the lock of hair joins with Legree's guilty dream of his mother and the sound of Cassy's singing to administer a kind of justice that could not come from a legal system that permitted and supported slavery.

While Eva's lock of hair exacts revenge on Legree even as it offers him potential salvation, Stowe attributes to the dead child benevolent spiritual impact as well. Daughter, wife, and sister of well-known evangelists whose antislavery efforts had been less than successful, Stowe suggests that death might provide a young woman opportunities not available to her in this world. When Tom thinks that Eva, after her death, appears to read the Bible to him, Stowe comments, "Was it a dream? Let it pass for one. But who shall say that sweet young spirit which in life so yearned to comfort and console the distressed, was forbidden of God to assume this ministry after death?" (499). Death thus offers the possibility of access to new power as well as enhancing feminine influence.

In addition to being a means to exercise power, Eva's death condemns a materialistic and individualistic culture that has caused too much pain for her sensitive nature. On the boat where she meets Tom, she looks at slaves with "perplexed and sorrowful earnestness" and woefully lifts their chains (232). Her heartbreak and her withdrawal from the world are revealed by her reaction to the story of Prue, the bread woman. Rather than weeping or exclaiming as Stowe says other children would, Eva's "cheeks grew pale, and a deep earnest shadow passed over her eyes" (325). "These things sink into my heart" (326), she tells Tom. The cook observes that horrors such as Prue's being left in the cellar until the flies got her should be kept from "sweet, delicate young ladies" because "it's enough to kill 'em" (327). Stowe says of her thoughtful heroine that the evils of slavery had one by one fallen into the depths of her heart. The broken heart from which she suffers and dies is in turn intended to break the hearts of readers, creating sympathy, the binding agent of community.

By dying, Eva also rejects the worldly life that awaits her as a privileged white adolescent, and her withdrawal from the position of the female as object/merchandise is itself an exercise of power. Although critic Ann Douglas places Eva in the category of women who are "far too young to be the objects of sexual interest" ("Introduction" 17), St. Clare's brother visualizes Eva as a sexually attractive woman, saying (ironically) that she will some-day make hearts ache; and her visiting twelve-year-old cousin, Henrique, is fascinated by Eva from the time he meets her. Objecting to the boy's cruel treatment of his slave, Eva already exerts womanly influence; Henrique responds earnestly, "I could love anything, for your sake" (396). The unworldly Eva gives no sign that she is attracted to her cousin and is apparently unaware of the nature of his attraction to her. She dies soon after his visit.

Eva's death figuratively substitutes for her marriage, and she thereby avoids further contact with the public world of privileged men, the world of business, politics, and slavery. Eva bears a remarkable resemblance to Karl Menninger's description of many tuberculosis patients as having a "certain wistful, ethereal beauty" (397), and she points toward his belief that tuberculosis often develops in response to sorrow, moral shock, and worry. Young patients, Menninger says, sometimes substitute "the dis-ease for an *affaire d'amour*" (396). Certainly the images used to describe Eva's death are resonant of marriage. Eva is to-tally surrounded by white on her deathbed. Waiting outside Eva's room as her death approaches, Tom says, "There must be somebody watchin' for the bridegroom" (425). Like death itself, Eva's disease is personified as a male figure who comes for the female. Miss Ophelia cannot be fooled by the illness; she "knew well the first guileful footsteps of that soft, insidious disease, which sweeps away so many of the fairest and loveliest, and, before one fibre of life seems broken, seals them irrevocably for death" (383). Stowe substitutes death for marriage and the worldly life it implies to emphasize that the life for which society intends Eva is incompatible with her communal values and her spiritual nature.

Stowe makes explicit what her heroine looks forward to in lieu of worldly affairs. When Marie St. Clare speaks of the jewels Eva will wear when she begins "dressing and going into company" (386), Eva wishes instead that she could sell the jewels intended to display her wealth and privilege. She would like to use the money thus gained to move the slaves to a free state and start a school for them, thus establishing a benevolent and democratic community. These aspirations are of course thwarted by her cir-cumstances; as a child she is in no position to make such deci-sions. Eva's death does, however, place her in another community. Rejecting her father's suggestion that she stay pretty to go visit Henrique, Eva replies, "I shall never go there, papa—I am going to a better country" (416). She will be transported to the "Savior's home" that is "sweet and peaceful" and "loving" (404), to the domestic heaven depicted by the cult of mourning and prominent in much mid-nineteenth-century women's writing.

Many of the slaves have much in common with Stowe's privileged white child and thus join Eva in her indictment of her culture. Like Eva, they exhibit personalities and behavior that are generally labeled feminine and that are compatible with communal values. Stowe says the slaves' interests center around the home, and their emotions rule them. Like women, their talents are domestic. Cooking is "an indigenous talent of the African race" (310), and the slaves who add "soft, poetic touches" to Eva's death room have the "nicety of eye which characterizes their race" (430). Their "instinctive affections" are "peculiarly strong," and they are "not naturally daring, enterprising, but home-loving and affectionate" (164). Especially "impressible," they cry easily, "after the manner of their susceptible race" (419). Attributing to her slave characters qualities associated with the feminine, Stowe means to elevate them and incorporate them into what to her is a superior domestic community, an effort that has often been misunderstood by readers who more readily identify with the competing set of values.

If the slaves generally are like nineteenth-century women, Tom is like the ideal woman. Elizabeth Ammons calls him the "supreme heroine of the book" and discusses his "feminine" characteristics ("Heroines" 173). He embodies the cardinal virtues of piety, purity, submissiveness, and domesticity, the Cult-of-True-Womanhood values that Barbara Welter found recommended repeatedly in women's magazines published between 1820 and 1860 (*Dimity Convictions*). Tom is known even to his oppressors for his religious devotion, and he remains faithful to his family though separated from them without reasonable hope of reunion. His submissiveness is illustrated by his willingness to sacrifice himself always for the good of others. Tom's domesticity reveals itself not only with his own family, but with his owners' families as well. In fact, he is allowed to assume symbolically the most exalted role of nineteenth-century woman—that of mother. As Eva is dying, she depends on Tom more than on anyone else. Marie St. Clare's selfishness precludes her playing a significant role in caring for her daughter; thus Tom is free to give Eva motherly care. The slave is sensitive to the child's needs, easing her suffering by carrying her from place to place, sitting with her, and singing their favorite songs.

Like the novel's women, Tom exercises power indirectly; and, like Eva, he gives his life for others and is most powerful when dying. As a kind of missionary, Tom begins to have a "strange power" (559) over the slaves on Legree's plantation, a power that is strange both because it is supernatural and because it is in complete contrast to the physical force by which Legree rules. Tom's passive response to his beating for refusing to reveal Cassy's and Emmaline's hiding place converts the tyrannical and sadistic slave overseers Quimbo and Sambo. Tom's death also inspires young George Shelby not only to free the Shelby slaves but also to vow to do "what one man can" to rid his land of "this curse of slavery" (593). Stowe comments directly on the parallel between Tom's death and Christ's: "But, of old, there was One whose suffering changed an instrument of torture, degradation and shame, into a symbol of glory, honor, and immortal life; and where His Spirit is, neither degrading stripes, nor blood, nor insults, can make the Christian's last struggle less than glorious" (583). Stowe's identification of Tom with Christ further reveals her concept of him as feminine. John Adams points out that Stowe believed Christ had an especially close affinity with women and saw him as the union of the feminine and the divine (81). Like Christ, Tom triumphs through death. His death demonstrates that he is not, as his society has assumed, a thing that can be owned but is instead a moral agent. In a world that excludes him from traditional power, he effects change, as does Eva. The ultimate passive acts of death, paradoxically seeming to remove these individuals from the community, affirm or create communal bonds more firmly secured against the marketplace values that have threatened them.

Tom's death, like Eva's, asserts the binding values of secular alliances and religious faith, both of which slavery threatens. Both condemn a materialistic world willingly left behind for a domestic heaven. On his way down the river (a journey toward death), Tom reads haltingly from his Bible: "In—my—father's—house—are—many—mansions" (229). Tom insists that he anticipates his approaching death eagerly and fearlessly; and when George Shelby arrives too late with the money to secure his freedom and take him home, the slave assures the son of the man who sold him that all is well. Legree, Tom says, has only opened the gate of heaven for him. But Tom's death has consequences for others in this world as well; his willingness to die rather than reveal their secret allows Cassy and Emmaline to escape.

Stowe and her contemporaries were perhaps no more preoccupied with death than their predecessors had been, but their responses to death had changed significantly, thus opening for Stowe the opportunity to use death as a means of asserting the values she associated with women. Philippe Ariès calls the nineteenth century "a period of impassioned, self-indulgent grief" (146); and Ann Douglas points out that, while excessive grief caused by a loved person's dying was often seen as a weakness in the seventeenth and eighteenth centuries, the nineteenth century made a cult of mourning ("Heaven Our Home" 56). Living in a world between that of the Puritans, who could not be sure of election, and the modern world, which cannot be sure of heaven, they could more nearly view death without fear and dread. Stowe's father, Lyman Beecher, had years before argued with Calvinist colleagues that the individual could choose God, not simply hope to be chosen. The fate of their souls was up to them, as it had not been up to their ancestors. Thus while Stowe's contemporaries expressed their grief more publicly, they could also more confidently perceive death as a moment of spiritual triumph.

In Stowe's narrative, such triumph is marked by the diminishing importance, even denial, of physical reality as the soul approaches eternity. Tom and Eva, who condemn the world's materialism, are appropriately rewarded by deaths in which the material plays little role and that are therefore divested of horror. St. Clare believes that his daughter has achieved "the victory without the battle—the crown without the conflict" (429); and Stowe denies that Eva's death is real. Because her "farewell voyage" was so "bright and placid," Stowe says, "it was impossible to realize that it was death that was approaching" (424). St. Clare too denies that Eva can die: "There is no death to such as thou, dear Eva! neither darkness nor shadow of death; only such a bright fading as when the morning star fades in the golden dawn" (429). Although he dies from a beating, Tom's death also is peaceful and beautiful; he falls asleep with a smile. Stowe's language diminishes the importance of the material and emphasizes the spiritual at a time when it seemed that her culture was engaged in the opposite activity.

Because Stowe's language strips death of what is in her context unimportant physical reality, her affirmations of death have frequently been perceived as the denial of reality often associated with the sentimental. Richard Allen's essay contrasting sentimentality and romanticism offers an example of a traditional view of sentimentality and is also helpful in illuminating Stowe's position. While Allen does not discuss Stowe specifically, *Uncle Tom's Cabin* provides an example of the anti-individualistic attitude the essay labels as sentimental. Allen says that sentimentality is always identified with groups on the fringes of a society and that it originates in the difficulty these individuals have in identifying with middle-class public life (122). Both the romantic and the sentimentalist reject the public identity, as Allen sees it; but whereas the romantic seeks an identity outside the social structure, the sentimentalist suppresses self even on the fringe or well beyond the bounds of social structure. Allen calls sentimentality "inhibited individualism" or "suppressed behavior" because it substitutes "self-sacrifice for self-assertion and sentiment for action" (121). Sentimentalism is an "alternative for those who, unable to identify with public life, are nevertheless unwilling to follow the logic of individualism to the point of overt defiance" (134).

Stowe of course cannot identify with the public life of business and politics that supports or at least condones slavery; and certainly she does not accept the "logic of individualism." Believing that self-sacrifice is the means to transform a society with which she will not identify, Stowe argues against the logic of individualism in *Uncle Tom's Cabin*. She rejects the romantic impulse to place oneself outside society not because she lacks nerve, as Allen's analysis of sentimentality would suggest, or because she lacks imaginative power. She does not place herself outside society because she believes that right feeling, which leads to self-sacrifice, can reform society.

The death scenes embodying Stowe's rejection of the profit motive constructed upon individualism and materialism and manifested in slavery and devalued women's activities are thus not sentimental in the traditional, derogatory understanding of that word. While the label of sentimentality has been used to describe a limited and fractured view of the world, Stowe's death scenes contribute to her unifying vision of an already fractured world. Racial distinctions begin to blur in her slaves that have more white blood than black, and gender differences lose their brutalizing edge in her male hero whose values and behavior seem female. Stowe reveals slavery as an analogue, even synecdoche, for Northern free labor; and regional differences disappear as Northerners' and Southerners' stance on the important issues generally mirror each other. Finally, Stowe bridges the secular and sacred with "feel[ing] right," with sympathy.

Philip Fisher offers a more useful approach to sentimentality, one that helps to explain how the deaths (Eva's particularly), intended to end slavery, were powerful to contemporary readers but have frequently seemed to call attention only to themselves and therefore to be ineffective to modern readers. Fisher argues that the sentimental novel, which he calls radical, does important cultural work, that it brings real change in the world. He says that the sentimental novel "arouses and excites action toward that part of the public future that is still open to decision and alternative" (*Hard Facts* 18), and he sees Stowe's engagement with the issue of slavery in America as a primary instance of this function. The images of the sentimental (Topsy and Uncle Tom, for example) were in their time so striking that they "became settled in the language and in the perceptual frame of the civilization" (20). They change "what the census of the human world looks like—what it includes or excludes" (3). They revise, in other words, people's perceptions of their world and thus have profound effect, for instance, creating the "inner resolve and moral bond that makes fighting the Civil War comprehensible" (20). But the change in perception is so thorough that to later audiences the images can seem "obvious, even stale" (20).

Still, Fisher's analysis accounts neither for the tension between Tom's and Eva's individual transcendence of limits and access to power and their escape from personal pain nor for the similar tension the novel creates for at least some twentieth-century readers. Just as dying enhances the individual powers of Tom and Eva but at the same time absorbs them into an otherworldly community and removes them from the necessity of exercising those powers, the novel calls for action but reveals the ultimate irrelevance of that action. This contradiction is perhaps inevitable in the work of a religious reformer of the secular world who seeks to change the world, but who must reveal its relative insignificance at the same time. Stowe perceives her age as one in which "nations are trembling and convulsed" and a "mighty influence is abroad, surging and heaving the world, as with an earthquake"; she warns of a coming judgment day when "injustice and cruelty shall bring on nations the wrath of Almighty God" (629). But she also suggests that endurance in this world is rewarded in the next. The next life that rewards Tom and provides Eva opportunities denied her in this world will compensate for the injustices suffered by Topsy as well; Eva tells her she can go to heaven and be an angel "just as much as if you were white" (410). The book's repeated, explicit message is that readers' emotions should lead to benevolent influence: "There is one thing that every individual can do, —they can see to it that *they feel right.* An atmosphere of sympathetic influence encircles every human being; and the man or woman who *feels* strongly, healthily and justly, on the great interests of humanity, is a constant benefactor to the human race" (624). Feeling, then, is basic to action, specifically the action of putting an end to slavery.

Stowe's means of communicating this message, however, is a novel that, though widely and heatedly discussed, was read and responded to for the most part in private. And, if grieving over the deaths of Eva and Tom because they remind readers of personal losses dissipates the emotions aroused by the images of slavery and thereby eliminates the impulse to social action and interaction, her means subvert her end. Such a conflict between means and ends is not peculiar to Stowe. In *No Place of Grace*, Jackson Lears says that Puritan and republican jeremiads as well as antimodernist protest have often reinforced the dominant culture by "reducing social conflicts to questions of individual morality and providing troubled Americans with an innocuous means of discharging half-conscious anxieties about the effects of expanding market capitalism" (6). Like the antimodernist critique of modern culture discussed by Lears, Stowe's protest perhaps unintentionally promotes the values she rejects. Attracted to the power (but not the isolation) implied by individualism, Stowe uses individualist appeal for anti-individualist ends.

The option of passive resistance, which at its most extreme ends in death and heaven, is the novel's most obvious alternative to accepting slavery and the individualistic and materialistic culture it symbolizes. As the preceding analysis suggests, this option is perhaps not as problematical as it often seems to the late-twentieth-century reader, given the nineteenth-century's restricted options for women and even more restricted options for slaves and its belief in the rewards of an afterlife. Even so, this passive resistance is not the only alternative Stowe envisions. The ideal that she offers as an alternative to either accepting the hegemony of the individualistic, materialistic world or to practicing passive resistance ending in death is an uncommon but real pattern of social organization—the agrarian Quaker family whose love of one another extends to their close community and outward to the larger human community, including of course runaway slaves. Rachel Halliday, the loving mother at the center of this family, is as capable as she is gentle; and unlike Mrs. Shelby, she has her husband's total respect. When her son worries that his father might go to jail for helping slaves escape their masters, Simeon Halliday reassures the child by reminding him that his mother can do anything that needs to be done. In this alternative community, men's and women's spheres may differ, but there is no division between their values. Stowe's portrayal of their daily life affirms their shared values of spirituality, engagement in community, and cooperative, agrarian work, thus successfully integrating the spiritual and the secular.

*Uncle Tom's Cabin* of course did not accomplish what Stowe intended; Southerners were not influenced to follow George Shelby's example and free their slaves, and the values her culture had restricted by identifying them as feminine were not given the authority that Stowe wished for them. In fact the book's political effect was divisive rather than unifying, and force rather than passivity or resistance through an alternative community settled the conflict over slavery. Emotions were awakened by *Uncle Tom's Cabin;* readers no doubt felt the sympathy and benevolence that Stowe intended. But she did not take into account emotions such as greed and pride, which were encouraged by individualism and which fueled the conflict over slavery. Her view of the emotions' positive power seems simplistic today and certainly would have been judged mistaken by her ancestors. Further, the novel's emotional appeal reconciles piety and indulged feelings, thus perhaps promoting the very concern with self that Stowe protested and thereby looking forward toward what Peter Homans calls the modern therapeutic type for whom "well being . . . replaces moral passion and social commitment" (227).

In important ways, however, *Uncle Tom's Cabin* did bring the nation together, did create the community Stowe envisioned. The phenomenal popularity of the book is well known: 3,000 copies sold the first day and 300,000 copies the first year (Banning 461). By 1861 it had sold more copies than any other American novel (Bode 185). Women writers of Stowe's time assumed an audience of women, but both sexes and all classes read *Uncle Tom's Cabin*. Evert Duychkinck's *Literary World* refers to an "Uncle Tom epidemic": "No age or sex is spared, men, women, and children all confess to its power. No condition is exempt; lords and ladies; flunkies and kitchen maids, are equally affected with the rage" (Hirsch 303). Emerson, uneasy about his own restricted audience, said *Uncle Tom's Cabin* was "read equally in the parlor and the kitchen and the nursery" (Matthiessen 67); and the *Albany Evening Journal* said the novel seemed likely to "make both ends of the world meet" (Hirsch 304). Stowe's affirmation of self-sacrificial death as a protest against the isolating individualistic and materialistic values of her time, while perhaps implicated in those values, contributed to the appeal of the novel that became one of the centers around which Victorian culture coalesced. By its power to join so many in a community of grief, it suggested (at least momentarily) that divisions between masculine and feminine values and therefore between men and women, between white and black, and between North and South might be healed. Modern readers' dismissal of *Uncle Tom's Cabin*'s death scenes as sentimental and therefore irrelevant is less a comment on Stowe's vision or her art than on the firm entrenchment of the individualistic and materialistic values against which the writer persuasively argues.

## N O T E S

An earlier version of this essay appeared in *American Studies* 24, no. 1 (1985). Copyright (c) 1985 Mid-America American Studies Association. Used by permission.

1. See also Herbert Brown, Lynn, and Fiedler (*Love and Death*).

2. Stowe, *Uncle Tom's Cabin*, ed. Douglas, 341. All subsequent quotations from the novel are from this edition, cited by page number in the text.

# 6
•

## Matriarchy and the Rhetoric of Domesticity

For readers of *Uncle Tom's Cabin* interested in Harriet Beecher Stowe's portrayal of women and her representation of what Jane Tompkins calls the "new matriarchy" (*Sensational Designs* 142) and Elizabeth Ammons calls her "radical script for social change" ("Stowe's Dream" 159), the kitchen of the Quakeress Rachel Halliday has provided a satisfying look at a utopian, matriarchal community. Here in the home, the center of activity, the women and children, guided by the loving influence of Rachel, work together to put sumptuous meals on the table while the patriarch of the family, Simeon Halliday, removed to the periphery of domestic activity, is "engaged in the anti-patriarchal operation of shaving."[1] Stowe draws a picture of the "neatly-painted kitchen . . . without a particle of dust," of the " 'creechy crawchy' " rocking chair that sings of "motherly loving kindness," and of the ample breakfast table at which Rachel presides, passing "a plate of cakes," pouring coffee, and infusing the scene with her "motherliness and fullheartedness" (214, 215, 223). Here Rachel is the moving force of her family, directing the activities of her home, a place of comfort and refuge from the cares of the world. Indeed, it is here under the aegis of Rachel's Christian, motherly love that the fugitive Harris family is reunited. But more importantly, it is here in Rachel's home and under her influence that George's spirit is revived, that he comes to know the meaning of the Gospel as he comes to know the meaning of the word *home:* "This, indeed, was a home—home, —a word that George had never yet known a meaning for, and a belief in God, and trust in his providence, began to encircle his heart" (224). The chapter that centers on Rachel Halliday's ideal community of home suggests an alternate society for the nation, in which women as nurturing mothers rule through their influence of love rather than by exploitation and competition. As Jane Tompkins has argued, Stowe's new matriarchy "constitutes the most politically subversive dimension of Stowe's novel" (*Sensational Designs* 142).

Yet the domestic scene that Stowe draws is informed by and infused with a rhetoric—and hence an ideology—that complicates her vision of a reformed America. For while she attempts social change—abolition and matriarchy—her politics and characterizations of women are constrained by a conservative discourse, the rhetoric of domesticity, that actually works against social change. Indeed, the two important rhetorics of *Uncle Tom's Cabin* work against each other and perplex Stowe's own discourse and paradigm for reform. While the abolitionist movement asserted the right of one segment of the American population to freedom and autonomy, domesticity advocated the enclosure of another group within the domestic circle and definitions of the self that worked to deprive women of the fullness of self-identity. Like the abolitionist movement, the ideology of domesticity was a social construct "that responded to changing social and economic reality" (Kerber 21) with its own agenda. That agenda, however, was not informed by women's desire for autonomy; rather, it was a discourse dominated by "the voice of the bourgeois male" that attempted to repress social change by asserting the traditional roles of women (Smith-Rosenberg 91). At a time when America was aflurry with competing rhetorics and social, industrial, and political reorientation, domesticity provided a stabilizing discourse that prescribed as it described women's roles and space in ways that limited women's competition with the current power hegemony. Moreover, as Linda Kerber observes, "The ideology of separate spheres could be both instrumental and prescriptive," a tool for maintaining women's social subordination and a tool women used as an emotional "hedge against secularization" (26), valorizing the home and women's domestic, sentimental, and religious charms. Indeed, Stowe demonstrates the ambiguity of the trope of domesticity when she uses it to create a matriarchy to counter the materialism of male-dominated politics and economics, the "radical script" that Tompkins and Ammons describe (Ammons 159). But the trope of domesticity strains and limits that script, for Stowe's "idealized matriarchal domain . . . has its boundaries drawn for it by the larger culture" (Askeland 789) and its characters circumscribed by readings that work to deprive women of full, rich personality.

The language of advice manuals for young women of the nineteenth century not only mirrored but engineered an image of women as domestic, dependent, and powerless. Written primarily by "the opinion setters of the new bourgeois world—male physicians, publishers, educators and religious leaders" (Smith-Rosenberg 25)—and by women who did "the dirty work of their society" (Douglas, *Feminization* 11), advice manuals for women, especially marriage manuals, described and inscribed a version of female deportment, self-concept, and social roles that contributed to the maintenance of a male-dominated social order. Wildly popular between 1820 and 1870, advice manuals for men and women constructed a version of America that emphasized gender differences as it ignored or blurred class and race differences, creating a version of America characterized by the values of the white male middle-class.[2] Unable or unwilling to write one discourse appropriate for both men and women, American advisers wrote separate discourses that not only mirrored and maintained the sexes' separate social spheres but marginalized female identity. At the same time that these "opinion setters" were advising young men to develop themselves, they were advising women to develop their domestic charms. While men told themselves that *"you may be whatsoever you will resolve to be"* (Alcott, *Young Man's Guide* 25), promoting for themselves the myth of the self-made man, women were reminded that they could neither make their own careers nor their own being. Thus this gendered version of American society contributed to the dichotomization of labor and power into public and private arenas, and to a static, flattened model of female personality accompanied and justified by a reading of the "inequality in the sexes" (*Female Friend* 196).

Characteristic of the rhetoric of the early decades of the nineteenth century, a piece of advice from *The Female Friend,* a book devoted to advising "Christian Virgins" and "A Young Married

Lady," demonstrates the culture's reading of the duality and inequality of the sexes: "There is an inequality in the sexes, and . . . for the economy of the world, the men who were to be guardians and law-givers, had not only the greater share of bodily strength bestowed upon them, but those also of reason and resolution. Your sex will be the better prepared from this necessary reflection, for the compliance and passiveness . . . for the better performance of those duties which seem to be most properly assigned to it by nature" (196).

The pervasiveness of such a reading of femininity is demonstrated in part by the use that women made of it and by their emotional investment in the domestic and religious paradigms the rhetoric supports. One of its striking paradoxes is that at the same time that women's work was devalued, homes and the women who managed them became idealized, often by women themselves, who advocated and sentimentalized their own oppression. Catherine Maria Sedgwick, for instance, exclaimed to her readers in 1839, "My young friends, thank God for your happy homes—and remember! it is 'woman's work' to make them happy" (100). Indeed, the rhetoric of the sacred and the rhetoric of domesticity often converged in descriptions of home and woman, as in this line from "Essay on Marriage": "O! what a hallowed place home is when lit by the smile of such a being" (qtd. in Cott 69), and in L. H. Sigourney's apostrophe, "Blessed Bride,—thou art about to enter this sanctuary, and to become a priestess at its altar" (26). In this conflicting and (con)fused rhetoric, women are transformed into angels and the home into a sacred sanctuary, and women's mission becomes no less than the divine salvation of the American people. In the hands of Catharine Beecher, leader of women's education reform and daughter of an old-time Calvinist, the home became analogous to the heavenly home and the mistress's duty that of saving the souls under her care. In *The American Woman's Home,* coauthored with her sister Harriet Beecher Stowe, she writes, "The family state then, is the aptest earthly illustration of the heavenly kingdom, and in it woman is its chief minister. Her great mission is self-denial. . . . She is to rear all under her care to lay up treasures, not on earth, but in heaven" (19). Like the ideal home posited by Beecher, the primary value in *Uncle Tom's Cabin* of Rachel Halliday's home, that "Paradise" in Indiana, is that it exemplifies the "living Gospel" and brings George Harris from "dark, misanthropic, pining atheistic doubts" to "a belief in God, and trust in his providence" (222, 224). For Mrs. Shelby, as for Stowe, home is the arena for teaching the true values of Christianity, as she has done with Eliza, whom she has taught to do her duty to young Harry "as a Christian mother" (83). Beecher's and Stowe's soteriology is a model not just for what Tompkins calls Beecher's "imperialistic drive" to colonize the world for Jesus (*Sensational Designs* 143–44) but also for the continued defense of existing "patterns of belief and value" (Geertz 231) that associated women with home and religiosity without directly challenging "the modern organization of work and the pursuit of wealth" (Cott 69).

Indeed, women and their sphere, the home, were ascribed the tasks of providing refuge from the world and of saving man from himself, of palliating, absorbing, and redeeming "the strain of social and economic transformation" (Cott 70). Woman's task, she was told by domestic advisers, is "to soften and humanize . . . to entertain and enliven" (*Female Friend* 197); the home "is a serene region in which a woman moves," and the wife's province is "to soften, to cheer, and to refresh that mind on which the weightiest cares of a family press" (Bean 10, 13), to influence her family with "gentle modifying power" toward moral, Christian living (Stowe, *Little Foxes* 140). As the author of *Buds for the Bridal Wreath* suggests, it is in the home that affection and morality germinate: "What God designed—a home of sweet affection, faithful love, and domestic peace,—a school of social culture, true refinement, pure endeavor, and sacred aspirations,—the birthplace, the cradle, the nursery, the school, of all those affections, graces, and virtues that belong to the children of God" (22).

At its best, then, the home is to be like Rachel Halliday's or Mrs. Bird's, the sphere of woman's influence of love and nurture, an orderly and comforting refuge from the world, and the training ground for future generations of Christian Americans. The opening sentence by which Stowe draws her reader into the Bird household illustrates the model home of an American housewife, for it presents an orderly but cozy environment, overseen by a delightful woman whose greatest heroism is the righting of moral wrong: "The light of the cheerful fire shone on the rug and carpet of a cosey parlor, and glittered on the sides of the tea-cups and well-brightened tea-pot, as Senator Bird was drawing off his boots, preparatory to inserting his feet in a pair of new handmade slippers, which his wife had been working for him while away on his senatorial tour" (141). This sentence oozes with the kind of physical comfort, the fire, teapot, and handmade slippers, that women could provide for their husbands weary from the vexations of the world. Indeed, Senator Bird acknowledges the curative quality of the home when he declares to his wife, anxious to nurse his wrangled nerves, " 'No, no, Mary, no doctoring! a cup of your good hot tea, and some of our good home living, is what I want. It's a tiresome business, this legislating!' " (141–42).

As comforting a view of home and of the woman's role as these examples present, Mrs. Bird has yet another, more important, role as female to perform: that is, to remind the senator of what his better self knows, to remind him of his humanity. This she does by appealing to the Bible and to right feeling as she remonstrates, "by entreaty and persuasion," against a law that would make aiding and comforting runaway slaves illegal. Though she convinces her husband to do the right thing, how she reminds him is problematic, for her method is constrained by a psychology of the female mind. She sounds her opposition to the proposed law not by appealing to logic, but by appealing to feelings, that special commodity of the female "mind" (Arthur 8, 129), and to Christian ethics. As T. S. Arthur puts it, "Feeling and perception [*and not thought*] are the peculiar distinguishing features of a woman's mind" (8). Drawing on compassion, then, for the fugitives, she declares to Senator Bird, "Things have got to a pretty pass, if a woman can't give a warm supper and a bed to poor, starving creatures, just because they are slaves, and have been abused and oppressed all their lives, poor things!" The senator, however, remains unconvinced by his wife's protestations, touching as they are, for they lack the logical disinterestedness that he values: "[T]here is such a state of public agitation rising, that we must put aside our private feelings" (144). What convinces the senator is not his wife's arguments, but the living drama of Eliza's "mournful and pathetic beauty" and his wife's "gentle and womanly offices" to "the poor woman." Only by such visualization, by the dramatic juxtaposition of the effects of an inhumane system against humane support, does the senator do the right thing and direct and effect the next stage of Eliza's rescue.[3] Like the ideal woman she represents, Mrs. Bird not only articulates but, more importantly, acts out the physical and moral resuscitation of those who come within her world.

Yet even the valorizations of home that we see in Stowe's

representations of Rachel Halliday and Mary Bird, as well as in the subliterature of domesticity, undermine the role and nature of women. As they make the home an ideal that cannot be realized, intensifying women's frustrations, they also point to woman's containment, passivity, and weakness. Though woman apparently has before her the all-important task of raising a nation of Christians, the rhetoric of domesticity actually works against her as it capitulates to the ideology of hegemonic masculine power. Though Mrs. Bird protests against the cruel treatment of fugitive slaves, she does not even think of extending her influence beyond her family circle by seeking a political, public voice. And though Mrs. Shelby has labored to teach her slaves Christian, family values, her work of years is undone in a moment, for her home is vulnerable to "the 'masculine' domain of materialism and commercialism" (Askeland 786). In both cases, the valued work of woman, providing and teaching Christian morality, is limited to her sphere and erased or canceled whenever it interferes with the designs of the larger, masculine sphere.

In fact, advice books often remind woman that although home is her special sphere, home is actually a masculine domain, subject to man's rule within and without, and a domain in which her presence and selfhood are liable to erasure. At the same time that she is expected to assume all the domestic and child-rearing duties, she is told that "the weightiest cares" of the family fall on the male (Bean 13). Even though "with her, home is everything," that world centers on the needs and presence of her husband: "Let her seek to make home the dearest spot on earth to him,— to spread around both it and him the sweet flowers of a chaste and pure affection" (*Buds for the Bridal Wreath* 38–39). Whatever winning ways a woman possesses, "sweetness, humanity, and tenderness" all go to maintaining the man's presence within the family and preserving his affections for her, for after all he "has been toiling all the day, principally, perhaps, with a view to her comfort" (Bean 10–12). Moreover, the truly feminine woman learns to submit gracefully to the advice, rule, whim, and even sullenness of her husband. While she may influence her husband, even advise him, the domesticated woman knows when to keep silent. Warning against "the first dispute," John Morison advises the wife, "If ever you attempt to rule, let it be by the force of character, by the well-known charm of female influence, by that gentleness of spirit and behavior which few men are able to resist" (38, 55). The anonymous author of *The Young Lady's Own Book* goes so far as to advise physical retreat and self-imposed silence over disagreement. By assigning to woman the Christian virtue of gentleness, Morison and his cohorts effectively disempower woman, erasing her presence from the kind of serious, intellectual debate that shapes the politics of the family and the nation. Indeed, as Judith Lowder Newton points out, the emphasis in advice literature on women's "influence" "functioned to sustain unequal power relations between middle-class women and middle-class men." Further, Newton asserts, "To have influence, in effect meant doing without self-definition, achievement, and control, meant relinquishing power for effacement of the self in love and sacrifice" (767). At the same time that the home as arena of Christian love is privileged, then, the rhetoric of domesticity contributes to disempowering woman physically and psychically, to containing woman within the home and convincing her of her inferior position and ability. Like Morison's ideal woman, the domesticated wife knows "her appropriate sphere, . . . where, silently and unobtrusively, she addresses herself, . . . to the conscientious discharge of her peculiar duties!" (57).

Again, Stowe's representation of the Bird family illustrates the point. For while Mrs. Bird wins the day by convincing the senator of the right attitude toward the law, subverting a degraded masculine notion of law and economy, she consistently persuades by conventionally feminine methods, relying on feeling rather than reason to make her point. Indeed, Stowe's own rhetorical method, like that of Mrs. Bird, is marked by emotion, by "exhibit[ing] [slavery] in a *living dramatic reality*" (622), rather than by polemic. While one might argue that Stowe extends her subversion to the entire masculine world by demonstrating the ineffectiveness of rationality with her own method and with Mrs. Bird's declared rejection of reason when she announces, "I hate reasoning" (145), Stowe's vision of woman's intellectual potential is clearly contained within and by the ideology of gender differences. Echoing cultural prescriptions against woman's voice, Stowe "exhibits" more than she speaks, and her women characters, as Barbara Bardes and Suzanne Gossett note, talk ineffectively, "powerlessly and inconsequentially" (54). Moreover, Stowe's language participates in the rhetoric of femininity, one that calls attention to women's meekness and diminutiveness, as when she describes Mrs. Bird as being "little," "timid," "mild," "gentle," "sympathetic." Even her character's name suggests something small and flighty. By the time the reader gets to Mrs. Bird's declaration that she will break fugitive slave laws, we have some trouble taking this little woman's "resolute air" and "determined tone" with complete seriousness (143). The effect of Stowe's use of these belittling adjectives makes Mrs. Bird a safe, conventionally feminine character who, though she breaks the law, continues to evoke the ideal woman rather than a dangerously subversive one.[4] Finally, while Stowe effectively demonstrates within the Bird home the morality of the private sphere in contrast to the public world of men, it is not her heroine but Senator Bird who makes inroads on that sphere by traveling the muddy roads of rural Ohio. Mrs. Bird remains contained, without a political voice, within her home, precisely because she is constituted by the cult of domesticity.

As the Bird scene demonstrates, the idealization of woman and home promotes a double-handed ideology of the feminine that at once raises woman to the level of angels and moral reformers, and yet contains woman within an ideology and a sphere that contribute to limiting and belittling her human potential. Aware that women do not have the same kind of access to the professions and education, and hence the power and self-definition, available to men, some proponents of domesticity like Catharine Beecher, Catherine Maria Sedgwick, and Lydia Maria Child urged the professionalization of domesticity as a way of untying the knot of the paradox that undermined women's work and identity. Beecher announced in the introduction of her book that if "the honor and duties of the family state are not duly appreciated, [it is because] women are not trained for these duties as men are trained for their trades and professions, and that, as the consequence, family labor is poorly done, poorly paid, and regarded as menial and disgraceful" (Beecher and Stowe 13). The solution, for all three authors, is to train women in the arts of housekeeping, cooking, and nursing so that they can maintain a home marked by economy and order. Like Stowe's Rachel Halliday, properly trained women would have a "neatly-painted kitchen," put together scrumptious meals, and nurse those, like the emotionally overwrought Eliza, who are in their care (214). Order, economy, regularity, and industry were the buzzwords for the period, dominating Henry Ward Beecher's

*Seven Lectures to Young Men* as well as his sisters' book on home economics. The shared use of the ideology and language of work contributed to the sense that running a house is in some ways comparable to running a business and that woman's "true profession" (Beecher and Stowe 13) is indeed a profession. Just such emphasis on the science of housekeeping is reflected in Ophelia Sinclair who, appalled at the "hurryscurryation" of Dinah's kitchen in Stowe's novel, declares she is going "to put everything in order" (317, 315). Given the keys to the various domestic closets of the St. Clare household, Miss Ophelia, good New Englander that she is, attempts to bring system and economy to the uneducated staff, who nonetheless are destined to wrench from her the exasperated complaint, "Such shiftless management, such waste, such confusion, I never saw!" (316).

But as Catharine Beecher makes clear, women have only one profession whereas men, confident in their power and position, told themselves, *"you may be whatsoever you will resolve to be"* (Alcott, *Young Man's Guide* 25). The consensus seemed to be with William A. Alcott: "Never were such immense results depending upon a generation of men as upon that which is now approaching the stage of action . . . to form by far the greatest nation that ever constituted an entire community of freemen" (*Young Man's Guide* 23). The work of the nation, the rhetoric of masculinity maintained, depended on the various talents and hard work of its men, of the capacity of each man to become a self-made man. Indeed, as men were advised to make their own success in the world, they were also enjoined to form their character, "making" themselves in more ways than one. Men's manuals not only overflow with practical advice for men entering the business world but emphasize the importance of character formation, which William Ellery Channing, Unitarian guru of self-culture, declares to be "the care which every man owes to himself, to the unfolding and perfecting of his Nature" (*Selected Writings* 226). Conflating moral and material success, Joel Hawes tells his young male readers, *"Character is power; character is influence; . . . [it] opens for [you] a sure and easy way to wealth, to honor and happiness. . . . On the character you are now forming hangs your own eternal destiny"* (111–16). Men's manuals are replete, as well, with strategies for forming character, emphasizing the importance of establishing positive habits early and of maintaining a temperate, moral, and industrious life. Yet, as important for temporal and religious well-being as they are, character formation and its consequences seem to be reserved for the male of the species.

Creating and celebrating the myth of the self-made man, men's advisers like Daniel Wise claimed self-culture to be a "slow, toilsome" task peculiarly fitted for the male because it required "manly strength of purpose" (72–73) and persever-ance, characteristics apparently not in the female repertoire, for women "rarely succeed in long works . . . their natural training rendering them equally adverse to long doubt and long labour" (*Evening Gazette* [Boston], March 27, 1830). The author of *The Young Lady's Own Book* told his readers, "It is seldom, indeed, that women are great proficients," and he advised them to realize their inferiority and dependence upon the male (19–20). In-deed, women were apparently hard-pressed to do their domestic work well, orderliness being labeled an inherently male trait by William Alcott as he warns, "Happy would be the condition of some husbands, could they escape the disorder produced by disorderly wives, and breathe freely once more their native ele-ment" (*Young Wife* 125). While women were told that a domestic education was necessary to better fit them for their peculiar duties, they were also often advised against intellectual pursuits, being told either that they had not the capacity for such work or that it is unfeminine and thus unattractive to men. Even when woman's academic education was proposed by some, its purpose remained tied to woman's peculiar sphere and what Frances Cogan calls a "survival ethic" (*All-American Girl* 4). (Cogan finds five rationales for women's academic education: romance and marriage, domestic economy and child rearing, cultural atmo-sphere and morality, vocational, and health and balance of self [74].)

Most debilitating about advice for women, however, is that it runs directly counter to the accepted prescriptions for charac-ter formation. Knowledge, reason, independence, perseverance, and competitiveness, the requisites for character formation, were consistently labeled as masculine or manly. Of the manuals for women surveyed for this essay, only a few mention character formation and then primarily in the context of women's domestic sphere and relation to men. They certainly do not discuss, as did Margaret Fuller, woman's need "as a nature to grow, as an intellect to discern, as a soul to live freely and unimpeded, to unfold such powers as were given her when we left our common home" (38). As is so often the case, what is absent is as telling as what is present; the lack of discussion in women's manuals about character formation, especially when it is so central to men's manuals, suggests a void in nineteenth-century concepts about the nature of woman. Although men were often told they held the power of self-formation and the chance for personal success in their own hands, self-cultivation and success were gender-specific tasks, women apparently being incompetent or fundamentally unable to realize either.

While one may wonder at the blatant misogyny of some male writers, especially when they are writing for an audience of women, the same sort of gendered reading of human potential is evident in Stowe's novel. Of all the characters in her novel, only George Harris is described as engaged in a program of self-cultivation. Stowe invites the reader into the Harris home, "a small, neat tenement, in the outskirts of Montreal," where George is seated in his study, a table in one corner of the room on which are piled paper and pen and over which hangs "a shelf of well-selected books." Stowe's narrator tells us that "[t]he same zeal for self-improvement, which led him to steal the much coveted acts of reading and writing, . . . still led him to devote all his leisure time to self-cultivation." But while George and even little Harry are engaged in self-cultivation, Eliza, now "more matronly than of yore but evidently contented and happy as woman need be," is ensconced in the female world of domesticity. Our view of Eliza shows her interrupting George's study to pull him back into the family sphere as she prepares dinner, with the blazing fire, snowy tablecloth, and tea kettle signs of her role and character: " 'Do put down that book, and let's talk, while I'm getting tea,—do' " (604). Though Eliza's incredible bravery and grit got her out of the clutches of slavery and brought her to the "true" realization of her sex as wife and mother, they apparently do not qualify her for self-cultivation. Eliza may be a survivor, one of Frances Cogan's "Real Women," a woman of intelligence, physical fitness, and self-sufficiency, but Stowe does not show her continuing to challenge her prescribed place, nurturing her human spiritual and intellectual potential, or gaining economic independence.

As Stowe draws the character of the matronly Eliza, William Alcott, outspoken advocate of self-formation and self-improvement for young men, constructs a model of the female self that not only does not include self-formation but that consigns woman's efforts in that area to the self-improvement of her husband and children. The wife, he insists in *The Young Wife*, is her husband's "help-meet"; she is created for the man and "is to assist him—cooperate with him—in the work of self-education" (22). Like Eliza, who attends to her husband's needs, following him first to Paris and then to Liberia as he works to improve himself and set about his life's work, Alcott's ideal partner "is . . . obviously fitted to be an assistant to her husband in the work of self-improvement, and the improvement of others" (27). Removed to the periphery of her own life, the domesticated woman sacrifices her own identity and self-culture so that others, like George, can improve themselves. Whatever sort of improvement Alcott's woman does gain is subsidiary to and a reflection of her husband's: "It also happens that in no way can she so rapidly promote her own improvement, as in promoting that of her husband; since the light and influence which she sheds on him is necessarily reflected upon herself" (23). Alcott suggests a model of the female self that not only places her in relation to others but that appears to deny or neglect woman's inner being, the central core from which would emerge her own character and identity. Apparently without individual and interior identity, women were consistently (could only be) described by their relations to others and by external signs of character, the tea kettle and snowy tablecloth, both methods of representation that further contribute to erasing women from the text(ure) of their own lives.

In the hands of the rhetoricians of domesticity, a wife not only derives her identity from her husband, merging "her own name in that of her husband" (Alcott, *Young Wife* 23), but her primary function seems to be enhancing her husband's life by creating a comfortable domestic space and by conforming to the external signs of agreeable femininity. The manuals not only demonstrate disproportionate attention to women's dress, complexion, accomplishments, and manners, but by omission they apparently deny women a private, internal life. Men were encouraged by a Lockean psychology of the self to shape their own characters, by an organicism that described character as "a plant which every one may cultivate" (Todd 57–58). Women, on the other hand, were urged to a "plastic" adaptation to others, to an external rather than internal transformation (*Young Lady's Own Book*

14). Given this way of looking at women, as rather hollow but potentially charming luminaries in the life of men, it is not surprising that the metaphor of the ornament occurs in the manuals as descriptive not only of women's accomplishments but of their identity. While most advisers were concerned that women's clothing be neat, healthful, and plain, the author of *The Young Lady's Own Book* acquiesces to women's "natural" interest in dress, rationalizing his position by arguing that because women ornament the lives of men, they should not be denied the use of ornament in their own attire: "Woman being the solace and delight as well as the helpmate of man, a moderate use of ornament seems reasonably allowable to her" (254). Mrs. Taylor more explicitly connects women with the metaphor of ornament when she calls the wife the "chief ornament" of the fireside whose charms are to please and domesticate the husband (114). As Mrs. Taylor seems to suggest, a primary reason women have for looking nice, for acquiring the usual accomplishments, for behaving with charm, modesty, and piety, is to attain and retain the affection of men. Perhaps this is why so much attention is focused on such things, because they constitute much of women's guarantee for economic stability. But women's concern for dress seems also to be a sign of their inherent moral shallowness and weakness. "Dress is, at best," the author of *The Young Man's Own Book* told his readers, "but a female privilege, and, in man, argues both of levity of mind, and effeminacy of manners" (137). This unbalanced attention on the externalities of women's character in advice manuals suggests not only a distrust of the feminine, but a flat reading of female personality, one that focuses the gaze on "the material surfaces of 'embodied selfhood' " (Sidonie Smith 83).

Indeed, in the advice manuals and in much nineteenth-century fiction, women are stereotyped as they are read, according to observable external signs. As David Reynolds demonstrates, nineteenth-century antebellum fiction employed "cultural stereotypes" with "dazzling diversity" (367, 339). Reynolds's survey of sentimental and sensational fiction turned up several kinds of female stereotypes, including the moral exemplar, woman victim, and adventure feminist (339–40). The broad category of moral exemplar, Reynolds finds, was further subtyped into the angel and the practical woman. Part of the huge success that *Uncle Tom's Cabin* enjoyed in its time, Reynolds explains, was that it "gave various moral exemplars uniquely re-demptive power" at the same time that it retained "a reassuringly simple division" of character types (388). For an audience used to finding female types in their literature, Eva could be readily recognized as the angelic moral exemplar, Miss Ophelia as the practical moral exemplar, and Eliza as the timid woman victim who, with her run from Haley across the icy Ohio River, emerges as the adventure feminist and ends the novel as a representative of white bourgeois culture, the practical moral exemplar. The power of stereotypes, as Reynolds and Clifford Geertz suggest, is that like other symbol systems they are "shared, conventional, or-dered, and indeed learned" ways of providing humans "a mean-ingful framework for orienting themselves to one another, to the world around them, and to themselves" (Geertz 250). But while stereotypes may be reassuring to the reading public and may facilitate the work of fiction as "instruments of cultural self-definition" (Tompkins, *Sensational Designs* xvi), they also partici-pate in the manipulation and containment of those they are intended to represent. By focusing attention on the external, material surfaces, Helene Cixous argues, stereotype "either obscures women or reproduces the classic representations of women" ("Laugh of the Medusa" 336), and, as Luce Irigaray adds, fails to break "the sharp edges of rigidity" that mark men's writing (qtd. in Person 14). Stereotypes do indeed do the work of their (patriarchal) culture. They provide a reassuring framework for human relations. But they also contribute to a reading that reinforces the notion that female characters and the women they represent lack depth, fluidity, or individuality, that women are best known by physical traits rather than by the mental, meta-physical definitions of selfhood men applied to themselves. By drawing a largely physical, external "blueprint" "for the govern-ing of [female] behavior" (Geertz 216, 44), stereotypes partici-pate in managing and limiting rather than liberating female behavior.

Thus, while Marie St. Clare may represent the worst type of woman, one who is self-centered and unaffectionate, marked by a "sallow" complexion and the "diamond bracelet on her slender wrist" (255, 275), she is not the only character in Stowe's novel who is stereotyped according to a semiotics of the self. Stowe also signals our reading of positive characters like Rachel Halliday by describing external appearances—her dress, complexion, and kitchen—metaphors of the self that divert the reader's gaze from the metaphysical self. The "plain white muslin handkerchief, lying in placid folds across her bosom,—the drab shawl and dress," Rachel's "rosy" complexion, "suggestive of a ripe peach," and her kitchen with its "rows of shining tin" (215, 223) are "details of physical description" that provide a code for reading personality and, like stereotypes, "have the simultaneous power of presence and absence, the ability to frame and to self-destruct" (Michie 86–87). Little Eva, one of the most memorable characters in the novel, not only represents a type of female character but disintegrates into typology as she disintegrates from life. "[H]er white dress, with her golden hair and glowing dress, her cheeks unnaturally bright" (401), signal her as an icon of sacrificial death, the angelic consumptive who dies before her time. And her death chamber, marked by statuettes and the white-draped bed, betokens a being who is not present, an icon among icons, a lifeless statuette, a "little sleeping form" "beneath the drooping angel-figures" (429). Like her room that is arranged for effect by Adolph and Rosa, Eva as character is arranged by Stowe for effect. Her function in the novel, emotionally touching as it may be, finally is ornamental. Her death does not do its office; it does not compel Augustine St. Clare to do what he believes should be done—to free his slaves—nor does it save the St. Clare slaves from misery. And she is unable to emerge beyond the rigidness of stereotype to become a complex character that readers know beneath the signs that mark her.

Victorian writers constructed an elaborate sign system whereby, theoretically, the inner self could be known by external signs such as manners and dress. In her own "philosophy of dress," Catherine Maria Sedgwick claims, "I should almost class neatness among the moral qualities of dress. It is a sign of self-respect. It is an indication that you appreciate the dignity of home. It is generally . . . a sign of inward purity" (195, 185). William Alcott claimed that "somehow or other, there is a very close connection between the purity of the body and that of the mind" (*Young Wife* 117), and T. S. Arthur pronounced that "[a] want of neatness, as well as a want of order, shows a defect in the mind" (40). Stowe, too, participates in this semiotic rhetoric, signaling with external images (the cozy fire, the shining teapot, the peachy complexion) the internal condition of her characters. But rather than illuminating the inner self as was supposed, the sign system of character actually subverts women's efforts to realize their own interiority. For by constructing a semiotics of character, writers of domesticity seem to have skewed the equation by confusing the sign with the referent and to have reduced (female) human complexity to a simple and manageable cipher or code that more clearly reflects an author's version of female character than actual female personality. Even when writers of the period realize that inner reality is not adequately represented by the external signs, they opt for the sign over the reality, especially when the sign conforms to their idea of feminine behavior. While "the smile of uncomplaining resignation" may belie the actuality beneath the surface (*Young Wife's Book* 16), writers nonetheless prefer the smile, and the submission it registers, rather than a contentious and complex inner character. Though Stowe wants to build a matrifocal universe centered on the sentimental and moral power of women, the rhetoric of domesticity, in which she is heavily vested, works against her agenda as it reduces the female character to a manageable "system of signs" (Michie 61), erasing or blurring women's interiority and constructing as the ideal woman a disempowered stereotype or cliché. Even as Stowe proposes motherhood as "the ethical and structural model for all of American life" (Ammons, "Stowe's Dream" 159), the rhetoric of domesticity has an "imprisoning effect" (Michie 89) on her characters and on the women who read her story. Both character and reader are rendered by Stowe abstractions and are figured by overused metaphors borrowed from the rhetoric of domesticity that oversimplify real womanhood. Though she valorizes them, Stowe's mothers—Mrs. Shelby, Mrs. Bird, and Eliza—and those "mothers of America" (623) whom she addresses in the last chapter are nonetheless clichés of motherhood and, like her vision of matriarchy, are imprisoned by the too familiar cultural constructions.

Disinherited from her natural right to inner reality, woman is moreover erased from the text of her own life, for the exemplary woman is to move through her home and through her life "silent, gentle, and often unperceived" (Alcott, *Young Wife* 23). From the moment of her marriage, her disintegration as an independent being begins, for with marriage she is "no longer her own," and "the aim of her existence" is renunciation of self (Sigourney 28). Compelled by custom to forsake her name and her aspirations, she is repeatedly admonished in the subliterature of domesticity to participate in her own erasure. She is told to remain silent or to quit the room rather than say something provoking (*Young Lady's Own Book* 201); to "let him see the smile of uncomplaining resignation" (*Young Wife's Book* 16); to "always acquiesce" (Freeling 29). "Silently and unobtrusively" (Morison 57), she is "to seek to live for others," "to practice self-denial for the good of others" (Arthur 13, 16).

Stowe endorses and problematizes the power and limitations of such erasure, for Mrs. Shelby knows the value of both strategic retreat and covert action. Though she remonstrates with Mr. Shelby about selling Tom and little Harry, she can do nothing to change his mind nor was she even consulted by her husband about the family financial situation or, as Mr. Shelby puts it, "my business" (82). In fact, Mr. Shelby tells his wife, "I didn't mean to tell you this Emily" (84). Her work and identity "as a Christian woman" teaching her slaves the "duties of the family" are canceled by one bill of sale (83). Though she has tried to maintain a Christian home, it remains vulnerable to the larger world of materialism. "[I]n a moment" her work is overturned; she and her charges are left to realize "that [the Shelbys] care for no tie, no duty, no relation, however sacred, compared with money" (83). Silenced by the ineffectiveness of her arguments to Mr. Shelby and by the swift erasure of her work, her only means of resistance lie with subterfuge veiled by "female artifice" (113), by whisper, innuendo, and physical removal to the balcony or veranda. Like the slaves Sam and Andy, other characters adept at manipulating their disempowerment and her accomplices in delaying Mr. Haley long enough for Eliza to make her escape, Mrs. Shelby must rely on covert action and "impression" rather than words to enact her will (109). By such means Mrs. Shelby survives the cultural silencing of women's voices and is able to continue as a moral influence in the life of her son, George, making her presence felt, even if in indirect ways. Similarly, Cassy manipulates her absence and enclosure in Simon Legree's house, assuming the white sheets of a ghost to haunt Legree's imagination and thus effect her escape and reemergence at the Harris home. Unfortunately, other characters, like the immature Eva and the alcoholic Prue, have not learned how to manipulate their position and are literally erased from the novel.

Problematic and troublesome about the rhetoric of domesticity as well is that while it effectually imprisons women within the home and within the culturally constructed blueprint for female behavior, it also undermines what is described as essentially female, religious sentiment. Supposedly by nature more religious and pious than man, woman was called on to Christianize and humanize those within her domestic circle, "for, in her influence upon the other sex, but mainly upon her children, lies the all-potent principle of social reformation" (Arthur 77). When one looks closely at the rhetoric of domesticity, however, one finds that even as it idealizes woman as mother and ascribes to woman the religious care of her family, the rhetoric trivializes women's religiosity. Like woman herself, who becomes in the hands of the moralists a figure, an ornament to grace men's lives, so woman's religious sentiment is figured as an ornament, a sparkling doodad pinned to the exterior of her person to make her more attractive. William Alcott asks, "Is there anything which can ornament female character . . . like deep, heart-felt, practical piety?" and he compares piety to a bright jewel: "Piety is like a diamond in the midst of pearls" (*Young Wife* 374–75). Another moralist writes to his female audience that "your great ornament must be that 'of a meek and quiet spirit'" (Morison 61). Like an ornament, and like woman, religion lacks real effectiveness against the demands of materialism and the world of men. While Mr. Shelby "reverenced and respected the consistency" of his wife's religiosity, he finds that "[w]e men of the world must wink pretty hard at various things, and get used to a deal that isn't the exact thing. But we don't quite fancy, when women and ministers come out broad and square, and go beyond us in matters of either modesty or morals" (53, 85). Though young George later acts from principles learned from his mother, it is he rather than Mrs. Shelby who does the work of morality, retrospectively justifying and authorizing his father's position, while his mother remains within her proper sphere. Moreover, religion operates to further erase woman's real presence, working against a view of her interiority and transcribing the feminine within the terms of patriarchy even in this her special sphere. Indeed, in the rhetoric of domesticity religion is devalued, "feminized," as Ann Douglas puts it. Like women, who are to be seen but not heard, women's religion is described as "full of repose," calm, and quietude (*Young Lady's Own Book* 160), and her influence of love and kindness, a "silent power" (Alcott, *Young Wife* 37), an influence deprived of real power and identity. While female piety exerts itself in acts of charity, the author of *The Young Lady's Own Book* finds such efforts to be "not very important," just as woman's life is made up of "little things," "little cares," and "little occurrences" (165–66, 280). Though woman is apparently the guardian of the heart/hearth, her religion is devalorized as more "a matter of sentiment than reasoning" (*Way to Get Married* 43) by men who reserve for themselves the empowering quality of mind, reasoning, and its religious field of endeavor, theology. While, as Stowe suggests, mothers may see to it that they and their charges "feel right" and demonstrate "the sympathies of Christ" (624), their religiosity is apparently limited by their nature, true religion (theology) being a masculine undertaking. Indeed, the author of *The Way to Get Married* tells his female audience not to exert themselves with difficult Scriptures but to "treat them with silent and becoming reverence" (43). The business of thinking through scriptural complexities appears to be beyond female capacities, reserved, like other realms of power, for the male.

Moreover, women apparently have a special need for religion, for as inheritors of the vanity and weakness of Eve they require the constraints of religion, just as they require the constraints of men's laws and men's metaphors to keep them in their "legitimate sphere" (Morison 53). Here the rhetoric becomes markedly strained, for while feminine sentimentality, to some extent, has been valorized, it also justifies social and legal restraints on women. Inheriting a very old tradition that blames "our first mother [who] was betrayed by the pride of knowledge," moralists persist, even as they praise women, in arguing her special proclivity to error: Because "she [Eve] chose wrong at first, . . . liability of error seems entailed upon her" (*Young Lady's Own Book* 29, 179). In the moral literature that men write for themselves, the pejorative language used to describe the feminine is even more obvious as they label the bodily appetites that would undo morality and industry "effeminate and perverted" (*Christian Examiner*, n.s. 22 [1832]: 4), contrasting an "effeminacy and corruption of morals" (Joseph Allen 10) with "manliness of thought and action" (Hawes 69). By labeling the feminine "degenerate," male opinion-setters evidence not only some confusion (and fear) about the nature of woman, whom they have also labeled as naturally pious, but they draw an image of woman that sustains their own sense of identity and justifies their own power at the cost of woman's. This kind of confusion about the nature of woman no doubt contributed to a strained if not jangled sense of self. It also underwrites Stowe's novel, perplexing her vision of a Christian matriarchy.

Although Stowe certainly has in mind the reformation of American society, inspired and influenced by the women whose hearts and whose pity for black mothers *Uncle Tom's Cabin* will touch, her vision of a matrifocal universe is constrained and problematized by the rhetoric of domesticity, a rhetoric marked by dissonance and disempowering strategies concerning the very institution of Christian motherhood that it appears to idealize. Though Stowe's women characters demonstrate the kind of loving affection and sisterhood requisite for the better world to come, they remain powerless to effect real change within the novel. Little Eva's death, sacrificial as it is, does not bring about the emancipation of the family slaves. Only Topsy escapes sale at the auction block or the cruelty of Marie St. Clare's rule after Augustine St. Clare's death. While Miss Ophelia, moved by love, insists that Topsy be given to her, she is nonetheless powerless on her own against the economic, legal, and political machinery of the slaveholding South and requires Augustine to actualize the transferal. Similarly, Mrs. Shelby is powerless in her own right to guarantee the safety of Tom, Eliza, and Harry against the authority of her husband and must wait for her son to come to his majority to enact her will by freeing the family slaves. Likewise, it took the instruments of men—the pen and the rifle—to free the American slaves. Though Mrs. Stowe may have been "the little woman who made [the] great war" (Stowe, *Life and Letters* 269), to call Stowe's novel a subversive rewriting of the text of gender difference sounds, to my mind, a bit too triumphant. Indeed, a contemporary of hers, angry at the condition of women in 1861, wrote a manifesto of women's rights in which she lambasts Harriet Beecher Stowe for not taking up the cause of women: "Mrs. Stowe told terrible yet truthful tales respecting the wrongs of the colored slave; but she quite overlooked the fact that the mother of Southern Slavery was a white slave, robbed, in the name of law and gospel, of her name, fortune, individuality, and the right of self-ownership. The Uncle Tom's Cabin of White Slavery—the history of Legalized Prostitution is yet to be written" (H. F. M. Brown 12–13).

# N O T E S

1. Stowe, *Uncle Tom's Cabin* (1986), 223. All subsequent quotations from the novel are from this edition, cited by page number in the text.

2. Arthur Schlesinger, Sr., estimates that by the 1840s and 1850s between thirty-six and thirty-eight different etiquette books were on the market in any one year and that an average of three new ones appeared each year before the Civil War (Cogan, *All-American Girl* 249–50).

3. Bardes and Gossett's discussion of women's methods of participating in helping the fugitives is helpful. Here they demonstrate the ineffectiveness of the female voice in Stowe's novel (56–57).

4. Askeland has an interesting discussion of the ways Stowe renders both Cassy and George "safe" characters (788–90).

# III
•
Religious Rhetoric and Biblical Influences
on Stowe

# 7

**●**

HELEN PETTER WESTRA

## Confronting Antichrist:
## The Influence of
## Jonathan Edwards's Millennial Vision

Harriet Beecher Stowe was, in her own words, heavily influenced by the "hearing and discussing of all the great theological problems of Calvinism, . . . always reverberating" through her parental home (*Lives* 572). A self-described product of Calvinism, she generally upheld its views of God's sovereignty, humanity's fall, Christ's redemptive work, and the Bible's infallibility. Although she eventually discarded the doctrine of election defended staunchly by Calvinist Jonathan Edwards, the eighteenth-century Great Awakening evangelist, what Harriet Beecher Stowe said of her brother Henry Beecher's relationship to Calvinism could generally describe her own: accepting "substantially the same ground with Jonathan Edwards but believ[ing] that Divine love is far more widely, constantly, and fully given to the children of men than did the old divine" (*Lives* 533).

Stowe's understanding of Calvinism's history and of Edwards as its spokesman was comprehensive. Though Vernon Louis Parrington likely overstates in saying that Stowe's "particular hero and saint was Jonathan Edwards" (215), biographer Charles H. Foster demonstrates her to be a precise and highly accurate representative of what he termed "Edwardean Calvinism" (x). John F. Wilson, exploring continuities between Edwards and Stowe, particularly notes Stowe's grasp of the role that Edwards's millennial theology played in shaping America's vision of itself as conscience and example to the world (81–82, 84, 90). Indeed, Edwards asserted that America was a country with a divine directive to overcome anti-Christian forces around the world—and thus to participate actively in the sacred work of redemption so that Christ could return and judge the nations. This theological concept permeates Stowe's thinking as part of a received tradition passed down by, among others, Edwards's son Jonathan Edwards, Jr., a theologian and editor of his father's chief millennial work, *A History of the Work of Redemption;* by Samuel Hopkins and Joseph Bellamy, both of whom were Edwards's students and authors of well-known dissertations on the millennium; by Timothy Dwight, Jonathan Edwards's grandson and biographer; and by Lyman Beecher, a student of Dwight, a powerful voice in the Second Great Awakening, and Harriet Beecher Stowe's father. This chapter will treat the significant continuities and adaptations from Edwards's millennialism, to the millenarian views and emphases of Lyman Beecher, to the modified millennial vision and rhetorical strategies employed with deliberate and powerful effect by Stowe in her most famous antislavery novel, *Uncle Tom's Cabin.*

Like Edwards's, Stowe's view of history was deeply informed by her yearnings for redemptive harmony on earth. She too believed that national and world history is holy history progressively moving toward a time when Christ's kingdom, established in the hearts and lives of those who are faithful to his example, will overcome the powers of evil and "bear the light of liberty and religion through all the earth and . . . bring in the great millennial day, when wars should cease and the whole world released from the thralldom of evil, should rejoice in the light of the Lord" (*Poganuc People* 197). Grounded on this vision of history, Stowe's *Uncle Tom's Cabin* is heavily sermonic, prophetic, and apocalyptic. Particularly in its concluding paragraphs it, like many of Edwards's imprecatory sermons, presses the question: on which side will an individual stand when the forces of righteousness and those of evil are arrayed for judgment before Almighty God? Indeed, Harriet Beecher Stowe's millennialism, adapted from Edwards's eschatology and that of his Calvinist successors, particularly her father Lyman Beecher, operates significantly in *Uncle Tom's Cabin* both as a theological framework and a rhetorical strategy to shape the work's language, imagery, and settings as well as its ultimate message and vision.

## Jonathan Edwards's Millennialism

Millennialism is an eschatological interpretation of history based on biblical prophecies and references (especially in Revelation 20) to Christ's reign of a "thousand years." One of millennialism's central concerns is forecasting events presumably related to overthrowing Satan and to the return of Jesus Christ and the end of time. While some millennialists read the phrase "thousand years" literally and others understand it symbolically, they generally believe world history will culminate with an extended period or millennium in which Satan will be constrained; Christ's church will triumph; global peace and prosperity will flourish; and the world as we know it will end with a final day of judgment.

During the Great Awakening, Jonathan Edwards's zealous hope was that America would be the place where the millennium would first signal its appearance. When the millennium begins to dawn, Edwards insisted, the "great [redemptive] work of God shall be brought to pass by the preaching of the gospel"; the news of salvation will noticeably "be preached with abundantly greater clearness and power than . . . heretofore" and will bring "vast multitudes savingly home to Christ" (*A History* 460–61). As one of the most prominent early American theologians to express the view known specifically as postmillennialism, that Christ's return to earth ("second coming") would not occur until *after* the Church inaugurates a millennial reign of peace and prosperity, Edwards came to be seen by many in the mid–nineteenth century as father and representative of the postmillennialist tradition in the United States ("History of Opinions" 655). Clearly, the millennial views Stowe employs in *Uncle Tom's Cabin* are an appropriation and adaptation of this legacy, her strategically personalized and telling revision of it brought to bear imaginatively on the lives of fictional characters and the life of a nation in crisis over the problem of slavery.

One of Edwards's most widely read and studied works among nineteenth-century Calvinists was the vigorously millennialist volume *A History of the Work of Redemption* (27). Its foremost purpose was to demonstrate that through the work of Christ and his Church, the whole of world history is gradually moving to the end of time by accomplishing God's redemptive plan of overcoming evil with righteousness. In positing a millennial triumph of the Church *followed* by Christ's return to earth and the last judgment, *A History* differs from premillennialist theories that Christ will *first* return to earth and then will establish his kingdom for one thousand years to be concluded by the day of judgment.

Like Edwards's, Stowe's postmillennial views projected a God who intended America to have an exemplary role in spreading the gospel and defeating evil in the world. But unlike Edwards's preoccupations with thwarting Catholicism, Mohammedanism, Arminianism, and Quakerism as major "antichristian" powers (*A History* 351, 411–16), Stowe's attention was focused on *slavery* as the great contemporary evil to be defeated. For Stowe, slavery was the chief anti-Christian institution opposing the advancement of Christ's kingdom and its promised peace and harmony. Using language reminiscent of Edwards's most heated, imprecating sermons, Stowe's *Key to Uncle Tom's Cabin* portrays the institution of slavery as utterly demonic: Its Satanic fire comes from "the lowest hell," threatening all of life "with sheeted flame and wreaths of sulphureous smoke" and "burning, burning, burning, over church and altar; burning over senate-house and forum; burning up liberty, burning up religion" (437).

In contrast to Stowe's emphasis on slavery, none of Edwards's discussions in *A History* of presumed evils make references to slavery in the colonies or to the colonies' expanding role in the international slave trade. A single pejorative comment on the present state of "Negroes" occurs in a passage that imagines a time when the gospel will reach Africa:

> Then shall the many nations of Africa, the nations of Negroes and others—heathens that chiefly fill that quarter of the world, that now seem to be in a state but little above the beasts in many respects and as much below them in many others—be enlightened with glorious light, and delivered from all their darkness, and shall become a civil, Christian, and an understanding and holy people. (472)

Here Edwards views Africans principally as uncivilized and savage "heathens" sorely in need of the gospel to bring light and civility to their lives. This narrow perspective seemed to prevent him from seeing the injustice and cruelty of buying and selling Africans and holding them in bondage for life. In fact, having read all of Edwards's published works and a large number of his unpublished manuscripts, I have found in them no discussion of slavery as a contemporary issue or anti-Christian practice.

During the 1740s, Edwards himself owned a "Negro Girle named Venus." Evidence of his purchase appears in his 1749 handwritten sermon on Ezekiel 44:9 (Beinecke Library) in which he used part of a discarded slave bill as scrap paper upon which to pen a portion of his sermon. The bill is both proof of Edwards's slaveholding status and a chilling reminder of how the institution of slavery, as well as the slave, was passed from one generation to another. What is left of the document reads as follows:

> To Have & to Hold the said Negro Girle named Venus unto the said Jonathan Edwards his heirs Exec[utors] Adm[inistrators] & Assigns and to their own proper use & behoof for ever. And I the said Richard Perkins do hereby for my Self and heirs, Exec[utors] and Adm[inistrators] covenant and promise & agree to and with the said Jonathan Edwards—his heirs Exec[utors] Adm[inistrators] and Assigns by these presents that I the said Richard Perkins at the ensealing & Delivery hereof have in my own name good Right, full Power & lawful Authority to bargain sell & deliver said Negro Girle named Venus unto the [ ? ] in manner & form aforesaid And shall & will warrant Defend the said Negro Girle named Venus unto the said Jonathan Edwards his heirs Exec[utors] Adm[inistrators] & Assigns against the lawful Challenge & demand of what manner of Persons whatsoever Claiming unto claim . . .[1]

There is sharp irony in the fact that the author of *A History of the Work of Redemption* remains silent on the issue of redeeming humans from chattel slavery while vociferously urging church leaders to be faithful collaborators in Christ's glorious work of spiritual "redemption." That Edwards permitted slavery and racism within his own household while insisting that ministers be exemplary Christians certainly reflects his ideological blind spots. Unlike Stowe, who viewed slavery as a consummate evil, Edwards and his Calvinist contemporaries failed to see slavery as an unjust, corrupting social ill.

Instead, Edwards believed that if the American church would be exemplary in its spiritual and doctrinal faithfulness and zeal, it would be gloriously instrumental in "bringing . . . the world from its present state, to the happy state of the millennium" (*An Humble Attempt* 411). Then "shall all the world be united in peace and love in one amiable society; all nations, in all parts, on every side of the globe, shall then be knit together in sweet harmony" (*A History* 483). A little more than a century later, this longing for a peacefully united, sweetly amiable world, most specifically for Stowe a world in which the institution of slavery would no longer dehumanize slave or master, was to become the central hope in *Uncle Tom's Cabin*.

## Lyman Beecher's Millennial Vision and Rhetoric

Describing his daughter Harriet, Lyman Beecher said, "No Jewish maiden ever grew up with a more earnest faith that she belonged to a consecrated race, a people especially called and chosen by God for some great work on earth" (Wagenknecht 135). As they were for Edwards and Beecher, millennial hopes and language were an integral part of Stowe's religious expression, her longing for Christ's "glorious" kingdom to be manifest on earth, and her profound sense of calling to participate in establishing that kingdom. For Stowe, the urgent task of overcoming the Antichrist and ushering in the millennial age did not focus on doctrinal purity extending to the ends of the earth, as it had for Edwards. Nor did it center on freeing the world from a tyrannical ruler, as it had for Americans fighting the Revolutionary War (Hatch, *The Sacred Cause of Liberty* 24–25, 86–87). Nor did it mean, as it did for Lyman Beecher, refashioning the nations of the world after the image of America's religious and democratic example. To Stowe, the millennium stood for a time when Christ's love, unquenchable in the hearts of faithful believers, would free the enslaved, the captive, and the oppressed and would bring peace to their lives.

Lyman Beecher developed an eschatological vision more suited to his nineteenth-century republican context and westward expansionism. Stowe likewise in *Uncle Tom's Cabin* adapts her inherited millennial traditions, pointedly revising Edwards's and her father's eschatological and millennial frameworks, rhetoric, and messages, and departing from them in significant ways. Stowe's antislavery novel, which she called "a work of religion" (Rourke, *Trumpets* 80), presents a theology of love, goodness, and redemption that has little connection with the patriarchal

146

ecclesiastical establishment Edwards and her father promoted so vigorously. There is in *Uncle Tom's Cabin* a "radical substitution of feminine and maternal for masculine values" (Ammons, "Heroines" 153) and an emphasis on the power of motherly love as a social corrective, and on the "traditional 'feminine' virtues of submissiveness, selfless love, compassion" (Berkson 244–45). Stowe's "ideal state in a millennial community" (*My Wife and I* 37–38) is matriarchal rather than patriarchal, authoritarian, or ecclesiastically directed. Accordingly, in *Uncle Tom's Cabin* Stowe pictures a world in which the work of redemption is chiefly represented and accomplished by slaves, women, children, and Quakers as the most vital bearers of Christ's image.

Beecher, like Edwards, was a theologian and a "relentless champion of Calvinist orthodoxy" (Henry 19). He was also a revivalist and a key figure in the Second Great Awakening. In his public role as an evangelist during an era of unprecedented national progress, he bouyantly expressed nineteenth-century American millennial hopes. "Soon," said Beecher, "will the responsive song be heard from every nation, and kindred, and tongue and people, as the voice of a great multitude, and as the voice of many waters, and as the voice of mighty thunderings, saying, Alleluia, for the lord God Omnipotent reigneth" (*A Reformation* 30).

Like Edwards, Lyman Beecher believed America would be the place as well as the instrument through which God would begin and establish his millennial kingdom throughout the earth. Thus, Beecher's message during the Second Great Awakening overtly stressed that "the millennium would commence in America" (*A Plea* 10). Filled with zeal to shape a nation able to launch the millennial age, he preached that it was God's "design," through the example of a Christian and democratic America, "to show the world by experiment, of what man is capable; and to . . . awake [around the world] the slumbering eye, and rouse the torpid minds, and nerve the palsied arm of millions" (*A Plea* 10).

America, as a free people and a liberated nation, will be able to do this, Beecher believed, because God has begun to

> pour out his Spirit upon the churches, and voluntary associations of Christians [have been] raised up. . . . to aid in the support of the gospel at home, to extend it to the new settlements and through the earth . . . [and] this great nation from her eminence begins to look abroad with compassion upon a world sitting in darkness, and to put

forth her mighty arm . . . to elevate the family of man. . . . And when we contemplate the unexampled resources of this country, . . . is it too much to be hoped that God will accept our powerful instrumentality and make it effectual for the renovation of the world? ("Memory" 103–4)

Consumed by ardour "to advance the cause of the Millennium" (Rourke, "Remarks" 83) and to educate pious pastors and godly citizens, Beecher tirelessly promoted the paraecclesiastical societies of his time—the American Bible Society, American Tract Society, American Education Society (to train ministers), and American Sunday School Union. The grand aim of these organizations was to build a Christian nation that would be empowered by God to inaugurate the millennium worldwide through piety and human instrumentality, for when America becomes fully faithful to its divine mission, then "will the trumpet of Jubilee sound, and the earth's debased millions will leap from the dust, and shake off their chains, and cry, 'Hosanna' " ("Memory" 19–20). In propagating this vision for America, Lyman Beecher was characteristically bold and outspoken. But in actions relative to slavery, he was cautious and understated. While president of Lane Seminary in Cincinnati, he "set the issue of slavery aside" as peripheral (Rourke, "Remarks" 83). His son-in-law Calvin E. Stowe described Beecher as a person who, without being conscious of it, held "not a little of the old Connecticut prejudice about blacks"; and further, because "his mind had been wholly absorbed by other themes," he did not specifically address slavery (Henry, 191). While he did not approve of slaveholding, Beecher was so preoccupied with proclaiming and expanding Christ's kingdom that he failed clearly to see the profound moral and spiritual consequences of slavery. Thus he preferred to compromise rather than take strong stands or choose sides in the abolition or colonization debates (Henry 190).

Harriet Beecher Stowe possessed much of her father's religious intensity and shared his passionate dream of a strong Christian nation. Most essentially for Stowe, however, the great "cause of Christ was the cause of the slave" (Charles Stowe and Lyman Beecher Stowe 289); for her the felicity and joy of the anticipated millennial age would come through a people and nation freed from the chains of slavery. For eighteenth-century Edwards, the Antichrist to be battled was apostasy, heresy, and paganism; he identified the "leviathan" of Isa. 27:1 as "Satan's

visible kingdom on earth," consisting of so-called religious dis-
tortions ranging from Deism to Judaism, Mohammedanism,
Catholicism, and Quakerism (*A History*, 467–69). Lyman Beecher's millennial dreams came increasingly to turn on a Protestant and democratic America evangelizing the world, saving it
from both spiritual *and* political oppression, and thus fulfilling
"the purpose of God to employ this nation in the glorious work of
renovating the earth" ("Memory" 104). Like his Calvinist predecessors, Beecher saw the papacy and canon law as a threat to
Protestant progress. Furthermore, as Catholic schools in America multiplied, Beecher viewed them as a hindrance to democracy; following one of his speeches in 1834, a mob actually
burned a convent in Charlestown, Massachusetts (Strout 128).

## Stowe's Millennialism in Her Battle against Slavery

In contrast to both Edwards and Beecher, Stowe named the
foremost anti-Christian force in her age to be the dehumanizing
institution of slavery (*Key* 438). She called it a full-grown "Leviathan" undermining the church and nation by ceaselessly resisting the spirit and claims of divine Love (*Key* 439–40, 402). No
evil is more hideous than slavery, insisted Stowe: "Nothing of
tragedy can be written, can be spoken, can be conceived, that
equals the frightful reality of scenes [of slavery] daily and hourly
acting on our shores, beneath the shadow of American law, and
the shadow of the cross of Christ."[2] For the church and nation
and each individual member and citizen, according to Stowe, the
ultimate test of faithfulness in advancing the kingdom of God
would be the quality of their responses to slavery and the enslaved. The right response is love felt and freely given—an inclusive and protective love, generous, healing, unconditional, class-
less, all-encompassing. Upon this point she departed markedly
from Jonathan Edwards and Lyman Beecher, for whom the
ultimate test of a church's or country's faithfulness in preparing
for the millennium would be the degree to which it promulgated
the gospel and theology of orthodox Protestantism.

With her keen sense of mission, Stowe uses *Uncle Tom's Cabin*
to present her version of the one right response to slavery: feelings and actions "in harmony with the sympathies of Christ"
(624). Hers is essentially a New Testament message; through the
gracious lives of those faithful to his law of love, the Savior brings

comfort, benevolence, and rest to the enslaved, oppressed, orphaned, widowed, suffering, and captive—to the Elizas, little Harrys, Georges, Evangelines, Topsys, Toms, Aunt Chloes, Emmelines, and Cassys of the world.

Stowe's message and millennial vision of a vital, triumphant American church was far more ecumenical than Edwards's or her father's. While Edwards grouped Quakers among "antichristian" heretics, Stowe portrayed the Quakers as exemplary in their compassionate demonstrations that "the love of God and the love of man are inseparable" (*Key* 439, 101). She singles them out for praise, among American religious denominations, as "the only body of Christians involved in this evil [slavery] who have ever succeeded in freeing themselves from it" (*Key* 426, 431). Accordingly, in *Uncle Tom's Cabin* most of the comfort and aid for runaway slaves comes from the hands and hearts of Quakers. They embody the true meaning of mercy—loving their neighbor as themselves (220, 224), gently teaching the lessons of righteousness (620–21), showing tenderness even to their enemies (542–44). It is among the Quakers that George Harris's "pining atheistic doubts, and fierce despair, melted away before the light of a living gospel, breathed in living faces" (225).

In her treatment of Catholicism, Stowe further demonstrates an ecumenicity that contrasts strikingly with Edwards's negative attitudes toward Papists and others outside the orthodox Protestant tradition. For the epigraph of her chapter titled "Liberty" (542), Stowe selects the words of the notable Catholic emancipator John Philpot Curran. She makes Augustine St. Clare's fondly remembered mother, the Evangeline for whom little Eva is named, a saintly woman who loved to sing and play the "fine old majestic music of the Catholic church" (334). Sensitive and generous, she had tried to convey to her children "an idea of the dignity and worth of the meanest soul" (337). St. Clare remembers his pious Catholic mother as "a direct embodiment and personification of the New Testament" (333), a woman who often voiced her faith in "a millennium that was coming, when Christ should reign, and all men should be free and happy" (345).

In their biography of Harriet Beecher Stowe, Charles and Lyman Stowe wrote that their mother had intended *Uncle Tom's Cabin* as "a sermon to be hurled against a great moral evil" (163). Like the preaching of Jonathan Edwards and her theological forebears, Stowe's message mingles alarms and reassurances—there will be "a day of vengeance" as well as a "day of grace" (629), and God will punish the wicked and forgive the penitent. Stowe's novel labors to awaken redemptive love and repentance in her readers' hearts (624). But it also sternly admonishes the hardhearted or timid who witness slavery "in silence" (583, 623, 624). With careful aim, Stowe combines the rhetoric of apocalypse with the Calvinist logic of exclusive disjunction used frequently by Edwards—for each person there will ultimately be eternal reward or eternal retribution. In her preface to the second French edition of *Uncle Tom's Cabin,* Stowe warns:

> When one breaks a human heart, . . . when the blood of the poor is spilled with disdain, HE [God] sees it, he takes note and remembers it. . . . For there is a day of retribution; the day promised to the redeemed approaches also. . . . A calm voice is heard . . . address[ing] to all oppressors . . . the following threat, "Whatever you have done to the least among those who are my brothers, you have to me." (1965, lxxv; my translation)

*Uncle Tom's Cabin's* apocalyptic conclusion similarly alternates the themes of divine grace and divine wrath in attempts to confront and arouse each reader with a ringing question: "Every time that you pray that the kingdom of Christ may come, can you forget that prophecy associates, in dread fellowship, the *day of vengeance* with the year of his redeemed?" (621; Stowe's emphasis).

"Great fiction," says Frederick R. Karl, occurs when the author "involves the reader in dramatic, crucially difficult moral decisions which parallel those [problems and decisions] of the central characters. It asks troublesome questions, disturbs, . . . forces curious confrontations, and possibly changes us" (123). Not unlike the deliberately hard-hitting interrogatives found in the application portion of many Calvinist sermons, Stowe's questions confront her audience directly with the moral and spiritual implications of her text. Her final chapter is especially noteworthy in marshaling dozens of questions, sometimes in clusters (622, 625), in her appeals to the reader's heart and conscience.

Stowe's questions are often placed in the mouths of enlightened or suffering characters. Little Eva, for example, asks beseechingly, "Papa, isn't there any way to have all slaves made free?" (403) and "Doesn't the Bible say we must love everybody?" (396). Upon learning that her husband's transactions with a slave trader will tear Tom from his family and wrest little Harry from his mother, Mrs. Shelby asks in anguish, "How can I bear to have this open acknowledgement that we [slave owners] care for no tie, no duty, no relation, however sacred, compared with money?" (83). Fleeing for his life, George Harris muses desperately: "There's a God for [white Christians], but is there any for us?" (191). Through pangs of agony, Tom cries, "O Jesus! Lord Jesus! have you quite forgot us poor critturs?" (515).

Strategically, some of the most urgent questions in the narrative echo the Bible or are taken directly from it. A description of Legree's evil treatment of Tom (480) is pointedly prefaced by a question from Hab. 1:13: "Wherefore lookest thou upon them that deal treacherously, and holdest thy tongue when the wicked devoureth the man that is more righteous than he?" When one of Legree's tormented slaves doubts that Christ's words—"Come unto Me, all ye that labor and are heavy laden"—were meant for her, the novel's narrative voice mingles questions with the rhetoric of scripture: " 'Is God HERE?' Ah, how is it possible for the untaught heart to keep its faith, unswerving, in the face of dire misrule, and palpable, unrebuked injustice? . . . AH, was it easy *here* to believe and hold fast the great password of Christian faith, that 'God IS, and is the REWARDER of them that diligently seek Him'?" (497–98; Stowe's emphasis). By invoking Holy Writ, these passages and their searing questions represent a moral framework and authority that transcend the novel's fictional elements.

Of great distress to Stowe was the fact that the language of Scripture and providential dispensation was being publicly manipulated (*Key* 402–4, 407–25) to demean Negroes and support slavery. Aggressive proslavery writers such as Alexander McCaine (*Slavery Defended from Scripture*), Thorton Stringfellow (*A Brief Examination of Scripture Testimony on the Institution of Slavery*), and Josiah Priest (*A Bible Defence of Slavery*) were arguing that Negroes were essentially uncivilized, barbarian, cursed. The biblical curse of Ham and his son Canaan (from Gen. 9:25) was used to assert that Ham was the father of the Negro race; from this evolved the argument that Americans and particularly Anglo-Saxons as an especially "blessed" and superior people were required by "intention of Providence" (*Uncle Tom's Cabin* 200) to keep Negroes subdued for the greater welfare of the nation and world. Demonstrating this distorted viewpoint in her novel, Stowe includes a description of Augustine St. Clare's father as a haughty, inflexible man who "considered the negro, through all possible gradations of color, as an intermediate link between man and animals, and graded all his ideas of justice . . . on this hypothesis" (355).

From Stowe's viewpoint, the 1850 Fugitive Slave Law, which outlawed all assistance to runaway slaves, penalized persons who performed deeds of conscience, compassion, and love. The terrifying implications of this legislation propelled her (Foster 28–29) to create a novel that publicly pressed what she perceived as the most compelling questions of the age: Who is your neighbor? and What will your feelings and behavior toward that neighbor ultimately mean in the course of personal, national, and holy history? Stowe's primary motive in highlighting these issues in *Uncle Tom's Cabin* was to move readers intimately to see, feel, and act upon the spiritual consequences of their own relationships to and responsibilities for their oppressed, enslaved neighbors. In keeping with her theological heritage and tradition of millennial rhetoric, Stowe uses an eschatologically framed narrative to transfigure "real" events and people and thus draw readers feelingly and affectively into lifelike experiences demonstrating that all persons are connected through their common humanity and, above all, that they touch each others' lives in ways that have profound and *eternal* consequences.

## Millennialism and Uncle Tom's Cabin

Stowe inaugurates the overarching millennial design in *Uncle Tom's Cabin* by creating a first chapter that immediately reveals the intersecting lives of three families (the Shelbys, the Harrises, and Uncle Tom's family) and establishes several key spiritual correlaries: slavery is an immoral institution, and each American citizen who supports it actively or passively will ultimately be accountable to God for his or her own behavior. Within "the grand design" of holy history, into which all human history fits, the glorious millennial kingdom of happiness and peace will be brought forth through the instrumentality of persevering Christians who resist evil and spread the gospel of Christ's redeeming love. Thus the first chapter of Stowe's novel names slavery as an anti-Christian institution from which "it is impossible to make anything beautiful or desirable" (51).

After Mr. Shelby completes his negotiations to sell Tom and

little Harry to a slave trader, Stowe emphasizes the gravity of Shelby's moral failure. Materialism and self-indulgence have rendered him ill-prepared to resist evil and exercise compassion. Shelby's incapacities threaten his soul, Stowe reminds her readers, as this shallow, self-gratifying man refuses to acknowledge his own culpability and seems "to fancy that his wife had piety and benevolence enough for two"; he makes the spiritually fatal error of harboring an "expectation of getting into heaven through her superabundance of qualities" (53). Stowe's sober implication is that Shelby himself must face the judgment of God for his lack of Christian mercy and compassion. But even Mrs. Shelby, with her "high moral and religious sensibility and principle" (52), through her lack of action endangers the slaves that serve her faithfully. She remains passive and "entirely ignorant" (52) of her husband's plan to sell little Harry and Tom. Until too late, she fails to see beneath her husband's superficial kindliness (52) and so naively dismisses Eliza's well-founded fears of separation from little Harry, preferring instead to put the "matter from her mind, without a second thought" (53).

The final pages of the novel underscore these themes of warning and judgment by repeatedly urging readers to awaken and repent of their failures relative to slavery. Stowe sounds the alarm against the collective sins of the American church and the American nation, each of which carries "in its bosom great and unredressed injustice" in ignoring the mounting groans "for man's freedom and equality" (629). Most of all, Stowe challenges Christians to accept their responsibilities to overcome slavery and establish Christ's kingdom of peace and liberty, for to deny that responsibility is to be on the side of evil. In her novel's final salvo, Stowe beseeches:

> O, Church of Christ, read the signs of the times! Is not this power the spirit of HIM whose kingdom is yet to come, and whose will to be done on earth as it is in heaven?
>
> But who may abide the day of his appearing? "for that day shall burn as an oven; and he shall appear as a swift witness against those that oppress the hireling in his wages, the widow and the fatherless, and that *turn aside the stranger in his right:* and he shall break in pieces the oppressor." (629; Stowe's emphasis)

The question from Mal. 3:2—"But who may abide the day of his appearing?"—is the same one Stowe had placed earlier in the mind of Augustine St. Clare as he recalled his mother's millennial dream of a time "when all men should be free and happy" (344).

This repeated text, as well as Stowe's use of other traditional millennial texts (Mal. 3:5, 4:1; Ps. 72:4) in *Uncle Tom's Cabin*, deliberately links her antislavery message with the coming of Christ's kingdom, in which evil will be thwarted and righteousness will triumph as God's faithful people "bear the light of liberty and religion through all the earth and . . . bring in the great millennial day, when wars should cease and the whole world released from the thralldom of evil" (Stowe, *Poganuc People* 197). Within Stowe's theological framework, then, resisting slavery is resisting the anti-Christian institution that most "confounds and confuses every principle of Christianity and morality" (*Uncle Tom's Cabin* 625). Thus Stowe's crucial test for the American nation and its people facing the signs of the times is: Are your responses to slavery in "harmony with the sympathies of Christ?" (624).

Language and typological imagery pointing to a new day, a day of redemption, a resurrection day, a new Jerusalem, or the golden "glory" of Christ's everlasting reign are very much part of the tradition of millennial discourse. Accordingly, in casting golden color and light on key scenes or passages in *Uncle Tom's Cabin*, Stowe attempts to show the millennial import of redemptive love and to direct her readers' vision to "a glory to be revealed—a wondrous something yet to come" (380) in the course of holy history. Consequently, during Eva's and Tom's reading from Revelation on the shores of Lake Pontchartrain and their talk of the New Jerusalem, the sky turns golden and glowing, ablaze with "glory" (380–82). Scenes surrounding Eva's sacrificial death are likewise abundant with references to light, "the break of day," the "glorious" smile on Eva's face, the "morning star," the "golden dawn," and "the day of our Lord Jesus Christ" (425–28, 433). Passages anticipating Tom's death as well as the Harris's freedom are also rich with the imagery of morning stars, brightening skies, birth, and a new day (536, 544).

In addition to millennial light, color, and imagery, Stowe employs Scriptures with strong eschatological overtones (from the Psalms, the Old Testament prophets, and Revelation) with increasing pointedness in the novel. Frequently the Bible is read or quoted by various characters to each other—young George Shelby to a gathering of slaves (78), Simeon the Quaker to

George Harris (212), Eva to Tom (380), Tom to St. Clare (308, 435), St. Clare to Tom (437), Tom to Legree's slaves (497), and Cassy to Tom (514). Augustine St. Clare's reading of Matthew 25 to Tom occurs in the light of "a warm, golden evening" (447), and it presents an account of the day when those who acted on Christ's behalf will be received in glory and those who disregarded Christ's mandates will be cursed (447–48).

Given her faith in God's cleansing and redemptive plan for the world, Stowe positions strategic scenes within her overarching millennialist framework to offer reassuring miniature images of the anticipated "great millennial day." In these scenes, she works figurally to create intimate environments where a type of millennial joy blossoms in the present and brings hope, a golden peace, and warm light to those it touches. These felicitous scenes foreshadow the extended millennial reign in which evil and oppression will someday be largely overcome by goodness and love.

Such a micromillennial environment appears in Rachel Halliday's kitchen where "there is a golden cloud of protection" as well as "the light of a living gospel, breathed in living faces" (225). Another millennial foretaste is found in the presence of Eva, who is "daylight and sunshine" to the slaves of the St. Clare household; when Eva begs her father to free all the slaves and to see that Christ's sacrificial love is the only example to follow, "the rays of the sun formed a kind of glory behind her, as she came forward in her white dress, with her golden hair and glowing cheeks" (401). Likewise, Eliza and George Harris's glowing hearth and cheerful home in Montreal become places where love flourishes, broken families are reunited, and haunted souls find freedom, serenity, and renewal (604).

Among the most remarkable of these micromillennial images are those linked with the spiritual poise, ministering goodness, and sacrificial love that radiate from Tom. Sometimes he simply sits next to Eva while he sings hymns, talks of heaven, and with her beholds "those intensely golden sunsets which kindle the whole horizon into one blaze of glory" (381–82). On an occasion when Tom expresses heartfelt love for his disconsolate master Augustine St. Clare and prays for him, "St. Clare felt himself borne, on the tide of [Tom's] faith and feeling, almost to the gates of that heaven he seemed so vividly to conceive" (438). Even in the barren, joyless atmosphere of Legree's plantation, Tom's life "overflow[s] with compassion and sympathy for the poor wretches by whom he was surrounded" (558). His sacrificial love comforts the disheartened; his tender voice falls "like dew" (562) on terrorized lives. As one who represents amazing grace and *spiritual* liberation in a nearly hopeless *physical* environment, he offers genuine foreshadowings of Christ's millennial "treasury of peace and joy" (558).

Much as Jonathan Edwards's *History of the Work of Redemption* had envisioned a worldwide millennial peace, so Stowe's novel anticipates global emancipation and change. *Uncle Tom's Cabin* contains glimpses of what Stowe hoped would be harbingers of the age in which slavery and oppression throughout the world would ultimately be defeated by love and justice. Through George Harris's dream of a Liberia that would nurture the "sublime doctrine of love and forgiveness" (611) and extend its "tide of civilization and Christianity" by planting "mighty republics" across "the whole splendid continent of Africa" (609), Stowe holds out her vision of a global millennium. Likewise, St. Clare links the millennium his mother had prayed for to the yearnings, "sighing, and groaning, and stirring" for freedom he believed were being felt in many parts of the earth: "[T]here is a mustering among the masses, the world over. . . . The same thing is working in Europe, in England, and in this country" (344). Later, St. Clare points to the contemporary example of "Hungarian nobles [who] set free millions of serfs" and did "not estimate honor and justice by dollars and cents" (451–52). Some chapters later, a similar spirit of justice and honor moves young George Shelby to free all his slaves, who respond with a song of "Jubilee" that foreshadows the liberation of the oppressed in America and the world over.

Certainly, then, *Uncle Tom's Cabin* is Stowe's creative attempt to resist anti-Christian forces in the church and the nation, to situate her campaign against slavery and for emancipation within a millennial context, and to employ biblical texts to underscore the eternal meaning of the work of redemption within her own age. Stowe's vision and rhetoric in *Uncle Tom's Cabin* promotes "the bright ideal" of what "true, generous, Christian love" (*Key* 435) could achieve as a salvific force against slavery. Her language and images, drawn from biblical and millennial traditions, challenge the nation and the church to submit to the cleansing, healing, and renewal she believes can occur when "the fires of a divine charity" melt "the chains of Mammon" (*Key* 436).

Commenting on the inherent limitations of fiction, Stowe stated in *Uncle Tom's Cabin:* "[I]n a novel, people's hearts break, and they die, and that is the end of it" (241). Yet she herself prayed that beyond "the end of it," her narrative would stir hearts to feel and act aright. Taking the millennial tradition she had received from Edwards and her father, she modified it to proclaim a gospel of compassion and benevolence; to demonstrate that maternal values and the redemptive power of "womanly" love are essential to a just and virtuous society; to portray an ecumenicity that included Quakers and Catholics as integral parts of the body of Christ; and to bring home the message that slavery is anti-Christian and must be abolished. Indeed, millions of Stowe's contemporaries found her narrative to be an unforgettable "illumination" that "nothing but the term 'mystical' will fittingly describe" (Francis Grierson, qtd. in Moorhead 22).

One explanation for the novel's obvious powerful hold on the popular imagination may be in the dramatic way Stowe personalized and humanized millennial images and recontextualized America's dreams of peace, harmony, and freedom. In speaking dramatically of an evil institution lodged within the nation's bosom and of the divine judgments that God-fearing people would wish to turn aside, the novel brought a greatly expanded definition and an eschatological relevance to the issue of slavery and the question of who is one's neighbor. Thus Stowe's use of the millennial framework, pointedly revealing the significance of every life and every deed in the light of eternity, by its very nature insisted that the novel's message of redemption transcend its fictional end.

# NOTES

1. The author expresses thanks to the Beinecke Library of Yale University for permission to transcribe and publish the Edwards slave indenture.

2. *Uncle Tom's Cabin* (1986), 623. All subsequent quotations from the novel are from this edition, cited by page number in the text.

# 8

•

MASON I. LOWANCE, JR.

# Biblical Typology and the Allegorical Mode:
# The Prophetic Strain

The purpose of this chapter is to examine Harriet Beecher
Stowe's employment of specific strategies of biblical hermeneu-
tics: typological figuralism, rhetorical tropes, prophetic and millennial modes of discourse, and allegorical character representation. The allegorical development of emblematic characters has,
of course, led to much of the controversy surrounding *Uncle
Tom's Cabin* because it is through the allegorical or stereotypical character that misrepresentation and exaggeration of the
black characters has occurred. Or so some critics, from Frederick
Douglass to James Baldwin, have claimed. In fact, Stowe has
carefully appropriated rhetorical modes from the Bible to reinforce her central argument about the essential evils of slavery,
and she carefully orchestrates biblical types, Platonic and allegorical figures, millennial and prophetic language to produce a
drama of antebellum slavery that is at once highly charged politically, in the context of contemporary arguments about biblical
sanctions and prohibitions of slavery, *and* essentially spiritual,
using character formation and narrative development to create a
picture of the future of America that is terrifying.

Unlike prophetic narratives of apartheid in South Africa, like
Alan Paton's *Cry, the Beloved Country*, Stowe's millennial vision
of America's decline is staged against the backdrop of America's
potential greatness, so that throughout the work there is a ten-

sion between what *is* and what *ought to be*. The idealism of Stowe's vision is juxtaposed against the essential pessimism of her graphic and realistic depictions of the conditions of slavery. To make her arguments cohere, she employs the Bible not only for the moral authority that only the Bible can invoke, but also as a rhetorical control, one that gives her text the authority of Scripture by recapitulating biblical characters and figures, and by renarrating episodes from the Bible that allow the reader to recognize predictable future events. Stowe thus develops a highly religious context for her story; Uncle Tom is the most obvious "suffering servant" or Messiah figure (as distinguished from a Christ figure) in the early portions of the narrative; however, he is gradually transformed into the crucified Christ by the end of the story, though it is precisely this crucifixion that is supposed to have inspired Stowe to write the novel. Her Sunday morning "vision" of the old black man being flogged to death combined with her sister's insistence that she write a narrative that would expose the evils of the "peculiar institution" to produce the most remarkable achievement in American literary history. Only twice in American history have fictional narratives been entered into the *Congressional Record*, and both had important influence in the transforming of laws to prohibit oppression. The first was the reading of Melville's account of Old Ushant from *White-Jacket* (1849), where a *retired* sailor was brutally flogged for refusing to shave his beard as he returned to America from England aboard a military vessel of the United States. This moving tribute to human endurance inspired the Congress to abolish flogging as a means of punishment aboard U.S. Naval vessels, and it was read aloud in the House of Representatives in 1849.

The second event was Stowe's achievement in *Uncle Tom's Cabin*, which did not need to be read aloud as practically every congressman in 1852 had read his own copy. Reference to the work, however, was made by both Northern and Southern representatives, who took essentially partisan lines in their critiques. What is important here is that the *veracity* of the book was regularly questioned and defended, and both sides used *character formation* and *character representation* to support their views. Particular and specific understanding of Stowe's method of writing character is therefore essential to an appropriate interpretation of the text. And her method was essentially biblical, an appropriation of style from the Mathers and from Jonathan Edwards. Prophetic and millennial figuralism informed her rhetorical style; biblical types became the foundation for her leading character formation; and the tension throughout between allegorical representation and typological or prophetic figuralism gives the narrative an added dimension of moral authority through specific, scriptural allusions.

It is important to understand that history for New England religious writers—including Harriet Beecher Stowe—was believed to be a related series of divinely inspired events, whereby the guiding hand of Providence might be perceived in the drama of human experience. The record of these historical events—the Bible—and the language employed in its composition became for New England writers a rich source for describing their own contemporary history. The Bible became the most prominent source of literal and metaphorical examples to illustrate providential intervention in human affairs, and its prophetic language became a primary vehicle through which later events of contemporary history might be comprehended and explained. The expression of historical developments in the language of the Bible became a means of associating the experience of America with literal, historical movements in ancient Israel. Moreover, it provided the writers with a method of predicting events, since all human history was ultimately contained between the creation in Genesis and the judgment in Revelation. The prophetic language of the Bible was essentially the language of revelation and eschatology, to which the events of all human history might be related through proper exegesis of scriptural metaphor and symbol.

In the previous chapter, Helen Westra has argued that millennialism, an interpretation of history based on biblical prophecies and references to Christ's reign of a thousand years at the end of human time, became the dominant theological force governing Stowe's vision of America's future. She convincingly shows how the millennial arguments of Jonathan Edwards and the New Light Calvinists of the Great Awakening were revitalized by ministers of the Second Great Awakening, preachers like Timothy Dwight, James Freeman Clarke, and Stowe's own father, Lyman Beecher. The purpose of this chapter is to show how another biblical formula, that of exegetical typology, was used by Stowe to develop character. Both millennialism as a visionary force and typology as a foundation of episode and character formation were derived from Stowe's immersion in biblical rhetoric and exegesis, not only from her own reading, but from her exposure to the Bible as the wife of one minister, sister of six, and daughter of one of the greatest ministerial orators of the century. Like millennialism, typology was as old as the earliest exegesis of the Bible, rooted in Scripture commentary and the subject of a variety of interpretations through the centuries of Christian history. However, as applied to historical narrative and to literature, it was quite specific and gave added interpretive force to the figures Stowe created in her novel. Uncle Tom, the married couples, the nurturing mothers, and the cruelty of Simon Legree all have antecedents in biblical figures on whose originals Stowe based her novel's characterization, just as she based her plot and "Concluding Remarks" on the millennial vision found in the apocalyptic books of the Bible—Ezekiel, Daniel, and Revelation.

## Biblical Types and Stowe's Characters

Basically, there are two kinds of prophetic symbols or "types" in literature. The first is a simple representative figure. In the rhetorical tradition of synecdoche, this type stands for the whole, for an abstract idea. Thus Adam is a type of humankind, who represents the process through which all human beings eventually go in falling from divine grace. His value in this classification is entirely symbolic; historical authenticity is of no relevance, though he may have coincidentally been historically real. Primarily, however, these types were abstractions, so that the essential relation between the type and that which it represents involves no historical continuity. Many notable fictional characters fit this classification, such as Bunyan's Christian, Milton's Comus, Marlowe's Faustus, the medieval Everyman, and Stowe's Uncle Tom. In the novel, Uncle Tom emblematically represents feminine virtue, the nurturing and sacrificial power that only women and feminized men are permitted by Stowe.

The second kind of type is more important for prophetic symbolism. While Stowe employed both kinds of figurative "types" in the composition of her novel, the rhetorical strategies of the work depend significantly on the abstract stereotyping of character (which has long been noted as a flaw in the dramatic and moral structure of the work, particularly by James Baldwin in the *Partisan Review* essay of 1949, "Everybody's Protest Novel") and, more subtly, on the readership's response to encoded meaning in the second kind of "type," the prophetic biblical figure.

Biblical or exegetical typology is derived from the practices of the early fathers and medieval theologians. They attempted to give continuity to the canon of Holy Scripture by demonstrating how the Old Testament prefigured the New through types and figures of which the New Testament persons and events were the antitype, or fulfillment. Thus, the historical Abraham became a type of God the Father in the sacrifice of his only son, Issac. In contrast to the purely representative type, the exegetical type exists in the historical context of linear time, and its relation to the substance it represents is that of foreshadowing, or adumbration, not of static, Platonic representation. The substance foreshadowed is denoted the antitype, and it usually exists in time, fulfilling the type. Rules for distinguishing the biblical figures— which are prophetic of Christ and his kingdom—from the Platonic, more allegorical symbolic representations, were written for each succeeding generation of Puritanism in England and New England. These crucial handbooks and sermons about exegesis have minor disagreements, but all concur on one central point: the most crucial distinction between the type and the allegorical trope involved a concept of linear time. The trope was a Platonic representation of one thing by another, but the type by definition preceded the antitype in the context of time, one element being instituted *by the same author* to foreshadow the other. Perry Miller has put it this way:

> In the type there must be evidence of the one eternal intention of one writer. The type exists in history and is factual. . . . By contrast, the allegory, the simile, and the metaphor have been made according to the fancy of men, and they mean whatever the brain of the begetter is pleased they should mean. In the type there is a rigorous correspondence, which is not a chance resemblance, between the representation and the antitype; in the trope there is a correspondence only between the thing and the associations it happens to excite in the impressionable but treacherous senses of men. (Miller, Introduction to *Images or Shadows of Divine Things*, ix)

Of course there are many shades of grey between these two extremes. Some conservative exegetes would regard as "types" only those Old Testament events and figures that are specifically instituted in the New Testament; others would be more liberal in their judgments, allowing such figures as Jacob's Ladder to adumbrate Christ's union of heaven and earth. Some go so far as to include the red cord of Rahab, the prostitute of Jericho, as a type of the saving blood of Jesus. From the beginning of typological rhetorical exegesis, in the second century, there have been schools among critics that reflect conservative or traditional tendencies, and these place great emphasis on the historical veracity of the type and the specific institution of the type and its antitype in Scripture. More liberal typologists sometimes border on using the Platonic, ahistorical symbol, and these exegetes are called spiritualizers or allegorizers.

Harriet Beecher Stowe was well acquainted with both schools of exegesis. The daughter of Lyman Beecher, who was one of the great thundering ministers of the Second Great Awakening in New England, and the wife of Calvin Stowe, who was a professor of moral philosophy and religion at Bowdoin College in Maine, Stowe was steeped in the rhetorical principles of the Bible, and her novel reflects a keen sense of biblical narrative. It was to be New England that would allow the appropriate conflation of historical fulfillment of those metaphorical and figural revelations made by the Divine Author in Scripture. In America—first in New England and later in the Revolution and early national era—the historical cycles of secular development could be fused with the biblical patterns of prophecy and fulfillment, so that the paradigm of Armageddon followed by a pastoral paradise could be demonstrated not only in contemporary events but also in the language of Scripture revelation. Both secular and sacred Americans of the late eighteenth and early nineteenth centuries were able to view their history and the events of their times in the traditional and orderly context of Jonathan Edwards's *History of the Work of Redemption,* which identifies the cycles of historical revolution with the inevitable patterns of regenerative process and progress. Stowe understood this perfectly, and she developed her narrative accordingly.

First, the evolution of the plot in *Uncle Tom's Cabin* follows a predestined pattern of inevitability, where Tom's final success in achieving sainthood is inextricably linked to his willingness to sacrifice for others, including Legree, who becomes just as inevitably his executioner. At the center of this spiritual plot lies the nuclear family and the institution of marriage, at once sacred and secular. The Shelbys, George and Eliza, the St. Clares, and Tom and Chloe become "representative types" of values concerning marital relationships with which Stowe endows each pair. The dynamic within these structures mirrors certain values Stowe observed in American society, or, as she put it herself in chapter 13 of *A Key to Uncle Tom's Cabin* ("The Quakers"):

> The writers's sketch of the character of this people has been drawn from personal observation. There are several settlements of these people in Ohio, and the manner of living, the tone of sentiment, and the habits of life, as represented in her book, are not at all exaggerated. These settlements have always been refuges for the oppressed and outlawed slave. The character of Rachel Halliday was a real one, but she has passed away to her reward. Simeon Halliday calmly risking fine and imprisonment for his love to God and man, has had in this country many counterparts among the sect. (256)

This disclaimer notwithstanding, Stowe's narrative follows a carefully planned but fictional representation of contemporary history. *A Key* was published in 1853 as a response to Southern attempts to discredit the veracity of *Uncle Tom's Cabin*, which had been published the year before. But in composing this valuable document, Stowe inadvertently revealed not only her sources for each character, but also her method of composition and her narrative strategies.

Nothing in the work was left to chance. Each character is not only a "representative" or allegorical type, thus leading to the intense contemporary criticism of Stowe's stereotypical representations of race and gender, but each character is also an exegetical type, appropriated from Scripture to represent some facet of the divine plan of prophecy and fulfillment. The most obvious of these prophetic figures is Evangeline, whose very name suggests a conflation of "Eve" from Genesis and "Angel" from the Book of Revelation. But Eva is more than a symbolic name; she is also a tragic figure who must be sacrificed in Stowe's plan to adumbrate the ultimate antitypical sacrifice of Tom by Legree's cruel execution of him. The tension, both dramatic and narrative, that exists between these two central characters throughout the novel is carefully planned and reflects the parallels designed in the Bible between typological adumbration and antitypical fulfillment.

Similarly, the mother figures in *Uncle Tom's Cabin* are modeled on biblical precedents and examples of motherhood, where Old Testament prefigurations foreshadow and adumbrate Mary's role as the mother of Christ. For example, in the Book of Judges, Hannah is the mother of Samuel, who is consecrated to God's service even before he is born, and Elizabeth, the New Testament mother of John the Baptist, recapitulates and advances the figural significance of Hannah's role as mother of a holy man. Both of these women are barren prior to their bearing of the divinely inspired men of destiny, and both prefigure the role of Mary in bearing God's son, Jesus Christ. Ultimately, the tensions in typological prefiguration and fulfillment are resolved in the incarnation, through which all prefigurative examples are abrogated and accomplished.

It is significant that Stowe avoids discussion of Eva as a "central character" in *A Key*. However, she cites among the sources for Uncle Tom, the Christ figure who is crucified both literally and figuratively at the conclusion of the novel, the real slave Josiah Henson, whose autobiographical slave narrative had been published in 1842 and whose relation to Tom is like that of Frederick Douglass to George Harris. The Douglass slave narrative, published in 1845, is clearly the character plan for George, who is, however, removed from *Uncle Tom's Cabin* relatively early in the narrative. It is Tom's character and narrative that continue to the end, and it is clear from *A Key* that Stowe intended this to be a moral and spiritual parallel to Christ himself.

> A last instance parallel with that of Uncle Tom is to be found in the published memoirs of the venerable Josiah Henson. His first recollections were of seeing his father mutilated and covered with blood, suffering the penalty of the law for the crime of raising his hand against a white man,—that white man being the overseer, who had attempted a brutal assault upon his mother. This punishment made his father surly and dangerous, and he was subsequently sold south, and thus parted forever from his wife and children. Henson grew up in a state of heathenism, without any religious instruction, till, in a camp-meeting, he first heard of Jesus Christ, and was electrified by the great and thrilling news that He had tasted death for every man the bond as well as the free. This story produced an immediate conversion. . . . Henson forthwith not only became a Christian, but began to declare the news to those about him; and, being a man of great natural force of mind and strength of character, his earnest endeavors to enlighten his fellow-heathen were so successful that he was gradually led to assume the station of a negro preacher; and though he could not read a word of the Bible or hymn-book, his

labors in this line were much prospered. *He became immediately a very valuable slave to his master* and was intrusted by the latter with the oversight of his whole estate, which he managed with great judgement and prudence. . . . When [his master's] affairs became embarrassed, he formed the design of removing all his negroes into Kentucky, and intrusted the operation entirely to his overseer. Henson was to take them alone, without any other attendant, from Maryland to Kentucky, a distance of some thousands of miles, giving only his promise as a Christian that he would faithfully perform this undertaking. (26; emphasis added)

Tom indeed reflects much of the character of Josiah Henson, and the duplicity with which Henson is subsequently treated is echoed in the promise to little Eva on her deathbed that her father will grant Tom his freedom, which St. Clare does not do before his own demise. Henson suffers being "sold South," just as Tom would later endure. Henson's story continues with moments of temptation, for example, the opportunity to kill his young master and escape, which he dismisses with the observation "What? Commit *murder?* and you a Christian!" (*Key* 29–30).

Stowe's appropriation of this narrative framework is obvious. However, she exceeds Henson's own account spiritually and artfully by linking Tom to little Eva, and by developing typological parallels between them that follow the exegetical patterns of prophecy and fulfillment. A close textual examination of the two chapters devoted to Eva and Tom in the novel will make these associations clearer, and we can also discern the author's intention to establish Tom as a representative of female, Christian, moral virtue from his earliest appearance in the narrative.

That *Uncle Tom's Cabin* employs the "representative type" of character is undisputed. Even critics who support and oppose the novel's narrative strategies and intent agree that Stowe exaggerated her characters so that they might "represent" certain values with which she endowed them. The principal objection to her rendering of character has been the racial stereotyping of the blacks, who often are given racially designated roles that conform to popular conceptions of black behavior, frequently perceived to be different from and inferior to qualities associated with the white characters. It would be incorrect to infer from these stereotypes that Stowe was unsympathetic with the Negro cause and wished to see the African remain in bondage to the white. But her clear sympathy with the various schemes by which Africans might be repatriated to Africa rather than integrated into American society on an equal basis with whites suggests that she may have been less optimistic and determined about equality for all citizens than she was certain of the evils of slavery as an institution and the need for immediate political and social emancipation. Richard Yarborough suggests that, "[a]lthough Stowe unquestionably sympathized with the slaves, her commitment to challenging the claim of black inferiority was frequently undermined by her own endorsement of racial stereotypes. . . . Of necessity, Stowe falls back upon popular conceptions of the Afro-American in depicting many of her slave characters. As one result, the blacks she uses to supply much of the humor in *Uncle Tom's Cabin* owe a great deal to the darky figures who capered across minstrel stages and white imaginations in the antebellum years (56).

The amusement and humor in *Uncle Tom's Cabin* is frequently at the expense of the black characters, as in the opening chapter when "Jim Crow" is required to dance and imitate white characters by his owner Shelby for the slave trader Haley. The visual image generated here, verbally, is of the minstrel dancer, replete with all those associated characteristics commonly held in the white antebellum imagination. Eliza's child is agile, well coordinated, animated, rhythmic, and above all slavishly obedient to the demands of his gentle master. The seeming harmony of this episode is about to be exploded into one of the most dramatic strategies of the entire novel, the attempt of the slave trader to rend asunder that sacred bond between mother and child. But in this scene, as in the scenes that follow with Sam and Andy, the black is exploited not only for the amusement of the white characters Shelby and Haley, but also for the audience of readers, who would have felt amused if slightly uncomfortable at this all-too-common scenario.

Similarly, Topsy is presented as a stereotypical figure, the pickaninny, but one whose innocence and impish behavior suggests the taint of original sin that needs Christianizing by Eva.

> The black, glassy eyes glittered with a kind of wicked drollery and the thing struck up, in a clear shrill voice, an odd negro melody, to which she kept time with her hands and feet, spinning round, clapping her hands, knocking her knees together, in a wild, fantastic sort of time, and producing in her throat all those odd gutteral sounds which dis-

tinguish the native music of her race; and finally, turning a summer-set or two, and giving a prolonged closing note, as odd and unearthly as that of a steamwhistle, she came suddenly down on the carpet, and stood with her hands folded, and a most sanctimonious expression of meekness and solemnity over her face, only broken by the cunning glances which she shot askance from the corners of her eyes.[1]

Throughout the narrative, Stowe clearly distinguishes characteristics of the Negro race from those of the Anglo-Saxons who own them, and she subtly weaves Christianity in and out of the contrast to show how moral virtue and piety are not the exclusive province of the whites. "Types" of Christian virtue, such as little Eva and the heroic mother Eliza, are on parade through the narrative, but Stowe carefully makes the associations between race and gender, good and evil, work interracially so that the stereotype of black inferiority is partly undermined by the action of the story. As Yarborough further suggests,

> Throughout *Uncle Tom's Cabin*, Stowe draws crucial distinctions in personality and behavior between full-blood and mixed-blood blacks. In her portrayal of the former—Sam, Andy, Topsy, Sambo, and Quimbo,—she emphasizes the racial gifts she saw as innately African. The traits of her mulatto figures, however, resemble those conventionally associated with whites. This is why, for example, Stowe stresses their physical attractiveness and why, in contrast to the dialect (or at least rough colloquialisms) of the full-blood blacks, the speech of the mulatto slaves is generally "correct." (51)

But Eliza's absurd argument for remaining a slave when George departs (that she's a Christian woman and must obey her master and mistress) is undermined by her later determination to disobey and run when her child's safety is threatened and the bonds of their sacred tie are jeopardized. Her virtue, in sum, consists of a human and maternal instinct that is primordial and archetypal. We are not far from those biblical mothers, like Sarah, Rachael, Hannah, Elizabeth, and of course Mary, whose archetypal presence in the biblical narrative reassures readers of the essential humanity of divine revelation.

It is in the narrative representation of Evangeline and Tom, however, that Stowe most fully realizes the biblical influences that pervade the novel, particularly in her strategies of characterization and association. Eva is presented not only as a representative type of Christian virtue (not unlike the sincerely devout Abraham in Genesis where his blind faith leads him to attempt the sacrifice of his only son, Isaac); she is also a prefigurative type of Christian redemption, of the sacrifice that Tom as Christ would make available to his white tormentors. Here, Stowe relies heavily on the readership's understanding of the biblical systems of typology and fulfillment, systems that not only were well understood by ministers and exegetical scholars, but would have been a commonplace in the literature of the ministry and the sermons they preached to their congregations. For example, when Jonathan Edwards wished to explain in *A History of the Work of Redemption* how God would ultimately redeem the entire world through the evolutionary cycles of history, he chose typological adumbration and antitypical fulfillment as a schema on which this prophetic system could rest:

> The setting up of the Kingdom of Christ is chiefly accomplished by four successive great events, each of which is in Scripture called Christ's coming in his Kingdom. . . . I would observe that each of the three former of these is a lively image or type of the fourth and last, viz., Christ's coming to the final judgement, as the principal dispensations of Providence before Christ's first coming were types of that first coming. As Christ's last coming to Judgment is accompanied with a resurrection . . . I would observe that each of those four great dispensations which are represented as Christ's coming in his Kingdom, *are but so many steps and degrees of the accomplishment of one event.* (247; emphasis added)

For Stowe, the progressive dispensations of God in history here articulated by Jonathan Edwards were a real and vital way of understanding her own times and the tensions between good and evil she perceived in antebellum America. America had been designated as the "elect nation," the "New English Israel" engaged on the "errand into the wilderness" in the model of ancient Israel entering the promised land. If popular contemporary images of this attainable paradise, such as the many paintings of "Peaceable Kingdom" by the artist Edward Hicks, were to have any real meaning in human history, then only a progressive and spiraling paradigm for the cycles of history would permit the alternations between backsliding and progress perceived in America's historical process. Therefore human history, which was the story of human beings engaged in the larger drama of providential teleology, could be best understood when God's dispensations were imperfectly revealed in earlier figures in a narrative that prefigures the events and qualities associated with

Christ and his judgment. Eva, who represents "spirituality" as a virtuous Christian type, is doomed not simply because she is too good for this evil world, but also because she is established, or instituted, by the author to recapitulate the dramatic climax of the incarnation drama, that sacrifice of Christ in martyrdom on the altar of evil that simultaneously gives evil a transient and temporary victory over good. It also makes possible the grace by which sinners (who repent, or who are elected for repentence) are able to achieve salvation. The epigraph of chapter 14, "Evangeline," suggests this dual role:

> A young star! which shone
> O'er life—too sweet an image for such glass!
> A lovely being, scarcely formed or moulded;
> A rose with all its sweetest leaves yet folded. (226)

Eva is represented as a neoclassic figure, a sculpture of ideal proportions though she is only six years old:

> Her form was the perfection of childish beauty, without its usual chubbiness and squareness of outline. There was about it an undulating and aerial grace, such as one might dream of for some mythic and allegorical being. Her face was remarkable less for its perfect beauty of feature than for a singular and dreamy earnestness of expression, which made the ideal start when they looked at her, and by which the dullest and most literal were impressed, without exactly knowing why. The shape of her head and the turn of her neck and bust was peculiarly noble, and the long golden-brown hair that floated like a cloud around it, the deep spiritual gravity of her violet blue eyes, shaded by heavy fringes of golden brown,—all marked her out from other children. . . . She was always in motion, always with a half smile on her rosy mouth, flying hither and thither, with an undulating and cloud-like tread, singing to herself as she moved in a happy dream. (231)

The reader has the immediate sense that little Eva is not long for this world, that her otherworldly qualities associate her clearly with some of Hawthorne's children, such as Priscilla in *The Blithedale Romance*, Pearl in *The Scarlet Letter*, or even Robin Molinieux, or Ibrahim in "The Gentle Boy." Indeed, it is only a matter of a few pages before the reader encounters Eva's ritual baptism, as she falls from the Mississippi riverboat on which she, her father, and Tom and the other slaves are traveling south. Eva's instinctive association with Tom is given in the exchange where "type" and "antitype" meet each other.

"My name's Tom; the little chil'en used to call me Uncle Tom, way back thar in Kentucky."

"Then I mean to call you Uncle Tom, because, you see, I like you," said Eva.

"So Uncle Tom, where are you going?"

"I don't know, Miss Eva."

"Don't know?" said Eva.

"No, I am going to be sold to somebody, I don't know who."

"My papa can buy you," said Eva, quickly; "and if he buys you, you will have good times. I mean to ask him, this very day."

"Thank you, my little lady," said Tom. (232–33)

This scene of tenderness and childish innocence in the face of institutional oppression, this momentary release from the horrors of the chattel slave system, is immediately followed by the first significant example of Tom's saving power, as Eva falls overboard and is ritualistically rescued, even resurrected, by Tom's strong arms:

Tom was standing just under her on the lower deck, as she fell. He saw her strike the water, and sink, and was after her in a moment. A broad-chested, strong-armed fellow, it was nothing for him to keep afloat in the water, till, in a moment or two the child rose to the surface, and he caught her in his arms, and, swimming with her to the boat-side, handed her up, all dripping, to the grasp of hundreds of hands, which, as if they had all belonged to one man, were stretched eagerly to receive her. (233)

The salvational power of Tom is temporary; Eva and Tom develop one of the most heavily sentimentalized relationships in all literature: it ends with Eva's death. Tom is there, by the bedside, with her father, St. Clare:

Tom had his master's hands between his own; and, with tears streaming down his dark cheeks, looked up for help where he had always been used to look. "Pray that this may be cut short!" said St. Clare, "this wrings my heart." . . .

"Eva," said St. Clare, gently.

She did not hear.

"O, Eva, tell us what you see! What is it?" said her father.

A bright and glorious smile passed over her face, and she said, brokenly,

—"O! love,—joy,—peace!" gave one sigh and passed from death into life!! (427–28)

This "passing from death into life" at the death scene is not only the stuff of the sentimental novel on which this trope is based; it is also orthodox Christian doctrine. Emily Dickinson was fond of this "death moment" in her poetry; it is one of the most highly sentimentalized moments in all of Victorian fiction, whether Dickens or Stowe. But here, and in the preceding episodes of the narrative, the apotheosis of Eva is paralleled by the transfiguration of Tom, who now assumes the role of Christian virtue and doomed martyr as the narrative proceeds toward his predetermined end.

The black characters in the novel prepare the way for the coming of Christ and the millennial kingdom. As Eliza escapes, she "dreamed of a beautiful country—a land, it seemed to her, of rest,—green shores, pleasant islands, and beautifully glittering water; and there, in a house which kind voices told her was a home, she saw her boy playing, a free and happy child. She heard her husband's footsteps; she felt him coming nearer; his arms were around her, his tears falling on her face, and she awoke! It was no dream. The daylight had long faded; her child lay calmly sleeping by her side; a candle was burning dimly on the stand, and her husband was sobbing by her pillow" (222). Here, millennial promises of the Twenty-third Psalm, with its "green pastures" and "still waters" are reinforced by the archetypal family: father, mother, and child. This trope of peace and harmony, love and family devotion, appears elsewhere in the novel, in virtually all of the family groupings, as an ideal to be sought, an ideal violated by the institution of slavery. It is also hinted in chapter 4, "An Evening in Uncle Tom's Cabin," where the Negroes are engaged in spiritual singing, and the lyrics of those millennial hymns conjure up visions of future paradise.

> "O, I'm going to glory,—won't you come along with me?
> Don't you see the angels beck'ning, and a calling me away?
> Don't you see the golden city and the everlasting day?"
> There were others, which made incessant mention of "Jordan's Banks" and "Canaan's Fields," and the "New Jerusalem" for the negro mind, impassioned and imaginative, always attaches itself to hymns and expressions of a vivid and pictorial nature; and, as they sung, some laughed, and some cried, and some clapped their hands, or shook hands rejoicingly with each other, as if they had fairly gained the other side of the river." (77–78)

This metaphorical construct of the "crossing of Jordan" is of course a conventional Christian type, a representation of the future glory made available to Christ and his saints. The eschatology of these hymns and spirituals is conventional Christian millennialism expressed in developmental typology; the future coming of Christ's kingdom is less a threat of punishment and judgment than it is a promise of glory for his saints: "O Canaan, bright Canaan, / I'm bound for the land of Canaan" (78).

Of all the characters in *Uncle Tom's Cabin*, Tom himself is represented as having true gifts of the spirit. His "learning" is wholly biblical; unlike Josiah Henson, on whom he is modeled, Tom is literate and is able to read and understand Scripture. It is the latter skill that elevates him above everyone else in the narrative, spiritually. God speaks through Tom, and Stowe arranges the entire story to conform to this oracular power.

> As for Tom's Bible, though it had no annotations and helps in the margin from learned commentators, still it had been embellished with certain way-marks and guide-boards of Tom's own invention, and which helped him more than the most learned expositions could have done. . . . he would designate, by bold, strong marks and dashes, with pen and ink, the passages which more particularly gratified his ear or affected his heart. His Bible was thus marked through, from one end to the other . . . his Bible seemed to him all of this life that remained, *as well as the promise of a future one.* (229–30)

Tom's power of perception is Edwardsean; Jonathan Edwards also relied upon "affections" and sense perception to communicate with God, rather than on the corrupted learning of ecclesiastical divines whose commentaries had polluted the libraries and churches of Europe and America since the times of the early Church fathers. Tom is a pure being; his vision of the future is unblemished, and his role as a Christian martyr about to be realized.

It is in the culminating scenes of Tom's agony before Simon Legree and in the death scene that ensues that Stowe's uses of biblical typological parallels are most readily perceived. Much critical work has been done on the necessity of transforming Tom into a representative type of Christian virtue, suggesting that Stowe had to "feminize" his character because her culture believed such virtue resided in the female (see O'Connell, this volume; Douglas, "Introduction"). However, although feminization of character is immensely important in the gender distinctions that Stowe's novel embraces, it does not completely answer all aspects of Tom's realization as a Christ figure. Tom-as-Christ is the *antitype* or fulfillment of all typological prefigurations that have gone before, such as Eva's transforming sacrifice.

Tom's "crucifixion" and flogging are used by Stowe to make some of the most poignant and dramatic statements about slavery that appear in the novel. Echoing Frederick Douglass's outrage when recalling his youthful witnessing of the flogging of his Aunt Hester, Stowe interrupts the narrative with these words: "Scenes of blood and cruelty are shocking to our ear and heart. What man has nerve to do, man has not nerve to hear. What brother-man and brother-Christian must suffer, cannot be told us, even in our secret chamber, it so harrows the soul! And yet, oh my country! these things are done under the shadow of thy laws! O, Christ! thy church sees them, almost in silence!" (583).

Like Christ at Calvary, Tom forgives Legree and expresses a deep concern for *his*, the torturer's soul. "Tom looked up to his master, and answered, 'Mas'r, if you was sick, or in trouble, or dying, and I could save ye, I'd give ye my heart's blood; and if, taking every drop of blood in this poor old body would save your precious soul, I'd give 'em freely, as the Lord gave his for me. O, Mas'r! don't bring this great sin on your soul! It will hurt you more than 't will me! Do the worst you can, my troubles will be over soon; but, if you don't repent, yours won't *never* end!' " (582–83). In true Christian humility, Tom asks, "Father, forgive [him], for [he] knows not what he does." With some of his last energy, Tom "opened his eyes and looked upon his master. 'Ye poor miserable critter!' he said, 'there ain't no more ye can do! I forgive ye, with all my soul!' and he fainted entirely away" (584).

This, of course, is not the death scene in the novel but is a recapitulation of the suffering of Christ on the cross. The apotheosis of Tom is reserved for the next chapter, where "Master George" has returned to set matters right. Millennialism is everywhere, and Tom greets George with the well-known phrase, "O, Mas'r George, ye're too late. The Lord's bought me, and is going to take me home,—and I long to go. Heaven is better than Kintuck" (590). Tom's final words are of love and forgiveness: "Give my love to Mas'r, and dear good Missis, and everybody in the place! Ye don't know! 'Pears like I loves 'em all! I loves every creature, everywhar!—it's nothing but love! O, Mas'r George! what a thing 'tis to be a Christian!" (590). And as he actually departs the earth, he again speaks of Christ's love, as it has been reflected in him: " 'Who,—who—who shall separate us from the love of Christ?' he said, in a voice that contended with mortal weakness; and, with a smile, he fell asleep" (591).

Thus Stowe brings to a close the narrative of Tom as Christian martyr. Biblical narrative functions in precisely the same way; the chosen people of God are assaulted on all sides by heathen peoples who do not understand their spiritual mission, and who punish and torture the "chosen people," rendering their history one of suffering and torment in an adversarial and hostile world. The Messiah himself was bruised and afflicted by men, and yet, as Isaiah reminds us, "with his stripes we are healed." It is on these prophetic, millennial, and typological prophecies of Isaiah that Stowe constructed her characterization of Tom, the martyr for Christian love and virtue, and it is with biblical rhetorical strategies that she develops her narrative of Christ among us in the person of a persecuted black slave who forgives his oppressors.

The denunciation of America for hypocrisy and for not having lived up to the principles of republican and Christian virtue, a fusion of neoclassical and biblical principles, was well known by the time Stowe preached her novel-sermon. Abolitionist pulpits rang with the rhetorical flourishes of ministers who denounced this grievous flaw in our system, and Frederick Douglass, in "What to the Slave Is the Fourth of July," delivered an oration that powerfully attacked American society for tolerating slavery when it preached another gospel of Christian love and republican equality of "all men." Stowe knew and used her Bible well and fused it with the traditions of the sentimental novel to create in *Uncle Tom's Cabin* a narrative of power, religious persuasion, and spiritual virtue. As she ended her sermon: "A Day of Grace is held out to us . . . the Christian Church has a heavy account to answer" (629).

## *The Prophetic Strain and Stowe's Millennialism: The Language of Canaan*

Helen Westra has argued that Stowe's millennialism, adapted and modified from Edwards's eschatology and that of his Calvinist successors, operates in the novel both as a theological framework and a rhetorical strategy to shape the work. She also traces the influences of Edwards's *History of the Work of Redemption*, especially the millennialism represented in that text, on Lyman Beecher and Harriet Beecher Stowe as "preachers" of the Second Great Awakening. *Language* and *rhetorical patterns* are critical in forging this connection. Millennialism is the central theological doctrine around which *Uncle Tom's Cabin* is developed; Stowe's vision in church of the old black man being flogged to death is a prophetic one, and her novel develops this ancient eschatological theme fully. However, the novel also incorporates the "language of Canaan," that prophetic vocabulary of episode and character known only to God's elect saints. This biblical language, appropriated by Stowe as typological prefiguration and fulfillment, shapes the novel's language, imagery, episodes, character formation, and dramatic settings, as well as its ultimate millennial vision and prophetic message. This eschatology, or vision of the last days, is not original to Jonathan Edwards, nor is its appropriation by Stowe unique; rather, both writers are assuming their audiences' specific knowledge of these tropes so that as writers they may employ the principles of Christian eschatology as rhetorical strategies and metaphorical controls in their own works.

Sacvan Bercovitch has demonstrated in *The American Jeremiad* that a sermon form devoted to a rehearsal of the sins of the people belongs to an Old Testament tradition that the New England Puritans appropriated for reinforcement of their self-representation as the "New English Israel." Bercovitch notes that

> the traditional mode, the European jeremiad was a lament over the ways of the world. It decried the sins of "the people,"—a community, a nation, a civilization, mankind in general,—and warned of God's wrath to follow. . . . The Lord required them to walk in righteousness, not to glory in the self; to follow His commandments, not the temptations of the flesh. So it had been in Eden, when Adam fell. So it had been in Jeremiah's time, when that most eloquent of Old Testament prophets railed against the stiff-necked Hebrews. So in Christ's time, when He denounced a generation of vipers and in the age of the apostles and at the fall of Rome. All of history proved it: humanity was naturally depraved. (10)

The language of the jeremiad is very present in castigations like Increase Mather's *Ichabod* (1702), a lamentation over the departed glory of the first and second generation of New England settlers. But the jeremiad might also be a visionary call to arms, a celebration of promise and hope, and the promise of a new beginning for God's new chosen people. Thus John Winthrop, in *A Model of Christian Charity* (1630), employs the rhetorical principles of the jeremiad to *inspire* his shipboard congregation, not only to condemn it:

> We shall find that the God of Israel is among us, when ten of us shall be able to resist a thousand of our enemies; when he shall make us a praise and glory that men shall say of succeeding plantations, "the Lord make it like that of New England." . . . The eyes of all people are upon us, so that if we shall deal falsely with our God in this work we have undertaken, and so cause him to withdraw his present help from us, we shall be made a story and a by-word through the world. . . . We shall shame the faces of many of God's worthy servants, and cause their prayers to be turned into curses upon us. (41)

Similarly, Stowe appropriates the rhetoric of the jeremiad to conclude *Uncle Tom's Cabin.* In this well-known rhetorical flourish, she threatens her readers not only as Americans but also as inheritors of the Christian faith. It was a strategy well known to the writers of slave narratives, from Olaudah Equiano to Frederick Douglass, who echoed the warning of antislavery, and to abolitionist preachers of the Second Great Awakening, who warned their listeners of the dangers of continuing to embrace republican and Christian principles while permitting the abhorrent practice of chattel slavery. Stowe vigorously warns:

> O, Church of Christ, read the signs of the times! Is not this power the spirit of HIM whose kingdom is yet to come, and whose will to be done on earth as it is in heaven?
>
> But who may abide the day of his appearing? "for that day shall burn as an oven; and he shall appear as a swift witness against those that oppress the hireling in his wages, the widow and the fatherless, and *that turn aside the stranger in his own right:* and he shall break in pieces the oppressor."
>
> Are not these dread words for a nation bearing in her bosom so mightily an injustice? Christians! every time that you pray that the kingdom of Christ may come, can you forget that prophecy associates, in dread fellowship, the *day of vengeance* with the year of his redeemed? (629)

Here, Stowe remarkably controls both language and imagery appropriated from the Book of Revelation to caution the United States against continued hypocrisy and degradation in the unChristian practice of slavery. Immediately, she follows with a return to the Old Testament prophets, to the language of adumbration and fulfillment, when her final paragraph of the "Concluding Remarks" warns:

> A day of grace is yet held out to us. Both North and South have been guilty before God; and the *Christian Church* has a heavy account to answer. Not by combining together, to protect injustice and cruelty [a clear reference to the Fugitive Slave Law and Compromise of 1850], and making a common capital of sin, is this Union to be Saved,—but by repentance, justice and mercy; for, not surer is the eternal law by which the millstone sinks in the ocean, than that stronger law, by which injustice and cruelty shall bring on nations the wrath of Almighty God! (629)

In this concluding passage, which has often been cited as one of the strongest warnings against slavery to appear in antebellum American writing, Stowe deliberately links the Old and New Testament doctrines of justice and mercy. She does so by noting that the salvation of humankind depends very much on how human beings respond to the teachings of Christ and subsequently treat their fellows. While this is hardly a return to "salvation by works," which the Protestant tradition rejected along with medieval iconography and stained glass, it does represent an emphasis on the importance of individual piety and morality in the salvational process. There is in Stowe, as there certainly is in Jonathan Edwards's writing, a restoration of covenant theology through which individuals may enter into a divine partnership to assist in effecting their own salvation. Humanity will ultimately be saved by grace; however, our behavior and principles will determine whether this predetermined grace can be made available to us. For Edwards, as for Stowe, repentance and transformation must precede regeneration, which does not come like a bolt out of the blue, but instead is the result of a lengthy process of reform and change.

Like Edwards, Stowe was a postmillennialist, a much abused term that means simply that Christ would most likely appear at the end of the thousand-years rather than as a wrathful judge at the beginning of it. Premillennialism argued that the harmony and prosperity sought by believers would only come as a result of the last judgment and the cleansing of the earth of all except God's elect saints. The optimist in Stowe's "Concluding Remarks" suggests that she was prepared to accept a transformed world, one that rejected slavery and embraced republican idealism, those dual cornerstones on which her Christian faith would rest. However, the rhetorical power of the jeremiad that she appropriates here places such a resolution in jeopardy, so that the reader is held suspended between two alternative modes of fulfillment. In so concluding the novel as a moral dilemma, she was positing alternatives very familiar to Great Awakening congregations—continued immersion in sin would lead only to death and destruction, where transformation and regeneration *might possibly* (though not *certainly* under the strict rules of Calvinism) lead to the gradual development of a utopian social order. Bercovitch also notes that for Edwards, "Regeneration . . . depended on conformity through grace to the principle of 'oneness' . . . American Protestants, after all, had a special role to play in God's plan. For them, above all other peoples, conversion, rebirth, and 'generic consciousness' were manifested typologically through the correspondence (which Edwards never tired of explaining) between personal fulfillment and social harmony (108).

Both Edwards and Stowe saw in America a promise for a new beginning, a restorative and regenerative transformation out of which a new world order would arise. But it was up to the present generation of Americans to effect this change. For both writers, the argument from tradition was applicable only insofar as it provided contemporary thinkers with a precedent for God's divine plan for the redemption of the world. Their visions depended, ultimately, on the revelation of God in Scripture, those sixty-six books of incarnate wisdom that through careful exegesis should reveal *to the saints* the plan of God's work of redemption. Writes Bercovitch, "New Israel, New World, new heavens and new earth; it was the common vision of the time, and it derived, unmistakably, from Puritan New England. . . . The 'star of empire' meant far more for [the eighteenth-century colonists] than the movement of civilization from the Old World to the New. It signaled the 'complete fulfillment' of the 'various ancient prophecies.' It was the morning star heralding the triumphant sun/Son that (in Edwards's words) would 'rise in the West, contrary to the course of . . . the world' " (113–14).

This *translatio studii*, the movement of the course of empire from east to west, was amply represented in the poetry and sermons of the late eighteenth and early nineteenth centuries, especially in the verses of Philip Freneau and Joel Barlow, whose "rising glory" epics echoed, like Stowe's novel, the biblical phrasing of Isaiah and Revelation. In "The Rising Glory of America," an epic poem that Freneau and his Princeton classmate Hugh Henry Brackenridge composed for the 1771 commencement, we find a fusion of secular imagery, biblical language, and biblical themes in a supremely optimistic "promise" of American prophetic fulfillment:

> A new Jerusalem, sent down from heaven,
> Shall grace our happy earth,—perhaps this land,
> Whose ample bosom shall receive, though late,
> Myriads of saints, with their immortal king,
> To live and reign on earth a thousand years,
> Thence called *Millennium*. Paradise anew
> Shall flourish, by no second Adam lost,
> No dangerous tree with deadly fruit shall grow,
> No tempting serpent to allure the soul,
> From native innocence. A *Canaan* here,
> Another *Canaan* shall excel the old. . . .
> the lion and the lamb
> In mutual friendship linked, shall browse the shrub,
> And timorous deer with softened tygers stray
> O'er mead, or lofty hill, or grass plain. . . .
> The fiercer passions of the human breast
> Shall kindle up to deeds of death no more,
> But all subside in universal peace. . . .
> And such AMERICA at last shall have,
> When ages, yet to come, have run their round,
> And future years of bliss alone remain. (77–78)

The system of exegesis by which such a prophetic passage would be interpreted by contemporary readers is called "typology," a schema for endowing Old Testament figures and events with prophetic value. Similarly, the New Testament was also believed to be endowed with prophetic power, so that the fulfillment of one testament was to be found in the first Incarnation, while the fulfillment of the New Testament would come in contemporary history and the second coming of Christ.

The Great Awakening and Jonathan Edwards had produced a revitalized typology transformed optimistically to explore the prophetic figures of the natural as well as the scriptural world. While rooting their conclusions in Scripture parallels, the Calvinists of the late eighteenth century in New England argued an eschatology that was derived from prophetic images found in history and current events, so that the millennial expectation became less a fear of the judgment than an awareness of God's transforming power over men's hearts. During the mid–eighteenth century, and just prior to the American Revolution, the force of the prophetic arguments was intense, and it animated reassertions of America's promising future in the writings of Edwards and his disciples, Joseph Bellamy, Timothy Dwight, and David Austin. The thousand years during which the forces of evil would be bound and the righteous saints were to enjoy abundance and plenty, peace and tranquility, became so dominant an image in sermons and literature of the eighteenth century that commentators throughout the Western world saw in contemporary events "signs of the times" that indicated the beginning of the grand and prosperous millennial period.

Edwards and his disciples paradoxically argued in sermons that doom awaited those who did not attend upon the Lord. The same pen that wrote "Sinners in the Hands of an Angry God" also stated that "it is not unlikely that this work of God's spirit is the dawning or at least a prelude of that glorious work of God, so often foretold in Scripture . . . and there are many things which make it probable that this work will begin in America. . . . And if we may suppose that this glorious work of God shall begin in any part of America, I think if we consider the circumstances of the settlement of New England, it must needs appear the most likely of all the American colonies" (Edwards, *Some Thoughts*).

All this sounds remarkably like Walt Whitman a century later, who would write, in the 1855 preface to *Leaves of Grass*, "The Americans of all nations at any time upon the earth have probably the fullest poetical nature. The United States themselves are essentially the greatest poem. . . . The American poets are to enclose old and new for America is the race of races (Whitman, *Leaves of Grass*, 2). Whitman's progressive optimism would give way to his "Drum Taps" lamentations and *Democratic Vistas* following his experience of the Civil War, much of the millennial optimism of the early national era was shattered on the battlefields of Gettysburg and Atlanta. But Harriet Beecher Stowe tapped the mother lode of prophetic imagery that filled the pages of sermons and poems composed between 1700 and 1850, and she artfully controlled the tension generated when a writer predicts a glorious future, if only the nation would steady its course.

Jonathan Edwards also saw in the coming millennium a vision of technological advancement and change. For Edwards and

Stowe, as for General Electric, "progress was our most important product." In Miscellany 262, one of the many unpublished manuscript fragments of Edwards now collected in the Beinecke Library at Yale University, we find the following fusion of civil and religious forces in the fulfillment of God's glory:

> *Millennium:* 'Tis probable that the world shall be more like Heaven in the millennium in this respect: that contemplation and spiritual enjoyments and those things that more directly concern the mind and religion, will be more the saint's ordinary business than now. There will be so many contrivances and inventions to facilitate and expidite their necessary secular business that they shall have more time for more noble exercise, and that they will have better contrivances for assisting one another through the whole earth by more expedite, easy, and safe communication between distant regions than now. The invention of the mariner's compass is a thing discovered by God to the world to that end. And how exceedingly has that one thing enlarged and facilitated communication. And who can doubt that yet God will make it more perfect, so that there need not be such a tedious voyage in order to hear from the other hemisphere? And so the country about the poles need no longer be hid to us, but the whole earth may be as one community, one body in Christ. (243)

Thus the millennial vision and progressive eschatology were joined in a comprehensive image of a future paradise in which human relations, scientific invention, and earthly achievement would be developed under the guidance of Providence. The vision was progressive and utopian. The proof of its revealed promise would be governed, however, by the truths that Edwards and Stowe received from Scripture and contemporary historical parallels to Scripture, and from the typological associations they perceived between the two.

Stowe brought to her contemporary drama of the institution of slavery a language so familiar to antebellum readers that little had to be added by way of explanation. When she published *A Key to Uncle Tom's Cabin* in 1853, she basically provided readers with examples of her sources, hundreds of them, to improve the veracity of the narrative. It is important that *A Key* provides very few explanations of the scriptural analogies in the text; most readers would have understood such parallels as those examined here between Eva and Tom as regenerative, sacrificial figures, and Stowe's contemporaries would have been well exposed to the "language of Canaan" that pervades the novel, in character formation and in the application of the millennial jeremiad, a sermonic form that Stowe appropriated not only from the Bible but from contemporary sermon rhetoric. *Uncle Tom's Cabin* stands today as one of the most rhetorically powerful of all American documents, and it owes much of this force to the appropriated power of biblical language, which Stowe consciously and intentionally used to the great effect the book's publication produced. Aware of this power, her "Concluding Remarks" indicate how she intended the work to be a warning to Americans that the "Day of Doom" was at hand if changes were not made to rid the country of the barbaric practice of chattel slavery. It was the Bible that provided the moral authority for such outrage, and the saturation of the population with the language and rhetoric of the Bible that gave her book even more force than its narrative line produces through sentimental and antislavery rhetoric.

## N O T E S

1. Stowe, *Uncle Tom's Cabin*, ed. Ann Douglas. (1981), 352. All subsequent quotations from the novel are from this edition, cited by page number in the text.

# IV

### Race and Slavery in *Uncle Tom's Cabin*

# 9

.

JAMES BENSE

# Myths and Rhetoric of the Slavery Debate and Stowe's Comic Vision of Slavery

In a critical tribute at the time of Harriet Beecher Stowe's death in 1896, Charles Dudley Warner called attention to the humorous appeal of *Uncle Tom's Cabin* (1852): "Distinguished as the novel is by its character-drawing and its pathos, I doubt if it would have captivated the world without its humor." Stowe's "humor of character in action, of situations elaborated with great freedom, and with what may be called a hilarious conception" impressed Warner with the amplitude of its ability to entertain "or to heighten the pathos of the narrative by contrast" (70).

Warner's observations may have been prompted in part by a passage from Stowe's 1878 introduction to *Uncle Tom's Cabin* quoted earlier in his essay. While aligning her novel's veracity with the factualism of the antislavery campaign, as in *A Key to Uncle Tom's Cabin* (1853; 5), in the introduction Stowe goes on to explain that "she sought to light up the darkness by humorous and grotesque episodes, and the presentation of the milder and more amusing phases of slavery," based on "her recollection of the never-failing wit and drollery of her former colored friends" (xxxi–xxxii). Stowe (referring above to herself) indicates here, as she had before (*Key* iii, 5), that without something to brighten the scenes of slavery there "would be a picture of such unrelieved horror and darkness as nobody could be induced to look at" (xxxi). Associating her text's humor with "grotesque episodes" and emphasizing the "unrelieved horror" to which it responds both imply farther reaching effects than the inclusion of amusement alone would suggest.[1]

A fundamental point of my argument is that Stowe's comic vision of slavery in *Uncle Tom's Cabin* is an intrinsic element of the textual "power" that Jane Tompkins has argued in *Sensational Designs* makes "the very possibility of social action . . . dependent on the action taking place in individual hearts" (128). If, as Tompkins points out, "modern readers" are not likely "to take seriously a novel that insists on religious conversion" in order to bring about "social change" (132), neither are they predisposed to recognize that the palpable effects of its humor, in particular of that humor which is politically most offensive, are an integral part of its conversionary operation. The importance of being able to locate the humor within what Tompkins calls a "schematization" that produces "a totalizing effect" (136) becomes apparent when comparing the critical findings of Myra Jehlen and Richard Yarborough regarding Stowe's slave characters. Like some other significant studies confined to the serious terrain of Stowe's text, Jehlen's offers formulations about its most impressive qualities without examining its humorous effects. As part of a broader purpose, her analysis demonstrates the novel's "transcendent power" through its "juxtapositions," one such being the "belief in individual self-possession" vis-à-vis "characters who are the property of other characters" (385), for which the dramatically serious portrayals of George Harris and Cassy serve as persuasive examples (386–88, 395–97). There is, however, in her observation that "the best of the slaves in *Uncle Tom's Cabin* are models of upward mobility" a suggested limit regarding how far one can go in attributing "power" (387) to others who are less exemplary. As a result, such an approach does not provide a sufficient answer to Yarborough's devastating survey of Stowe's slave characters, beginning with her comic figures. Stowe's "endorsement of racial stereotypes" and perplexity about "the Negro" provide a basis for him to argue that her humor in connection with slave characters fatally limits what her artistic sincerity could accomplish: "Of necessity, Stowe falls back upon popular conceptions of the Afro-American in depicting many of her slave characters. As one result, the blacks she uses to supply much of the humor in *Uncle Tom's Cabin* owe a great deal to the darky figures who capered across minstrel stages and white imaginations in the antebellum years." Apparently taking Sam and Andy as easy comic targets, Yarborough notes their importance in aiding Eliza to escape but points out that their motivation does not stem from "any real desire to help the fugitives" but is merely "to please their mistress." Despite "their tricksterlike" role, "they ultimately seem little more than bumptious, giggling, outsized adolescents" (47).

In response to Yarborough's dismissive criticism, I would argue that the humorous dimension of Stowe's treatment of slavery reflects a conscious artistic strategy that responded effectively to the slavery debate of the 1830s and 1840s. As the case of Sam will also show, Stowe worked subversively within the rhetoric and culturally invented myths that held sway over slavery propaganda to convert the most egregious kind of slave stereotyping among her contemporaries into a shape-shifting, encompassing figure who would, through his words and enactments, deflate major tenets of American ideology that had made his "creation" possible. The surprising effects of Sam's language suggest that Stowe was confident in the power of vernacular humor to serve a serious artistic purpose. As a result of combining the subversion of slavery's myths with an examination of celebrated American values that were slavery's antithesis, Stowe's invention entraps superior-minded readers into a self-reflective identification with "Black Sam," also referred to as "Master Sam," a figure whose irrepressible drive toward selfhood challenges the inauthenticity of an unregenerate culture.

Stowe's comic appropriation of one of slavery's most cherished stereotypes—a "childlike" creature exhibiting "obedience," "loyalty," and "happiness"—was consistent with her larger strategy of giving full expression to the cultural constructs of slaveocracy in order to expose them from within. As historical evidence regarding the slavery debate suggests, antislavery indictments and proslavery replies had created an impasse in the "court" of Northern public opinion. For more than a decade prior to the publication of *Uncle Tom's Cabin*, the abolitionist campaign had focused much of its publicity, in the form of testimonies from slavery's observers and its fugitives, into an attack on the immoral conduct of slave owners and an exposé of slave degradation and abuse. The defense of slavery, on the other hand, rested importantly on the South's image of idyllic plantation life with slaveholders as patriarchs of their slave "families." The "ambiguities" of the "Negro 'domestication' " myth, as George M. Fredrickson delineates them, informed the prevailing antebellum perceptions of slaves that influenced both antislavery and proslavery campaigns. Fredrickson notices "an important cleavage" in the racial and economic views of the institution, which implied such questions as "whether the model for the ideal slave was taken from the realm of the subhuman, with the slave as a high type of domesticated animal . . . or from the human family as a 'domestic' and domesticating institution, with the slave in the role of a child, responding with human affection to a kindly master." Regarding "the nature of the plantation: was it a commercial enterprise with the blacks as a subhuman labor force, or a small patriarchal society?" (55–56).[2]

Slavery's defenders expressed a variety of views. Those who regarded slaves as subhuman, such as T. W. Hoit, asserted that "it is right that barbarism should subserve civilization" (10). Others pragmatically maintained that, whether viewed as racially inferior or as culturally conditioned products of servitude, slaves were not prepared for freedom (Fredrickson 44–46). When pressed with "[t]he abolitionists' charge that slavery was inherently sinful," defenders (such as John C. Calhoun) advanced "the unequivocal claim that slavery was 'a positive good,' " a position that developed "in tandem" with "the doctrine of permanent black inferiority" (Fredrickson 46, 47). The affirmation of slavery's "positive good" was supported by the stereotype of the happy slave, who "was not only unfit for freedom but was ideally suited to slavery" (Fredrickson 52).

The conflicted ambiguities of the South's familial myth resonated with the tensions of Northern paternalism. Referring to "[w]hat Ann Douglas has called 'the feminization of American culture,' " Mason I. Lowance, Jr. explains the impact of this development on the slavery debate: "[T]he identification of the slave culture with docility, domesticity, and above all, with Christian meekness and acceptance provided the proslavery advocates with a version of American society that did not correspond to the impulses toward freedom articulated by democratic principles and the rhetoric of abolitionist literature" ("Slave Narrative" 402–3). Moreover, the abolitionist argument that the rights of freedom and self-determination could no longer be denied to the slave population in the South was seriously undermined by the North's own undisguised practices of racial prejudice. Describing the ostracism of "free Negroes in the South," Dwight Lowell Dumond states, "Their status in the North was, in many localities, little better than in the South, race prejudice operating through force of public opinion supplying the deficiencies of less severe legal restrictions" (9). The encounters with Northern segregation practices related by Frederick Douglass (Andrews, ed., *My Bondage* 214–15, 223–24, 238–39, 245–47) and Harriet Jacobs (162–63, 175–77) amply illustrate the validity of Dumond's historical observation.

In addition to the resistance generated by contradictions between democratic values and racial prejudice in the North, the antislavery movement was confronted with other prohibitive barriers in the South. After the Nat Turner rebellion in 1831, "slaveowners were extraordinarily careful to maintain absolute control over their 'people' and to quarantine them from any kind of outside influence" (Fredrickson 53). The isolation of plantation slaves, as Douglass indicated, kept outsiders from forming unfavorable opinions (*My Bondage,* Andrews ed. 44–46). As Northern abolitionism gained momentum, the South's reactionary suppression of free speech on the subject "closed the public forums to all antislavery doctrine" (Dumond 39).

These defenses did not prevent the American Anti-Slavery Society in New York from recruiting unsympathetic witnesses of slavery to publish testimonial evidence of its barbarities. In 1839, Theodore Weld's *American Slavery As It Is: The Testimony of a Thousand Witnesses* presented evidence of widespread cruelty on the part of slaveholders. Published with the testimonies were statements from citizens who could vouch for the credibility of the contributors. An "Advertisement to the Reader" announced the inclusion of slaveholder "testimony . . . taken, mainly, from recent newspapers, published in the slave states" (iii). The Society combined the empirical case against the South's proslavery mythology with the metaphor of a court of public opinion: "Reader, you are empannelled as a juror to try a plain case and bring in an honest verdict" (7). The reader's sensibilities were called upon, much as they would be later in *Uncle Tom's Cabin,* to imagine the sufferings of the slave and of the slave family.

Although deflected somewhat by the Southern claim of exaggeration, the weight of evidence in *American Slavery* made a lasting public impression. The courtroom metaphor appears years later in a Southern assessment of the overwhelming impact of *Uncle Tom's Cabin*. George Frederick Holmes observed despairingly, "We have not the ear of the court; our witnesses are distrusted and discredited, and in most cases, they are not even granted a hearing" (qtd. in Gossett, *"Uncle Tom's Cabin"* 209). The shocking nature of Southern newspaper advertisements for runaway slaves, often describing scars or other evidence of brutality, led Stowe to exhibit some in *A Key*, as did Charles Dickens in his *American Notes* in 1842. In keeping with a conventional requirement of slavery testimony, Douglass in 1855 would still mock-seriously resolve "to relate and describe; only allowing myself a word or two, occasionally, to assist the reader in the proper understanding of the facts narrated" (*My Bondage*, Andrews ed. 69).

Along with its compelling qualities, *American Slavery's* propagandist elements are also apparent. The "factual" emphasis of the testimonies does not provide much in the way of "understandable" explanations for common practices of inhuman abuse. In contrast to the pale figures of wanton cruelty who parade across the pages of *American Slavery*, Stowe's legendary Simon Legree, as Kenneth S. Lynn points out in his 1962 introduction to *Uncle Tom's Cabin*, "is, despite his beastliness, a human being."[3] Moreover, as explained by Dumond, plantation life on a factual level could not be reduced to a "typical" case: "There was too much diversity, and the human element entered in too largely to permit even a highly centralized picture. To attempt it is to become lost in a labyrinth of qualifications" (37).

Following Weld's book of testimonies in 1839, and prior to the coming of age of fugitive-slave autobiographies, as exemplified by Douglass's 1845 *Narrative*, James Freeman Clarke's 1842 Thanksgiving Day sermon further reveals the paralysis of the slavery debate in the North a decade before the appearance of *Uncle Tom's Cabin*. The resistance to talking about slavery is strongly implied in his opening remarks: *"But what good will it do to consider this subject at all?"* (3–4). Placing his listeners "before the judgment-seat of Christ," he continues with withering irony: "Will it do to say then, that it was an exciting subject,— one which the majority of the respectable citizens disliked to hear mentioned,—that the agitation of it might disturb our political, ecclesiastical, or social organizations?" (4).

Clarke's sermon shows that, despite the unparalleled influence of *Uncle Tom's Cabin* in antislavery literature, Stowe added nothing substantially new to what had long been known in the North about slavery. Moreover, aspects of Stowe's novel associated with its extraordinary appeal are foreshadowed in Clarke's own insightful approach to the subject. A major premise of Clarke's sermon, that Northerners must bear their responsibility for the perpetuation of slavery in the South, anticipated Stowe's later appeal to her readers. Clarke also combined an awareness of the Southern slave code with a strategy to undercut the best representations of slavery, a rhetorical pattern that Stowe would later incorporate in her novel. A former resident in the South, Clarke adopted the *American Slavery* strategy of presenting background credentials, thus establishing himself as a slavery witness. His sympathetic views of North and South enabled him to use a conciliatory rhetoric (as Stowe later would) to negotiate between opposed sectional loyalties. Initially attempting to deprogram his audience of the irreconcilable claims of Northern and Southern propagandists—of the slave's unendurable sufferings, on the one hand, and of the slave's "fitness" for slavery, on the other—Clarke's juggling of sentiments provocatively appropriates the atmosphere of ambivalence and skepticism. He concedes that an outsider's perceptions of slavery are subject to exaggeration. Conjuring up horrors from testimonies in *American Slavery*, the "misery" of slaves constantly "whipped and worked" and "dripping with blood," Clarke dispels this imagery by speculating that a Northern visitor may "perhaps" remain in the South "for months without hearing the sound of the lash. . . . Yet," he adds, "the *real* evils of slavery never have been, and hardly can be exaggerated" (5–6).

Rather than dwell on the "cruelties" of slaveholders covered by Weld's book, Clarke proceeds to the slave's "moral degradation" (8) and a sequence of stereotypes. Balancing traits associated with the slave trickster ("Falsehood, theft") and other "vices" against the purity and honesty of "tenderly pious slaves," he underscores "one evil so inherent in the system, that no care can obviate it. The slave's nature never *grows*. The slave is always a child" (8–9). While "God has made Progress and Freedom inseparable," Clarke continues, "the slave has no motive to look forward," or to be "industrious, diligent, skilful, and faithful" (9). These malignant consequences of the slave-as-child myth indicate the importance that Benjamin Franklin would assume as a countervailing symbol for Douglass and other fugitive slaves.

Clarke's survey of economic, political, and religious areas of the debate concludes with refutations of final "objections," which reveal the North's denial of responsibility for slavery and state the conventional myths that perpetuated racist stereotyping: "Objection 3. *'But the blacks cannot take care of themselves.'*" "Objection 4. *'They do not wish to be free. They are very happy as they are.'*" "Objection 5. *'But they are not intended to be free. They are an inferior race'*" (21, 22).

Clarke's appeals to "conscience" and "public opinion" (25) were amplified by the lecturing and writing of fugitive slaves. But while the truth claim of factualism and the rhetoric of moral suasion would continue to shape the antislavery campaign of the 1840s and 1850s, the extension of these strategies to slave testimonies heightened the contradictions of Northern racial prejudice. Because the ex-slave could not assume the same authority as a white author, "[t]he reception of his narrative as truth depended on the degree to which his artfulness could hide his art" (Andrews 3). As Douglass explains in *My Bondage and My Freedom*, his believability as a lecturer could not be maintained without an appearance of uneducated simplicity, coached if necessary by advisers (Andrews ed. 220–21) who regarded him as being "better fitted to speak than to write" (240). Such were the limitations imposed on Douglass even after he had demonstrably outgrown and continually defied them.

Against the persistence of proslavery arguments, which were not dispelled by the grotesqueries of the factual testimonies, "pathos and humor" played an important role in the discourse between slave lecturers and their audiences (Blassingame 123). Despite the insistence on a slave lecturer's inferiority, "the public," observed John A. Collins, "have itching ears to hear a colored man speak, and particularly a *slave*" (qtd. in Blassingame 123). Lewis Clarke responded to his audience's curiosity by humorously subverting slave stereotypes: "The slaves used to debate together sometimes, what could be the reason that the yellow folks couldn't be trusted like the dark ones could." They "concluded it was because they was sons of their masters. . . . You laugh; but that's what the *slaves* concluded was the reason" (qtd. in Child 154). Lydia Maria Child's transcription of Clarke's wit belies her description of a mind struggling to express itself (151). Having "promised to resume the thread" of Clarke's speech in a second installment, Child later tells her readers, "His discourse, however, *had* no thread, but was as discursive and uncertain as the movements of fallen leaves in the autumn wind" (159). Clarke in particular stands out as a likely influence on Stowe. He is the first to be introduced, along with Douglass and Josiah Henson, in her *Key* chapter on George Harris, and he was "an acquaintance" who had "related personally" to Stowe some of the "incidents of his life" (13–14).

Like Lewis Clarke, Stowe used humor to challenge the assumptions from which slave stereotypes were derived. In *Uncle Tom's Cabin,* she first presents "Black Sam" while he wonders aloud about the consequences of Uncle Tom's departure "with a comprehensiveness of vision and strict outlook to his own personal well-being, that would have done credit to any white patriot in Washington" (47–48). Having learned of the sale of Tom, Sam's thoughts are not concerned with the tragic plight of a fellow slave being sold south but are focused instead on the opportunity of being promoted to Tom's position as manager of Shelby's business affairs.

The appropriateness of Sam's initial appearance as a stage soliloquist becomes clear as he subsequently assumes what amounts to a host of dramatis personae. The manifold allusiveness of his shape-shifting career infuses the stereotype of the submissive "child" of slavery with the power not only to reveal the incompatibility of slavery's "justifications" with human values, but also to unmask the cultural chauvinism of antebellum North and South. Thus Sam's role contributes to Stowe's larger purpose of calling for a profound reform of American values as a whole. Operating within the idyllic "family" myth used by pro-slavery propagandists, he combines tricksterism *and* piety as a best-of-both formula for self-advancement. Through his performance as a speaker, Sam's roles as providential agent, self-taught orator, community protector, bragging humorist, and homespun philosopher result in significant humor at the expense of white male authority.

As suggested by James Freeman Clarke's sermon, tricksterism and pious behavior were both responses to the intolerable condition of a life without personal meaning or certain hope of eventual liberation. Stowe's humorous approach to this realization proves to be more effective than its pratfall foolishness at first lets on. As Eliza flees from the Shelby farm to keep her child from being handed over to the slave trader Haley, Sam's trickster talents come into play in the service of Mrs. Shelby, who fervently desires to help Eliza escape. When he admonishes Andy with mock seriousness, "This yer's a seris bisness. . . . Yer mustn't be a makin' game" (61), his verbal irony signals the savvy youngster and the reader that a "game" is precisely what he will invent to confuse and mislead the slave trader. Although Sam's easy triumphs over Haley can only occur within a world of facile comedy, within this domain his wit and timing are brilliant, exemplifying in masterly strokes what Edgar Allan Poe's narrator in "The Purloined Letter" describes as "an identification of the reasoner's intellect with that of his opponent" (1432). Presenting the slave trader with a choice between two roads, Sam manipulates Haley through a sequence of psychological reversals, tricking him into choosing the wrong one and reinforcing his resolve to pursue it. Once the trick is up, the design of this plan, exploiting the trader's own sense of fairness, forces him "to pocket his wrath with the best grace he was able" (64). Sam's triumph results from a rhetorical reversal similar to that observed by William L. Andrews in a passage from Douglass in which "[t]he slaveholder's reductive reading of his slave is ironically reversed to reduce *him* to the level of a comic grotesque" (134). Sam underscores the point by asking Haley, "How does strange gentleman spect to know more about a country dan de natives born and raised?" (64).

Sam's reporting of events in the Shelby parlor reenacts the developing "egocentrism in black autobiography of the 1840s," a departure from "self-effacement" that was possible with growing "public sympathy" encouraged by "the antislavery movement" (Andrews 100). During his account of Eliza's river crossing, not only does he proclaim the special providence that made it possible, he identifies himself as God's intervening agent: "Thar's allers instruments ris up to do de Lord's will. Now, if't hadn't been for me to-day, she'd a been took a dozen times" (77–78). Here and elsewhere, Sam's burlesquing gestures telegraph the disconcerting contradictions of the cultural realities that his playfulness invokes. Thus, when he has underscored his own providential part in assisting Eliza, Sam also has enacted the pious egocentrism of the Puritan tradition, simultaneously aggrandizing himself while subsuming his achievement under the glory of God's sovereignty. Although his self-appropriation depends upon the sanction of his mistress, who "has allers been a instructin' " Sam and the other Shelby slaves in the ways of God's beneficence (77), Stowe's text leaves little doubt about the intended veracity of his interpretation of events. Mr. Shelby plays the role of a skeptic, initially calling Sam's account of Eliza's fleeing across the river's ice "apocryphal," but Mrs. Shelby, we are informed, "sat perfectly silent, pale with excitement, while Sam told his story" (77).

In response to Mr. Shelby's disapproval of the nature of these "providences," Sam reformulates his ethos into a measured blend of penitence and pride: "[A] poor nigger like me's 'mazin' tempted to act ugly sometimes, when fellers will cut up such shines as dat ar Mas'r Haley; he an't no gen'l'man no way; anybody's been raised as I've been can't help a seein' dat ar" (78). While seeming to affirm the "family" myth upon which slavery was defended, his strategic retreat to pride in his upbringing continues to highlight the manner in which the oppressiveness of slavery would inevitably produce dishonesty—by revealing how "the demands of truthfulness and self-preservation were often at odds in the experience of blacks in America" (Andrews 3). As all three characters in the parlor are swept up by the extraordinary events, the scene displays them entrapped in a self-conscious acting out of master-slave relations comparable to the "charade" that Herman Melville created in *Benito Cereno* (Sundquist, *"Benito Cereno"* 111). Melville's text presents a sinister version of the Shelby parlor scene, Babo's "masquerade of devotion to Benito Cereno" revealing "the complexly layered qualities of rebellion and submission—of 'Nat' and 'Sambo' roles—that historians have detected among the accounts of slave behavior" (Sundquist 110).[4]

Stowe's comedy, though it does not have the veiled complexity of Melville's narrative, originates from a similarly compelling insight. Mrs. Shelby's determination to subvert the slave code, in order to preserve the union between Eliza and Eliza's son, effectively unveils the travesty of human relations upon which slavery depended. To use Nancy Walker's terminology, Mrs. Shelby's "whispered" code countermands the "announced, articulated" code of her husband (105). As a result, both have become partners with Sam in a game of mock propriety of which he is the master, though the rules of behavior are cultural inventions imposed by his owners. In conformance with masculine rules, Mr. Shelby goes through the motions of correcting Sam in order to maintain his "honor," revealing a hypocritical level of self-illusion that eviscerates his moral substance. Mrs. Shelby happily participates in her newly subversive role as she congratulates Sam for having gained "a proper sense" of his "errors," then sends him off to his reward in Chloe's kitchen (78).

When the false nature of master-slave relations has become absurdly apparent, Stowe's narrator invokes but also questions the wisdom of the North's "romantic racialist view" (Fredrickson 102), implying that Sam is the equivalent of a "child" too knowing to be misled by falsehood: "Now, there is no more use in making believe be angry with a negro than with a child; both instinctively see the true state of the case, through all attempts to affect the contrary; and Sam was in no wise disheartened by . . . [Mr. Shelby's] rebuke, though he assumed an air of doleful gravity" (78). By locating her narrative consciousness within what Fredrickson has elucidated as the "ambiguities" of "domestication," Stowe combined the most powerful associations that she could summon to override the " 'hard' racism that manifest[ed] itself in the image of 'the Negro as beast' " and that "vied for supremacy in Southern propaganda with the 'soft' image of the black slave as beloved child" (Fredrickson 58). Stowe's repeated soteriological references to Sam's palm-leaf hat also symbolically identify him as a "rakish" (78) version of those "spirits bright" with "conquering palms" of whom Uncle Tom later sings to Eva (266).[5] While these mediating gestures also may have provided assurance against the South's fears of slave insurrections, Sam's conscious mastery of his trickster role is very unchildlike: "Mas'r's quite right, —quite; it was ugly on me, —there's no disputin' that ar; and of course Mas'r and Missis wouldn't encourage no such works" (78). His renderings of Caesar's image to Caesar, like the "alacrity" of his departing "bow" (78), suggest his potential to assume the sinister role of Melville's Babo in a different setting.

When Sam leaves the Shelby parlor, Stowe's comic tour de force expands into another subversive agenda as the narrator reiterates that "Master Sam had a native talent that might, undoubtedly, have raised him to eminence in political life" (78). The idea of Sam as a human being is momentarily held up to view, as though to highlight the "moral degradation" of the slave described in Clarke's sermon. But Sam is too much a grotesque invention to be plausible as a politician manqué. As the final act of his performance unfolds, his "talent of making capital out of everything that turned up, to be invested for his own especial praise and glory," (78) enables him to comically recapitulate the emergence of the self-made American hero from Benjamin Franklin to Ralph Waldo Emerson.

Following Franklin's habits of self-education, Sam takes advantage of opportunities to observe political speakers in order to imitate their style. Among "brethren of his own color," he "would edify and delight them with the most ludicrous burlesques and imitations, all delivered with the most imperturbable earnestness and solemnity" (79). Sam's aspirations reflect not only Franklin's importance as a model for Douglass and other fugitive-slave authors but also Franklin's status as a "role player" known for his "shrewd manipulation of appearances" (Andrews 116). As suggested earlier by James Freeman Clarke, however, the very idea of personal growth was antithetical to the slave-as-child myth. Because, as Andrew argues, white editors and readers sometimes compared an ex-slave to "a Franklin or a Washington" only to measure the "absence of what 'might have been,'" Sam's nonrealistic status effectively highlights this habit of inverse perception as well (42).

Arriving in Aunt Chloe's kitchen, Sam performs as an orator who will "speechify" his own people, a trope suggesting both the potential empowerment of language and Stowe's own subversive program of disempowerment through her comic attack on oratorical manners and rhetoric. Only the manner of Sam's narrative is related, but his version of the day's events provides an occasion for remarks touching upon the principle of solidarity. Their didactic function, however, turns out to be inseparable from their effect of elevating him as community protector, "fendin' yer all, —yes, all on yer" (80). Andy, who had accompanied Sam earlier in the day, reappears here as the ineffectual debunker of the yarn spinner, reminding Sam that he had been ready to help catch Eliza until he learned that Mrs. Shelby wanted her to escape with her child. Sam responds to the challenge with two linguistic maneuvers. The first is to invent a word that will at once mystify and disfranchise the opposition: "[B]oys like you, Andy, means well, but they can't be spected to *collusitate* the great principles of action" (80; emphasis added). The second humorously lays out the political art of righteously defending the indefensible. Calling upon the argument of a spiritual reversal, Sam claims "conscience" as the unassailable reason for his first position. Then in response to Mrs. Shelby's wishes, he elevates his claim to "conscience *more yet,*—cause fellers allers gets more by stickin' to Missis' side" (80). Because Sam's "conscience" has been metaphysically appropriated by his master and mistress—according to the Southern slaveholder's "religion," slave obedience was commanded by God—this shifting of allegiance does not produce any "moral" contradiction. In other words, Sam's status as a chattel slave has oppressively bracketed truth and falsehood as exploitative instruments of appropriation.

This defense of "conscience" is probably not what Emerson in "Self-Reliance" had in mind for "a great soul" when he wrote, "A foolish consistency is the hobgoblin of little minds, adored by little statesmen and philosophers and divines" (265). But Sam's "conversance" with political, philosophical, and theological subjects adds to the suggestion that he has in some manner appropriated Emerson's passage. Although he substitutes the willful act of persistence for the mere appearance of consistency, his elision of the prefix indicates that from his perspective they need not be differentiated: "[D]is yer 'sistency's a thing what an't seed into very clar, by most anybody" (81). Sustaining the parallels between Emerson's reflections and his own, Sam also expresses his concern over the misapprehensions of little minds—"Now, yer see, when a feller stands up for a thing one day and night, de contrar de next, folks ses (and nat'rally enough dey ses), why he an't persistent" (81). With the inspired assurance of a metaphysical optimist, he delivers an analogy: "I'm a tryin' to get top o' der hay. Wal, I puts up my larder dis yer side; 'tan't no go'—den, cause I don't try dere no more, but puts my larder right de contrar side, an't I persistent? I'm persistent in wantin' to get up which ary side my larder is; don't you see, all on yer?" (81). Through Sam's emblematizing of self-reliance, success, and salvation, Stowe projects a comically conceived, inward view of the North's popular mind, its self-congratulatory compounding of the influences of Emerson and Franklin with the religious tradition of exemplary "perseverance."

The figure of a ladder was introduced earlier by Andy to correct Sam's egregious error in interpreting the unfolding events: "[C]an't ye see through a ladder, ye black nigger? Missis don't want dis yer Mas'r Haley to get Lizy's boy; dat's de go!" (49).

Sam's obtuseness when it comes to seeing through the rungs of masculine constructs to the affairs of a mother's heart is his comic flaw. As the narrator states, "[B]etween Sam and Aunt Chloe there had existed, from ancient times, a sort of chronic feud, or rather a decided coolness" (79). His masculine chauvinism, however, does not prevent him from being "eminently conciliatory" with "the cooking department" when it comes to restoring "the balance in his solids and fluids" (79). The image of a ladder, from which Sam derives his "principles," opens and closes his performance as he rises from the table "full of supper and glory" to wave "his palm-leaf" and bestow a "pathetic benediction" upon his audience (81).

Assessing differences between Douglass's 1845 *Narrative* and his 1855 *My Bondage and My Freedom*, Andrews has observed the compelling quality that Douglass achieves by introducing humor into his revised autobiography. Of Douglass's 1855 persona, Andrews writes, "We gain a glimpse of our common, undignified humanity with this hero, the climax of whose life moves us to comic empathy as well as respect, not just awe of or fear for him" (287). The connections Andrews touches upon between the artistic "vitality" of "dialect" and the roles of antebellum humorists and "antebellum black southern writers" as "harbingers of American literary realism" (289–90) add to the importance of appreciating Douglass's humor. But these developments suggest that just as Stowe was indebted to Lewis Clarke and other black abolitionists, so is it likely that her enormously popular novel would have exerted a creative influence on Douglass (see Levine 73) and on other American practitioners of literary realism.

Sam's exhibition of self-inventiveness not only saves him from mere farce but empowers his performance with the concentrated force of a comic hyper-realism. Just as importantly, Stowe's "realism" with Sam is poignantly *felt* through the humanizing effects of humor, which reinforce the sentimental effects found elsewhere in the novel. Sam himself is a skillful storyteller, as Stowe's narrator underscores by describing his manner and its humorous effect on his "compeers" and "smaller fry": "Roars of laughter attended the narrative" of the day's events. "Sam, however, preserved an immovable gravity, only from time to time rolling his eyes up, and giving his auditors divers inexpressibly droll glances, without departing from the sententious elevation of his oratory" (80). As Samuel Clemens would later record in "How to Tell a Story," the American humorist "does his best to conceal the fact that he even dimly suspects that there is anything funny about it" (216). Referring to the frontier humor in "Crocket *Almanacs*," which "appeared all over the country (1835–56)," F. O. Matthiessen observed "how much that we have connected with Mark Twain really belonged not to any one man but to the frontier soil" (638).

Stowe's conception of Sam drew upon the appeal of Southwestern humor, with its boastful manner and colorful speech. Her narrator affirms the representative quality of his "ornament and varnishing" by comparing him to "some of our fashionable dilettanti" (80). Later in Sam's speech, this association with popular humor of the period is strengthened by a malapropism alluding apparently to *The Spirit of the Times*, "a sports magazine that became the receptacle for masculine anecdotes and humorous sketches sent from every part of the country" (Harold Thompson 739): "I has principles, —I'm proud to 'oon 'em, — they's perquisite to dese yer times, and ter *all* times" (81). In the same passage on "principles," Sam's claim—"I sticks to 'em like forty, —jest anything that I thinks is principle, I goes in to 't" (81)—forms an ironic parallel with Johnson J. Hooper's Simon Suggs, who "had a single principle, 'It is good to be shifty in a new country' " (Harold Thompson 740; cf. Andrews 289–90, 331n).

The revelatory impact and resonance of Sam's language suggest that Stowe shared the attitude of James Russell Lowell that artistic power could be derived from the intense and picturesque qualities of humor that he regarded as "symptoms of the imaginative faculty in full health" (qtd. in Harold Thompson 735), a judgment that cannot be reconciled with the perception of Stowe's condescension toward her comic slave characters. As passages even from "Song of Myself" suggest, the enactments of Whitman's "robust soul" (like the playfulness of Sam's boastful egotism) at times humorously exaggerate Emerson's celebration of self-reliance as a masculine American virtue. Matthiessen draws a similar connection: "Though Emerson did not know it, the 'frolic health' he wanted in our poets was the best description of the mood that produced the tall tale" (636). Moreover, Stowe could direct her comic wit at her own deeply held convictions. Sam's emphasis on "dese yer times" and "*all* times" adds a millennial tone to his pronouncements that projects Stowe's overriding religious faith into an oracular voice of comic utterance.[6]

Master Sam's comic performance turns slavery's "child" into a chimerical emblem of American ideology suspended between its actual fallen condition and its potential regeneration.[7] In the fallen world of slaveocracy, he represents an idealized figure of slave "property" who ironically reflects the pseudovalues that the master culture most esteemed in itself. Above this fallen world, Sam's comic foolery sustains Stowe's millennial assurance that slavery was neither "natural" nor a reflection of God's design. Two paths to regeneration, one through resistance, the other through martyrdom, are briefly projected by Sam. First announcing himself as protector against "any one o' these yer drivers that comes smelling round arter any our people," he promises to "stand up for yer rights" and "fend 'em to the last breath!" (80). At the close of his speech, Sam provides a loquacious rendition of his own self-sacrifice, nonetheless foreshadowing the real spiritual strength of Uncle Tom: "I wouldn't mind if dey burnt me 'live, —I'd walk right up to de stake, I would, and say, here I comes to shed my last blood fur my principles, fur my country, fur der gen'l interests of society" (81).

Although Sam's self-serving heroics operate above and below the complexities of the human universe, the fact that he is, in this respect, a nonrealistic figure should not be viewed as resulting from Stowe's inability to transcend the culture-bound notions of slave stereotypes that she appropriates. With apparent deliberateness, Stowe extended Sam's performance until his comic antics had deflated celebrated strains of nineteenth-century American ideology. The achievement of this consciously humorous strategy transcends the reductive cultural consciousness that celebrated freedom while perpetuating slave stereotypes. Stowe's projection of the aspirations of American culture onto a figure with the epithets "Black" and "Master" suggests that "pious" tricksters could prove to be the defining element of an unregenerate culture—a culture that could, as Douglass had emphasized, make "a man" into "a slave" (*Narrative* 97). While Sam's worship of success importantly reflects the influence of exploitative "values" within the slavery environment, his spirited appeal leaves the reader to contemplate not only the illusions but also the promises of life itself.[8]

# N O T E S

I would like to thank Ellen Westbrook and Sheila Coghill for their helpful responses to earlier drafts of this article.

1. This "picture of such unrelieved horror" brings to mind James Baldwin's assertion that the novel "is activated by what might be called a theological terror" (Ammons ed. 94); the evident integrity of the book's laughter, however, as much as its other compelling qualities, keeps Baldwin's well-known indictment from being convincing.

2. *Uncle Tom's Cabin* addressed the implications of the questions raised by Fredrickson. Stowe's envisionments of slaveocracy demonstrate that the slave "family" could not be maintained against the disruptive economic forces upon which chattel slavery was based. Theodore R. Hovet has provided an illuminating view of how Stowe initially unites visionary ideals of both the North and South "to create a shadowy American version of Eden" (506), then introduces "the counterforce or satanic agent" of "modern business, which looks upon the world, even human beings, only as commodities . . ." (509).

3. Stowe, *Uncle Tom's Cabin* (1962), xiii. All subsequent quotations from the novel are from this edition, cited by page number in the text.

4. Philip Fisher also compares *Uncle Tom's Cabin* and *Benito Cereno* ("Democratic Social Space" 80–81 and *passim*).

5. Stowe defines Sam's status "soteriologically," as Tompkins has indicated regarding the novel's characters in general, "according to whether they are saved or damned" (135). Referring to the hymn scenes, Tompkins has described how linkages of this type within Stowe's text form "a system of endless cross-references" (136), giving "the impression" that "every kind of detail" can have "a purpose and a meaning which are both immediately apprehensible and finally significant" (139).

6. This language echoes that of earlier millennialism in New England. See Lowance's historical comment on "signs of the times" (*Language of Canaan* 180).

7. This dichotomy in the comic domain correlates with other dimensions of Stowe's vision observed in the studies of Tompkins, Jehlen, and Hovet (cited previously).

8. With regard to the examination of Sam's language in relation to Emerson, discussed above, see also Christina Zwarg's "Fathering and Blackface in *Uncle Tom's Cabin*" (*Novel* 22 [1989], 274–87), which includes an excellent analysis.

# 10
•

SARAH SMITH DUCKSWORTH

## Stowe's Construction of an African Persona and the Creation of White Identity for a New World Order

On faith, I think, most people generally assume, without actually reading *Uncle Tom's Cabin* by Harriet Beecher Stowe, that the book must contain a certain vision of humanity encompassing racial equality and brotherhood. But a close reading of the text reveals that the author's antislavery sentiments, though sincere and full of righteous condemnation, do not include notions of parity between white and black people; and that her real concern in writing the novel was not to raise lowly Africans up to a position of equality in American society, but to help bring an end to slavery for the sake of white salvation. When filtered through a cultural lens, *Uncle Tom's Cabin* reveals a conservative bias that does not at all conflict with racial beliefs and attitudes held by the majority of nineteenth-century white Americans.

By Stowe's own admission, *Uncle Tom's Cabin* represents her understanding of unpleasant and painful issues surrounding the "peculiar institution" of chattel slavery, her acceptance of shared white guilt in upholding it, and her decision to campaign against the evils inherent in the system. Before taking up the antislavery cause, she recalls using religion to insulate herself from the unsavory political and social realities of her day, and she tells how she sought solace in her dream of the millennium, a vi-

205

sionary time of peace and love divinely promised. According to Stowe, her faith in an impending new world order, a golden future, permitted her to hope that the "advancing light and civilization would certainly live down" the evil of slavery.[1] But with the passage of the Fugitive Slave Law of 1850, which effectively made slave catchers of all white citizens, including those in the North, Stowe says she became convinced that her creative voice was urgently needed. Consequently, she launched a campaign against the evil system in the only way she knew how—with pen and ink as weapons. At that time "the fictive dream took palpable form in Stowe's own life. When challenged in a letter from her sister-in-law to 'write something that will make the whole nation feel what an accursed thing slavery is,' Stowe is said to have risen to her feet and declared, 'I will write something. I will if I live' " (Sundquist, Introduction 7). From June 5, 1851, through April 2, 1852, her serialized story depicting downtrodden victims of chattel slavery created waves of controversy throughout the country.

Since *Uncle Tom's Cabin* was conceived by its author as a sermonic tract aimed at correcting specific transgressions of nineteenth-century white Americans, some contemporary scholars, witnessing the novel's reappearance on college reading lists, question whether the book should be used in modern classrooms. Their reservations stem partly from their belief that classes should prepare students for the twenty-first-century world—a society in which multiethnic students will not only change the look of the learning environment but will also dictate a curriculum reflecting cultural diversity. Citing social scientists who predict the "browning of America," these critics argue that the university is obliged to stress the common humanity of all people and that a book such as *Uncle Tom's Cabin* that dredges up past ills and prejudices could prove inimical to this multicultural challenge of the future.

A different kind of objection to the novel comes from those who believe, with James Baldwin, that *Uncle Tom's Cabin* "is a very bad" and "dishonest" novel. In a well-known essay, "Everybody's Protest Novel," Baldwin explains that Stowe's book is "bad" for its "self righteous, virtuous sentimentality," and "dishonest" for both its failure to probe into white motivations for brutality toward blacks and its libelous depictions of stock Negro characters (Baldwin [1964; 1984] 14). From Baldwin's perspective, *Uncle Tom's Cabin* misrepresents reality by presenting dis-tortions that were for Stowe "more palatable than the truth." Baldwin argues that fallout from Stowe's false depictions has been far from benign, since they have been "handed down and memorized" and still persist "with a terrible power" to shape attitudes (Baldwin [1964; 1984] 16).

After considerable deliberation and soul-searching, I have reached my position on *Uncle Tom's Cabin,* which is (with all due respect to Baldwin and other astute critics) that the suppression of the novel on the bases of possible irrelevancy and dishonesty is insupportable. When I consider the book's profound impact upon writers down through the years and upon artists working in other media who have borrowed subject matter from *Uncle Tom's Cabin* for use in paintings and in song-and-dance routines, I am convinced that the novel should not be censored. And if the past is truly prologue as Shakespeare suggests, I believe there must be relevances and linkages that can be established between now and then that a new audience can discover.

Of course, *Uncle Tom's Cabin* cannot be read in today's classrooms the same way people read it in 1852. Changes in Americans' life-styles have so distanced the book that our reconsideration of it must now include both analyses and comparisons of constructs that have evolved across intervening decades. Since modern constructs of race are likely to contrast sharply to past constructs of racial "truth," the resulting reality gap could open up Stowe's fictional world to intriguingly new interpretations.

To convince her peers to change a system as ingrained in the social and economic fabric of America as chattel slavery, Stowe sets out to prove to this audience that the system of chattel slavery is both morally wrong and personally degrading to them. Her argument hinges on her ability to sell the idea that changing the rules of slavery is in the best interest of white people, and that they, not blacks, have the larger stake in creating the new world order. To this end Stowe uses two strategies: (1) She presents a number of familiar white types to demonstrate how degrees of involvement in brutalizing slaves produce reciprocal and commensurate dehumanizing effects upon diverse members of the "master race"; and (2) she presents what Toni Morrison calls the "black persona," which functions, with numerous deformities, to define the ideal white prototype. Upon close inspection, these two strategies reveal Stowe's novel as a social tract, reinforcing the values of nineteenth-century mainstream white culture.

Stowe first introduces her readers to two familiar white types who play key contrasting roles within the institution of slavery in the opening scene of the novel. She presents the slave trader Haley as a "low bred fellow" who carries the mark of coarseness in his thick features and in his gaudy dress. Seasoned in his profession, Haley has been further corrupted by both his lust for material gain and his zeal to make a fortune on the backs of Africans. Characteristically, his crude, officious manner leads him to rationalize any ill-treatment of blacks as a surface unpleasantry that he skillfully avoids. Explaining his modus operandi to Mr. Shelby, a gentleman planter who had objected to selling a slave child from his plantation, Haley responds: "I understand perfectly. It is mighty onpleasant getting on with women, sometimes. I al'ays hate these yer screechin' screamin' times. They are mighty onpleasant; but, as I manages business, I generally avoids 'em, sir. Now, what if you get the girl off for a day, or a week, or so; then the thing is done quietly, —all over before she comes home. . . . These critters an't like white folks, you know; they gets over things, only manage right" (5).

In drawing a sharp contrast between Haley's pragmatic outlook on slave trading and Mr. Shelby's reluctance to sell a piece of helpless "property," Stowe suggests that a critical moral consciousness separates the two types. Delineating both their psychological and physical attributes, Stowe makes qualitative differences between them even more apparent. In contrast to Haley, Mr. Shelby has "the appearance of a gentleman." By nature he is "disposed to easy indulgence of those around him" and is concerned about "the physical comfort of the negroes on his estate" (8). Indeed, selling slaves is against his principles; yet he sells two because, as Stowe stresses, bad investments force his hand—he perceives his choice to be to sell a couple of slaves or to risk losing his entire "stock."

Stowe explores further the systemic inconsistency in the behavior of a benevolent white master type as she directs Shelby, who represents the group, to stress his reason for engaging in slave traffic. His acts of expediency, which go against the grain of his conscience, substantiate the writer's vision of a "portentous shadow" brooding over even the most humane plantation in the real world. Using as an example Shelby's dilemma, she points out that any "misfortune or imprudence" of a true-to-life Southern master could likewise result in his well-conditioned and kindly used slaves being sold into a life of "hopeless misery and toil" (8). In an act of affirmation and contrition, the fictional Mr. Shelby summarizes his regret for his part in such uncharacteristic and distasteful transactions: "If anybody had ever said to me that I should sell Tom down south to one of those rascally traders, I should have said, 'Is thy servant a dog that he should do this thing?' And now it must come, for aught I see. And Eliza's child, too!" (7–8).

Stowe continues to invert the myth of a "good" slave master as a type who can hold fast to his principles in the face of a corrupt institution when she presents, approximately a third of the way into the story, Mr. St. Clare as her best example of a mature white gentleman. This basically good person has come into the "rough bark of manhood" retaining a sensitiveness of character "fresh . . . at the core" more akin to the softness of women than the ordinary hardness of his own sex" (150). Naturally, St. Clare's innate virtue is matched by handsomeness and excellent deportment. Stowe describes him as having "a noble cast of head" and carrying an "air of free-and-easy superiority." Nevertheless, she notes, he can be moved to good humor and compassion, as evidenced by his ready compliance to angelic little Eva's request that he purchase Uncle Tom just because she, his darling daughter, wishes to make the slave happy (146).

Understandably, due to the ingrained morality and sensitive nature of his type, St. Clare is ridden by a deep sense of guilt for the role he plays in the system. He frequently ruminates over the suffering of slaves and shows his unease through his indulgent, inconsistent dealings with blacks who serve him. For example, when St. Clare's wife upbraids him for allowing the mulatto houseboy, Adolph, to appropriate his toiletries and clothes, St. Clare responds, "Why after all, what's the harm of the poor dog's wanting to be like his master; and if I haven't brought him up any better than to find his chief good in cologne and cambric handkerchiefs, why shouldn't I give them to him?" (174).

In sharp contrast to St. Clare, Stowe dredges up from the bowels of humanity her conception of a slave master to represent the most brutish and debased sort of white man. This is Simon Legree, who has been utterly ruined by his total immersion in the dark world of slave culture. By cutting himself off from the beneficent influence of the white race, Legree has sunk into an abyss of iniquity that, in Stowe's estimate, is about as low as a white man can go. His almost exclusive dealings in black flesh have blunted all of his original racially inherited sensitivities. Only brief intimations of his lost innocence come back to haunt him from time to time when, during infrequent intervals, faint rays of light penetrate his murky depravity. Caught up in a dark world of passion, excess, and chaos, Legree is a veritable beast of a man who forces slave women to lie with him and drives field hands beyond their endurance, using whip and lash to cut them into submission. Characteristically, Legree boasts to an appalled white gentleman, "I don't go for savin' niggers. Use up and buy more's my way, —makes you less trouble, and I'm quite sure it comes cheaper in the end" (338).

Hovering over Uncle Tom's long ordeal like a bright promise on the horizon is young Master George Shelby, the son of the gentleman planter already introduced. He represents for Stowe the kind of white leadership the new world order will require. George makes his appearance early in the book when, as a lad of thirteen, he visits (as was his custom) Aunt Chloe and Uncle Tom in their lowly cabin. Despite his age at the time, Master George "appears fully to realize the dignity of his position as instructor" to the adult slaves who literally adore him (21).

Stowe provides several examples to show how young Master George has become the pride and joy of the Shelby plantation's slaves. For example, Uncle Tom exclaims admiringly, while comparing his own poor writing to the letters Master George "flourishingly scrawled" on a slate, "La sakes, now, does it?" and his wife, Aunt Chloe, pridefully rejoins, "How easy white folk al'us does things! . . . The way he can write, now! and read too! and then to come out here evenings and read his lessons to us, — it's mighty interestin'!" (21). Later, at a slaves' prayer meeting, Master George is encouraged to read the Scripture for the congregation; and, as he complies, the blacks react with gratitude and awe. Moved by his wonderful chanting of Bible verses, these Africans cannot hold back from interrupting and exclaiming such things as "The *sakes* now!" "Only hear that!" "Jest think on't!" "Is all that a-coming sure enough?" (28).

As a type of future savior, but one who still needs tutelage, young George Shelby is helpless in his desire to stop Uncle Tom from being sold. Therefore, when the youthful Master George makes his second appearance in the story, it is to bid his old servant farewell and to round out the first third of the action.

Deliberately, at this point, young George's leadership potential is emphasized through Tom's prophetic words: "O, Mas'r George, you has everything —l'arnin', privileges, readin', writin' —and you'll grow up to be a great, learned good man, and all the people on the place and your mother and father'll be so proud on ye!" (99). The audience now realizes that it will be just a matter of time before George returns to take his destined place in the scheme of plantation life and bring radical correction to the ailing system. His parting words are a promise to both Uncle Tom and to Stowe's readers: "I'll be real good, Uncle Tom, I tell you. . . . I'm going to be a first rater; and don't you be discouraged. I'll have you back on the place, yet" (99).

Master George has attained all the virtues of his type—decency, wisdom, and a hefty inheritance—when he reenters the story near the end of the book. As a full-grown man of substance and power, he has the means to save his old friend from cruel chains and brutality, but by the time Master George reaches Uncle Tom it is too late for him to preserve the slave's physical life. At the end of his long search, George can only give words of comfort to the dying African. Watching Uncle Tom's painful death throes, Master George is overwrought, but, in his maturity, he is able to suppress murderous emotion and substitute manly forbearance.

In depicting the ideal white leader's emotional flexibility and natural predilection to make the wisest and most generous decision, Stowe has Master George leave Uncle Tom's heart-rending death scene and grave site and go home to do the right thing by the plantation blacks whose lives he still holds in his hands. In the spirit of human decency, he offers his slaves their freedom. Not surprisingly, Master George's attempt to confer liberty upon these Africans is met with resistance from the slaves themselves. Not a one wants to leave the plantation. In unison they plead: "We don't want to be no freer than we are. We's allers had all we wanted. We don't want to leave de ole place, and Mas'r and Missis, and de rest!" (436). Mercifully, the benevolent white gentleman summons up his mother-instilled womanly compassion. He now sees no reason to force good slaves, who will need the care and direction he can give them better than they can give themselves, to leave their shacks against their wills. So Master George assures them: "There'll be no need for you to leave me.

The place wants as many hands to work it as it did before. We need the same about the house as we did before. But . . . I shall pay you for your work, such as we shall agree on" (436).

From this scene, readers can logically conclude that Stowe's concept of the ideal system, accommodating both blacks and whites, involves slaves becoming declassified from their status as "property" and reclassified as "permanent workers." And as author of this "best of all solutions" for the "best of all worlds" to come, Stowe celebrates a new day heralding the new world order prefigured by the Shelby/American plantation. As the story now attains its "proper conclusion," Stowe leaves the reader with the image of an unchained plantation as the model for paradise on earth, wherein all the cruelty inherent in owning slaves has been expunged, and a good, God-fearing white master has reached his manifest destiny: rescuing his share of the heathen horde and receiving in return his much deserved reward of eternal service and devotion from willing and grateful servants.

In modeling the new white leader upon the character of a mature Master George Shelby, Stowe reiterates her faith in the white race's ability to rise above the sins of slavery and to inherit paradise. Conversely, by targeting specific types of white male participants in the system, ranging from the worst to the best intentioned, Stowe sends a message to "good" white people all over the country who may have felt unconnected to the evil of slavery. Her message is that they, through both their silence and hypocrisy, also share the blame for the crimes of slave dealers. She then charges all upstanding white citizens with a God-given duty to agitate against the chattel system in order to save their own souls and recover the auspicious promise of America's golden future.

Further consideration of the array of white types failing to measure up to the white ideal also clarifies Stowe's concept of the awesome responsibility devolving to all whites who would inherit the millennium. She singles out generally the self-righteous who may feel exempt from the sins of slavery because they own no human property, and she berates particularly missionaries who go off to Africa to Christianize Africans while, she maintains, heathens of the same race flounder in ignorance and suffer abominable treatment in America. Such sentiment the author highlights with good effect in a scene where she permits Mr. St. Clare to scold his cousin, Ophelia, when she momentarily shirks her responsibility to train the unruly black gal in her charge: "That's you Christians, all over!—you'll get up a society, and get some poor missionary to spend all his days among such heathens. But let me see one of you that would take one into your house with you, and take the labor of their conversion on yourselves! No; when it comes to that, they are dirty and disagreeable, and its too much care, and so on" (238).

Slave types appear in the novel just as stiffly drawn as their white counterparts, but unlike those of the white stereotypes, their roles are functional rather than prescriptive. Stowe's multiform black characters define with great clarity the nature of the problem whites face in facilitating the peaceful future. Depictions of blacks' faults create for whites a greater understanding of and appreciation for the innate good qualities of their race, which they must nurture to a level of excellence in preparation for the hour of manifest destiny.

The idea that the road to white ascension was through understanding and controlling savagism did not begin in America with Europeans justifying their domination of Africans. This idea was transported to this country by the first colonizers of the New World and first applied in their treatment of Native Americans. Roy Harvey Pearce develops this thesis in great detail, significantly concluding, "The Indian became important for the English mind, not for what he was in and of himself, but rather for what he showed civilized men they were not and must not be" (*Savagism and Civilization* 5). He further asserts, "For giving God and civilization to the Indian, the colonial Englishman was to receive the riches of a new world. . . . In America, from the very beginning the history of the savage is the history of the civilized" (8). Based on Pearce's conclusions and in the light of succeeding history, it appears reasonable to extrapolate that once Native Americans ceased to be a major threat to European settlers and after Africans took over the role of beasts of burden for the creation of the New World, Africans became the new savages next to whom whites could define themselves.

On the surface, Stowe's slave characters appear as stick figures that the writer manipulates into a variety of grotesque shapes to illustrate the different postures of slave people. On the one hand, Stowe depicts black victims reacting to one hard lot after the other: scuttling across rivers on ice floes, jumping off the sides of boats, poisoning hapless black babies, and trying to blunt the pain of their maltreatment with liquor. On the other hand, she creates black characters whom she passes off as "everyday slave people." These run-of-the-mill negroes twist and gyrate like quaint puppets, creating a kind of general confusion that is supposed to simulate plantation culture.

Apparently these African humanoids, who seem so unrealistic to most people today, not only served the writer's purpose but fulfilled the expectations of Stowe's mainstream audience as well. In light of the wide nod of recognition nineteenth-century readers gave these fictional types, they do indeed warrant a closer look beyond mere acknowledgment that they are bogus. Instead of homing in on what these black characters *are* (figments of a white cultural imagination), we might readjust our spotlight on the story to ask *what* they represent and *how* they function in the novel.

Indeed, by shifting the reader's attention from a preoccupation with the dilemma of white folks to a consideration of what the black presence could mean in the book and how these meanings may define the behavior of the novel's white characters, one just might, as Toni Morrison suggests, gain keener insight into the psyche of a nation driven by racial prejudices. Morrison recommends in her recent book *Playing in the Dark* a focused rereading of novels written by white authors wherein the black presence seems oddly constructed. Her own rereading of such texts has convinced her that many white writers, in imagining the African persona, reveal "an extraordinary meditation on the self; a powerful exploration of the fears and desires that reside in the writerly conscience" (17).

Morrison's conclusions have merit and validity when *Uncle Tom's Cabin* is subjected to the kind of analysis she recommends. Under close cultural scrutiny it seems all too apparent that Stowe does, in fact, use African types to model "alien" behavior that flies in the face of "civilized" white behavior. As her slave characters stumble across the pages and fall off various perches to exhibit their latest transmogrification of decorum, Stowe positions white characters close by to demonstrate sharply contrasting patterns of action. Using this Frick and Frack strategy, Stowe reveals slaves as both foils for and inversions of their white counterparts. They appear as distorted mirror images of whites, painted in various shades of bronze and ebony, acting black according to their degree of tint.

Stowe sets out to "prove" the superiority of whites over blacks through her development of children characters from both races. The first black children she introduces as personalities are Pete and Mose, the two young sons of Uncle Tom. For as long as these boys are allowed to pounce across the pages of the novel, they rattle the minds of their parents and disrupt every loosely observed routine designed to bring a little order to their Kentucky cabin home, located on the Shelby's plantation. A few scenes before the appearance of Tom's rambunctious sons, Stowe has already shown how two little white boys can participate calmly and compassionately in a domestic scene roughly parallel to the one the black boys will soon face. As actors on Stowe's stage, the white children establish the standard for normalcy before readers witness the confusion that will be left in the wake of Pete's and Mose's travesty on civilization.

For their uncouth demonstration of counterwhite behavior, Tom's youngsters, Pete and Mose, tumble away from a lot of hard to differentiate pickaninnies—who lie, "in any quantity, about on the floor, or [perch] . . . in every corner (73)—to add to the drama of Tom's farewell scene. The slave boys stretch themselves out, disrupting conversations, meals, and bedtime preparations. In keeping with their heathen natures, Pete and Mose laugh and gambol about without any apparent external motivation. When the boys' behavior escalates to banshee level, their good-natured mammy, Chloe (whose few brains must be wrapped up in the flaky pie dough for which she is famous), tries to impose discipline on them by aiming a kick in their general direction. Later, she pushes away their woolly heads and gives them a slap that resounds formidably but only succeeds "to knock out so much more laughter from the young ones" (25).

More indicative of Pete's and Mose's inferior natures than their irrational behavior is their inability to reason abstractly and to project into the future. Stowe reveals their mental and emotional shallowness by juxtaposing their father's forced departure from home against the boys' preoccupation with breakfast.

Between the time Shelby sells his two articles of human chattel to Haley and the time scheduled for the trucking away of the slave merchandise, Tom has only one night and a few early morning hours to huddle with his wife, Chloe, and their four children. In just a few paragraphs, Stowe rushes readers through the period prefacing the dissolution of the black family. The next morning, Pete and Mose sense nothing about the impending disaster, but, despite the fact they have not been told directly, Stowe implies that if the boys were rational creatures, they would grasp the situation from the general confusion the news creates around them. In any case, even as Chloe—with the unhappy, clamorous style of a lower primate—puts out the last meal the family will take together, Pete and Mose seem unaffected.

As Chloe dishes the food, Pete and Mose look at the groaning table of delectables. Then, luxuriating in their seeming good fortune, the boys just want to celebrate:

> "Lor, Pete," said Mose, triumphantly, "han't we got a buster of a breakfast!" at the same time catching at a fragment of the chicken. Aunt Chloe gave him a sudden box on the ear. "Thar now! crowing over the last breakfast yer poor daddy's gwine to have to home!" "O Chloe," said Tom, gently. "Wal, I can't help it, said Aunt Chloe, hiding her face in her apron; "I's so tossed about it makes me act ugly." The boys stood quite still, looking first at their father and then at their mother, while the baby, climbing up her clothes, began an imperious, commanding cry. "Thar!" said Aunt Chloe, wiping her eyes and taking up the baby, "now I's done, I hope,—now do eat something. This yer's my nicest chicken. Thar boys, ye shall have some, poor critturs! Yer mammy's been cross to yer." The boys needed no second invitation, and went in with great zeal for the eatables. (94)

Pete and Mose remain dry-eyed until they actually see their father being led away by the slave trader. Only at that moment do they cling to Chloe's skirts, "sobbing and groaning vehemently" (96). The comic tones Stowe has painted over Tom's leave-taking make the young boys' sudden bawling seem quite laughable and prohibit her audience from dwelling on Pete's and Mose's tears.

Stowe's painting of the Bird family's home in Ohio a few scenes earlier portrays the joyous hearth. Despite the author's brief mention of frolicking Bird family juveniles, the children of this home are cast in the mold of all descendants from the flood—white and Christian, in Stowe's view. The childish antics of the little Bird boys do not even disturb their mother's composure. She handles their little pranks with aplomb, all the while "looking the very picture of delight" (75).

In contrast to Uncle Tom's family's departure scene, the Bird family has a reception scene. The white family has been very deliberately placed in a situation where they can display their superior humanity by giving aid and comfort to a couple of poor, downtrodden, runaway slaves—a mother and child. Reconsidering the roles played by the two dissimilar families in the novel, it becomes clear that Stowe intends to create for the Birds a problem that is the mirror image of the black family's dilemma. The comparisons that readers will inevitably draw between the behaviors of the two families in the analogous scenes serve as preamble to her argument for racial inequality.

Although it was impossible for Stowe to set up scenarios that were identical for the black and white families, the outlines of their predicaments are sufficiently similar to serve the author's purpose. Both scenes portray a victim or victims and sympathizers. And in each instance the tragic event causing the separation of victim from family has been imposed by "superior" others. Because Stowe wants her audience to focus particularly on the responses of the racially different young boys to similar stimuli, the roughly parallel situations suffice. Through her careful depictions, Stowe successfully creates the illusion that a great qualitative disparity exists in the reactions of white and black boys (with blacks revealing clear deficiencies), even as they face almost the same situation. And she directs her readers to conclude that if the ability to empathize with a victim is so radically unequal in blacks and whites—even when blacks have the more urgent reason to be empathetic—there must be some biological basis for the difference. Surely, through the interactions Stowe fabricates in the story to reveal blacks' low-level sensibilities, she intends to impress upon her audience that such density must be racially encoded, not learned.

By way of contrast to the rowdiness of Pete and Mose, the white boys do not interfere as they watch their mother fuss over two pitiful strangers who have been rescued from the Ohio River and brought into their home by a neighbor. These strangers are none other than "near white" Eliza, from the Shelby plantation, and her "near white" son, Harry. The reader already knows that Eliza has made the dash for freedom with the child in her arms after she accidentally learned that Mr. Shelby was planning to sell Harry along with Uncle Tom. At the point of her rescue, readers are perhaps relieved to see good white people ready to act with compassion.

Stowe's enthralled nineteenth-century audience must have been impressed by the intelligence and sensitivity of the Bird

family children to Eliza's and Harry's plight, for soon after unobtrusively absorbing information about the runaways, the little Bird boys start to comprehend and empathize with the situation. The more they hear, the more their little hearts break. Soon
they begin to rummage in their pockets, searching for pocket-
handkerchiefs. When they fail to find anything to wipe their
tears, Stowe allows the dear little boys to throw themselves "dis-
consolately into the skirts of their mother's gown, where they . . .
[sob and wipe] their eyes and noses, to their hearts' content" (82).

Actions do indeed speak volumes about differences between
the races, and based on their actions, Stowe reveals that the most
significant way the Bird boys differ from Pete and Mose is in their
contrasting abilities to learn from experience and to correct their
errant ways. It is unthinkable that mindless Pete and Mose can
ever regret causing their mammy to slap them about, but the
Bird boys can and do regret the time they caused their mother to
discipline them. Stowe proves this unparalleled white capability
for remorse in the following summarized anecdote:

Since the white boys do not need to be disciplined in the scene
where they are part of a sympathetic audience, Stowe reaches
outside the story to advance their maturity; then she allows them
to look back in retrospect at the most "vehement chastisement"
they ever received from the "timid, blushing little woman" they
call Mother (76). From the Bird boys' reverie, the audience
learns about the time Mrs. Bird caught her sons throwing stones
at a cat. Even though this activity had not been the children's
original idea, when they were caught, they meekly submitted to
their whippings. After applying the strap as vigorously as she
could. Mrs. Bird sent the boys to bed without supper. Then,
overcome by the realization that she had hurt her own sons, even
for their own good, the kindly mother lingered outside their
bedroom and cried. Through the closed door, the boys could
hear Mrs. Bird's sobs. Feeling so sorry to be the cause of her
tears, the youngsters repented and never forgot the lesson they
learned. As Master Bill would say later, "[W]e boys never stoned
another kitten" (77).

Side by side, Mrs. Bird's boys and Uncle Tom's boys are as
different from each other as day and night. Stowe's juxtaposition
of such typed children strongly implies that the line of demarca-
tion separating the races is color, and that color is the attribute
that predetermines every aspect of white and black character.

Based on the presumed unequal endowment nature gives the races, Stowe suggests that inevitably each race takes a different path in life and shoulders a unique set of responsibilities.

A close look at Aunt Chloe and the two white women introduced in the first part of the novel, Mrs. Shelby and Mrs. Bird, unmasks Stowe's views on how black and white women function within their separate and dissimilar families. Indeed, the mothers of both races are the magnets holding together their distinct cultures, but the pull each has upon her respective charges is very different. Evidently Stowe believes, based on the importance she attaches to motherhood in the story, that the quality of the very difference between black and white mothers assures the races' basic, never-to-be-abridged inequality.

The impression the novel creates is that the woman of the "superior" white race possesses a strength of character likened to a powerful field of light with both penetrating and sublime qualities, which she uses to guide her less perfect male partners and sons along the path of righteousness. Conversely, the black mother has no light to shine. She is all force and "brick house," supporting a childlike mate and muscling uncouth sons into some semblance of calm. But she is able to repress their natural exuberance only temporarily. The white woman's superior intellect and influence is employed to uplift permanently the white males within her sphere of operation, while the black woman's limited intellect and lack of influence is used to keep the progress of her whole race in check. Indeed, Stowe must assume, this state of affairs was ordained by God, for she contends that Chloe is "[a] cook . . . in the very bone and centre of her soul" (19), just as other blacks are natural sowers and reapers of harvests, hewers of wood, and drawers of water. On the other hand, both Mrs. Shelby and Mrs. Bird are "ladies"—intelligent and morally tough despite their genteel ways.

According to Stowe, Mrs. Shelby is "a woman of high class both intellectually and morally" with a "natural magnanimity of mind." Additionally, she has "high moral and religious sensibility." And in all undertakings of principle, she is able to turn her "great energy and ability into practical results." Mr. Shelby, who is not as principled as his wife, holds only reverence and respect for those qualities in Mrs. Shelby and gives her "unlimited scope in all her benevolent efforts" to improve the slaves. He seems to believe that his wife has "piety and benevolence enough for two," and he keeps "a shadowy expectation of getting into heaven through her superabundance of qualities to which he made no particular pretension" (9–10).

In equally complimentary fashion, Stowe depicts Mrs. Bird as a little woman "of about four feet in height, and with mild blue eyes and a peach blow complexion, and the gentlest, sweetest voice in the world" (76). On the surface, Stowe acknowledges, Mrs. Bird may seem timid, but, the author warns, if an issue involving some principle—especially cruelty—arises, Mrs. Bird's rallying effort to see the right thing done can be frighteningly forceful. Of course Mr. Bird, like Mr. Shelby, knows exactly when to back down and let his wife have her way. Specifically, even after he has spoken eloquently for and voted in favor of the Fugitive Slave Law of 1850, Mr. Bird is coerced by his wife to help Eliza and Harry find a safe haven from the slave runners.

For both white women, their husbands and children are their whole world. They know when to push their menfolk along the path of progress and virtue and when to allow them their stubbornness. These white women just wait patiently and wage quietly their moral campaign, knowing that one day their correct imperatives will be realized either through their husband's acquiescence or through the actions of their well-trained sons. Mrs. Shelby's victory is her son's benevolent stewardship of blacks at the end of the book; Mrs. Bird's victory is her success in getting Mr. Bird to sympathize with the runaways and to allay their misery.

These white women know full well their spiritual mission as shepherdesses for God. But Chloe can only identify herself in terms of the physical services she performs. She focuses always on tangibles—abstract concepts of evil and good are beyond her mental grasp. Consequently, the one thing that makes Chloe's "fat sides" shake with honest pride and merriment is not a favorite child or a pious husband, but knowing that her baked goods are better than those of her "compeers" (20). Chloe may seem proactive when she urges Uncle Tom to run north with Eliza: "Well, old man! . . . Why don't you go too? Will you wait to be toted down river, where they kill niggers with hard work and starving? I's a heap rather die than go there any day! There's time for ye—be off with Lizzy" (37). But in reality, Chloe does not command much consideration from her man. While, "[t]he heaviest load on [Mr. Shelby's] . . . mind, after his conversation with the trader, lay in the foreseen necessity of breaking to his wife the arrangement contemplated [selling Tom and Eliza's son]" (10), Tom can only think of his duty to white people. So, rather than listen to Chloe's advice, he asserts with great pride, "Mas'r a'ways found me on the spot—he always will. I never have broke trust, nor used my pass in no ways contrary to my word and never will" (37). By the time Tom is scheduled to leave his family, he is eager to exonerate his former master of all blame. However, as reality sets in and Tom comprehends more fully his fate, he sobs "heavy, hoarse, and loud." Stowe uses this emotional moment to sermonize. She suggests that Tom's grief is just as strong as that of any white man or woman who has had a child die: "For, . . . in life's great straits and mighty griefs, ye feel but one sorrow!" (38).

Just as Chloe knows that her value is based on what she can physically accomplish, she also feels that her husband has to be assessed in the same way. Of course, she is grief stricken to lose the companionship of her "old man," and she is willing to hire herself out as a baker to get him back. But the money she earns from her job is as tangible to her as the body of her husband, and, in her mind, it can be used as a fair exchange. So when death denies her the return of Uncle Tom in the flesh, the money she has given Mrs. Shelby to repurchase her husband (the same bills paid for her services) now seems to her useless. Chloe cannot imagine any abstract benefit from the money. Seeing the cash "lying on the table," Chloe gathers it up "with trembling hand" and gives it to her mistress saying, "Thar . . . [I] don't never want to see nor hear on't again" (435).

The idea that blacks are naturally impulsive and quixotic and do not experience emotional trauma was common wisdom in nineteenth-century white America. But as we read through all the scenes in which Stowe juxtaposes white and black families, we can safely conclude that Stowe does not share the sentiment wholeheartedly; for during the course of the novel, her slave characters do suffer genuine pain when separated from their loved ones, albeit their pain has a source different from that of white pain. In the place of white sensitivities Stowe imputes to slaves strong "attachments" and "terror":

> In order to appreciate the sufferings of the negroes, it must be remembered that all the instinctive affections of that race are pecu-

liarly strong. Their local attachments are very abiding. They are not naturally daring and enterprising, but home-loving and affectionate. Add to this all the terrors with which ignorance invests the unknown, and add to this, again, that selling to the south is set before the negro from childhood as the last severity of punishment. The threat that terrifies more than whipping or torture of any kind is the threat of being sent down river. . . . This nerves the African, naturally patient, timid, and unenterprising, with heroic courage, and leads him to suffer hunger, cold, pain, the perils of the wilderness, and the more dread penalties of recapture. (93)

Stowe's concern for fractured slave families must lead modern-day readers to wonder why the writer herself turns Tom's departure scene into a joke. For an answer, I believe, one can follow Morrison's suggestion and look into the sociohistorical reality of the times. It has been well documented in the annals of entertainment history that, in its early years, the white American comic tradition relied very heavily on buffoon black characters. In fact, during the nineteenth century, "coon" jokes were so much a part of Americana that it probably never occurred to Stowe that creating any joke involving blacks, even one based on a tragic situation, could be offensive. Indeed, Stowe probably felt (consciously or unconsciously) that spoofing comical blacks would be welcomed by her mainstream audience and that by including such "interesting and funny insights" into slave culture she would keep her readers turning the pages, and thereby gain a better chance of promoting her overall antislavery goal. Moreover, based on her consistent derogatory depictions of common slaves throughout the book, Stowe must have truly believed that shallow emotionalism and frantic confusion, the most "unwhite" responses she could imagine, accurately characterized primitive blacks.

In most instances, Stowe strongly disapproves of the white slavers' practice of fracturing black families not only for economical expediency but for the exercise of their white skin prerogatives as well. By exposing the selfishness of Marie St. Clare, the mother of pure white little Eva and the wife of gentleman St. Clare, Stowe reveals, with little sympathy, how cavalierly a young white woman coming from a slave-owning family can marry, leave her paternal home, and take with her a pet slave woman to attend to her personal needs and desires. Marie at one point explains to her Yankee cousin, Ophelia, her particular annoyance with Mammy, the black maid she has uprooted. In Marie's opinion, Mammy has stubbornly refused to be happy in their new home. The fact that the slave woman was forced to leave her husband and children in order to live with newlyweds on a strange plantation is, in this white woman's mind, no reason for the slave to act unhappy. When Miss Ophelia suggests that maybe Mammy feels lonesome for her family, Marie refutes the idea as absurd: "Mammy couldn't have the feelings that I should. It's a different thing altogether, —of course, it is—, and yet St. Clare pretends not to see it. And just as if Mammy could love her little dirty babies as I love Eva! Yet St. Clare once really and soberly tried to persuade me that it was my duty, with my weak health, and all I suffer, to let Mammy go back, and take somebody else in her place. That was a little too much even for *me* to bear" (172).

Recognizing the radical antislavery position such a critique of whites posits, Stowe pushes forward, tempering her hard-line positions with her placating conviction that abolishing or, at least, changing the terms of slavery could produce an ideal future for America—one that would not only be free of all the evils produced by slavery but would be glorified by God. In this visionary society, the writer foresees the continued tractability of Africans. Essentially, to those whites willing to unchain slaves and usher in the millennium, Stowe gives her assurance that blacks will remain true to form: naturally simple, good-natured, and forgiving. On this point, Stowe waxes eloquent: "The negro race, no longer despised and trodden down, will, perhaps, show forth some of the latest and most magnificent revelations of human life. Certainly they will, in their gentleness, their lowly docility of heart, their aptitude to repose on a superior mind and rest on a higher power, their child-like simplicity of affection, and facility for forgiveness" (178).

Stowe's argument against slavery's cruel practices includes showing white people that they can live in harmony with inferior blacks, if only whites would educate them properly. To illustrate her point Stowe creates a scenario in which a black character, Topsy, goes through various training stages, culminating with her appropriation of good manners at a level commensurate with her racially inherited miming abilities.

Although Eva does not take on the day-to-day training responsibilities for Topsy, she is the key to Topsy's conversion. Cast in stark contrast to the devilish, rude Topsy, Eva is the standard Stowe creates to define the white ideal. As Stowe carefully paints the two girls, one sooty black and the other creamy white, she rationalizes the bases for her comparisons, pointing to equality in age and gender as their common ground. Then, presenting as a given the notion that the young retain their racial purity until life experiences begin to modify their personalities, Stowe reasons that Eva and Topsy are the clearest common denominators of their respective races; therefore, all the analogies she, as an objective transcriber of natural phenomena, will henceforth draw are to be received as scientific—verifiable truth.

In one of the novel's most defining and memorable scenes, Topsy engages in a perfectly heathenish exhibition of her power to turn civilization upside down by wrecking Miss Ophelia's bedroom. Afterwards, her bewildered and indignant mistress, taking seriously her "white [wo]man's burden," tries to make Topsy understand that this destructive activity has been absolutely, unforgivably barbaric. But Topsy, having no ability to relate to the lecture, stays calm; it is the white woman who becomes frustrated and finally has to comprehend that wailing at a "brick wall" is useless. At this point, little Eva enters the scene. All sweetness and light, Eva pleads with Topsy to be good because, contrary to all Topsy has learned from life, there is one person who can love something as ugly and evil as a black imp, and that person is Eva herself. Then, by some miracle, Eva penetrates Topsy's mortared skull and something clicks inside. Topsy, strangely enthralled by the solemnity of the moment, and Eva, touched with her own kindness, stand facing each other. During this holy interlude, Stowe commands her readers to realize the significance of this breakthrough. She steps away from her fictional world and explains: "There stood the two children, representatives of the two extremes of society. The fair, high-bred child, with her golden head, her deep eyes, her spiritual, noble brow, and prince-like movements; and her black, keen, subtle, cringing, yet acute neighbor. There stood the representatives of their races. The Saxon, born of ages of cultivation, command, education, physical and moral eminence; the Afric, born of ages of oppression, submission, ignorance, toil, and vice!" (244).

From the moment of her uncouth appearance to the time of her conversion to civilization, Topsy dominates the story, defining in depth her "unwhiteness," which is, of course, more than skin deep. Stowe plops Topsy down on a page at the beginning of chapter 20—more than halfway into the novel—introducing her as an open-mouthed, very black little girl with "round shining eyes, glittering as glass beads" and woolly hair fixed in a "do" of "sundry little tails" (236). How different Topsy appears from the fair-skinned Eva with the violet-blue eyes and rosy mouth, whose noble head is encircled by "long golden brown hair . . . [that] floated like a cloud" (143). Just as Topsy's appearance is as startling as a bolt from an alien world, Topsy's manner is equally foreign. Topsy tumbles in exotic confusion, whereas Eva glides in white beauty.

As much as Topsy is an odd sight to behold, she is a force with which to be reckoned. Soon after Topsy enters the scene, St. Clare whistles a command and she starts to produce "those odd guttural sounds which distinguish the native music of her race," keeping time all the while like one possessed by an "unearthly" spirit (237). Following this "entertainment," Topsy gives an account of herself and reveals that she has no conception even of what it means to be human. In her mind, she has "just growed" like a weed of the earth (240).

Stowe proves that Topsy's queer idea about her conception is fundamentally correct; for, in many ways, the little darky really is like a weed bending in response to a wide range of stimuli—including the good example of the "superior race." Naturally, Eva is the sunshine that causes Topsy to become receptive to Miss Ophelia's instructions. As a perfect mime who has been shown the light of "Eva love," Topsy traces, in shadow, white behaviors and becomes proof positive that any black, starting out in life as a barbarian, can have his/her act "whitened up."

Leaving no stone unturned, Stowe examines the other side of the issue, which pertains to the effect of white depravity on primitive blacks. She theorizes that a white man who mistreats slaves not only produces chattel unfit to bear even the inferior human label of slave but damns himself in the process. Simon Legree, the cruel slave driver, demonstrates this ultraheathenization principle in a worst-case scenario.

Because of his extreme cruelty and low-class demeanor, Simon Legree presents a brutish mirror image for his slaves to reflect. As his likeness impresses itself upon the primitive personalities of the slaves in his service, Stowe imagines an egregious debasement of the African personality. The slaves who become most degraded by Simon Legree are the two black over-seers who have been especially groomed by the slave master to help him maintain order at his plantation.

Upon meeting Legree's black henchmen, Stowe's nineteenth-century audience was probably thoroughly repulsed by their raw animal-like natures. Nevertheless, in spite of these slaves' dog-gish appearance, Stowe conceives of their redemption, and she manipulates their puppet strings to show that somewhere deep in their savage hearts still resides a racial inheritance of sim-plicity and kindness. Indeed, by calling upon what she conceives to be the black race's susceptibility to spiritually moving ex-periences, Stowe allows the two sooty villains to undergo con-versions consequent to their witnessing Uncle Tom's Christlike suffering.

After vigorously assisting Simon Legree flog stoic Uncle Tom, the black brutes take a respite. They watch Simon Legree, who also hesitates for a moment under a strange heavenly spell; then they see him give in to the "spirit of evil . . . with seven-fold vehemence . . . [foam] with rage . . . and [smite] his victim to the ground" (411). At this point the blacks obtain a "born-again" understanding of good and evil and, soon after, they share their uncommon feelings with Uncle Tom: " 'Sartin, we's been doin' a drefful wicked thing!' said Sambo; 'hopes Mas'r'll have to 'count for it, and not we.' . . . 'O Tom!' said Quimbo, 'we's been awful wicked to ye!' 'I forgive ye, with all my heart!' said Tom, faintly. 'O Tom! do tell us who is Jesus, anyhow?' said Sambo; —'Jesus, that's been a-standin' by you so, all this night! —Who is he?' " (412). These former beasts now only have to mention Jesus' name and they get religion. Sambo cries out, "[B]ut I do believe! —I can't help it; Lord Jesus, have mercy on us!" (412).

As a main character, Uncle Tom is Stowe's ultimate example of worthiness embodied in an unmixed African. As a Christ figure, he is allowed to reach spiritual perfection. Uncle Tom's ascension adequately refutes the contrary notion by which some period whites justified slavery—that blacks do not have souls. And Tom's sainthood becomes the centerpiece of Stowe's argu-ment that blacks not only have souls, some do, in fact, have souls so pure that they may be chosen by God to live in paradise.

Stowe sees no contradiction to her theory that even though ra-cial inequality is real in the secular sphere, perfect racial equality is not impossible in the spiritual sphere. Quite simply, Stowe maintains, spirituality and intellect are two different things. To prove her total acceptance of this axiom Stowe concedes that Tom is in fact more spiritually talented than most white ministers she has known. To account for such an apparent oxymoron, she rationalizes that Uncle Tom's special piety emanates from his possession of a simple mind that has been enhanced by a "child-like earnestness," allowing him to pray "right up" (29). Stowe implies that white preachers do not easily match the thrilling beauty of the black man's devotionals perhaps because their higher intellect makes them more calculating. Stowe therefore exhorts whites to see that, despite the African's mental dullness, black men like Tom have lily-white hearts that the Savior accepts. The end of the novel does not even question whether or not Uncle Tom will join Eva in heaven. Of course, he does.[2]

The relationship Stowe depicts between Uncle Tom and little Eva is, from my point of view, the hardest for most African Americans to swallow. As an African American myself, I marvel at how fantastically credulous the nineteenth-century reading audience must have been to accept Stowe's suggestion that the aura of spiritual perfection surrounding Tom, a strapping, burly, childlike Negro, was strong enough to make feasible the scenes in which he entertains the very flower of the white race in private rooms and in quiet gardens full of bushes. And, I wonder, how could they have read the passages dealing with these two characters' mawkish displays of affection without a mustard seed of suspicion that Tom, though simpleminded, could have been a dangerous pedophile?

Surely, something is strange about Tom's behavior if from the moment he sees little Eva, he cannot stop watching her: "Tom, who had the soft, impressionable nature of his kindly race, ever yearning towards the simple and childlike, watched the little creature [Eva] with daily increasing interest. To him she seemed something almost divine; and whenever her golden head and deep blue eyes peered out upon him from behind some dusky cotton-bale, or looked down upon him over some ridge of packages, he half believed that she was one of the angels stepped out of his New Testament" (144).

Throughout the period of their special friendship, Uncle Tom and Eva spend a lot of time together in private. Often they sit together in the arbor "on a little mossy seat" (258) just laughing and talking; and again they share a writing table, sitting in such close proximity that Eva can put "her little golden head close to his" (234). Eva even goes into Uncle Tom's private chambers to "[hear] him sing" (183) when, apparently, nobody but Uncle Tom knows she's there.

I think it is very peculiar that no white character in the story ever expresses anxiety over the unusual relationship between Eva and Tom. Looking at one scene in particular—where St. Clare and Ophelia happen to spy from a window Eva sticking flowers into Tom's beard and hair before leading him off happily to God knows where—I wonder how this kind of behavior could be seen by the white male parent as just fine. Why, I wonder, is St. Clare so trusting? The only comment about this ridiculous scene comes from Ophelia who finds Eva's display of affection for the African disgusting on account of the old boy's color. But Stowe quickly has St. Clare point out to Ophelia that she has an attitude problem and probably would not feel such distaste if Eva were "caressing a large dog" (176). At last, Stowe has supplied the rationale that begs for acceptance of this unlikely duo and trust in their innocence: Eva is simply the purest specimen of her race; and Tom, representing a class of subhumans not to be ranked above dogs, can be rendered pure of heart, and, strangely, asexual and innocuous.

Finally, in trying to puzzle through the fascination this unusual attraction between a little white girl and a muscular adult African male slave could have held for the first readers of *Uncle Tom's Cabin*, I can only speculate that it must have fulfilled some fantasy of racial harmony for them. I can only imagine hopeful responses coming from Stowe's well-intentioned white audience, agreeing that the relationship between Eva and Tom shows how pure hearts will bridge generations and overcome racial barriers.

It is indeed interesting to speculate on the reasons why Stowe chooses Eva and Tom to be her ambassadors of change for their respective races. In the case of Eva, I believe, the novel itself provides adequate clues for the use of a little white girl as the millennial figure who comes to earth at a critical time to awaken a sinning race of people. For it is clear from Stowe's depiction of feminine qualities that she believes white women are the "gentler and kinder" and better half of the "superior" race. Throughout the book, white women alone assume the role of moral leaders, patiently prodding their men to do the right thing and encouraging them to live more prudent and Christian lives. Even Simon Legree shudders when he remembers his "pale, loving mother rising by his bedside" (370) to remind him that he has blackened his soul beyond repair. Since Stowe reveals in all her depictions of children a belief that the young possess their racial inheritance in the most immaculate and ingenuous form, a white girl would be naturally, in Stowe's mind, the one most likely to commune with God before all others of her race.

Now, turning to Stowe's choice of Tom as the black saint to evoke the sympathies of white sinners, the rationale is not so apparent. There are no internal clues in the story to suggest why Uncle Tom should represent the black solution to racial strife. But once again, I believe, the answer to the question about the utility of Uncle Tom, like the answers to so many other puzzles about African types in the book, can be uncovered by probing the sociocultural realities of the times.

Historians specializing in pre–Civil War history assert that the "purity" and "innocence" of black females living on antebellum plantations could not be guaranteed once the slave girl passed age ten, so common was the sexual abuse of black females in those days (Bennett and Genovese). Eugene D. Genovese writes about the "fancy girl market" in which "young, shapely, unusually light in color" girls were sold at auction "as house servants with special services required." He further reports that "a particularly beautiful girl or young woman might bring $5,000 . . . [and] these sales, private and public went on in full view, drew attention but not much censure from the southern press" (417). Harriet Jacobs, in her classic narrative dealing with her own case of sexual harassment beginning when she was merely thirteen, writes that "a man nearly forty years my senior daily [tried] his utmost to corrupt the pure principles my grandmother had instilled" (27). And she laments that, generally, the slave girl "will become prematurely knowing in evil things. Soon she will be compelled to tremble when she hears her master's footfall" (28).

In light of such common knowledge regarding the despoiling of African slave girls, perhaps Stowe felt that only a black male made out to be as pious as Uncle Tom could function credibly in the highly spiritual capacity of a black Jesus. Besides, it only took a literary sleight of hand for Stowe to turn this prime Negro into a eunuch. And, once that trick was accomplished, Stowe only needed to invoke Christian Scripture that promises passage through the pearly gates to anyone who approaches its portals as a child. Certainly, by this biblical standard, Uncle Tom qualifies for celestial robes.

Uncle Tom becomes the principal actor in Stowe's fantasy that exhorts the silent white multitude to break the physical chains of slavery. After playing out this drama of liberation on the stage of fiction, as Stowe promises, Tom, the black Christ, is more than willing to absolve whites of their sins and to help them better understand what a special gift they have: whiteness—which quality alone can inspire in the simple hearts and minds of the earth's natural servants such feelings and propensities as love, gratitude, and, above all, a willingness to serve and to entertain. Only such an alluring vision, utilizing a forgiving and unresentful victim, willing to commit his life for the eternal happiness of undeserving sinners, can explain why pious Uncle Tom, along with angelic little Eva, has continued to frolic into the twentieth century, appearing in such popular venues as Shirley Temple movies and "Song of the South."[3]

Even as Stowe assures her white contemporaries that their salvation depends on loving black primitives and treating them with kindness, she realizes that one problem with half-breeds must be addressed. In Stowe's day, America had spawned a large community of human beings sharing both black and white genes: the tragic mulattoes. From Stowe's point of view, the plight of this limbo group would not be easily solved. According to the mainstream nineteenth-century theory of white racial superiority to which Stowe subscribes, no person with a drop of black blood could be considered white. Nevertheless, Stowe maintains that slaves with varying amounts of "white blood" inherit different levels of sensibilities in direct proportion to the amount of white blood they carry. Stowe also imagines that this inheritance from the superior race makes mulattoes hate their outcast status. The mulattoes' dilemma in America, as Stowe conceives it, is to be superior to unmixed blacks, but always to be doomed by "the impress of the despised race upon [their] . . . face[s]" (79).

The three mixed slave characters Stowe uses in the novel to show the positive effects of white blood upon this new breed of humans are the married couple George and Eliza and their little son, Harry. From Stowe's perspective, much of the mulattoes' white inheritance is manifest in their physical appearance. Consequently, the three mulattoes in the story are all beautiful, having distinctly white markers of beauty: fair or rosy complexions, narrow features, and silky curly hair. Stowe envisions no beauty in blackness; and, indeed, none of her dark-skinned characters are pleasant to look at. In fact, quadroons with "silky curls" laugh maliciously at unattractive dark-skinned servants like Dinah, St. Clare's disorganized black culinary genius, who cannot join the near-white pretenders to white purity at their high-toned balls. The house slave, Rosa, vain and high yellow, mocks Dinah as she points to the cook's unmixed African's hair, derisively saying that the poor woman "greases her wool every day to make it lie straight . . . while it will be wool, after all" (214).

According to Stowe, many of the good traits mulattoes inherit from white fathers are intellectual and will cause such civilized behavior in these half-breeds that they inevitably become malcontent with their slave condition. So it is that Eliza acts well-bred and proper not just because a good white woman has raised her, but mainly because her genetic code has been altered by "white blood." And Harry, having inherited only the trick of mimicry from his black side, is, above all, "white" in his sensitivity to danger and in his protective attitude toward his mother. Finally, Eliza's husband, George, "a bright and intelligent young mulatto," owes his "adroitness and ingenuity" to the infusion of Anglo-Saxon blood in his veins (11). Not only is he beautiful like the rest of his family, but he has inherited "from one of the proudest families in Kentucky . . . [his] set of fine European features" (107). Of course, these mulattoes do not speak the rude dialect of their black kin. Naturally, they have encoded access to the prestige language of the dominant culture.

Another unfortunate consequence of mixed blood for mulattoes is that the very beauty, high spirits, handsomeness, and fluency it produces in them are, Stowe maintains, their fatal flaws. It causes pretty quadroon girls endowed with "natural graces" to fall victim to "temptations" (11), handsome light-skinned slave boys to be used and sold as "fancy articles" (5), and high-yellow young slave men to become so resentful of bondage that they cry out like George, "I'm willing to go with the case to [God], and ask him if I do wrong to seek my freedom. . . . [and I willingly accept] six feet of free soil . . . if it comes to that" (108).

Ultimately, Stowe contends, the most devastating side-effect of mixed blood is the mental acuity it produces. Because white blood causes mulattoes to think and feel more intensely than their full-blooded African counterparts, and because a certain amount of the taint from their lowly black relatives dictates that they must live their lives forever cut off from the salubrious influence of pure whites, Stowe considers the dilemma of mixed slaves to be critical. The author's solution for the nearly white pariahs in the novel is for them to return to Africa; and, interestingly enough, this is also her solution for unmixed blacks, like Topsy, who have been successfully "educated" by whites. Stowe proposes to send both the artificially civilized Africans and the naturally superior mulattoes back to the Dark Continent where they can do a lot of good, uplifting heathens. In Topsy's case, Stowe reasons, "the same activity and ingenuity which, when a child made her so multiform and restless in her development [can be] employed in a safer and wholesome manner, in teaching the children of her own country" (433).

As *Uncle Tom's Cabin* began in controversy, so does it end with opposing forces finding their comfort zones disturbed at both ends of the book. The nineteenth-century men and women who believed slavery was an economic necessity abhorred the intent of the novel; but, perhaps, if they had considered the inevitable downfall of the system, they would have found the novel's ending, which holds out the prospect of so many "uppity" blacks returning to Africa, pleasing. On the other hand, those of Stowe's era who had long agitated to end chattel slavery would have celebrated the intent of *Uncle Tom's Cabin* but could not have appreciated the writer's suggestion that progressive blacks, both mixed and unmixed, go back to Africa.

Left out of the saber crossing of proslavery and antislavery forces, I feel, were many who kept silent about their displeasure with the author's unsavory use of fictitious Africans. For surely, from the novel's first appearance, an undercurrent of dislike for the book meandered among African Americans, masked by the gratitude most felt compelled to offer due to its antislavery theme. Understandably, prominent educated free blacks like William Wells Brown, a Harvard graduate credited with writing the first African-American novel, and Frances E. Watkins Harper, the prolific orator and writer, celebrated the book as a touchstone for victory in the cold war against slavery; and even Frederick Douglass was politic in expressing his belief that the novel was the most effective weapon to date in the struggle. Yet history shows that even in the wake of appreciation for Stowe's antislavery support, the portrayal of a passive Uncle Tom was problematic for blacks who believed that every human being's highest duty is to resist the tyranny of oppression. The words of such free blacks as preacher J. B. Smith, teacher William G. Allen, and medical doctor and journalist Martin R. Delany reveal both disaffection and anger toward the behavior ascribed to Uncle Tom. Statements by these blacks are contained in a recent article by Yarborough, who cites from a period black newspaper the following excerpt of a letter angrily denouncing Stowe's resolution for the "Negro problem": "Uncle Tom must be killed, George Harris exiled! Heaven for dead Negroes! Liberia for living mulattos. Neither can live on the American continent. Death or banishment is our doom, say the slaveocrats, the Colonizationists, and, save the mark—Mrs. Stowe!!"[4]

As blacks moved further away from the days of chains and shackles, and as they became more empowered by their hard-won social and political gains, the seething disdain for Uncle Tom as a character grew into open declarations of hostility against Stowe's entire novel and its whole cast of darky stereotypes. The biggest idiot in the black world becomes known as an Uncle Tom, a model for every emasculated, servile, simple-minded, self-hating black person in America. This widespread rejection of Uncle Tom as a universal type among black people has been immortalized by writers like Richard Wright, who satirically called his first collection of stories, based on culturally abused blacks living in the South, *Uncle Tom's Children* (1940), and Ismael Reed, whose novel *Flight To Canada* (1976) is a biting burlesque on the fictive descendants of Uncle Tom.

Although Stowe wrote her widely known and discussed novel in response to what she perceived to be the great evil of her society—slavery—the foundation upon which she created her masterpiece was the master culture. At bottom, her racial ideology was replete with the same pseudoscientific theories motivating whites who actively participated in the "peculiar institution." Where she parted company with the unredeemed purveyors of human misery was in her belief that the black person, a creation of God, had been given an immortal soul. This article of faith made it impossible for Stowe to remain silent on the systematic victimization of the black race. By linking her antislavery position to her conviction of racial inequality, Stowe articulated the hope and belief of great numbers of whites who evidently felt as burdened as the writer by the sinful weight of slavery. Stowe's vision of a new world order offered them a perfect way to attain their manifest destiny and to control the host of lowly Africans in their midst.

In a twentieth-century classroom, *Uncle Tom's Cabin* could be used to dramatically introduce students to one of the darkest eras in America's past, details of which have been either masked or excluded from mainstream history texts. However, in presenting this novel to modern students, I believe, professors must try to insure that the stereotypes Stowe invented will not reinforce the lingering racial misconceptions and deep-rooted biases still nurtured by many in the country who continue to harbor ideas of racial superiority. By emphasizing the utility of the novel as a political tract in its day, a teacher can set the tone for an alternative rereading of the text that goes beyond literary interpretation to an analysis of its cultural context with the African persona in focus. Keeping in mind the generally accepted view that present situations are shaped by history, the teacher can suggest to students that a cultural rereading of the book should not only shed light on the past but may also lead to a better understanding of the new American dilemma that is developing around issues of multiculturalism. Indeed, stereotyping may be as much a problem for our contemporary society as it was for people of the nineteenth century. Notions of "otherness" still complicate interactions among the various ethnic and racial groups who live in close proximity and comprise a new American mosaic in which the colors seldom blend yet frequently clash. I believe that *Uncle Tom's Cabin,* viewed as a cultural product, may be useful as a cautionary tale to help students recognize not only how truly self-deceiving the concept of a "degraded other" can be, but also, on a larger scale, how collective self-images enhanced beyond reason and laws of nature perpetuate social injustice against those with the least power to protect themselves.


N O T E S

1. Stowe's statement is contained in "Concluding Remarks" in the original 1852 edition of *Uncle Tom's Cabin,* reprinted in the Bantam Press edition (1981) with an introduction by Alfred Kazin (440). All

subsequent quotations from the novel are from this edition, cited by page number in the text.

2. Yarborough cites a passage from *A Key to Uncle Tom's Cabin* to show that Stowe backs up the views she expresses in the novel, that blacks have a special talent for religion: "The negro race is confessedly more simple, docile, childlike, and affectionate than other races; and hence the divine graces of love and faith when in-breathed by the Holy spirit find in their natural temperament a more congenial atmosphere" (57).

3. Bogel says that white stage performers' presentation of the black character "as either a nitwit or a childlike lackey . . . had existed since the days of slavery and such stereotypes were . . . popularized in American life and arts" (4).

4. See Yarborough (68–72) for a discussion of period reactions from African Americans that contained both praise and reservations about Stowe's depictions of blacks.

# 11

MICHAEL J. MEYER

## Toward a Rhetoric of Equality: Reflective and Refractive Images in Stowe's Language

One critical strain of argument that has emerged since the publication of Harriet Beecher Stowe's novel in 1852 places *Uncle Tom's Cabin* in a corner. Essentially this argument suggests that Stowe engaged in racial stereotyping to such an extent that the novel's antislavery, abolitionist purpose cannot be redeemed or recuperated through any kind of textual study or commentary. From the very early critical reviews in 1852 to James Baldwin's 1949 essay in *The Partisan Review*, Stowe has been unfairly accused of subverting her ostensibly Abolitionist purpose by creating characters that exhibit significant and culturally powerful racial stereotypes. Her text, the argument runs, is basically a racist tract in sheep's clothing. Arguments that stereotypes in *Uncle Tom's Cabin* subvert racial equality also suggest that readers can perceive only Stowe's latent prejudice in the text. To attest that more than this occurs, however, one has only to reread the novel, being sensitive to inherent personal biases that are rightfully labeled "myopic" (Riggio 150). Such readers will find reflective and refractive images as Stowe employs powerful mirroring techniques to her rhetorical advantage. These images themselves argue that Stowe attempts to establish a *rhetoric of equality* rather than unconsciously revealing biases that would destroy her stance on equanimity between blacks and whites. When read with the heart, the pathos of the plot convinces. This essay contends that despite the tradition of negative assessment focusing on stereotypical misrepresentation, the characters in *Uncle Tom's Cabin* reinforce Stowe's antislavery position rather than deliberately subvert her intent.

In an unpublished essay delivered at a 1992 MMLA forum on "The Validity of Texts about Minorities Written By Majorities," Mark Scarbrough argues that many of today's critics are "still trying to determine who best 'got it right' through the essentialist rhetoric of mimetic functionality." Consequently, Scarbrough contends, although a diversity of American voices has been made audible, such voices have been heard only "at the cost of (re)building fences around turfmaking soloists where the cultural rubric demands polyphony" (1). In fact, Scarbrough uses *Uncle Tom's Cabin* as just one example of his argument for a polyphonic rather than monophonic canon, noting that it is certainly one work exemplifying the inadequacy of labels and their fluctuating acceptance.

As he discusses texts about blacks written by white authors, Scarbrough further deplores critics' failure to acknowledge that race itself is a fabricated rather than an essential discourse, and he stresses the futility of arguments over which nineteenth-century authors had a fully correct version of the American experience or which books reflect the culture of the time. Specifically, Scarbrough's point is that to move forward truly into accurate new modes of literary analysis, critics must do more than examine the Other side of binary oppositions. Instead they must incorporate and reconcile contradictions while recognizing that no author's vision (whether a minority's or a privileged majority's) is inherently either "bad" or "good." Unfortunately, *Uncle Tom's Cabin* has experienced just such a polarized reaction.

After its initial publication, Stowe's novel received unconditional praise, leading best-seller lists and even earning international acclaim for its advocacy of the abolitionist cause. However, more recent assessments of the novel have plummeted it into the depths of disrespect, especially those by critics who believe that no middle-aged white woman could possibly have captured the black experience of slavery with any honesty. Instead, such critics express resentment about "the weight [Stowe's] imprimatur carried in establishing the credibility of black authors" and "the immense power she wielded as an interpreter of black life" (Yarborough 70).

Variant responses abound in recent criticism. Stowe's rhetoric can be seen as positive and "correct," from a twentieth-century viewpoint, in that it upholds a matriarchal approach in a patriarchal society. But according to these same perspectives, the novel is negative and "incorrect" by subverting its own declared intention of abolishing slavery and by using inherently racist language and racial stereotypes. Thus while a feminist might appropriately try to recuperate this text and include it in the canon, many African-American critics only with great difficulty can see *Uncle Tom's Cabin* as anything but a novel by a white woman writing about a topic about which she knew nothing. In fact, many have espoused the ideas of Martin Delaney, who asserted in an April 1853 letter to Frederick Douglass the belief that no white person can truly know a black, and that only violence, not passivity, can solve the black question in America (Yarborough 70).

If readers accept these increasingly negative assessments of Stowe's novel as a vehicle for presenting valid nineteenth-century observations about racial barriers and how to eliminate them, they will be forced to admit that the initial moral gain and the historical effect of *Uncle Tom's Cabin* has deteriorated into significant artistic loss and setback. In fact, Scarbrough warns, readers may even be caught castigating and avoiding such a "white" text because its attitudes on race relations seem at first glance petty and dangerous. Readers may even agree with the assessment that the novel is a mere portrayal of "Negro" life and character, overlaid with stereotypes by Stowe. Yet if *Uncle Tom's Cabin* is neither a satisfactory artistic portrait nor an accurate representation of the racial equality so desired by African Americans, one must try to decide where it falls short and where it succeeds. To deny its power, influence, and significance is to try to change a historical fact. Yet denying the novel's power and denigrating its worth has been precisely what has occurred.

As current readers struggle with claims that Stowe deliberately suggests African Americans need not be treated as equals until they become white, they must carefully examine both positive and negative possibilities in the narrative's portrait of race. If such contentions about Stowe's innate racist bias are the *only* truth about Stowe and her text, then it is no wonder that African-

American readers have reacted to the book with rage, bitterness, and a desire for revenge. Specifically, such readers would have to redirect such rage at the years of white oppression and perceived superiority (which some claim the novel's discourse actually advocates) in order for a racial Other to become a candidate for the American mainstream. Consequently, a search for more "representational" fiction, written by minorities themselves and thus mirroring a "truer" slave and master experience, would be both believable and expected.

However, negative critics have polarized the "issues" by seeking African-American texts that more "accurately" depict Negro characters as well as their familial and cultural milieu, thereby creating "white" texts that "got it wrong" and African-American fiction that "got it right." As R. Allen Harris notes in *College English*, the arguments illustrate that critics with very distinct agendas . . . and consequently with distinctive interpretative interests, can find support [for their interpretations] without any systematic attempt to load the data" (658). Consequently, such critics ignore the potential to see Stowe's honest attempt to fashion a rhetoric of equality in *Uncle Tom's Cabin* that would allow critics to value the novel's intrinsic worth while maintaining skepticism about its roots and its obvious flaws as art. By closely examining previously overlooked textual elements, readers will perceive that *Uncle Tom's Cabin* does qualify as an admirable abolitionist novel, despite the fact that Stowe at times guides inadequately developed characters through the motions of empty ritual.

It is undeniable that during a portion of the 1860s, even African Americans greeted Stowe's work as a monumental achievement and hailed her as the creator of ever more white support in the North for abolition, even though it required a Civil War to attain it. For example, Frederick Douglass, the freed slave who spoke for his race in the mid-1800s, initially at least saw Stowe as a kindred spirit. In one of his letters, he writes that the book was "a flash to light a million camp fires in front of the embattled hosts of slavery" (Hughes 102) and that he "saw no reason to find fault with well-meant efforts for our benefit" (Yarborough 71). In addition, black poet Paul Laurence Dunbar's 1898 sonnet labels Stowe as "Prophet and Priestess" and extols her as fearless and daring. The poem continues by blessing Stowe for paving the way for the end to slavery and for exhorting her country and the world to rise up against the white slaveholders who suppressed both the "niggers" and freemen (73).

Unfortunately, Dunbar's and Douglass's praises were short-lived. Over the next forty years, the reputation of Stowe's work seemed to diminish and weaken as *Uncle Tom's Cabin* was perceived as mere propaganda or as sentimentalized prose written for a pulp magazine. Later critics tended to dismiss even its artistry, evaluating it as a series of short sketches tied together loosely by a narrative voice that at times was intrusive if not offensive. Because she addressed the reader in didactic language, Stowe was assessed as merely another writer whose "popular" fiction would have no lasting power.

These controversies about the text's aesthetic value have caused critics to avoid or disregard the positive images Stowe employs. In fact, Harris states that although critics are aware of the book's dual nature, they often focus on its negative traits at the expense of the positive ones. At times, according to Harris, this attitude results in willful misreadings by individuals "who pursue [their own] rhetorical ends rather than [trying to] understand the novel" (658). One element such negative critics have left unexplored is Stowe's use of reflective and refractive images in order to establish a rhetoric of equality. Unfortunately, readers who refuse to assimilate a "white" text into African-American discourse while at the same time insisting on the assimilation of African-American texts into the dominant culture will miss this possibility.

Such readers fail to realize what Scarbrough stresses in his argument: that "all writers, both black and white, imagine race" and "refigure it in a strategy of discourse."

> No text mirrors race. Race in itself is a discourse, most specifically a discourse of power that promotes and fosters racial tension and discrimination, and so may 'only' function at the level of imaginative construction. . . . It is both encoded in texts and (ironically) disembodied in texts. It finds its way into textual production and escapes the very confines of the text. Racism is part of the discourse of race . . . and race itself is a metaphoric construction of power in our society—those who are "white" are so because of their place in the power hierarchy. (5)

Thus the construct of *Uncle Tom's Cabin* cannot avoid dealing with racism. But that fact does not warrant the conclusion that the novel intentionally promotes and fosters racial tension and discrimination.

For instance, one way *Uncle Tom's Cabin* works toward a rhetoric of equality is through Stowe's use of reflective naming, emphasizing identical names in order to establish parallels and contrasts. Unfortunately, no one has examined yet why Stowe names her characters as she does and what might be suggested by her practice. One of the most surprising techniques is Stowe's repetition of several given names when she could have easily used alternatives that would have made the novel clearer and would have helped the reader to keep the characters straight. For example, there are two Georges in the book, one white and one black; two Toms, one white and one black; and two Henrys, one white and one mulatto. Surely these choices are not by chance. In one case the naming suggests similar identities; in the other two, naming evokes a significant contrast of personalities. Given the fact that several psychological studies have asserted the power of naming to develop personality traits and determine a strong self-image, this so-called "coincidence" demands more attention.

Stowe's use of reflective naming indicates her attempt to see whites and blacks as equals. If stereotyping by race is invalid, it is logical that both black and white characters can share the same given name. Moreover, the text suggests that inheriting a "white" name does not necessarily suggest inheriting a racist ideology. For example, George Shelby, the young son of the slaveholder, does not follow his father's pattern but applies the racial sympathy he learns from the matriarchal figure in the novel, his mother, Mrs. Shelby. The younger Shelby's compassion indicates that whites do have the potential to recognize the sins of their fathers and to change because of this recognition. The other George, Eliza's husband, though part black, is comparable to the young Shelby in his assertions that members of the Negro race also have inherent rights and that he wishes his family to be free at any cost, just as Shelby wishes to free his slaves at the end of the novel. Considering the large repository of names from which Stowe could have selected, her choice of parallel names suggests racial equality and also provides a parallel to the early framers of the Constitution, George Washington and Thomas Jefferson. Seen in this way, the black George has the potential to become a new "father of his nation" while the docile servant Uncle Tom is presented as an individual who is essential in the framing of a new concept of freedom and independence for his race.

The Toms of the novel—Tom Loker, the slave catcher, and Uncle Tom—also provide evidence of the characters' names as mirror images of blacks and whites; however, in this case the image is refractive rather than reflective. Tom Loker, the man Haley hires to track down George and Eliza, thus serves as the distorted mirror in which the evil in one Tom is paralleled by the loving concern of another. The dual naming also enables Stowe to ironically invert the actions of the black Uncle Tom and the white Loker. The slave is willing to risk violence to his person in order to protect his extended family which includes whites (St. Clare and little Eva) as well as the mulatto woman Cassy. In contrast, Loker bitterly complains about the wounds inflicted by George Harris as he attempts to destroy an African-American family and return its members to bondage. Uncle Tom's sense that humane treatment and love transcend color lines dominates his actions toward others, while Loker's deep-seated prejudice governs his divisive rejection of the Negro race as equal.

The two young boys in the novel also reflect Stowe's pervasive use of refraction in her mirroring technique. Despite their similar names, Henry and Henrique are different personalities. Henrique, St. Clare's nephew, is independent, and he acts rude and superior to his cousin, his uncle, and even his own father. The other Henry, Eliza and George's child, is dependent, polite, and humble. Through these characters, Stowe would have her readers know that race does not predetermine personality. Again Stowe inverts racial stereotypes, since nineteenth-century white readers would expect the white child to possess the positive traits while the black child should have a negative attitude and actions. Thus, as Stowe works toward the rhetoric of equality, identical and similar names serve her purpose, since their repetition creates confusion among her readers' expectations and suggests the inability to forge universal claims based either on "nomos" or on racial makeup.

Another opportunity for twentieth-century readers to affirm Stowe's rhetoric of equality lies in reevaluating past attacks on *Uncle Tom's Cabin.* For example, Richard Yarborough argues that Stowe employs derogative Negro stereotypes in the novel and that her work negatively influences future writing about the African-American race. Yarborough then cites four examples to prove his point. He begins with the characters of Sam and Andy, the Shelbys' servants, who lead the slaver Haley on a wild-goose chase to save Eliza. Calling them "bumptious, giggly outsized adolescents," Yarborough sees their trickster actions as motivated merely by their desire to please whites. The narrative renders their uneducated speech as comic, a factor that Yarborough argues diminishes the African-American image (47). Tremaine McDowell's critical reaction in 1931 anticipates this criticism of Yarborough's and expresses a similar negative reaction against Stowe's attempt to portray Negro dialect, noting the resemblance between speech by whites and "mulattos" as opposed to the "darky" dialect which he declares is full of "barbarisms" (88–91).

But Yarborough and McDowell both fail to acknowledge that Stowe's portrayal of African-American existence was the first to center on black characters who were of major significance to the plot. Initially, this may seem a superficial point, but Stowe's own sense that this was a major accomplishment suggests that the dialogue between Sam and Andy was an honest attempt to imitate a Negro dialect as it must have sounded to a white. As such, *Uncle Tom's Cabin* acknowledges blacks as a race with its own speech patterns. While the dialogue might appear deprecatory of blacks at times, Yarborough's and McDowell's criticisms are only valid from a twentieth-century perspective and reveal more about the interpreter than the text. Suggestions that Stowe's portrayals of dialect were intentionally derogatory and demeaning also ignore the possibility that Sam's and Andy's speech patterns may satirize the many whites who denied the possibility of black equality, choosing rather to judge individuals they considered inferior on the basis of their language. Stowe's use of dialect suggests instead the inaccurate stereotyping of individuals based on a hierarchy of dialect and conversely the accurate perception of the wide variety of speech patterns among African Americans as well as among whites. In fact, Sam's and Andy's use of dialect and language depicts them as far more clever than does the speech of the slaver Haley, precisely because their verbal banter enables the two slaves to thwart Haley's attempt to capture Eliza by employing reverse psychology and by anticipating his lack of trust in black advice.

Yarborough's second criticism is of Topsy, whom he sees as the stereotypical pickaninny. The grotesque freakishness of

Topsy, Yarborough contends, evokes not only typical concepts of African-American folk music and dance but also a dangerous lack of self-control and restraint that suggests domination by the devil. Thus to be born black is to be considered pagan (48). Once again, Yarborough's criticism fails to perceive the possibility of a rhetoric of equality, examining only one side of the issue. If Topsy is indeed stereotyped in this way, Stowe's portrait reflects less an inherent racism than a simple recognition that such actions were expected from black children by bigoted whites. Since Topsy conforms her life to these expectations, *Uncle Tom's Cabin* criticizes whites who failed to realize the potential that lay beneath the surface of characters of all races if they receive the love and attention that Topsy obviously lacks. Stowe returns to the rhetoric of equality by demonstrating that when a child, either white or black, loses a parental figure's love and care, there is no difference based on race. Although Topsy is aware of her separation from her parents and suggests that she just "growed up," she is not the sole African American who suffers from separation from parental figures. In fact, Stowe stresses the important influence of loving guardians and role models for both races when she mirrors Topsy's loss in several other plot occurrences that affect black characters as well as whites. For example, Stowe repeats the image of loss in Emmeline's separation from her mother, in Tom's separation from his children, and in little Eva's and Marie St. Clare's lack of bonding.

Stowe extends this domestic rhetoric of equality by examining positive family relationships as well, again asserting that race is an invalid measure for determining and maintaining them. Stowe persuades readers that positive families transcend racial barriers through the admirable relationship of Aunt Chloe and Uncle Tom, the marriage of George and Eliza, and the white Quaker household that helps Eliza escape. Each demonstrates Stowe's ideal vision of the human race as unalarmed by racial judgments and divisions. Moreover, when such families face forced separations, both races make adjustments by finding surrogates. Witness how Ophelia finally "feels" for Topsy, how Cassy helps Emmeline to cope, and how St. Clare assumes the motherly role with little Eva that Marie is incapable of assuming.

Stowe also fosters her rhetoric of equality by stressing that the loss of a child is felt deeply in both black and white cultures. Several episodes repeat Eliza's reaction to the possible loss of her child when Uncle Tom is sold, including the story of the woman aboard the ship to New Orleans and the story of Prue. Such a possibility is also played out in the white culture when St. Clare loses little Eva. In all cases, the pain is felt deeply, indicating Stowe's recognition of still another human trait shared by both the black and white races. Such parallel experiences of loss and its accompanying feelings refute claims about Stowe's intentional and innate racial bias.

The next characters Yarborough examines are Sambo and Quimbo, Legree's slaves, who as Yarborough notes only need more positive influence from whites to attain salvation. He also points out that Stowe conceived the two characters as particularly susceptible to white influence and holds that as real characters they are improbable. Their personalities suggest to Yarborough Stowe's deliberate implication of deficiencies in the black race (50) and suggest that racial identity predetermines negative personalities. However, the narrow focus of this critique fails to acknowledge that Sambo's and Quimbo's deficiencies may result from flaws in their own characters rather than from white influence. There were and still are African Americans as well as whites who betray their own race to attain selfish ends. Readers might compare Sambo and Quimbo to today's gang members of all races, who destroy their own kind and kin while disregarding their responsibilities to raise and uplift. Their negative personalities need not be associated with their racial identities, and they do have the ability to change. Once exposed to Uncle Tom's admirable resistance to Legree's demands, Sambo and Quimbo are able for the first time to respect a brother who values his own moral code above that of a white master, and whose defiance labels him a man of independent thought despite his role as slave. Although Sambo's and Quimbo's redemption may be improbable in real life, a member of their own race, not a white, motivates the change in their characters and extends Stowe's reflective strategies into the realm of spiritual redemption.

Yarborough then proceeds to mixed-blood characters, Eliza and George Harris, pointing out that Stowe's mulattoes are somehow better than the full-blooded African Americans. Dialect, physical attractiveness, and moral restraint are but three criteria he perceives in Stowe's novel as defining this superiority. To Yarborough, George especially reveals Stowe's reluctance to portray the pent-up rage of the intelligent, strong-willed mulatto male without a Christian restraint (50–52). Such restraint, which Stowe particularly admired, and which is embodied in Uncle Tom himself, is a trait that Yarborough claims today's African Americans associate with passivity and a simple mind. He also criticizes Tom's lack of aggressive traits, which are replaced by the feminine qualities Stowe admired in the Negro race. According to Yarborough, this shift to femininity creates a stereotype of Africans that emphasizes childlike innocence and purity of spirit. Yarborough suggests true freedom would be difficult if not impossible to attain for such a "Negro" (58). Yet as Harris reminds us, this perspective misses the mark by a good deal, since "Tom is far more a type of Christ than a type of Black. . . . he lives in imitation of Christ" (659).

Finally, Yarborough concludes that Stowe's distinction between mixed blacks and full-blooded blacks does little to support claims that African Americans are equal to whites and thus deserving of equal treatment. Quoting critic H. J. Simms, Yarborough suggests that Stowe renders the genius of George as Caucasion, not Ethiopian, and that Stowe attributes his success to the influence of his white blood (59). Yet the concept of polarities suggests that even Yarborough's final criticism has a positive corollary. Myra Jehlen specifically demonstrates this when she argues that George's accomplishments are quite significant and that Stowe's major emphasis in her portrayal is on his right to self-possession, his ability to become himself and to contend and compete with others to increase both his status and property. George's intellectual capacity as well as Uncle Tom's position as the Shelbys' right-hand man indicate that an individual's worth is self-created and that Stowe felt that this opportunity ought to be open to all (386–87). Moreover, George's status as a mulatto should hardly be a factor in the reader's analysis of his accomplishments, since miscegenation was a given result of slavery. After a century of mixing blood lines, few blacks, if any, could claim a pure African heritage.

Still another negative critic whose views are countered by uncovering Stowe's rhetoric of equality is James Baldwin. In a 1949 article, Baldwin calls *Uncle Tom's Cabin* a very bad novel that contains a self-righteous, virtuous sentimentality "associated with dishonesty" (Ammons ed. 92). However, his denunciation of Stowe's presentations of black characters as passive and lacking power does not indicate that the novel's portrayal of race is flawed. Baldwin notes that most of the Negroes in the novel are merely "lovable figures presenting no problem," while two of the three major characters, Eliza and George, are "as white as she [Stowe] can make them" (94). Later, he asserts that Stowe

> could not cast out the blacks—a wretched huddled mass, apparently, claiming, like an obsession, her inner Eye—she could not embrace them either, without purifying them of Sin. She must cover their intimidating nakedness, robe them in white, the garment of salvation; only thus could she herself be delivered from ever-present sin, only thus could she bury, as St. Paul demanded, "the carnal man, the man of flesh." Tom, therefore, her only black man, has been robbed of his humanity and divested of his sex. It is the price for that darkness with which he has been branded. (94)

Since Baldwin views the black characters in *Uncle Tom's Cabin* as stereotypes of a condescending, forbearing race whom Stowe can only accept by robing them in Christianity and salvation, he concludes that this robing implies that negroes are inferior, not made in God's image, and that they require racial transformation into whites in order to attain equality. Baldwin also accuses white writers of the American protest novel of "being forgiven, on the strength of their good intentions, whatever violence they do to language, whatever excessive demand they make of credibility" (95). He particularly criticizes white audiences' primary concern with writers' avowed aims to bring greater freedom to the oppressed, regardless of the inaccuracy of their concepts. J. C. Furnas echoes Baldwin's sentiments about passive, forbearing African Americans when he objects to Stowe's gentle Christian Negroes, and contends that she portrays African-Americans with "white blood" as more intelligent, enterprising, and sensitive. Furnas also reacts to Stowe's portrayal of blacks as happier in dependent or subordinate roles and nearer to animals than to humans (Ammons ed. 110).

Baldwin condemns Stowe even more than Furnas, suggesting that *Uncle Tom's Cabin* does not affirm black identity but instead confirms the monstrous legend it was written to destroy. He contrasts Stowe's novel with Richard Wright's *Native Son* to suggest that blacks, rather than exhorting and submitting as did Uncle Tom, should curse the white power structure, as Bigger Thomas did in Wright's novel. Baldwin's ultimate assessment is that *Uncle Tom's Cabin* lacks the equality of human rights for which Stowe hoped, since the text deconstructs itself by implied biases Stowe represents (Ammons ed. 96).

However, Baldwin's critique is marred by a perspective which blinds him to a positive interpretation of Stowe's use of passive characterization. Harris points out that although Baldwin is right to look for motive force in Stowe's people, "his mistake is looking for it with realist tools; the various forces that impel Stowe's figures are more allegorical than psychological" (660). Baldwin also fails to acknowledge that not all black men in the novel are totally restricted to passivity, nor are all whites invariably active and aggressive. The picture Stowe paints of aggressiveness is far from complimentary. Rather, she shows that it too possesses duality. George Harris's anger offers no positive alternatives or solutions to his own racial dilemmas. Similarly, Legree, as a result of his violence toward Tom and Cassy, must pay the price of horrendous fear before his impending death at the novel's close. Finally, Baldwin's criticism ignores the fact that passivity characterizes white men as well as men of color. Consider, for example, St. Clare's apathy and his unwillingness to make decisions, or Senator Bird's duality in voting one way and acting another. Similarly, the older Master Shelby is unwilling to do the right thing and stand up for his slave. Instead he passively succumbs to the slave trader Haley's wicked offers. The passive actions by these white characters are indeed intended by Stowe to suggest weakness.

Yet critics who conclude that all passivity necessarily flaws Stowe's characterization or who infer that Stowe's subliminal intent was to suggest racial inferiority in Tom's character fail to realize that passivity can be either a weakness or a strength, as Thoreau's doctrine of civil disobedience convincingly illustrated in 1849, three years before the publication of Stowe's novel. Uncle Tom's reluctance to strike out against Legree does not establish his weakness as an African American, because he demonstrates that strength can be shown in his refusal to act as well as in action. In later generations, both Mahatma Gandhi and Martin Luther King continued to assert the power of passive resistance. Tom's passive resistance to Legree need not be seen as either a flaw or a stereotype of the way whites want African Americans to act. Rather, passive resistance demonstrates the innate power of matriarchal actions such as compassion and education by example. Again, many critics who fluctuate in their opinions of whether aggressiveness is positive and passivity is negative or vice versa have ignored the mirror image of white and black characters who possess this personality trait. Stowe does not advocate either alternative as an absolute. Rather she admirably balances the two states, indicating her own ambivalence about them as well as her feelings that neither race can determine which is better; the paradoxical duality dominates.

Since the narrative posits passive resistance as a strength possessed by the feminine, the so-called weakness of Tom that is deplored by Baldwin cannot be read as a negative trait, and the cultural claim that Tom no longer fits his gender and is thus emasculated by Stowe cannot be supported by the text. Instead, the feminine is exalted by Stowe, as the acts of Mrs. Shelby, Mrs. Bird, and Tom's wife, Aunt Chloe, indicate. The rhetoric of equality is also evident here, since the male is no longer dominant; female traits seem more favorable in Stowe's eyes. The narrative values women's tenderness in its portrayal of female characters attempting to teach their sons to follow their examples.

In fact, following the example of several white women in the novel, white men also demonstrate God's mercy and compassion. In addition, both male and female African-American characters practice the feminine tenderness and sympathy so associated with Uncle Tom, traits of the ideal and uncommon Christian hero. These positive qualities appear to rub off on all characters Tom approaches, including Cassy, Emmeline, George Shelby, St. Clare, Sambo, and Quimbo. His femininity affects others for their good rather than lowering their self-esteem. Moreover, the impassivity Uncle Tom exhibits in his death balances his aggressive defiance of Legree's demand that he flog others. Thus by avoiding stereotypic masculinity and its demands of violence and retribution, Uncle Tom becomes a Christ figure who in his servanthood and slavery obtains freedom both by turning the other cheek and by refusing to seek revenge for the atrocities committed by Legree.

Stowe's rhetoric of equality is most evident in her depiction of Christianity and its effect on believers. Her use of religion might initially seem to suggest that her belief in equality does not apply finally to blacks, since she continually characterizes blacks as rejected by God and without a real country of their own (see *Uncle Tom's Cabin*, [1986] 290, 298, 323, 487, 502, 512, 523). Yet

Stowe reiterates through both little Eva and Tom that God does not and has not forsaken any of His people, including the black race. Though the white St. Clare as well as blacks may sense desertion by God, the narrative proffers deliverance, whether by entering a new world (both temporal and eternal) or by receiving strength to endure all trials one must face. George Harris, the younger Shelby, and Cassy each illustrate the potential to overcome racial oppression by means of faith.

Finally, both white and black characters share the Christian belief in an afterlife where they can finally attain justice and equality. George Harris, Prue, St. Clare, and the woman on the riverboat who jumps overboard, all come to believe Uncle Tom's and little Eva's hope that death is a positive release from the oppression and problems that real life inevitably brings. Through these characters, Stowe reiterates an ultimate truth, that only heavenly bliss will *really* end *all* types of suffering: the oppressive pasts of Ophelia and St. Clare, the oppressive entrapment based on gender inferiority experienced by Mrs. Shelby and the African-American woman Cassy, and, finally, the oppressive racism so evident in the novel's main story line. Stowe's continued emphasis on death as the only true release might have evolved from her own recognition that, despite attempts to attain social equality, the vestiges of racial, gender, sexual, and ethnic discrimination would remain. Thus Yarborough might be accurate in his criticism that Stowe appeals for the colonization of Liberia for blacks (63) because people could not construct a truly just, interracial society on this continent. Yet perhaps Stowe's inability to envision a just society in America is positive rather than evidence of inherent bigotry. Her solution of a new black nation in Africa recognizes that only a new country like Liberia or heaven could help slaves so inculcated with inferiority by their master's condescension and by their lack of education that they relegated themselves to roles of dependency. Such a recognition, rather than weakening the novel, strengthens it with a prescient realization that even 100 years later, and no matter what the reason, America would have achieved no permanent solution to enslavement of the Other. Stowe anticipates that, as long as human history continues, people will perceive inequalities among themselves and claim the inherent superiority of one to another.

Despite Stowe's attempt to establish a rhetoric of equality, critical opinion continues to call for suppression of her work.

In 1956, the University of Chicago's children's librarian, Mary Eakins, defiantly advocated censoring rather than reassessing the text. Eakins writes that the novel

> probably has a place in [the] high school library as an original document in America but it has no place in an elementary school collection nor should it be recommended for general reading in high schools. Mrs. Stowe has employed stereotypes to which there is the greatest objection. Immature readers will not recognize the book as a social document but will accept it at face value [which] can do much harm in perpetuating stereotypes and fostering misunderstandings. (qtd. in Furnas 109–10)

Similarly, Furnas suggests that *Uncle Tom's Cabin* merely aggravates racism and accounts for whites' continued ignorance and presumption of superiority. He condemns Stowe's novel for broadcasting and perpetuating notions that created "fresh debts of viciousness as fast as old ones were paid" (105). Labeling the novel as "irresponsibly sententious and God's instrument for punitive ends on the Negro race" (106–7), Furnas also states that the sweeping generalities of *Uncle Tom's Cabin* have encouraged racist doctrines to "plump out their previous inchoate notions" (108). He goes so far as to claim that *Uncle Tom's Cabin* is racist propaganda designed "to instill or strengthen racist ideas" (107). Since the sermonizing associated with Uncle Tom's character still shapes white attitudes toward Negroes, Furnas submits that the novel is a mildly vulgar, subtly tainted piece of cultural subversion, as was Charles Dodson's *Alice in Wonderland*.

Although the story is not the work of a novice and (as Stowe's *Key to Uncle Tom's Cabin* documents) was written from an immense mass of accumulated thought and material, critical biases (themselves shaped by racial ideology) continue to obscure our assessment of *Uncle Tom's Cabin* and make it difficult to admit that, whether created by a white skin or a black, the text expresses genius. Nevertheless, just as Henry Louis Gates discovers "binary oppositions" in his reading of Frederick Douglass, this trait is also evident in Stowe. Despite its flaws, readers continue to be moved by the novel and, as Gates states, "to be transfixed by the passages that read [themselves]" (2). The novel continues to offer a positive reading experience because it moves readers not only to outrage but occasionally to a social consciousness that results in action instead of mere recognition of and lip service to a cause. If it produces such reactions, how then can it be intentionally racist in character? As the first novel that presented blacks as central characters, it continues to deserve a place in the canon and can be recuperated from its lower-echelon status. Despite Stowe's co-opting of the voices of the Other, to suspect that subversion was her intent requires a willful overlooking of the other elements of black and white equality signaled by other events in the novel.

If readers look at the message of *Uncle Tom's Cabin* with moderation, they will recognize the flaws (the authorial intrusion, the didacticism, the over-idealization of the angelic Eva), but they will also continue to assert the value of discourse by nonminorities about minorities, whether it is centered on social, ethnic, sexual, or racial differences. This moderate approach is exemplified in Leslie Fiedler's reading of the novel. Fiedler calls *Uncle Tom's Cabin* "a various and complex book" while pointing out that "Uncle Toms" have been unfairly labeled contemptuously, while the advocates of force are not called "Georges." Fiedler also suggests that both Uncle Tom's and little Eva's archetypal stature is evidence of the cultural hope for forgiveness and mutual love and that their personalities provide the twin images of guilt and reconciliation that represent the truth of slavery for many Americans ("Harriet" 113).

Perhaps Edmund Wilson's commentary is most accurate; he argues that the novel has declined in popularity not as a result of its own flaws but primarily because of the dramatizations of its text, which in the late 1800s had become half-minstrel show and half-circus (117). Wilson praises the vitality of the characters, who leap into being despite the occasional ineptitude of Stowe's style. He also points out that, of all the religious people in the novel, only Uncle Tom adheres to the principles of faith espoused by the white characters. Wilson concludes that "it is hard to imagine what other book of the period compares with Stowe's" (121) and agrees with novelist Anthony Burgess that even in Tom's hammiest postures as a slave, his character is totally convincing (124).

Although the text exposes both paternalism and proprietorialism as flaws of the white system, Stowe's major contribution was "taking the Negro seriously as subject matter and 'attempting' an accurate transcription of their dialect" (Burgess 126–27). As Stowe argues for abolition through the text, she convincingly illustrates that African Americans are not innately inferior to whites either intellectually or spiritually. If the novel degrades one race, it attributes such degradation to the slave system and does not suggest the author's intent to maintain it. Society's inculcation of self-hatred in individuals is shown by the novel to stunt both mental and moral development, and Stowe pleads for tolerance rather than encouraging such latent prejudices. The text suggests that for Stowe, African Americans were fully human beings caught in a system that denied their humanity and violated their most ordinary sensibilities. To argue otherwise, that Stowe was inherently racist and that the novel subverts its primary intention, is to miss the argument of the novel for full and equal humanity. Such an argument denies that Stowe minimizes innate or genetic racial differences and stresses social and environmental factors in the formation of character.

Although some critics contend that the situation of slavery in America has changed only minimally since 1852, we cannot judge Stowe's novel as unsuccessful and unreadable because we have not attained its ultimate goal of liberation and equality. Refusing to look at such a complex work that on first examination may appear to be "politically incorrect" can seriously endanger potential dialogue on social, gender, ethnic, and racial issues. Just as both positive and negative elements characterize America as a nation, so too they characterize *Uncle Tom's Cabin*. Consequently, readers must examine both poles before asserting the novel's "truth." Such consideration reveals the text's movement toward a rhetoric of social and racial equality. Only by continuing to discover the many facets of *Uncle Tom's Cabin* can Stowe's critics perceive the power of the whole.

Then and only then will the critical revolution advocated by the political correctness movement be complete rather than fragmented. Critics must recognize the thick political discourse that has led to how America imagines race. As Scarbrough concludes:

> If we recognize race as a political discourse, then we can see that the old questions of mimesis are no longer tenable. They have held their position longest in studies of race relations in America, but they are only part of an older network of hegemony that prefers solos or choruses to polyphony. Voice is in itself a construct, one full of games and co-optings which hearken back as they pull forward, and race becomes a game of representational constructions by which authors (re)form the parameters of discourse. (7)

By noticing the points at which critics begin to misrepresent their own (not the culture's) agendas, we can avoid confrontations about how whites answer the black question or how African Americans re-answer the white question. As Harris reminds us, we must realize that

> critics have axes to grind. Interpretations often say as much about the interpreter as they do about the text. Once these axes are identified—as silly, deluded or irrational, on the one hand, or reasonable and relevant on the other—the worth of an interpretation is much clearer. Some critics are, by the nature of their interests, blind to certain elements of the text. Others, for the same reason, are particularly perceptive to some elements. . . . Mapping one interpretation against another brings both the text and the criticism into clearer focus. (661)

# 12

SUSAN MARIE NUERNBERG

## The Rhetoric of Race

One cannot be proslavery and for racial equality at the same time; but acceptance of racial equality is not a necessity for being antislavery. An illustration of this is that African Americans in this country did not achieve civil rights until one century after emancipation.

Readers of Stowe who reject *Uncle Tom's Cabin* because it portrays African Americans in an offensive way should not discard the book.[1] In the first place Stowe's purpose in writing it is not to advocate racial equality in the secular and social sphere. Her aim is to put an end to slavery, to what stood in opposition to her traditional notions of Christian morality. In the sense of putting an end to moral injustice, Stowe's novel does contribute positively to the cause of abolition. Of all the books written for the cause, it was the one most widely read and discussed. As Ralph Waldo Emerson notes in "Success," *Uncle Tom's Cabin* "encircled the globe, and was the only book that found readers in the parlor, the nursery, and the kitchen in every household" (286).

Readers of Stowe who endorse the novel but are disappointed with her failure to envision a society where whites and Africans live as equals should know that the purpose of her book is not to promote social equality. The abolition of slavery is necessary from Stowe's point of view to purify the nation of sin. Stowe's desire to see slavery abolished derives not from ideas about earthly equality but from the concept of equality before God. Her ideology is conservative in essence because it calls for a retreat to traditional religious and moral values. While she spoke out in *Uncle Tom's Cabin* against the injustices of slavery, she said nothing with real meaning about racial injustice.

To understand why this is so, we should look into the prevailing ideas on race during Stowe's period. In the first half of the nineteenth century, racial thought in the United States attempted, among other things, to justify the enslavement of blacks and the expulsion and possible extermination of Native Americans. During this period, popular periodicals, the press, and many American politicians eagerly sought scientific proof for racial distinctions and for the prevailing American and world order. As Reginald Horsman states in his study of American racial Anglo-Saxonism, *Race and Manifest Destiny*, "The intellectual community provided the evidence they needed" (3). Like other popularizers of racial thought in American letters, such as Mark Twain and Jack London, Stowe helped set the tone for the American understanding of race and contributed to the discussion of the topic even though she herself avoided the subject of racial equality on the economic and political level.

Pre-Darwinian scientific theories of racial difference debated whether differences were innate or the product of environment. Environmentalism, the idea that all races were members of the same species and had a common remote ancestry (also known as "monogenesis"), attributed differences in color, anatomy, intelligence, temperament, and morality to differing physical and social environments, especially to climate and to ways of life produced by "savagery" and "civilization." This view of environmentalism, or monogenesis, was articulated by Samuel Stanhope Smith in his 1787 *Essay on the Causes of the Variety of Complexion* and exemplifies the dominant view of eighteenth-century science on the origin of racial differences.

In 1830, Smith's view of environmentalism was challenged by Charles Caldwell's theory of polygenesis, or the separate creation of the races as distinct species, which appeared in his book *Thoughts on the Original Unity of the Human Race*. The view accepted in scientific and intellectual circles in the 1840s and 1850s was that the races of humankind had been separately created as distinct and unequal species of the *genus homo* and not simply as varieties of the same species. The assertion that racial differences were innate and not the product of environment gave proslavery advocates a scientific basis for viewing blacks as members of separate and permanently inferior species.

The theory of polygenesis, as George M. Fredrickson observes, "amounted to a scientific apology for Negro slavery and Indian extermination" (77), and its leading exponent, Dr. Josiah C. Nott, was stridently proslavery. Although recognized as a leading scientist, Nott described his field of study as "the nigger business" or "niggerology," and his supposed research supported a white racial supremacist justification for slavery and for imperial expansion.[2] Nott was a quack practitioner of a pseudoscience; however, his views are indicative of the racial preconceptions of many scientists and intellectuals in the 1840s and 1850s who defended America's racial status quo. *Types of Mankind*, the eight-hundred-page study of separate species of humankind by Nott and Gliddon, sold out immediately in 1854. Its main thesis is that pure-blooded nonwhite races are incapable of high intelligence or of civilization without the infusion of some white blood.

The monogenic-origin theory had no real champion among scientists in the middle of the nineteenth century. They tended to dismiss it as murky theology or superstition. Louis Agassiz, the Swiss biologist who emigrated to America in 1846 and joined the Harvard faculty in 1848, accepted the doctrine of the plural origins of humankind, which complimented his hypothesis that specific differences within the plant and animal kingdom were the result of separate creations brought about by the environment of differing regions of the earth.

Given the widespread acceptance of the theory of polygenesis at this time, one wonders why proslavery advocates did not attempt to justify slavery on the grounds that blacks were of a separate, in other words inferior, species from whites. Apparently, such a position was perceived as undermining the Bible. The *Richmond Enquirer* on July 6, 1854 declared that some slaveholders might accept the "infidel" doctrine of diversity because it seemed to be an excellent defense of slavery, but they would be wrong. Southerners could afford no such defenders as Nott and Gliddon if the Bible was to be "the price it must pay for them" (qtd. in Gossett, *Race* 66). Neither abolitionists nor Southerners embraced the arguments of the polygenesists because both groups perceived the doctrine of diversity as contradicting the Bible. Stowe, who saw herself and her audience as followers of Christ in America, carefully, and understandably, avoided any reference in *Uncle Tom's Cabin* to the scientific discourse on race.

In her preface to *A Key to Uncle Tom's Cabin*, Stowe explains that this work "has so far overrun its limits that she [Stowe] has been obliged to omit one whole department;—that of the characteristics and developments of the colored race in various countries and circumstances" (iii). Nowhere in her writings does Stowe exhibit her awareness of the widespread search going on in the scientific community to measure and classify human races. Nor does Stowe question the superiority of the Anglo-Saxon "race," even though she portrays Uncle Tom as a true Christian and through George Harris declares her view that the African "race" is higher morally than the Anglo-Saxon. Stowe gives the blacks moral superiority but not social equality, and she depicts whites as aggressive and dominant, not as docile, meek, or "Christian."

Fredrickson points out that at this time in Europe, "intellectuals associated with the romantic movement in thought and literature were turning away from the universalism of the Enlightenment and embracing, at least implicitly, concepts of inbred national character and genius that could readily be transmuted into concepts of 'racial' superiority" (97). Notions of white or Anglo-Saxon superiority are common among abolitionists. Theodore Parker names the supposedly hereditary traits of the Anglo-Saxon in his sermon on "The Nebraska Question" of February 12, 1854. These traits include the Anglo-Saxon's "restless disposition to invade and conquer other lands; his haughty contempt of humbler tribes which leads him to subvert, enslave, kill, and exterminate; his fondness for material things . . . ; his love of personal liberty . . . [his] most profound respect for . . . established law. . . . And his . . . inflexible, industrious, and unconquerable will" (qtd. in Fredrickson 100). As Fredrickson points out, such descriptions of the Anglo-Saxon were being formulated and popularized at the very time when the slavery controversy focused attention on the African character.

Roy Harvey Pearce argues in *The Savages of America*, his study of the Indian and the idea of civilization, that whites writing about "savages" were writing for other whites about whites, using the Indians to represent all that the white is not. The same applies to Stowe in that she is writing for other whites about whites (in urging them to abolish the sin of slavery), and her black characters represent all that whites are not. Tom becomes a symbol of the Christian virtue and piety that is lacking in white America, as evidenced by passage of the Fugitive Slave Law that forced the North to police and return the South's black runaways.

Although Stowe forges a link between alleged Negro virtues and Christian ones, she was not the first to do so. This was the theme of a series of lectures given in Cincinnati, where Stowe lived, during 1837 and 1838 by Alexander Kinmont and published in 1839 as *Twelve Lectures on Man.*

In Kinmont's scheme, it was the blacks and not the whites who would first achieve millennial perfection because he imagined that blacks, unlike whites, had the divine attributes of mercy and benevolence.[3] The whites had a divinely appointed mission, according to Kinmont, but it was limited to the development of the arts, sciences, and intellect. Blacks were destined to develop a "far nobler civilization" than whites, Kinmont reasoned, because the white's "innate love of dominion" rendered him or her "almost constitutionally unable to be a true Christian" (qtd. in Fredrickson 105).

Stowe appropriates Kinmont's rhetoric of the black as a natural Christian in her portrayal of Uncle Tom as childlike, affectionate, docile, and patient. In addition, George Harris's claim that "the African race has peculiarities, yet to be unfolded in the light of civilization and Christianity, which, if not the same with those of the Anglo-Saxon, may prove to be morally, of even a higher type" clearly echoes Kinmont's vision of millennial perfection.[4]

Kinmont's rhetoric of the moral superiority of the enslaved black appealed not only to Stowe but to other abolitionists, among them William Ellery Channing, who in his 1840 essay "Emancipation" expands upon Kinmont's idea of black potentialities. Omitting the visionary or prophetic quality of Kinmont's lectures that appealed to Stowe, Channing emphasized the idea that since the African nature was "affectionate and easily touched," they were peculiarly susceptible to religious experience. Channing argued that Africans were natural candidates for Christian perfection because they "carr[y] within [them], much more than we, the germs of meek, long-suffering, loving virtue" (qtd. in Fredrickson 106).

Of course there is no germ or gene for "loving virtue" or for "meekness" in any race or individual. Rather, Stowe, Channing, and Kinmont all misinterpret social reality between whites and blacks as racial differences. Slaves were made to suffer, to endure, meek and obedient, by force of slavery; it is not in their culture or in their genetic makeup to do so. Blacks, whether slaves or free, always appear to whites such as Stowe and Kinmont to lack a culture of their own. As a result, their behavior is always misunderstood by them. Stowe signals her own cultural distance in the preface to the American edition of *Uncle Tom's Cabin*, where she explains that "the scenes of this story . . . lie among . . . an exotic race, whose ancestors . . . perpetuated to their descendants, a character so essentially unlike the hard and dominant Anglo-Saxon race, as for many years to have won from it only misunderstanding and contempt" ([1965] 1).

Next to Tom's excessive meekness, the most controversial aspect of Stowe's rhetoric of race, and the one that many blacks feel they cannot afford to let pass uncriticized, is her apparent endorsement of emigration when she depicts George Harris relocating his family to Liberia in search of "an African nationality" at the end of the book. The rationale for this cultural and fictional endorsement is rooted in the period's confusion of social reality and racial differences.

Both Stowe and Kinmont express the idea that "it is the inherent meekness of the blacks which gives them a special talent for religion" (qtd. in Gossett, *"Uncle Tom's Cabin"* 83). And both describe the future of Africa in the language of the millennium. Kinmont declared that the blacks had been "dragged" away from their "homeland" in Africa to which they were naturally attached, and that "the destined seat of [their] future glory and civilization" was Africa. In the "sweet and mellow light" of Africa would flower "the attributes of divine beneficence" of the blacks. There they would create a civilization "from the cultivation of innocence, simplicity and virtue" (qtd. in Gossett, 85).

Like Kinmont, Stowe saw Africa in terms of the millennium as the home of a future high civilization. She argues through the character of George that blacks *ought* to return to Africa. In the chapter "Results," Stowe quotes a letter of George's. In this letter, George embraces colonization and rejects social equality as his goal. George writes, "The desire and yearning of my soul is for an African *nationality*. I want a people that shall have a tangible, separate existence of its own" (608).

The American Colonization Society, founded early in the nineteenth century, was supported largely by Protestant clergy who hoped to establish a colony of converted ex-slaves in Liberia to contribute to the conversion and redemption of Africa.[5] The aim of colonization, besides the physical removal of free blacks, was gradual elimination of slavery. This was to be accomplished by encouraging voluntary manumission and by offering a way of freeing slaves without augmenting the number of free blacks on American soil. Many of the members of colonization societies believed that blacks could not be assimilated into American society and, if freed, would remain an alien and troublesome presence. Free blacks, however, would thrive in Liberia because they would no longer be hampered in their efforts to improve themselves by white prejudice and discrimination, which were seen as fundamental facts of American life that could not be changed. Stowe embraces this stance when she has George reject social equality with white Americans. George's letter continues:

> But, you will tell me our race have equal rights to mingle in the American republic as the Irishman, the German, the Swede. Granted, they have. We *ought* to be free to meet and mingle, —to rise by our individual worth, without any consideration of caste or color; and they who deny us this right are false to their own professed principles of human equality. We ought, in particular, to be allowed *here*. We have *more* than the rights of common men; —we have the claim of an injured race for reparation. But, then *I do not want it*; I want a country, a nation, of my own. (610)

Stowe appropriates the ideas and language of the colonization movement to talk about the desirability of expatriation for free blacks from the perspective of George. We may ask what is her purpose in having George, obviously the most "white" of her black characters, declare he does not want social equality with whites in America?

In 1830, colonization failed to get government subsidy, and the movement was replaced by abolitionism. William Lloyd Garrison, in 1831 and 1832, denounced the colonization society as a proslavery plot designed to rid the South of the troubling presence of free blacks. This position was endorsed by the American

Anti-Slavery Society. According to Fredrickson, the actual function of colonization had been to provide an outlet for humanitarian feelings at a time when slavery was in fact developing and flourishing in the South (28). In contrast to proponents of colonization, who saw white prejudice as an insurmountable obstacle, the abolitionists saw slaveholding as an individual sin.

At a meeting of the American and Foreign Anti-Slavery Society in New York on May 11, 1853, which Stowe did not attend, "the evil influence of the last chapter of *Uncle Tom's Cabin* in the matter of Colonization" was discussed (Gossett, *"Uncle Tom's Cabin"* 294). Dr. Leonard Bacon, a close friend of the Beecher family, arose and reportedly said that "Mrs. Stowe had told him [Bacon] that if she were to write *Uncle Tom's Cabin* again, she would not send George Harris to Liberia" (qtd. in Gossett, 294). However, in her next antislavery novel, *Dred* (1856), Stowe once again embraces colonization.

Many abolitionists shared Stowe's stand on colonization, as evidenced in their wide acceptance of her novel. However, her position was only one among many articulated within the abolitionist movement of her day. Clear alternatives are presented in the writings of Frederick Douglass and Martin R. Delany. Both Douglass and Delany were, like Stowe, critics of the Fugitive Slave Law, but unlike her, they were both opposed to the aims and methods of the colonization movement. Frederick Douglass rejected colonization, as he bluntly told Stowe in a letter of March 8, 1853 (published in *Frederick Douglass' Paper* in December 1853), for the reason that "we are *here*, and we are likely to remain. Individuals emigrate—nations never. We have grown up with this republic, and I see nothing in her character, or even in the character of the American people as yet, which compels the belief that we must leave the United States" (qtd. in Levine 82).

In March 1853 Douglass visited Stowe at her home in Andover, Massachusetts, to solicit her support for his project, which was to open a trade school for free blacks in Rochester, New York. Douglass saw that education in industrial and mechanical skills was needed for blacks to overcome racist practices in apprenticeships (such as the one he recounts in his *Narrative* that prevented him from working in the New Bedford shipyard as a caulker), and he reasoned that such education would "elevate" blacks from a forced dependency on merely servile occupations

(Levine 79). Douglass argued in his *Paper* of December 2, 1853, that "the most telling, the most killing refutation of slavery, is the presentation of an industrious enterprising, thrifty, and intelligent free black population. Such a population I believe would rise in the northern states under the fostering care of such a college as that proposed" (qtd. in Levine 79). Douglass insists that racist practices in apprenticeships are a real obstacle to the abolition of slavery, which can be overcome in practical ways. He is in touch with a real need to "elevate" blacks in America through practical education from their condition of poverty, ignorance, and degradation. His reliance on Stowe's help to realize the industrial school that was at the center of his plan for the elevation of blacks in America doomed him in the eyes of Martin Delany, who emphasized black self-determination without white philanthropy—and for good reason.

In the fall of 1850, Delany was denied entrance to Berkshire Medical School in Pittsfield, Massachusetts, because he had no intention of practicing medicine in Liberia under the auspices of a colonization society. Delany then applied to Harvard Medical School and was admitted for the fall term in 1850, but he was not allowed to return for the second semester (along with two black students who were sponsored by the Massachusetts Colonization Society) because some students protested.[6]

Delany's disenchantment with America can be linked not only to the refusal of Harvard to allow him to complete his medical studies. It also coincides with the passage of the Fugitive Slave Law in 1850, which led some blacks to fear that slavery would be nationalized; this fear caused emigrationist sentiment to grow among Northern free blacks. In his 1852 book *The Condition, Elevation, Emigration, and Destiny of the Colored People of the United States*, Delany writes that "a people capable of originating and sustaining such a law as this, are not the people to whom we are willing to entrust our liberty at discretion" (156). Because Delany saw equality as unobtainable for blacks in America, he embraced an emigrationist stance. When William Lloyd Garrison raised some objections to this book, Delany simply pointed to America's failure to treat whites and blacks with equality. In the *Liberator* on May 21, 1852, Delany defended the belief expressed in his book that it was impossible to find a solution to the unequal status of black people within America. He wrote, "I have no hopes in this country—no confidence in the American people—with a few excellent exceptions—therefore, I have written as I have done, Heathenism and Liberty, before Christianity and Slavery" (qtd. in Griffith 16).

In his 1852 book, which Douglass did not review in his *Paper*, Delany points out that white antislavery leaders had failed to support the upward mobility of blacks and that within their own circles they had made no real effort to allow African Americans equal status. "We find ourselves occupying . . . a mere secondary underlying position, in all our relations to them," he wrote (27). Delany felt that blacks could overcome white racism only by developing a separate course of action for themselves. This was necessary because he saw the primary goal of whites to be the subjugation of blacks.

Delany envisioned black economic determinism through the development of large-scale cotton, sugar, and rice enterprises in the Caribbean that would successfully compete against and destroy the economy of the Southern states where these goods were produced with slave labor. Delany's embrace of back-to-Africa differs from Stowe's in that Delany saw the regeneration of Africa as thwarting white racial domination, whereas Stowe saw it as fulfilling a prophecy of millennial perfection on earth. Most African Americans, however, such as Douglass, felt that blacks should continue to work for equality in America (Griffith 28).

William Lloyd Garrison, who achieved recognition as the most radical of American antislavery advocates, founded the New England Anti-Slavery Society in 1832, helped organize the American Anti-Slavery Society in 1833, and published a weekly paper, the *Liberator*, from 1831 to 1865. In the early 1830s he had called for the repeal of a 1705 law in Massachusetts forbidding interracial marriages. He also advocated women's rights and nonresistance. The Civil War forced Garrison to choose between his pacifist beliefs and emancipation, and he supported freedom for slaves at the expense of his pacifist beliefs. Emancipation, however, brought to the surface the latent conservatism in his program for freed blacks, whose political rights he was not prepared to guarantee immediately.

Garrison's response to *Uncle Tom's Cabin*, published in the *Liberator* of March 26, 1852, reflected his support of emancipation over pacifism during the Civil War. He questioned Stowe's stance on nonresistance by pointing out that for her and other whites it is acceptable to return blow for blow, but that blacks must turn the other cheek. He found her use of different standards of conduct for whites and blacks objectionable, as well as her use of religious principles to discuss social injustices. "[W]hen [blacks] are spit upon and buffeted, outraged and oppressed, talk not then of a non-resisting Savior—it is fanaticism! Talk not of over coming evil with good—it is madness! Talk not of peacefully submitting to chains and stripes—it is base servility! Talk not of servants being obedient to their masters—let the blood of the tyrants flow" (qtd. in Gossett, "*Uncle Tom's Cabin*" 170). Garrison's critique of Stowe's elevation of black character through the portrayal of Uncle Tom as a flawless and "non-resisting Savior" anticipates the most devastating criticism *Uncle Tom's Cabin* would receive in the twentieth century.

James Baldwin in his now famous 1949 essay "Everybody's Protest Novel" says that Stowe robbed Tom of his humanity and of his sex. Why? Stowe distorts and rejects Uncle Tom's humanity and his sex because she conceives of him as a spirit and not as a body. She imagines him as extraordinarily forbearing, not as suffering. Uncle Tom's triumph is "metaphysical" and "unearthly" since, as Baldwin notes, "he is black, born without light, it is only through humility, the incessant mortification of the flesh, that he can enter into communion with God or man" (Ammons ed. 94). Furthermore, Uncle Tom is denied that "something resolutely indefinable, [and] unpredictable" that is, according to Baldwin, "nothing more than the disquieting complexity of ourselves" (93) because Stowe's prime concern or frame of reference as a novelist is not (as it should have been) "a devotion to the human being, his freedom and fulfillment" (93).

Rather, the "virtuous rage of Mrs. Stowe," Baldwin writes, "is motivated by nothing so temporal as a concern for the relationship of men to one another—or, even, as she would have claimed, by a concern for their relationship to God—but merely by a panic of being hurled into the flames, of being caught in traffic with the devil" (94). Instead of revealing some vast reality or "truth" that has the power to "free us from ourselves" (93), Stowe's book exhibits, in Baldwin's words, a "theological terror, the terror of damnation."

> Here, black equates with evil and white with grace; if being mindful of the necessity of good works, she could not cast out the blacks—a wretched, huddled mass, apparently, claiming, like an obsession,

her inner eye—she could not embrace them either without purifying them of sin. She must cover their intimidating nakedness, robe them in white, the garments of salvation; only thus could she herself be delivered from ever-present sin, only thus could she bury, as St. Paul demanded, "the carnal man, the man of the flesh." (94)

Baldwin presents an opposing image of a black man from *Native Son* in the figure of Bigger Thomas—an image of bitterness, hatred, and fear—a character whose fear drives him to murder and his hatred to rape, and who through this violence redeems his manhood. The tragedy for Bigger is not his being born black in America, Baldwin says, but "that he has accepted a theology that denies him life, that he admits the possibility of his being sub-human and feels constrained, therefore, to battle for his humanity according to those brutal criteria bequeathed him at his birth" (97). Unlike Uncle Tom, Bigger Thomas resorts to violence to establish his identity. Violence is still a necessary part of black strategy for identity and survival because blacks are still categorized as subhuman and denied a fully human complexity. Baldwin clearly identifies with Bigger, who is not willing to pay white culture's price of being black, a price constituted by his humanity and his manhood—the price Stowe extracted of Uncle Tom. Baldwin presents a new perspective—from one who identifies himself with Bigger Thomas and not with an emasculated Uncle Tom.

Black writers prior to Baldwin and Richard Wright had, of course, created alternatives to Uncle Tom, but with Baldwin we come full circle in a sense to impassioned acceptance of precisely what was denied the black male in American culture as captured and frozen by Stowe. This does not, however, prevent Baldwin from recognizing *Native Son* as "a continuation, a complement of that monstrous legend it was written to destroy" (97). Bigger Thomas's violence is like Uncle Tom's meekness—excessive and ultimately life denying.

Writing after Baldwin, J. C. Furnas is one of the first critics to call into question the kind of sweeping statements Stowe makes in *Uncle Tom's Cabin* about both the "African race that can never have existed" and the "Anglo-Saxon race that never did either." Furnas comments on how the Uncle Tom image has evolved from a symbol of that which is best in Christian society, as Stowe portrayed Uncle Tom, to a boot-licking, servile black in his relationship with whites. The Uncle Tom type also says yes to anything proposed by whites that does not seem to favor blacks. Furnas defines the term as meaning "a weakling or a coward, a traitor, a wily manipulator, one who engineers a race sell-out or one who for any reason failed to 'speak up' for his race at an important point" (Ammons ed. 105).

Besides tracing the evolution of the connotation of an Uncle Tom, Furnas identifies as an error Stowe's assumption of an "African race" that was consistent in appearance and spirit. He argues that such illusions about Africa and an "African race" begot the curious colonization movement aimed at somehow solving the problem of the American Negro. A second error in Stowe's conception of race that Furnas points out is her belief that miscegenation or crossbreeding would create mulattoes who owed their energy to "white blood." Furnas has access to new genetic evidence suggesting that much crossing and re-crossing has gone on among various "races" of homo sapiens (321–27).

While Furnas is one of the first generation of literary critics armed with knowledge of what the study of genetics might potentially be able to demonstrate, he admits that "promising approaches is about all that genetics yet offers" (314). Nevertheless, he brings to Stowe criticism the awareness that "you can ponder nature and nurture as ingeniously as you please, but without the basic concepts of genetics you will never make head or tail of what actually goes on" (314). Besides pointing out that as a popular work Stowe's book broadcast and perpetuated notions of race that were simply wrong, he also acknowledges that those same notions of race "plague us today" (105).

Stowe's ideas are confused and contradictory, and they are representative in general of ideas and attitudes held by others in the abolitionist movement and in antebellum American culture. But we need not downgrade Stowe because she shared many of the misconceptions about race common in her day, nor need we underestimate her humanitarian point of view.

While early critics tended to feel that Stowe had abused whites in order to elevate blacks, the modern reader is likely to find that Tom has racial features that now connote a degrading stereotype. Tom does in fact have religious traits that Stowe admired—and not just in blacks. As Gossett points out, "Stowe would be intensely surprised, were she alive now, to discover the opinion that she had denied Tom humanity by making him excessively meek"

("*Uncle Tom's Cabin*" 103). Tom does show strength of character late in the novel by refusing to deny his faith or to betray his fellow slaves who were in hiding. Stowe's contemporary critics thought that nobody could be so noble—especially no black could. Thus, they thought Stowe had evaluated the character of Tom too high, not too low. He represents Stowe's idea that the highest virtue is Christian love. According to Gossett, "Tom's religion amounts to the proposition that since God loves mankind, people should love one another" (104). Stowe herself claims to have had a vision while taking communion in church in February 1851 of a saintly black man being mercilessly flogged and praying for his torturers as he died. Her vision of a black Christ inspired both the character of Uncle Tom and the story's climax in Tom's death/victory (Douglas, "Introduction" 8).

Tom *is* too noble, meek, and forgiving to be a realistic character, and Stowe presents Tom as if these are qualities that blacks have naturally. In *A Key*, Stowe states her attitudes on the spiritual character of blacks explicitly: "The Negro race is confessedly more simple, docile, childlike and affectionate, than other races," she said, "and hence the divine graces of love and faith, when in-breathed by the Holy Spirit, find in their temperament a more congenial atmosphere" (41). Obviously this description was meant as a compliment; we see that if blacks are like this because of their racial character, why credit them for it? Stowe did not hold the "good" whites in the novel to any such standard of virtue and holiness. Gossett is correct in noting that Stowe's white characters are presented as "all the more admirable because they do not take the blows of fate meekly" ("*Uncle Tom's Cabin*" 107).

Stowe's book makes a powerful appeal for abolition and for the equality of all souls in the eyes of God. But Stowe is not a revolutionary. Stowe's goal, which is to purify Christianity, is a moral reform. As the September 3, 1852, London *Times* review of *Uncle Tom's Cabin* was quick to reprove, "she should surely have contented herself with proving the infamy of the slave system, and not been tempted to establish the superiority of the African nature over that of the Anglo-Saxon and of every other known race" (qtd. in Ammons, *Critical Essays* 27). In elevating the black as thoroughly virtuous, she spells out what is lacking in the white and makes virtue very acceptable to readers because while blacks are elevated, they are no threat. Uncle Tom is not threatening because, as Baldwin points out, he is not a human being. Rather he is an inspiring myth.

What did *Uncle Tom's Cabin* accomplish on the social level? Nothing. It does nothing for social justice and the promotion of racial equality. It does not contest white political superiority or any of the real issues that needed to be addressed that this book could have discussed. A good debate would have focused on racial equality and social equality. What were the problems? Once free, what was the place of blacks in American society? Stowe prefers not to deal with that but instead to solve the problem of slavery by sending free blacks to Africa. They are elevated in fiction; in reality, they are not high enough to be part of society.

The positive contribution Stowe's book makes is to vilify slavery and by so doing to help the cause of abolition, because the novel was so popular and widely read. The book was popular because Stowe does not question the political and racial dominance of whites, nor does she envision participation of free blacks in American life, and because the book preaches an ideal of high and pure faith. Stowe's novel is not threatening to whites in the sense that it does not disturb their status. She says slavery is wrong morally and equates it with sin. She thus allows proslavery whites to feel guilty but not threatened because she is not advocating racial equality on the economic and political level.

Like other abolitionists, Stowe tended to see herself as a moral and religious reformer, not a social reformer. In a letter of January 6, 1853, to the Earl of Shaftsbury, Stowe explains her purpose in writing *A Key to Uncle Tom's Cabin:* "It is God's will that must be told, and I am the unwilling agent" (qtd. in Katz ii). In her role as instrument of God, she works to abolish slavery, which she sees as a sin, a violation of God's law. Stowe writes in the preface to *A Key* that her goal in writing is "to bring this subject of slavery, as a moral and religious question, before the minds of all those who profess to be followers of Christ in this country" (iv). In doing so, we might note, she could fulfill her own religious responsibilities and help to reassert clerical influence over the nation at large.

At a time when race was debated in scientific communities to prove equality (the monogenesis theory) or inequality (the polygenesis theory), and in literary circles, thought shifted from eighteenth-century universalism to nineteenth-century romantic endorsement of national character. Stowe went straight to the public. She understood that by bringing this debate from scientific or literary fields to the religious ground, her voice could carry further and would bring social change regarding slavery. Her strategy was to depict a flawless black character, Uncle Tom, a sexless human and a monument of religious virtue and devotion to God. Uncle Tom is perceived as too virtuous and too noble to be real, and thus he is not threatening.

Stowe writes about innate virtue and disposition to religion in the black race to emphasize what the whites lack or must acquire, which are precisely those virtues and the inclination to worship God the way blacks could. Her goal of helping free blacks from slavery was a cleansing of the Christian religion. She abuses the white by elevating the black to teach her white readers a moral lesson. However, she also alleviates white fear of a racially mixed society by offering the image of a free black, but at home in Africa.

# NOTES

1. For more information on the reception of *Uncle Tom's Cabin*, see Ammons, *Critical Essays*, and Levine.

2. For more information on the racial views of Nott, see Fredrickson 78–82.

3. For more information on Alexander Kinmont, see Fredrickson 104–6 and Gossett, *"Uncle Tom's Cabin"* 83–85.

4. Stowe, *Uncle Tom's Cabin* (Douglas 1981) 610. All future quotations from the novel are from this edition, cited by page number in the text.

5. For more information on the colonization movement, see Fredrickson 8–11 and Griffith 109–12.

6. For more information on the Harvard Medical School episode, see Griffith 13–14.

●

R. C. DE PROSPO

# Afterword/Afterward:
# Auntie Harriet and Uncle Ike—
# Prophesying a Final Stowe Debate

A woman in the black power movement was
considered, at best, irrelevant. A woman asserting herself was a pariah. A woman attempting the role of leadership was, to my
proud black brothers, making an alliance
with the "counterrevolutionary, man-hating,
lesbian, feminist white bitches." It was a violation of some black power principle that was
left undefined. If a black woman assumed the
role of leadership, she was said to be eroding
black manhood, to be hindering the progress
of the black race.

—Elaine Brown, *A Taste of Power*

"I'm tired of black Uncle Toms telling us to
lay down our guns when the police are out
there killing us," he said to enthusiastic ap-
plause. "I'm not dumb. Check this out: If you
are going to go out and fight a war for the
white man, you better damn sure stand up
and fight for yourself."

—Keith Peddler

271

# I

This conclusion will consist primarily of meditations on racism and tolerance, canonicity and marginality, relevance and irrelevance, and so I will begin, following closely the example of Thoreau's play on the appropriateness of his readers' expectations in the opening of *Walden*, by digressing.

The delicate and potentially explosive issue of Faulkner's racism and sexism is also not impertinent here, so I must confess a troubled recognition that the book by Faulkner that I am enlisting as a powerful critique of the reactionary ideologies—including white racism—that underlie sentimental WASP abolitionist noblesse oblige, as well as its later WASP liberal and radical counterparts, contains the following example of vintage Southern gentry humor: "[T]he Negro he was shooting at outed with a dollar-and-a-half mail-order pistol and would have burned Boon with it only it never went off, it just went snicksnicksnicksnicksnick five times and Boon still blasting away and he broke a plate-glass window that cost McCaslin forty-five dollars and hit a Negro woman who happened to be passing in the leg only Major de Spain paid for that; he and McCaslin cut cards, the plate-glass window against the Negro woman's leg" (227). When Huck Finn, in a novel that has been banned because of its supposed racism, blurts out in response to Mrs. Phelps's "Good gracious! anybody hurt?" "No'm. Killed a nigger" (Clemens, *Adventures* 173), both Huck and Huck's author are at least partially shielded by Huck's having immediately before "trust[ed] to Providence to put the right words in my mouth when the time come" (171), also by Huck's presently "going a good deal on instinct" (173), finally by Huck's being about to assume the disguise, immediately after he tells this particularly callous stretcher, of Tom Sayer (175).[1] The parable of decadent Southern patrician mastery comically beset enjoys fewer contextual safeguards in *The Bear* and can more easily be taken as a cheap racist masculinist joke told exclusively at the expense of its victims, not at all of its teller.

What Faulkner seems to me to get exactly right in *The Bear*, however, both retrospectively and prophetically, is the ambivalence—personal and cultural self-satisfaction alternating with personal and cultural guilt and self-hatred—that can be driving privileged white advocacy of black underclass virtue and power: a kind of limousine liberalism that a white Southern male shabby aristocrat literary descendant of Faulkner would later famously deride when it surfaced in the guise of fundraisers for Black Panthers held in Manhattan penthouses by Leonard Bernstein and his circle. Faulkner's version of "radical chic" in *The Bear* is of course neither so politically liberal nor quite so socially pretentious as Tom Wolfe's. When Faulkner adds on to the first three chapters of *The Bear* a structurally protuberant and stylistically exorbitant chapter four, and then superadds on to that a coda that only seems to return to the stylistic conventionality that only seems to be adhered to in the first three chapters, he not only alerts inattentive readers to the psychological and cultural density that had always been implicated in the motivation of the hunters. Faulkner serves notice also that the child prodigy, the Mozart, of all hunters has grown up to become more than just a virtuoso woodsman. Destined ultimately to age into the sad prototype of avuncularity, "uncle to half a county and still father to none" (287), Ike McCaslin even at twenty-one is capable of prolonging chapter four with tireless, interminable, contrarian, ideologue fanaticism:

> He used a simple egg to discover to them a new world where a nation of people could be founded in humility and pity and sufferance and pride of one to another. . . . He saw the land already accursed even as Ikkemotubbe and Ikkemotubbe's father old Issetibbeha and old Issetibbeha's fathers too held it, already tainted even before any white man owned it by what Grandfather and his kind, his fathers had brought into the new land which He had vouchsafed them out of pity and sufferance, on condition of pity and humiliation and sufferance and endurance, from that old world's corrupt and worthless twilight . . . and no hope for the land anywhere so long as Ikkemotubbe and Ikkemotubbe's descendants held it in unbroken succession. Maybe He saw that only by voiding the land for a time of Ikkemotubbe's blood and substituting for it another blood, He could accomplish His purpose. Maybe he knew already what that other blood would be, maybe it was more than justice that only the white man's blood was available and capable to raise the white man's curse, more than vengeance when . . . He used the blood which had brought in the evil to destroy the evil as doctors use fever to burn up fever, poison to slay poison. . . . Maybe He knew that Grandfather himself would not serve His purpose because Grandfather was born too soon too, but that Grandfather would have descendants, the right descendants; maybe He had foreseen already the descendants Grandfather would have, maybe He saw already in Grandfather the

seed progenitive of the three generations He saw it would take to set
at least some of His lowly people free. (248–49)

Which "lowly people," reached finally at long last at what is
not even nearly the end of Ike's ingenious reconstruction of
Southern history, are the African Americans whom Ike's grandfather had not only owned and kept and exploited as chattel
slaves; with whom Ike's grandfather had not only miscegenated
and fathered myriad unacknowledged mulatto children; but with
whose unacknowledged mulatto children Ike's grandfather undeniably and abhorrently had committed incest. Destined ultimately to be more than just set free, African Americans are
the people chosen to inherit America, according to Uncle Ike's
private hybrid teleology, which seems initially an astonishing
gumbo of vulgar Whig historicism, cryptofundamentalist Protestantism, neo-American exceptionalism, and proto-Afrocentrism.
But what Faulkner can be said to warn in compounding Ike's
tirade of such apparently disparate zealotries as the conventional
Western historiographico-religio-nationalist three on the one
hand, and the renegade Afrocentrist one on the other, is that all
WASP advocacy of one of the two peoples whom white America
has perenially laid most low must always already be white racism
in disguise—white racism disguised, especially and most perni-
ciously, from itself.[2]

Ike will eventually bring himself up short, realizing that the
very ferocity of "his repudiation . . . to him, too, even in the act of
escaping (and maybe this was the reality and the truth of his need
to escape), was heresy: so that even in escaping he was taking
with him more of that evil and unregenerate old man who could
summon, because she was his property, a human being because
she was old enough and female, to his widower's house and get a
child on her and then dismiss her because she was of an inferior
race" (282). But even long before this slight, guilty, hesita-
tion, even while Ike's righteous anger is at its peak, his pride in
his own race and his contempt for the other are easily detect-
able: in Ike's unquestioning acceptance of the divine providential
rectitude of the Columbian conquests; in Ike's minimizing of
the ethical significance of the introduction of chattel slavery to
America by implying vaguely that some prior Native American
practices were just as bad (tribal warfare? the acquisition of
trophies and captives being supposed by Ike to have made Native

Americans particularly vulnerable to the corruptions of cupidity
and pride?); in Ike's honoring "Grandfather"—old Carothers
McCaslin who mates with his mulatto daughter, Tomasina,
which issues in Tomey's Terrill, the firstborn of the African-
American branch of the McCaslin family tree, and which issues
also in both Tomasina and Tomasina's mother, Eunice, commit-
ting suicide—with the same orthographic and syntactical deference with which Ike honors God;[3] in Ike's finally, and most
patronizingly, attributing the liberation and ascension of the
black race entirely to the labors and sacrifices of whites, even old
depraved Carothers an instrument of God, even the impudent
reckless Southern Confederacy the means to ensure that the
white race be thoroughly, fratricidally, extirpated, and of course
finally ascetic backwoods Ike himself, the third-generation
"right descendant" (249) of old Carothers who identifies with the
one just white man, John Brown, "simple enough to believe that
horror and outrage were first and last simply horror and outrage
and was crude enough to act upon that" (273).

What prompts Ike to bring himself up short, and what will end
this lengthy detour of my own, is Ike's attempt to counter the
whole massive weight of his culture's white supremacism with
a recitation of African-American racial advantages: "Endurance . . . and pity and tolerance and forbearance and fidelity and
love of children . . . whether their own or not or black or not. And
more" (282–83). "This is Harriet Beecher Stowe territory," as
Bryan J. Wolf comments in what may seem a very different
context, an unearthing of the sentimentalism and feminism that
may just as unexpectedly be seen to underlie Emanuel Leutze's
huge 1848 historical canvas, *The Storming of the Teocalli by
Cortez and His Troops* (425). But Ike's reconstruction of Southern
history is as gaudily tendentious and sensationalist as is Leutze's
of Spanish colonial history, and Leutze's purely masculinist, bor-
derline pornographic representations of rape and pillage dominate the painting as obviously as Ike's purely masculinist, bor-
derline gynophobic and antidomestic celebrations of the hunt
dominate Ike's fanaticism ("There was always a bottle present . . .
which not women, not boys and children, but only hunters
drank" [Faulkner 186]), and so it is fair to suggest that the tension that Wolf discovers between the marginal domestic elements of the painting and its central antidomestic elements—
"the self-sacrifice of mothers in the background and at the

canvas's sides" versus "[m]ale acts of violent struggle in the foreground" (425)—is analogous to a tension in Ike's fanaticism between a hesitant and conflicted approbation of traditional feminine attributes in African Americans on the one hand, and a predominating celebration of the traditional masculine ones of the hunters on the other. But Wolf would situate Leutze, the painter, in "Harriet Beecher Stowe territory," or perhaps as not quite having reached it yet, really, because the tension that Wolf discovers in Leutze makes the painting "more an allegory of gender than of politics" (425) only according to Wolf's, and perhaps also implicitly to Stowe's, understanding, not according to Leutze's, who is implicitly after something a bit lesser, and lower; I am trying to situate only Ike, the character, there, and would thus advance Faulkner to some territory ahead of the rest. Recall Ike's private hybrid teleology, even more mongrel than that tiny fyce dog with whom Ike identifies, who knows no better than to rush the enormous bear (Faulkner 204), more mongrel even than Old Carother's progeny; add now to the conventional Western three ideologies—Whig historicism, Protestant fundamentalism, American exceptionalism—a conventional Western fourth: sentimentalism and the cult of domesticity. Faulkner, dead white male sexist racist canonical American master ne plus ultra, creating in the febrile demogoguery of Uncle Ike the very figure of co-optation.

It's all co-opted, all white racist, even the feminism, even, especially and most discouragingly, the non-Western, nonconventional Afrocentrism.

## II

Of course it remains possible still today to go backwards and pursue some reactionary goal of reinstating the old white male chauvinist Americanist scholarship, and the old canon of nineteenth-century dead white male, for the most part contemporaneously underappreciated, culturally alienated, and thus predominantly antisentimental and ironist, dead white male writers whom this scholarship canonized—and who, symbiotically, propped this scholarship up in turn. But it is impossible to do so without going backwards, being reactionary, being white, being male chauvinist, and, if not necessarily being quite dead, then at least being quite old.

The high quality and sophistication of every one of the essays in this volume are sufficient proof that hitherto nontraditional study of hitherto noncanonical figures has become, somewhat paradoxically, rather highly evolved in the scholarly culture of the United States. The position of Stowe, and everything that Stowe has come to represent in contemporary American literary and cultural scholarship, is really by now well past the point of being established; Stowe's position is in the process, rather, of being consolidated and enhanced. We have come so far, in fact, that we can today identify the predominant agon of *Uncle Tom's Cabin* as neither an ethical, nor a regional, nor a historical one; critical attention to what is being represented in the novel, which used to be the cynosure of whatever scholarship the novel inspired, is being superseded by critical attention to the process of representation itself. When, for prime example, Catherine O'Connell in the introductory essay establishes as the conceptual framework for all of the essays to follow the heteroglossic interplay among rhetorics of religion, republicanism, and sentimentality, she is confidently taking for granted that the criticism of Stowe has moved through the provinces of homiletics, intellectual history, aesthetics, even through those of canon formation and race debate in the United States, to emerge into the realm of the infralinguistic. The world of *Uncle Tom's Cabin* that will concern the majority of these essays is a richly semiotic one in which all manner of varying and antagonistic sign systems conflict.

Thus Jan Pilditch will dramatize a Stowe struggling with the quasi-oedipal, gender-bending anxieties that accompany Stowe's appropriation of the genre of satire, that for Stowe was not only potentially unladylike in its Billingsgate invective, but which for Stowe was unmistakably and indelibly marked as the exclusive preserve of male authority. Thus Bradley Shaw discovers "pliability" as a pattern of discourse so deeply implicit in Stowe, and also, necessarily, in antebellum American culture generally, that it can control equally both sides of even the most divisive political debates, a discourse so dominant in its capaciousness that it frequently seems in Shaw's characterizations to be itself writing the authors, rather than being written by them, a discourse that is in effect way beyond "rhetoric," at least as rhetoric is conventionally defined. And thus Melanie Kisthardt will detect in the polyvocalities of *Uncle Tom's Cabin* a staging of the whole, supranational, semiotic interplay between patriarchy and its subversive feminist Other, opening up a text that used to be of interest exclusively to Americanist intellectual historians and, more recently, to Americanist scholars of women's literature, for theorizing at the highest, the most current, international, feminist, and intertextual levels.

The charge that Stowe's rhetoric is merely sentimental or merely racist is confronted only obliquely by these first four essays, each of which discovers rhetorical complexities that implicitly make this, the most common charge against Stowe, seem either trivial or moot. The charge is met head-on by Isabelle White, James Bense, and Michael Meyer, whose concentration on the aesthetics and the ethics of Stowe's rhetoric remains still very finely focused, however, on literary values. For White, the discourse of death is to be understood not as a stigma of the maudlin, unconsidered exploitation of grief in Victorian popular culture, but as an important sign of the popular cultural desire for—and anxiety about—community; White closely rereads death scenes in *Uncle Tom's Cabin*, as well as the conventional obsequies of the entire period, to uncover a very serious, a very interesting, a virtually Nietzschean premonition of a-theism and anomie—and all of this to be found in one of the apparently least sophisticated and most meretricious of nineteenth-century popular cultural phenomena. Bense confronts what is probably an even more vulnerable aspect of Stowe's rhetoric, her black racial stereotypes, finding them not only effective and necessary given Stowe's mass readership—Bense shows at length that mere mimetic or verisimilar representations of slavery did not, historically, move the mass readership—which is to defend Stowe according to the definition of rhetoric, old style; Bense also goes on more audaciously to claim that a darker, a virtually Melvillian, indeterminacy and deviousness can be seen to complicate Stowe's representations, such that even the servile manners of Black Sam are imbricated with subversive rage, which is to defend Stowe according to a much more current, much more expansive theoretist definition of rhetoric. And Meyer dares forensically to counterattack against those whom he depicts as condemning the novel as sufficiently racist to invalidate its avowed abolitionist aspirations, first by recalling Stowe's prolific statements of purpose in writing the novel, as well as the equally clearly documented historical consequences of its publication, second by teasing out of it a still genuinely affective stylistics that continues to elicit responses of outrage and compassion even from contemporary readers.

The essays by Helen Westra and Mason Lowance on Stowe's connection to American religious tradition may appear to deviate significantly from the underlying theoretical orientation that I have identified in all of the essays I have discussed thus far. But, although written for the most part in a more familiar new critical and intellectual historical idiom, they both provide yet another example of the linguistic emphasis announced in O'Connell's introductory essay, this one within a more strictly Americanist framework. The rhetoric of Puritan millennialism, especially as it was developed in eighteenth-century Massachusetts Bay Colony by Jonathan Edwards and carried down by Edwards's New Light ministerial descendants, is not just absorbed by Stowe at the feet of the scores of ministers who fathered, mentored, and, finally, married her, although this sort of direct interpersonal influence on Stowe was of course massive and is massively documented by Westra; the rhetoric itself, as is also massively documented by Westra, contains a nascent American nationalism that can only come to detest with a missionary zeal the chattel slavery that had been permitted to compromise America's national virtue, and that must be eradicated not only in order to fulfill, but as an integral part of the fulfillment of, the theologo-nationalist dream that America, among all other, older, nations, is destined to be the only one pure enough to host Parousia, rapture, millennium. Lowance, similarly but more broadly, focuses on a more generally biblical rhetoric, that of typology, as prophesying not only eschatologically the first and second comings of Christ, but also—implicitly, tropologically—the persistence of itself perennially as a rhetoric of interconnectedness and reconciliation, thus making a claim no less linguistically oriented in its way than those of O'Connell, Pilditch, Shaw, and Kisthardt for the existence of a rhetoric—a "language of Canaan"—so powerful and lasting as to join together texts as apparently disparate as those of the poets of the Old Testament, Freneau, Barlow, Franklin, Edwards, Dickinson, Whitman, and Stowe.

After having said all this about these essays' success in making it new on the subject of Stowe, I must go on to concede that all of these essays are indebted to a rich and varied scholarly culture of modern literary history, contemporary cultural and ethnic studies, and feminist theory in the United States. All of the essays in this volume, in particular those in part 2 by Shaw, White, and Susan Roberson, as well as those in part 4 by Bense and Susan Nuernberg, can be placed within the very long U.S. scholarly tradition of cultural criticism, one that might be said to extend all the way back at least to the work of Perry Miller; I refer here not only to Miller's final, overtly popular cultural essay on nineteenth-century commercial publishing, *The Raven and the Whale*, but also to his earlier seminal work on Puritan theology and rhetoric, which can still be said, no matter how much scholarship on early American material and folk culture has recently been done, fairly to represent the world that common people in Massachusetts Bay Colony shared with Harvard-educated ministers and wealthy merchants.[4] And the essays by Westra and Lowance in part 3 build on an even older American literary historiographical tradition of tracing continuities between Puritan origins and various nineteenth-century literary and cultural outcomes—a scholarly tradition that extends at least as far back as Frederick Lewis Pattee, and perhaps even farther, to the nineteenth-century amateur and popular American literary historical efforts of George Putnam, Samuel Lorenzo Knapp, Samuel Kittel, James Freeman Clarke, and Henry T. Tuckerman, and extending all the way forward to the very latest comprehensive American literary history to be published, the *Columbia Literary History of the United States*, edited by Emory Elliott. Finally, the essays of O'Connell, Pilditch, and Kisthardt in parts 1 and 2 are certainly the most untraditional in the volume, but even these essays, in their very deftness and security, rely on the currency of feminist theory and discourse analysis that have become such a scholarly lingua franca that even the most traditionalist of scholars—and there are plenty of them, especially in Americanist circles—must prove themselves competent in them in order to continue publishing. The new, methodologically diverse, countercanonizing scholarly culture is still very much in the process of growing and articulating itself—in such forms as, among a great many others, a 1992 NEH summer seminar whose title named only a single book, Stowe's *Uncle Tom's Cabin*, as well as the present collection of new essays devoted just to Stowe's *Uncle Tom's Cabin*, all of which derived from work done during that seminar.[5]

Thus the current status of the very late-twentieth-century

scholarly debate over Stowe's worthiness to be read or taught, or talked or written about in scholarly venues, seems to me to be approaching the current status of the mid-nineteenth-century political debates over slavery (Who is going to argue today that slavery was not wrong?) or the biological inequality of the races (Who is going to argue today that the races are not biologically equal?) or the veracity of Stowe's representation of slavery in *Uncle Tom's Cabin* (Who is going to argue today that Stowe deliberately perjured herself?): the result no longer being very much in doubt, the debate seems less appealing to those who would take sides than to those who would study the taking of sides—that is, theorists, who have known since at least the work of Foucault that controversy never forecasts the death of the subject of controversy but, quite the contrary, proves its vitality.

## III

And yet . . .

There remain nonetheless unstilled ominous, even biblio-cidal, murmurings. There remains, for example, in so many of the essays a pianissimo sounding of that old, stubbornly undead 1949 racialist denunciation of *Uncle Tom's Cabin* by James Bald-win, which seems to haunt the entire volume—Meyer's passion-ate defense of the novel cites not only Baldwin but several other detractors, quoting them all copiously enough to risk letting them make the case he wants so earnestly to counter; even O'Connell's high theorizing contains sotto voce allusions to Baldwin in both her opening and her closing. And realize that the Baldwin who is so troubling in this regard is a very, very, early, tightly packed and conflicted Baldwin—tightly packed and con-flicted at least about masculinity and sexual preference, which must of needs qualify and complicate in about a hundred ways anything angry and bitter that Baldwin is saying about the dis-semination of black male racial stereotypes in a universally pop-ular abolitionist fiction written by a female sentimental writer in the antebellum United States. That Baldwin's 1949 essay still lives, even among the most advanced scholarly advocates of Stowe, even at the advent of the third millennium, must certainly say less about the seminal status of the 1949 essay in Baldwin's corpus, or even about the seminal status of Baldwin in the canon of American literature, than it does about lingering defensiveness and uncertainty among white U.S. intellectuals over continuing to promulgate the novel that Baldwin felt inclined, for whatever deeply ambivalent reasons, so vigorously to attack. And consider that such hesitations in this regard may be a luxury only of scholars; consult less scrupulous arbiters of the popular cultural historical understanding and you find that the new "American Adventure" pavilion at Disney World's EPCOT selects as the hallmark of Frederick Douglass's career Douglass's endorsement of . . . *Uncle Tom's Cabin!*—an endorsement that, in the context of Douglass's entire, difficult and tactical, involvement with the abolitionist movement, must be suspected to represent something less than the unequivocal faith in the possibility of racial harmony in the United States than Disney wants its visitors to believe.[6]

Slightly more overt, but still only implicit, is the potential for damage to *Uncle Tom's Cabin* permitted by Susan Roberson's findings, based on a truly comprehensive survey of popular cultural texts, which confirm that Stowe's definition of femininity seems to be quite unambiguous and monovocal, indeed, at least when placed in the context of the rhetoric of domesticity that prevailed in the popular culture of Stowe's time. Although perhaps only affirming the theoretist axiom that truth is context-bound, and that Stowe's rhetoric in the company of contemporaneous popular cultural women's texts is a genuinely different phenomenon from the phenomenon it becomes when placed in that of anachronistic ones by Kristeva and Bakhtin, Roberson's work nonetheless at least gives pause to anybody who would extol *Uncle Tom's Cabin* as revolutionary in its representation of gender.[7] Somewhat less covert are the damaging implications of Susan Nuernberg's scrupulous intellectual historical reconstruction of the antebellum rhetoric of race, which must restore for us a specialized and ultrafine theological distinction between the temporal and eternal status of human beings, and also a related, neotheological one between slavery and racial inequality. Again, with all theoretist contextualist axioms aside, Nuernberg's depiction of Stowe's racism, which makes Stowe seem not much more fundamentally humane in her plans to repatriate manumitted African Americans than are our own current Balkan or Israeli ethnic cleansers, is about as sobering to those who would bring to the surface Stowe's underlying racial egalitarianism as Roberson's depiction of Stowe's sexism is to those who would have Stowe protofeminist.

Most dangerous of all to the continuing viability of *Uncle Tom's Cabin*, and most explicit in its challenge to this viability, is the perspective of Sarah Ducksworth—who is, not coincidentally, the single African-American contributor to the volume. Despite being about as forgiving as Bense or Meyer toward Stowe's racial stereotypes, being at least as mindful as they of the historical strictures constraining both Stowe's own and the white antebellum popular culture's perception of African Americans, Ducksworth cannot help but give voice to a minority opinion on the novel to which all of the other contributors have only indirect access: that is, of course, that of the contemporary African-American descendants of those African-American slaves racially stereotyped throughout *Uncle Tom's Cabin*, contemporary African can Americans who must, even as they are in the process of reading *Uncle Tom's Cabin*, revise, renarrate, correct, speak back to the novel in order to restore the dignity and humanity that the novel so often denies their African-American forebears. It is no accident that Ducksworth, more than any of the other contributors, works hard to include alongside her discussion of Stowe discussion of an archive underrepresented in the other essays, and undervalued by the white supremacism that Stowe undeniably—undeniably to all but her most loyal defenders—upheld: first, albeit only implicitly in Ducksworth's exposition, there are the nineteenth-century African-American slave narratives that modern scholarship is still only in the process of recovering; second, there are the modern and contemporary African-American writings that Ducksworth cites, and that seek in the slave narratives their own independent ethnic, literary, and ethical foundations.

So there is, after all, an interested party to the Stowe debate who tends to be excluded from it, and for an excellent reason: his participation would not perpetuate the controversy, and thereby its subject, but threatens to end it, thereby putting into question the very existence of *Uncle Tom's Cabin*, thereby forcing the contemplation of the novel's disappearance. This interested party, of course, is hardly obscure or unlikely; he would almost undoubtedly be identified as the prime interested party by anybody—anybody in the United States surely, maybe anybody anywhere, in accordance with the nearly universal knowledge of at least the bare plot of *Uncle Tom's Cabin* that proponents of the novel so often cite, by now almost obligatorily, as evidence of the novel's great appeal. This interested party of course constitutes a whole category of late-twentieth-century aggrieved U.S. person, a category of aggrieved person who of course has urgent claims on our attention, and who is not so easily dismissed as the backwards reactionary old white male chauvinist scholars whom I earlier declared moribund in today's scholarly climate. That this category of aggrieved person is of course known to exist, and to be not only formidable but very threatening, is proven indirectly by his relative invisibility in these essays—even Ducksworth only seldom concentrates on him specifically. What I call in my title a final Stowe debate prophesies the eventual participation of this hitherto excluded category of aggrieved person, and so is therefore on the one hand not really a debate, but on the other hand, extremely final. If this final Stowe debate is to take place, there may be no more debating *Uncle Tom's Cabin* for a very, very, long time to come.

Everybody knows to whom I am referring. We just cannot forget James Baldwin; we just cannot ignore the still very current, and still wholly unambiguous, idiomatic meaning of "Uncle Tom" (as both Nietzsche and after him Heidegger knew, language, even especially colloquialism, has a mind, and voice, of its own: *die Sprache spricht*); and we just cannot underestimate the fury of "proud black brothers" recalled by Elaine Brown, former lover of Huey Newton, former head of the Black Panthers, current partner of a rich French companion living in comfortable retirement in Paris, but still raging and frightened over that proud black male fury nearly a generation after the fact, whose anger and fear I quoted as my first epigraph.

To say that there is gender conflict in contemporary African-American culture in the United States vastly understates the case. African-American writer Ishmael Reed makes more than a small living following—sometimes literally following around—successful African-American woman writers, most notoriously Alice Walker, like a one-man truth squad determined to correct their supposedly prejudiced and untruthful representations of African-American males; Reed fueled the controversy over Anita Hill's allegation that she had been sexually harrassed by Supreme Court Justice Clarence Thomas, made during her testimony at the latter's U.S. Senate confirmation hearings in 1992, by criticizing those who would defend Hill and attack Thomas as perpetuating racist and sexist assumptions about the violent sexuality of African-American males.[8] Conversely, African-

American scholar and theorist Henry Louis Gates, Jr., who has spent a significant portion of his scholarly energies sponsoring the recuperation of lost or neglected African-American women's literature, probably enjoys the greatest potential to become a reconciler of African-American men and women, especially in the academy, and thereby is probably the person most capable of balancing and maybe even counteracting Reed's confrontational black masculinist partisanship. But even Gates has been frequently attacked as insensitive to African-American women and not long ago found himself, along with his fellow African-American theorist Houston Baker, implicitly labeled a sexist of a particularly low order in a particularly nasty exchange with the African-American scholar Joyce Joyce, and in of all places the usually high-theorist pages of *New Literary History*. "[N]othing," according to Joyce, "better illustrates the spiritually impoverished predicament in which Black America finds itself than Tina Turner's song 'What's Love Got to Do with It?' and its accompanying video" (322). Gates had adduced the song as an ironic commentary on Joyce's unquestioning idolatry of the love of African-American literature; Joyce missed the irony—not just Gates's, but also Turner's, who is singing, in this her first major hit after she left the abusive relationship with husband Ike, ironically about the abuse of the discourse of love in African-American male courtship, and African-American procuring, as well. Joyce continues, now widening her aim to include not just Tina, but Gates, Baker, and literary theory in general: "The song suggests to our young people not only that sex for sex's sake (like writing for writing's sake or 'the "free movement" of writing itself') is a legitimate or healthy attitude, but also that the biological satisfaction the sex act brings is the ultimate fulfillment" (322). Joyce concludes what has now become a furious attack with the African-American woman's coup-de-grace; Gates and Baker "failed to demonstrate love and respect for a Black Sister" (382).

Who would venture to introduce *Uncle Tom's Cabin* into the mainstream of contemporary literary and cultural scholarship in the United States certainly risks spreading to the academy the gender warfare that already afflicts African-American culture—risks provoking a confrontation between two academic constituencies with many common interests, and which have frequently allied themselves in the common cause of liberalizing the structure not only of the curriculum but of the institution itself. That African Americanists and white feminists have as yet to my knowledge not skirmished in any major way over *Uncle Tom's Cabin* I will guess is attributable to the forbearance of the former. This forbearance may prove to be less than eternal. I would not want to have the obligation to explain, certainly not to Ishmael Reed or Amiri Baraka, not even to Henry Louis Gates, Jr. or Houston Baker (Spike Lee? Mike Tyson? Rodney King?), that the tender docility of Uncle Tom is to be read just as an illustration of the feminizing of identity, the floating of gender, or just as an example of one of the voicings of the carnivalesque polyvocalities of the novel; nor would I like to have the task of explaining to them the novel's purging of the angry and violent George as just some sort of historically defensible concession to contemporaneous abolitionist nervousness, or the novel's conversely relishing the minstrel subserviency of Black Sam as just the novel's sly endorsement of the African-American folk culture of subversive tricksterism. Consider the response of the contemporary African-American man in the United States, even the highly cultured and educated African-American man, to all of these characterizations of African-American manhood in light of the response of the "proud black brothers" to Elaine Brown's ascendancy to the head of the Black Panthers, and in the light also of African-American gang leader Keith Peddler's scorn for "black Uncle Toms" which I quoted as my second epigraph. And consider the response even to some of the novel's most prominent, positive, racially unobjectionable or racially neutral, attributes, this time in light of Faulkner's exposure in *The Bear* of the virtually omnipotent power for co-optation wielded by the various articulations of dominant American nationalist ideology. The enormous popularity of the novel, connecting it through Stowe's sentimentality to virtually the entire literate world of the nineteenth century, and beyond, coupled with the novel's obvious citation of Protestant sermonic, theological, and ecclesiological tradition in New England, connecting it through Stowe's intellectual lineage to what is still accepted by most American scholars as the main source of modern American culture, can be combined to substantiate a claim for *Uncle Tom's Cabin* that is much more grand, and much more potentially racially divisive today, than just that the book was responsible for the Civil War. I often suspect that just as all great fortunes, according to Balzac's

famous aphorism, conceal a great crime, so do all great popu-
larities conceal a great complacency. Suppose the dual filiations
of *Uncle Tom's Cabin* to both nineteenth-century U.S. popular
culture and Puritan New England to represent an implicit, irre-
sistable reassurance that the second, the more recent, and the
more stubbornly indelible of the two great crimes on which
America was founded was just an aberration; that deeply imbed-
ded in America's colonial Puritan history, and ubiquitously dis-
seminated throughout America's early nationhood, there is to
be found not racism but racial toleration, not systematic vi-
cious inequity but spontaneous virtuous equality, America from
the beginning now and forever innocent and humane at heart.
White culture, including white scholarly culture, in the United
States too often forgets that self-determination (which may be
culturally predominantly gendered male but which can of course
float between the sexes) and underprivilege (which may be historically predominantly African-American in the United States
but which can—and is currently beginning to—float among any
number of ethnicities) can be more infuriated by being vouch-
safed a gift of freedom than by being oppressed. Abolition, which
is the white race's great glory, can offend African-American
pride a great deal more than can slavery, which is the white race's
great shame.

## IV

I find it curious and stimulating that such meditations as these,
on the end of America, perhaps on the end of nationality in
general, on the end of a book, perhaps on the end of literature
in general, can commence not only with readings of marginal
literary phenomena but also with a reading of what are perennially considered American masterpieces by American masters. I
began with Thoreau and Faulkner, and colaterally with Mark
Twain, not to counter countercanonizing with the restoration of
the original canon. Quite the opposite. I sought, like Frank
Lentricchia, to find at the very center of American literary canonicity—for Lentricchia it is Frost's "The Road Not Taken"—"a
savage little undoing of our mainline literary and political sentiments" (86–87), and thereby to decenter as forcefully, maybe
more forcefully, from the inside out rather than from the outside
in. What I want to do now, in conclusion, in what is really only a

postscript to this postscript, is to explore a bit farther the theoretical implications of this "undoing" or decentering for the definition of the subject matter of literary study, and simultaneously to speculate on the odd blindness to our own popular culture often exhibited by even the most apparently liberal, even permissive, scholarly attentiveness to the popular cultures of the past.

Beyond the understandable professional tact and self-protectiveness that prompts many literary studies of the traditionally noncanonical—especially those that dare to consider the non- or the subliterary—to present themselves as hyperdisciplined, virtually disciplinarian, the disparity between the hedonism of popular culture on the one hand and the sobriety of many studies of popular culture on the other might be attributed to what seems today an invidious distinction between the way in which contemporary popular culture is produced and consumed and the way in which contemporary scholarship is produced and consumed. The former is made by opportunist entrepreneurs of unreliable employment and unfixed residence who gamble on achieving short-term celebrity, and who then capitalize on it with what often seems frenzied and short-sighted greed; the former is consumed by a fickle, browsing audience with the attention span of . . . whatever hyperbolic figure of lazy inattentiveness happens to reign at the current moment for the proponents of cultural literacy; the pace of exchange is hip-hop, relentless, hypnotic, prolonged without effort, and promiscuously accepting of external beats—so long as they are brief. The latter is made by persons either employed for life or aspiring to be (although this situation is rapidly changing, at both the top and the bottom of the profession), who are usually rewarded for conformism and punished for trying to single themselves out, whose earnings are distributed more-or-less evenly over the course of a lifetime, and whose life's work is structured identically and done from a sedentary position; the latter is consumed by readers of serious books, a group constituted either by volunteers who consider themselves members of an elite and embattled minority, or by conscripts drafted into either unwilling or indifferent brief service in the ranks of college students; the pace of exchange is glacial, and xenophobically unadmitting of extraneous distraction.

If anything like this disparity holds true, then the contemporary scholarship of popular culture can only possess a fundamental underlying commitment to transform its subject matter. This is most readily, and invisibly, accomplished by focusing on a popular culture that is not presently a popular culture, either a culturally exotic one or, as in the case of Stowe studies, a past one. Thus cultural studies in the United States, and incidentally foreign-language study as well, which very frequently present themselves as in especially close touch with a living, grass-roots subject matter, are revealed to have very divided and impure loyalties. Both convert phenomena that they themselves promote as valuable precisely because capable of being acquired first-hand, either involuntarily or inadvertently, into second-hand school subjects that can be learned only by students who must somehow be kept by teachers off the streets.

*Uncle Tom's Cabin* is not just currently a former best-seller. It is currently no kind of best-seller at all, the contrary of a best-seller. This not because it is too long: length is no barrier to sales, now no more than then, as witness, for a comparable, middle-brow, racially alert, almost currently popular example, *The Bonfire of the Vanities;* length is actually more a barrier to canonization, as witness the perennial exclusion from anthologies of American literature of *Moby-Dick*—all the masterpieces that fit, we print. *Uncle Tom's Cabin* is other than a best-seller, rather, because it is foreign, in need of mediation, of instruction, is a school text that makes work for schoolteachers. I would not minimize the importance and necessity of this work—especially if we are going, god help us, to teach this novel to Keith Peddler and other contemporary young black males in the United States, for instance. But I would note that occasional glancing aside at the popular culture our students walk into the classroom already knowing—probably better than their teachers do—can yield insights as interesting as, and sometimes more troubling than, a fixed stare at the school text at hand, or a glassy-eyed one at the impossibly voluminous archive of related historical materials in the library. Glancing aside notices that *Uncle Tom's Cabin* may have just been edged out of first place as the biggest best-seller of all time, excepting the Bible, of course, by *The Road Less Traveled* by M. Scott Peck, M.D., which is the longest-running title on the *New York Times* best-seller list, so long-running that the Guinness people are considering it for the world championship;[9] more than an idle fact for statistics fans, the extraordinary popularity of this notorious melange of pseudo-psychobabble and feel-good confectionary religiosity, combined into a sort of social-scientific theodicy to justify pain, death, and evil to a credulous contemporary U.S. readership, might contribute valuably to a general critique of popular culture in the United States and the epiphenomena of best-sellerdom and might lend itself also, of course, to a specific critique of the popularity of *Uncle Tom's Cabin.* Glancing aside notices also that the late Alex Haley's "Queen," the unfinished book that was produced as a televised miniseries, seems, as the story of Haley's white roots, to be very much more assimilationist, and less angry and Afrocentric, than Haley's best-selling fictional representation of his black ones; "Queen," which Haley's friends and family have gone on record in the *New York Times* (Feb. 14, 1993: II 29) to say reveals more directly Haley's own racial views than *Roots* did, could encourage a revision of *Roots* with an eye to its underlying acceptability to white audiences, could encourage also revision even of Haley's *Autobiography of Malcolm X* with similar suspicions, and could expose subtle restrictions on the representations of race in the popular culture of the United States, restrictions that would presumably apply even more for Stowe in the 1850s than for Haley in the 1970s and 1980s.[10] The co-optation that I read back into Stowe and into her reception via a painfully close reading of a few passages from Faulkner's masterpiece could commence also from elsewhere—even from a popular cultural phenomenology of *Roots* and "Queen."

To encourage glancing aside is to encourage a kind of attentiveness that I recognize can seem merely undisciplined, merely inattentive, and can seem modeled after the casual, barely receptive receptivity enabled by the technology of the remote control. Submission to the popular culture of the sound bite, video game, and MTV might, I recognize, seem perverse, philistine, even professionally suicidal to many scholars and teachers. To consider such a submission is, to be sure, to consider the end of conventional reading and writing. But if we learn anything as scholars, we learn that meditations on the deaths of things—of God, of the novel, of ideology, of the author—never eventuate in the deaths of the things, no more so than does controversy signal even the possibility of the demise of the object of controversy. To contemplate the end of traditional reading and writing, like contemplating the end of nations and of books, is always already to meditate in the most intense way possible on reading and writing. Glancing aside is not a bad figure for the kind of nonlinear, unfixed eye movement that has been recorded in many experiments by physiologists during which very absorbed reading is taking place; nor is it a bad figure for the production of the *lexias* into which Roland Barthes famously "cut up" and then rearranged Balzac's short masterpiece *Sarrazine* in *S/Z* (3–15); nor is it a bad figure for the structure of what is certainly one of the newest, and what may prove to be the most powerful, contemporary reorganizations of knowledge, hypertext, a system instantiated through available computer technology in which all boundaries among all individual texts, and even the boundary between the consumer and the producer of text, can disappear.[11] Today such a massive integration as this last remains still theoretical, even utopian. But to end here by prophesying an afterward, after word, when all inequities among the participants in discourse disappear, is to end, appropriately and at long last, by glancing back at Protestant millennialism, at abolitionism, at sentimentalism and the cult of domesticity, at American ideology, and at Stowe.

# NOTES

Epigraphs: Elaine Brown 357; Peddler, a member of the Piru Nation Gang, spoke at the national African-American gang summit, Kansas City, Mo., April 30–May 2, 1993 (Mydans 38).

1. The issue of racism will remain as perennial a *topos* in critiques of *The Adventures of Huckleberry Finn* as it is in socially responsible critiques of American culture in general. See, for example, the Fall 1984 special issue of *Mark Twain Journal* devoted to African-American scholars' debate over Mark Twain's racism; eight essays from the special issue were recently republished in Leonard et al. Or see, on the other hand, the sensationalist white apologetics of Fishkin.

2. It is more than curious that Ike displays no sympathy whatsoever for Native Americans as victims of white genocide, no matter how much filiopietistic reverence he pays to his teacher Sam Fathers, "son of a Negro slave and a Chickasaw chief" (Faulkner 199). Native Americans function for Ike as the mere preliminary victims of his crude version of Whig, neo-Hegelian evolutionary historicism, the red race that is purged necessarily and ineluctably from the land by the white race before the white race in turn purges itself in fratricidal warfare, thus making way for the blameless, pacific, millennialist ascendency of the black.

3. And with which Ike also honors his Native American father, Sam Fathers, and honors also the wilderness, itself, that Ike's Native Ameri-

can father taught Ike to negotiate with such virtuosity. The wilderness "coalesced" once, and most magnificently, for Ike in the form of his first encounter with Ben, the eponymous Bear of the novel's title (Faulkner 202); when it does so for Ike one last time, in the reduced form of the rattlesnake that Ike almost steps on during his final trip to the wilderness before the timber company begins harvesting it, Ike stood "with one hand raised as Sam had stood that afternoon six years ago when Sam had led him into the wilderness and showed him and he ceased to be a child, speaking the old tongue which Sam had spoken that day without premeditation either: 'Chief,' he said: 'Grandfather' " (315).

4. This is the same Perry Miller who has been recently recalled by one of his earliest and most successful students, David Levin, as having "long before Jane Tomkins," in Miller's Harvard College course in American romanticism in the 1950s, routinely emphasized the achievement of both Stowe and Susan Warner (7, 10). Of course we might also regret that there weren't more women in that Harvard class to appreciate Miller's proto-feminism.

5. And many somewhat broader collections, as well. See, for a single, very recent, very prestigious, example, *The Culture of Sentiment*, edited by Shirley Samuels of Cornell University and just published by Oxford University Press, which collects essays by a number of young female scholars, all variously on the related subjects of sentimentalism, domesticity, and race in the nineteenth-century United States, and which is being promoted by Jane Tomkins of Duke University in the jacket copy as "feminist, new historicist, race-class-gender oriented, and theoretically sophisticated without being jargon-ridden."

6. "[T]he more recent 'American Adventure' Pavilion at EPCOT actually tries to highlight some of the struggles in United States history which had racial, sexual, and ethnic difference at the core. Chief Joseph, Susan B. Anthony, and Frederick Douglass all have their say . . . [but] abstracting their words from the context in which they were made effectively neutralizes the acknowledgement of difference intended by their inclusion. Douglass, for example, extolls the virtues of Harriet Beecher Stowe's *Uncle Tom's Cabin*. This is something he might have done in public for highly strategic reasons, but the truth is that Douglass was highly ambivalent, to say the least, about Stowe's book, and wrote his own *Heroic Slave* in large part to counter her portrayal of black heroism" (Kuenz 76–77).

7. Recall also the way in which Stowe positions herself, fifteen years after the publication of *Uncle Tom's Cabin*, in the interminable controversy that probably threatened definitions of gender, sexuality, and domestic arrangements more than any other, at least among the privileged and educated. In answer to Byron's angry riposte to Thomas Moore's 1830 denunciation of Byron's behavior toward Lady Byron leading up to their separation, Stowe wrote her long-forgotten, highly conventional, even reactionary *Lady Byron Vindicated*.

8. See, for example, the profile of Reed in the *Chronicle of Higher Education* Feb. 17, 1993: A5. The opposite page of this issue prints a feature story about "an ambitious new reference work, *Black Women in America: An Historical Encyclopedia*" (A6). Just in case.

9. *New York Times* Nov. 8, 1992: V 11. Lentricchia might take pause over Peck's title the next time he wants to "undo" American literary or political conventions with one of Frost's best-known poems.

10. Malcolm was famous for his scorn for fiction, after he had discovered his true, serious, vocation. His famous exception to this rule is really no exception: the decision to include *Uncle Tom's Cabin* on the autodidactic almost exclusively nonfiction reading list was of course prompted by an interest in something other than the novel's aesthetic or entertainment values.

11. See Landow, especially "Hypertext and Critical Theory" 2–34.

# Works Cited

Adams, John. *Harriet Beecher Stowe.* New York: Twayne, 1963.

Ahlstrom, Sydney. *A Religious History of the American People.* Vol. 2. New York: Doubleday, 1975.

Alcott, William A. *The Young Man's Guide.* 2d ed. Boston, 1834.

———. *The Young Wife, or Duties of Woman in the Marriage Relation.* 3d ed. Boston: Light, 1837.

Aldern, Raymond Macdonald. *The Rise of Formal Satire in England under Classical Influence.* Philadelphia: Norwood, 1978.

Allen, Joseph. *The Sources of Public Prosperity. A Discourse Delivered in Northborough, April 9, 1829.* Worcester, Mass.: Griffin and Morrill, 1829.

Allen, Richard. "If You Have Tears: Sentimentalism As Soft Romanticism." *Genre* 9 (1975): 119–45.

American Anti-Slavery Society. "Disunion." New York: American Anti-Slavery Society, 1845.

Ammons, Elizabeth, ed. *Critical Essays on Harriet Beecher Stowe.* Boston: Hall, 1980.

———. "Heroines in *Uncle Tom's Cabin.*" *American Literature* 49 (1977): 161–79. Rpt. in Ammons, ed. 152–65.

———. "Stowe's Dream of the Mother-Savior: *Uncle Tom's Cabin* and American Women Writers before the 1920s." Sundquist, ed. 155–95.

Andrews, William L. *To Tell a Free Story: The First Century of Afro-American Autobiography, 1760–1865.* Urbana: U of Illinois P, 1988.

"An Appeal to the Reason and Religion of American Christians against

the American Anti-Slavery Society, by a Citizen of New York."
New York, 1838.

Ariès, Philippe. *Western Attitudes toward Death from the Middle Ages to the Present.* Trans. Patricia M. Ranum. Baltimore: Johns Hopkins UP, 1974.

Arnon, Robert D. "Wit, Humor, and Satire in Seventeenth-Century America." *Tennessee Studies in Literature.* Knoxville: U of Tennessee P, 1976.

*The Art of Good Behaviour: and, Letter Writing in Love, Courtship, and Marriage.* New York: Huestis and Cozans, 1850.

Arthur, T. S. *Advice to Young Ladies on Their Duties and Conduct in Life.* Boston: Phillips and Sampson, 1848.

Askeland, Lori. "Remodeling the Model Home in *Uncle Tom's Cabin* and *Beloved.*" *American Literature* 64 (December 1992): 785–805.

Auerbach, Nina. "Introduction: The Communal Eye." *Communities of Women: An Idea in Fiction.* Cambridge, Mass.: Harvard UP, 1978. 1–32.

Baker, Houston. "*Commentary.* In Dubious Battle." *New Literary History* 18.2 (Winter 1987): 363–69.

Bakhtin, Mikhail. *The Dialogic Imagination.* Austin: U of Texas P, 1981.

———. "The Problem of the Text in Linguistics, Philology, and the Human Sciences: An Experiment in Philosophical Analysis." *"Speech Genres" and Other Late Essays.* Trans. Vern W. McGee. Ed. Caryl Emerson and Michael Holquist. Austin: U of Texas P, 1986. 103–31.

Baldwin, James. "Everybody's Protest Novel." *Partisan Review* 16 (June 1949): 578–85. Rpt. in Ammons, ed. 92–97. Also in *Notes of a Native Son,* 1964; 1984. 13–23.

———. *Notes of a Native Son.* New York: Bantam, 1964; reprint, Boston: Beacon, 1984.

Banning, Margaret. "*Uncle Tom's Cabin* by Harriet Beecher Stowe." *Georgia Review* 9 (1955): 461–65.

Bardes, Barbara, and Suzanne Gossett. *Declarations of Independence: Women and Political Power in Nineteenth-Century American Fiction.* New Brunswick, N.J.: Rutgers UP, 1990.

Barlow, Joel. *The Columbiad.* Philadelphia, 1807.

———. *The Vision of Columbus.* Hartford, Conn., 1787.

Barthes, Roland. *S/Z.* Trans. Richard Miller. New York: Hill and Wang, 1974.

Baym, Nina, et al., eds. *The Norton Anthology of American Literature.* 3d ed. 2 vols. New York: Norton, 1989.

———. *Woman's Fiction: A Guide to Novels by and about Women in America, 1820–1870.* Ithaca, N.Y.: Cornell UP, 1978.

Bean, James. *The Christian Minister's Affectionate Advice to a Married Couple.* New York: American Tract Society, 1815.

Beauvoir, Simone de. *The Second Sex.* Ed. and trans. H. M. Parshley. New York: Knopf, 1971.

Beecher, Catharine E. *An Essay on Slavery and Abolitionism, with Reference to the Duty of American Females.* Philadelphia: Perkins, 1837.

——, and Harriet Beecher Stowe. *The American Woman's Home.* 1861. New York: Arno, 1971.

Beecher, Lyman. "The Memory of Our Fathers, a Sermon Delivered at Plymouth, Massachusetts, December 22, 1827." *Nationalism and Religion in America.* Ed. Winthrop S. Hudson. New York: Harper, 1970. 99–105.

——. *A Plea for the West.* New York, 1835.

——. *A Reformation of Morals Practicable and Indispensable.* Andover, N.H., 1814.

Bennett, Lerone, Jr. *Before the Mayflower.* New York: Penguin, 1984.

Bercovitch, Sacvan. *The American Jeremiad.* Madison: U of Wisconsin P, 1978.

Berkson, Dorothy. "Millennial Politics and the Feminine Fiction of Harriet Beecher Stowe." Ammons, ed. 244–58.

Berlant, Lauren. "The Female Complaint." *Social Text* (1987): 237–59.

Birney, James Gillespie. *American Churches: The Bulwarks of American Slavery.* New York: Arno, 1968.

Blassingame, John W., ed. *Slave Testimony: Two Centuries of Letters, Speeches, Interviews, and Autobiographies.* Baton Rouge: Louisiana State UP, 1977.

Bloch, Ruth H. "American Feminine Ideals in Transition: The Rise of the Moral Mother, 1785–1815." *Feminist Studies* 4 (1978): 100–126.

Blumenthal, Walter Hart. "Barbs and Bludgeons." *American Book Collector* 7.9 (June 1957): 23–31.

Bode, Carl. *The Anatomy of American Popular Culture: 1840–1861.* Berkeley and Los Angeles: U of California P, 1959.

Bogel, Donald. *Toms, Coons, Mulattoes, Mammies, and Bucks: An Interpretative History of Blacks in American Films.* New York: Continuum, 1992.

Bond, Adrienne. "Disorder and the Sentimental Model: A Look at *Pudd'nhead Wilson.*" *Southern Literary Quarterly* 13 (1981): 59–71.

Bradley, Joseph. *Ladies Repository* 10 (Feb. 1850): 61–62.

Brodhead, Richard. "Sparing the Rod: Discipline and Fiction in Antebellum America." *Representations* 21 (1988): 67–96.

Brown, Elaine. *A Taste of Power: A Black Woman's Story.* New York: Pantheon, 1992.

Brown, H. F. M. *The False and True Marriages: The Reason and Result.* 2d. ed. Cleveland: Viets and Savage, 1861.

Brown, Herbert Ross. *The Sentimental Novel in America 1789–1860.* Durham, N.C.: Duke UP, 1940.

# Works Cited

Brown, William Wells. *Clotel, or The President's Daughter.* 1853. New York: University Books, 1989.

*Buds for the Bridal Wreath.* Boston: Crosby, Nichols, 1856.

Burgess, Anthony. "Making de White Boss Frown." Ammons, ed. 22–27.

Caldwell, Charles. *Thoughts on the Original Unity of the Human Race.* New York, 1830.

Camfield, Gregg. "The Moral Aesthetics of Sentimentality: A Missing Key to *Uncle Tom's Cabin.*" *Nineteenth-Century Literature* (1988): 319–45.

Chafe, William F. *Women and Equality: Changing Patterns in American Culture.* New York: Oxford UP, 1977.

Channing, William Ellery. *William Ellery Channing: Selected Writings.* Ed. David Robinson. New York: Paulist, 1985.

———. *Works.* Boston, 1849. Vol. 6.

C[hild], L[ydia] M[aria]. "Lewis Clarke: Leaves from a Slave's Journal of Life." Blassingame, ed. 151–64.

*Christian Examiner* 22 (1832): 4.

Cixous, Hélène. *"Coming to Writing" and Other Essays.* Ed. Deborah Jenson. Trans. Sarah Cornell, Deborah Jenson, Ann Liddle, and Susan Sellars. Cambridge, Mass.: Harvard UP, 1991.

———. "The Laugh of the Medusa." *Feminisms: An Anthology of Literary Theory and Criticism.* Ed. Robyn R. Warhol and Diane Price Herndal. New Brunswick, N.J.: Rutgers UP, 1991. 334–49.

Clarke, James Freeman. *Slavery in the United States: A Sermon Delivered in Armory Hall on Thanksgiving Day, November 24, 1842.* Boston: Greene, 1843.

Clemens, Samuel. *The Adventures of Huckleberry Finn.* New York: Norton, 1962.

———. "How to Tell a Story." Baym, ed. 2:215–19.

Cogan, Frances B. *All-American Girl: The Ideal of Real Womanhood in Mid-Nineteenth-Century America.* Athens: U of Georgia P, 1989.

———. "Weak Fathers and Other Beasts: An Examination of the American Male in Domestic Novels, 1850–1870." *American Studies* 25.2 (1984): 5–20.

"A Condensed Anti-Slavery Bible Argument; By a Citizen of Virginia." New York, 1845.

Cott, Nancy. *The Bonds of Womanhood: "Woman's Sphere" in New England, 1780–1835.* New Haven: Yale UP, 1977.

Cox, Samuel H. "Letter of the Rev. Dr. Samuel H. Cox against the American Colonization Society." Boston, 1834.

Delany, Martin R. *The Condition, Elevation, Emigration, and Destiny of the Colored People of the United States.* Philadelphia, 1852.

Douglas, Ann. *The Feminization of American Culture.* New York: Knopf, 1977.

———. "Heaven Our Home: Consolation Literature in the Northern

United States, 1820–1880." *Death in America.* Ed. David E. Stannard. Philadelphia: U of Pennsylvania P, 1975.
———. "Introduction: The Art of Controversy." *Uncle Tom's Cabin; or, Life Among the Lowly.* By Harriet Beecher Stowe. 7–34.
Douglass, Frederick. *Life and Times of Frederick Douglass.* New York: Macmillan, 1962.
———. *My Bondage and My Freedom.* New York: Dover, 1969; reprint, ed. William L. Andrews. Urbana: U of Illinois P, 1987.
———. *Narrative of the Life of Frederick Douglass, An American Slave.* Ed. Benjamin Quarles. Cambridge, Mass.: Harvard UP, 1960.
Dumond, Dwight Lowell. *Antislavery Origins of the Civil War in the United States.* Ann Arbor: U of Michigan P, 1939; reprint, with foreword by Arthur Schlesinger, Jr., 1959.
Dunbar, Paul Laurence. "Harriet Beecher Stowe." Ammons, ed. 73.
Eastman, Mary. " 'A Negro's Passion for a Ruffled Shirt.' From *Aunt Phillis's Cabin, or Southern Life As It Is.*" *Eclectic* 3 (1852–53): 68–69.
Edwards, Jonathan. *A History of the Work of Redemption.* Ed. John F. Wilson. Vol. 9 of *The Works of Jonathan Edwards.* New Haven: Yale UP, 1989.
———. *An Humble Attempt.* In *Apocalyptic Writings. Works of Jonathan Edwards.* Ed. Stephen Stein. Vol. 5. New Haven: Yale UP, 1977.
———. "Miscellaneous Notebooks." Ms. Ed. Thomas A. Shafer for the Yale UP edition of *The Works of Jonathan Edwards.* Beinecke Library, Yale U, New Haven, Conn.
———. *Some Thoughts Concerning the Present Revival of Religion in New England.* Hartford, Conn., 1742.
———. *Typological Writings of Jonathan Edwards.* Ed. Wallace Anderson, Mason Lowance, and David Watters. Vol. 11 of *The Works of Jonathan Edwards.* New Haven: Yale UP, 1993.
Elliot, E. N., ed. *Cotton Is King and Other Pro-Slavery Arguments.* Augusta, Ga., 1860.
Elliott, Emory, ed. *Columbia Literary History of the U.S.* New York: Columbia UP, 1988.
Elliot, Robert C. *The Power of Satire.* Princeton, N.J.: Princeton UP, 1960.
Emerson, Ralph Waldo. *Ralph Waldo Emerson: Essays & Lectures.* Ed. Joel Porte. New York: Library of America, 1983.
———. "Success." *The Complete Works of Ralph Waldo Emerson.* Ed. Edward Waldo Emerson. 12 vols. Boston: Houghton Mifflin, 1903–4. Vol. 7.
*Evening Gazette* (Boston), March 27, 1830.
Faulkner, William. *The Bear: Three Famous Short Novels.* New York: Vintage, 1961.
*The Female Friend; or the Duties of Christian Virgins; To Which Is Added Advice to a Young Married Lady.* Baltimore: Keatinge, 1809.

## Works Cited

Fiedler, Leslie. "Harriet Beecher Stowe's Novel of Sentimental Protest." Ammons, ed. 112–16.

——. *Love and Death in the American Novel.* 1960. New York: Stein and Day, 1966.

Fisher, Philip. "Democratic Social Space: Whitman, Melville, and the Promise of Transparency." *Representations* 24 (1988): 60–101.

——. *Hard Facts: Setting and Form in the American Novel.* New York: Oxford UP, 1985.

——, ed. *The New American Studies: Essays from "Representations."* Berkeley and Los Angeles: U of California P, 1991.

Fishkin, Shelley Fisher. *Was Huck Black? Mark Twain and African-American Voice.* New York: Oxford UP, 1993.

Fladeland, Betty. *Men and Brothers: Anglo-American Antislavery Cooperation.* Urbana: U of Illinois P, 1972.

Foner, Eric. *Free Soil, Free Labor, Free Men: The Ideology of the Republican Party before the Civil War.* New York: Oxford UP, 1970.

Forrest, Wilson. *Crusader in Crinoline: The Life of Harriet Beecher Stowe.* Philadelphia: Lippincott, 1941.

Foster, Charles. *The Rungless Ladder: Harriet Beecher Stowe and New England Calvinism.* Durham, N.C.: Duke UP, 1954.

Franklin, John Hope. *From Slavery to Freedom.* New York: Knopf, 1947.

Fredrickson, George M. *The Black Image in the White Mind: The Debate on Afro-American Character and Destiny, 1817–1914.* New York: Harper and Row, 1971.

Freeling, Arthur. *The Young Bride's Book: An Epitome of the Domestic Duties and Social Enjoyments of Woman As Wife and Mother.* New York: Wilson, 1845.

Freneau, Phillip, and Hugh Henry Brackenridge. "The Rising Glory of America." Philadelphia, 1809.

Frye, Northrop. *An Anatomy of Criticism.* Princeton, N.J.: Princeton UP, 1971.

Fuller, Margaret. *Woman in the Nineteenth Century.* Ed. Bernard Rosenthal. New York: Norton, 1971.

Furnas, J. C. *Goodbye to Uncle Tom.* London: Secker and Warburg, 1956.

——. "Goodbye to Uncle Tom: An Excerpt." Ammons, ed. 105–11.

Gates, Henry Louis, Jr. "Whose Canon Is It, Anyway?" *New York Times Book Review,* February 26, 1989: 43–44.

——. " 'What's Love Got to Do With It?': Critical Theory, Integrity, and the Black Idiom." *New Literary History* 18.2 (Winter 1987): 345–362.

Geertz, Clifford. *The Interpretation of Cultures: Selected Essays by Clifford Geertz.* New York: Basic, 1973.

Genovese, Eugene D. *Roll, Jordan, Roll: The World the Slaves Made.* New York: Vintage, 1975.

Goen, C. C. "Jonathan Edwards, A New Departure in Eschatology." *Church History* 28 (1959): 25–40.

Gossett, Thomas F. *Race: The History of an Idea in America.* Dallas, Tex.: Southern Methodist UP, 1963.

———. *"Uncle Tom's Cabin" and American Culture.* Dallas, Tex.: Southern Methodist UP, 1985.

Griffith, Cyril E. *The African Dream: Martin R. Delany and the Emergence of Pan-African Thought.* University Park: Pennsylvania State UP, 1975.

Hale, Sarah Josepha. *Northwood, or Life North and South: Showing the True Character of Both.* 2d ed. New York: H. Long & Brother, 1852.

Haley, Alex. *The Autobiography of Malcolm X.* New York: Ballantine, 1992.

———. *Roots.* New York: Doubleday, 1976.

Hall, Stuart. "Cultural Studies: Two Paradigms." *Media, Culture, and Society.* London: Academic, 1980. 57–72.

Halttunen, Karen. *Confidence Men and Painted Women: A Study of Middle-Class Culture in America, 1830–1870.* New Haven: Yale UP, 1982.

Harris, R. Allen. "'The Man That Was a Thing': Criticism and Uncle Tom." *College English* 50 (October 1988): 649–53.

Hatch, Nathan. *The Democratization of American Christianity.* New Haven: Yale UP, 1989.

———. *The Sacred Cause of Liberty: Republican Thought and the Millennium in Revolutionary New England.* New Haven: Yale UP, 1977.

Hawes, Joel. *Lectures to Young Men, on the Formation of Character.* Hartford, Conn.: Cooke, 1829.

Hendrick, J. T. "Union and Slavery: A Thanksgiving Sermon." Clarksville, Tenn., 1851.

Henry, Stuart. *Unvanquished Puritan: A Portrait of Lyman Beecher.* Grand Rapids, Mich.: Eerdmans, 1973.

Higonnet, Margaret. "Speaking Silences: Women's Suicide." *The Female Body in Western Culture.* Ed. Susan Suleiman. Cambridge, Mass.: Harvard UP, 1986. 68–83.

Hirsch, Stephen. "Uncle Tomitudes: The Popular Reaction to Uncle Tom's Cabin." *South Atlantic Review* 43 (1978): 303–30.

"History of Opinions Respecting the Millennium." *American Theological Review* 1 (November 1859): 644–55.

Hoit, T. W. *The Right of American Slavery.* Southern and Western ed. St. Louis, Mo.: Bushnell, 1860.

Holmes, George F. "Notices of New Works: *Uncle Tom's Cabin: or Life Among the Lowly.*" *Southern Literary Messenger* 18 (1852): 630–38.

Homans, Peter. *Theology after Freud.* Indianapolis, Ind.: Bobbs-Merrill, 1970.

Horsman, Reginald. *Race and Manifest Destiny: The Origins of American Racial Anglo-Saxonism.* Cambridge, Mass.: Harvard UP, 1981.

Hovet, Theodore R. "Modernization and the American Fall into Slavery in *Uncle Tom's Cabin.*" *New England Quarterly* 54 (1981): 499–518.

Hughes, Langston. "Introduction to *Uncle Tom's Cabin.*" Ammons, ed. 102–4.

Humphreys, Nancy K. *American Women's Magazines: An Annotated Historical Guide.* New York: Garland, 1989.

Irigaray, Luce. *This Sex Which Is Not One.* Trans. Catherine Porter and Carolyn Burke. Ithaca, N.Y.: Cornell UP, 1985.

———. "Women-Mothers, the Silent Substratum." *The Irigaray Reader.* Trans. David Macey. Ed. and intro. Margaret Whitford. Cambridge: Basil Blackwell, 1991.

Jacobs, Harriet. *Incidents in the Life of a Slave Girl.* Ed. Jean Fagan Yellen. Cambridge, Mass.: Harvard UP, 1987.

Janeway, Elizabeth. *Man's World: Woman's Place: A Study in Social Mythology.* New York: Morrow, 1971.

Jay, William. "Reply to Remarks of Rev. Moses Stuart." New York, 1850.

Jehlen, Myra. "The Family Militant: Domesticity versus Slavery in *Uncle Tom's Cabin.*" *Criticism* 31 (1989): 383–400.

Joswick, Thomas. " 'The Crown without the Conflict': Religious Values and Moral Reasoning in *Uncle Tom's Cabin.*" *Nineteenth-Century Fiction* 39 (1984): 253–74.

Joyce, Joyce A. "The Black Canon: Reconstructing Black American Literary Criticism." *New Literary History* 18.2 (Winter 1987): 335–43.

Kaplan, Cora. *Sea Changes: Essays on Culture and Feminism.* London: Verso, 1986.

Karl, Frederick R. "Introduction to the Danse Macabre: Conrad's *Heart of Darkness.*" *Joseph Conrad, "Heart of Darkness": A Case Study in Contemporary Criticism.* Ed. Ross C. Murfin. New York: St. Martin's, 1989. 123–38.

Katz, William Loren. Introduction. *A Key to Uncle Tom's Cabin.* By Harriet Beecher Stowe. New York: Arno, 1968.

Kazin, Alfred. Introduction. *Uncle Tom's Cabin.* By Harriet Beecher Stowe. 1852. Reprint, New York: Bantam, 1981.

Kelley, Mary. *Private Woman, Public Stage: Literary Domesticity in Nineteenth-Century America.* New York: Oxford UP, 1984.

Kerber, Linda. "Separate Spheres, Female Worlds, and Woman's Place: The Rhetoric of Women's History." *Journal of American History* 75 (1988): 9–39.

Kernan, Alvin. *The Cankered Muse.* New Haven: Yale UP, 1959.

————. *The Plot of Satire.* New Haven: Yale UP, 1965.

Kuenz, Jane. "It's a Small World after All: Disney and the Pleasures of Identification." *South Atlantic Quarterly* 19.1 (Winter 1993): 63–88.

Landow, George P. *Hypertext.* Baltimore: Johns Hopkins UP, 1992.

Lang, Amy Schrager. "Slavery and Sentimentalism: The Strange Career of Augustine St. Clare." *Women's Studies* 12 (1986): 31–54.

Lears, Jackson. *No Place of Grace: Antimodernism and the Transformation of American Culture, 1880–1920.* New York: Pantheon, 1981.

Lentricchia, Frank. "Lyric in the Culture of Capitalism." *American Literary History* 1.1 (Spring 1989): 63–88.

Leonard, James S., Thomas A. Tenney, and Thadious M. Davis, eds. *Satire or Evasion? Black Perspectives on "Huckleberry Finn."* Durham, N.C.: Duke UP, 1992.

Lerner, Gerda. *Black Women in White America.* New York: Pantheon, 1972.

Levin, David. *Forms of Uncertainty: Essays in Historical Criticism.* Charlottesville: U of Virginia P, 1992.

Levine, Robert S. "*Uncle Tom's Cabin* in *Frederick Douglass's Paper:* An Analysis of Reception." *American Literature* 64 (1992): 71–93.

Livermore, Elizabeth D. *Zoë, or The Quadroon's Triumph: A Tale for the Times.* Cincinnati: Truman and Spofford, 1855.

Loveland, Anne C. *Southern Evangelicals and the Social Order.* Baton Rouge: Louisiana State UP, 1980.

Lowance, Mason I., Jr. *The Language of Canaan: Metaphor and Symbol in New England from the Puritans to the Transcendentalists.* Cambridge, Mass.: Harvard UP, 1980.

————. "Religion in Puritan Poetry." *Puritan Poetry and Poetics: Seventeenth- and Eighteenth-Century American Poetry.* Ed. Peter White. University Park: Pennsylvania State UP, 1986. 33–46.

————. "The Slave Narrative in American Literature." *African-American Writers.* Ed. Lea Baechler and A. Walton Litz. New York: Scribner's, 1991. 395–412.

Lynn, Kenneth S. "Mrs. Stowe and the American Imagination." *New Republic,* June 29, 1963: 20–21.

Matthiessen, F. O. *American Renaissance.* 1941. New York: Oxford UP, 1966.

McCaine, Alexander. "Slavery Defended from Scripture against the Attacks of the Abolitionists." Baltimore, 1842.

McDowell, Tremaine. "The Use of Negro Dialect by Harriet Beecher Stowe." Ammons, ed. 88–91.

Menninger, Karl. *Man against Himself.* New York: Harcourt Brace, 1938.

Michie, Helena. *The Flesh Made Word: Female Figures and Women's Bodies.* New York: Oxford UP, 1987.

Miller, Perry. Editor's introduction. *Images or Shadows of Divine Things.* By Jonathan Edwards. New Haven: Yale UP, 1948.

## Works Cited

———. *The Raven and the Whale.* New York: Macmillan, 1961.

Moorhead, James. *American Apocalypse: Yankee Protestants and the Civil War 1860–1869.* New Haven: Yale UP, 1978.

Morgan, Edmund S. *American Slavery, American Freedom.* New York: Norton, 1975.

Morison, John. *Counsels on Matrimony; or, Friendly Suggestions to Husbands and Wives. . . .* Brookfield, Mass.: Merriam and Cooke, 1842.

Morrison, Toni. *Playing in the Dark: Whiteness and the Literary Imagination.* Cambridge, Mass.: Harvard UP, 1992.

*The Mother's Hymn Book. Compiled from Various Authors and Private Manuscripts. For the Use of Maternal Associations, and for Social, Family, and Private Worship.* Ed. Thomas Hastings. Revised ed. New York: Ela, 1851.

"The Mother's Vision: The Birth-Day in Heaven of Mary Ann. Her Second Year among the Angels." *Southern Literary Messenger* 19 (1853): 306–7.

Mott, Frank Luther. *A History of American Magazines: 1885–1905.* Cambridge, Mass.: Harvard UP, 1957. Vol. 4.

Mydans, Seth. "Gangs Go Public in New Fight for Respect." *New York Times,* May 2, 1993: 1, 38.

Newton, Judith Lowder. "Power and Ideology of 'Woman's Sphere.'" *Feminisms: An Anthology of Literary Theory and Criticism.* Ed. Robyn R. Warhol and Diane Price Herndl. New Brunswick, N.J.: Rutgers UP, 1991. 765–80.

Nott, J. C., and George R. Gliddon, eds. *Types of Mankind, or Ethnological Researches.* Philadelphia, 1854.

Parker, Theodore. "The Nebraska Question." *Collected Works.* Ed. Francis P. Cobbe. London, 1863–70. Vol. 5.

Parrington, Vernon Louis. *Main Currents in American Thought: An Interpretation of American Literature from the Beginning to 1920.* New York: Harcourt Brace, 1958.

Parsons, C. B. "Woman's Power and Influence." *Home Circle,* 1855: 352–56.

Pearce, Roy Harvey. *The Savages of America: A Study of the Indian and the Idea of Civilization.* 1953. Baltimore: Johns Hopkins UP, 1965.

———. *Savagism and Civilization: A Study of the Indian and the American Mind.* Berkeley and Los Angeles: U of California P, 1988.

Peck, M. Scott. *The Road Less Traveled.* New York: Simon and Schuster, 1976.

Person, Leland S., Jr. *Aesthetic Headaches: Women and Masculine Poetics in Poe, Melville, and Hawthorne.* Athens: U of Georgia P, 1988.

Pickering, James H. *The World Turned Upside Down.* New York: Kennikat, 1975.

Pilditch, Jan. *The Growth and Development of American Satire.* Diss. Hamilton, N.Z.: Waikato U, 1990.

Poe, Edgar Allan. "The Purloined Letter." Baym, ed. 1425–37.

Pope, Alexander. "Essay on Man." *The Poems of Alexander Pope.* Ed. John Butt. New Haven: Yale UP, 1963.

Priest, Josiah. *A Bible Defence of Slavery.* Glasgow, Ky. 1852.

Reynolds, David S. *Beneath the American Renaissance: The Subversive Imagination in the Age of Emerson and Melville.* Cambridge, Mass.: Harvard UP, 1989.

Rich, Adrienne. *On Lies, Secrets, and Silence.* New York: Norton, 1979.

Riggio, Thomas. "*Uncle Tom* Reconstructed: A Neglected Chapter in the History of a Book." Ammons, ed. 139–51.

Roth, George L. "An American Theory of Satire: 1790–1820." *American Literature* 29 (Jan. 1958): 399–407.

Rourke, Constance Mayfield. "Remarks from *Trumpets of Jubilee.*" Ammons, ed. 77–87.

———. *Trumpets of Jubilee.* New York: Harcourt Brace and World, 1963.

Ruether, Rosemary Radford, and Rosemary Skinner Keller, eds. *Women and Religion in America: The Nineteenth Century.* San Francisco: Harper and Row, 1982.

Ryan, Mary. *Cradle of the Middle Class: The Family in Oneida County, New York, 1790–1865.* New York: Cambridge UP, 1981.

Samuels, Shirley, ed. *The Culture of Sentiment: Race, Gender, and Sentimentality in Nineteenth-Century America.* New York: Oxford UP, 1993.

Sanchez-Eppler, Karen. "Bodily Bonds: The Intersecting Rhetorics of Feminism and Abolition." *Representations* 24 (1988): 28–59.

Scarbrough, Mark. "A Case for Polyphony." *The Validity of Texts about Minorities Written by Majorities.* St. Louis, Mo. Presentation, MMLA Forum. 1992.1–8.

Sedgwick, Catherine Maria. *Means and Ends, or Self-Training.* Boston: Marsh, Capen, Lyon and Webb, 1839.

Sigourney, L. H. *Whisper to a Bride.* Hartford, Conn.: Parsons, 1850.

Smith, Samuel Stanhope. *An Essay on the Causes of the Variety of Complexion and Figure in the Human Species.* 1787. Ed. Winthrop Jordan. Cambridge, Mass.: Harvard UP, 1965.

Smith, Sidonie. "Resisting the Gaze of Embodiment: Women's Autobiography in the Nineteenth Century." *American Women's Autobiography: Fea(s)ts of Memory.* Ed. Margo Culley. Madison: U of Wisconsin P, 1992. 75–110.

Smith-Rosenberg, Carroll. *Disorderly Conduct: Visions of Gender in Victorian America.* New York: Knopf, 1985.

Stowe, Charles, and Lyman Beecher Stowe. *Harriet Beecher Stowe: The Story of Her Life.* New York: Houghton, 1911.

Stowe, Harriet Beecher. *A Key to Uncle Tom's Cabin.* Boston: John P. Jewett, 1853.

# Works Cited

————. *Lady Byron Vindicated.* Boston: Osgood, Fields, and Co., 1870.

————. *Life and Letters of Harriet Beecher Stowe.* Ed. Annie Fields. Boston: Houghton Mifflin, 1988.

————. *Little Foxes, or The Insignificant Little Habits which Mar Domestic Happiness.* London: Bell and Daldy, 1866.

————. *Lives and Deeds of Our Self Made Men.* Hartford, Conn.: Worthington, Dustin, 1872.

————. *My Wife and I.* New York: Ford, 1877.

————. *Poganuc People: Their Loves and Their Lives.* New York: Fords, Howard, and Hulbert, 1887.

————. *Uncle Sam's Emancipation: Earthly Care, A Heavenly Discipline and Other Sketches.* Philadelphia: W. P. Hazard, 1853.

————. *Uncle Tom's Cabin.* Ed. John Woods. New York: Oxford UP, 1965.

————. *Uncle Tom's Cabin; or, Life among the Lowly.* Ed. Ann Douglas. N.Y.: Penguin, 1981.

————. *Uncle Tom's Cabin.* 1852. With an introduction by Alfred Kazin. Reprint, New York: Bantam, 1981.

————. *Uncle Tom's Cabin; or, Life among the Lowly.* Ed. Kenneth S. Lynn. Cambridge, Mass.: Belknap Press of Harvard UP, 1982.

Stringfellow, Rev. Thornton. *Slavery: Its Origin, Nature, and History, Considered in the Light of Bible Teachings, Moral Justice, and Political Wisdom.* New York: John F. Trow, 1861.

Strout, Cushing. *The New Heavens and New Earth.* New York: Harper, 1974.

Sundquist, Eric J. *"Benito Cereno* and New World Slavery." *Reconstructing American Literary History.* Ed. Sacvan Bercovitch. Cambridge, Mass.: Harvard UP, 1986. 93–122.

————. Introduction. Sundquist, ed. 1–44.

————, ed. *New Essays on "Uncle Tom's Cabin."* New York: Cambridge UP, 1986.

Taylor, Mrs. *Practical Hints to Young Females, on the Duties of a Wife, a Mother, and a Mistress of a Family.* 3d American ed. Boston: Loring, 1826.

Taylor, William R. *Cavalier and Yankee: The Old South and American National Character.* New York: Braziller, 1961.

Thompson, Harold W. "Humor." *Literary History of the United States.* Ed. Robert E. Spiller et al. Revised ed. in one volume. New York: Macmillan, 1953.

Thompson, John R. "Uncle Tom's Cabin." *Southern Literary Messenger* 18 (1852): 721–31.

Tiffany, Joel. *A Treatise on the Unconstitutionality of American Slavery.* Cleveland, Ohio [1850].

Todd, John. *The Young Man. Hints Addressed to the Young Men of the United States.* 2d ed. Northampton, Mass., 1845.

"To Mrs. H. B. Stowe." *Eclectic* 3 (1852–53): 249.

"To the People of the United States. *Annual Report of the American Bible Society: With an Account of Its Organization.* New York, 1836. Vol. 1.

Tompkins, Jane. *Sensational Designs: The Cultural Work of American Fiction, 1790–1860.* New York: Oxford UP, 1985.

———. "Sentimental Power: *Uncle Tom's Cabin* and the Politics of Literary History." *Glyph* 8 (1981): 79–102. Rpt. in *The New Feminist Criticism.* Ed. Elaine Showalter. New York: Pantheon, 1985. 81–104.

Turner, James. *Without God, without Creed: The Origins of Unbelief in America.* Baltimore: Johns Hopkins UP, 1985.

"*Uncle Tom's Cabin.*" Review. *Times* (London), Sept. 3, 1852: 5.

"A Voice from a Sufferer." *Eclectic* 3 (1852–53): 5.

Wagenknecht, Edward Charles. *Harriet Beecher Stowe, the Known and the Unknown.* New York: Oxford UP, 1965.

Walker, Nancy A. *A Very Serious Thing: Women's Humor and American Culture.* Minneapolis: U of Minnesota P, 1988.

Warner, Charles Dudley. "The Story of *Uncle Tom's Cabin.*" Ammons, ed. 60–72.

*The Way to Get Married: and the Advantages and Disadvantages of the Marriage State. . . .* Philadelphia: Johnson, 1806.

Weber, Brom. *The Art of American Humor.* New York: Crowell 1962.

[Weld, Theodore Dwight.] *American Slavery As It Is: Testimony of a Thousand Witnesses.* New York: American Anti-Slavery Society, 1839. With a foreword by William Loren Katz. New York: Arno and *New York Times,* 1968.

Welter, Barbara. "The Cult of True Womanhood: 1800–1860." *American Quarterly* 18 (1966): 151–74.

———. *Dimity Convictions: The American Woman in the Nineteenth Century.* Athens: Ohio UP, 1976.

Whitman, Walt. "Preface to *Leaves of Grass.*" *Anthology of American Literature.* Ed. Geroge McMichael et al. New York: MacMillan, 1989. Vol. 1.

Williams, W. R. "True Sphere of Woman." *Mothers' Journal and Family Visitant* 16 (1851): 303–4.

Williston, John. "Balm of Gilead for a Diseased Land." Boston, 1742.

Wilson, Edmund. "Harriet Beecher Stowe." Ammons, ed. 117–21.

Wilson, John. Editor's Introduction. *A History of the Work of Redemption.* Vol. 9 of *The Works of Jonathan Edwards,* by Jonathan Edwards. New Haven: Yale UP, 1989. 1–109.

Winthrop, John. "A Model of Christian Charity." Baym, ed. 31–42.

Wise, Daniel. *The Young Man's Counsellor: or, Sketches and Illustrations of the Duties and Dangers of Young Men. . . .* New York, 1850.

Wolf, Bryan J. "How the West Was Hung, Or, When I Hear the Word

## Works Cited

'Culture' I Take Out My Checkbook." *American Quarterly* 44.3 (September 1992): 418–38.

Wolfe, Tom. *The Bonfire of the Vanities.* New York: Farrar, Straus, and Giroux, 1987.

———. *Radical Chic and Mau-Mauing the Flack Catchers.* New York: Farrar, Straus, and Giroux, 1970.

"Woman's True Mission, or 'The Noble Ladies of England.'" *Southern Literary Messenger* 19 (1853): 303–6.

Yarborough, Richard. "Strategies of Black Characterization in *Uncle Tom's Cabin* and the Early Afro-American Novel." Sundquist, ed. 45–84.

Yellin, Jean Fagan. "Doing It Herself: *Uncle Tom's Cabin* and Woman's Role in the Slavery Crisis." Sundquist, ed. 85–105.

*The Young Lady's Own Book: A Manual of Intellectual Improvement and Moral Deportment.* Philadelphia: Key, Mielke, and Biddle, 1832.

*The Young Man's Own Book.* Philadelphia: Key and Biddle, 1833.

*The Young Wife's Book: A Manual of Moral, Religious, and Domestic Duties.* Philadelphia: Lea and Blanchard, 1841.

Zanger, Jules. "The 'Tragic Octoroon' in Pre–Civil War Fiction." *American Quarterly* 18 (1966): 63–70.

Zuckerman, Mary Ellen. *Sources on the History of Women's Magazines, 1792–1960: An Annotated Bibliography.* Westport, Conn.: Greenwood, 1991.

# Notes on Contributors

James Bense is assistant professor of English at Moorhead State University in Minnesota. His publications include an article on Nathaniel Hawthorne in the Best from American Literature series.

R. C. De Prospo chairs American studies at Washington College in Maryland. He is the author of *Theism in the Discourse of Jonathan Edwards* as well as various articles on early and nineteenth-century American literature, American literary historiography and pedagogy, and literary theory.

Sarah Smith Ducksworth, assistant professor of English at Kean College of New Jersey, is the author of various articles for reference books such as *McGill's Survey of World Literature, Masterpieces of African-American Literature,* and *The African-American Encyclopedia.* Currently, she is working on a book based on Ida B. Wells's antilynching campaign of the late nineteenth century and on short fiction.

Melanie J. Kisthardt is instructor of English at Temple University. She is completing a study of Sarah Orne Jewett, *Beyond Local Color,* and is working on a study of Harriet Beecher Stowe's influence on Jewett.

Mason I. Lowance, Jr., is professor of English and American literature at the University of Massachusetts, Amherst. He has written *Increase Mather* (1974), *Massachusetts Broadsides of the American Revolution* (1976), *The Language of Canaan: Metaphor and Symbol in New England from the Puritans to the Transcendentalists* (1980), and *The Typological Writings of Jonathan Edwards* (1993). He has been a Guggenheim Fellow and Fellow of the National Humanities Institute, Yale, and he is a member of the American Antiquarian Society, Worcester. He has written articles on the slave narrative, Frederick Douglass, Herman Melville, Nathaniel Hawthorne, Increase and Cotton Mather, Jonathan Edwards, Emerson, and Thoreau, and he is an editor of *Early American Literature.*

Michael J. Meyer is the chair of the English department at Hong Kong International School. He has contributed chapters to three recent studies of John Steinbeck and is assistant editor of the *Steinbeck Quarterly.* He is presently editing a book of essays on the modern grotesque and working on a study of Steinbeck's use of the Cain-Abel myth. He has also written articles on children's literature and young adult fiction and served as guest editor of *Children's Literature Quarterly.*

Susan Marie Nuernberg, assistant professor of English at the University of Wisconsin at Oshkosh, is currently editing *The Critical Response to Jack London.* She is the recipient of two NEH awards and has recently completed a study entitled *The Call of Kind: Race in Jack London's Fiction.*

Catherine E. O'Connell is assistant professor of English at St. John Fisher College. She is currently at work on a book about the cultural meanings of women's sentimental literature in antebellum America.

Jan Pilditch is a lecturer of English and American studies at the University of Waikato, New Zealand. She has published on British and American satire and on writing by women. She is currently editing *The Critical Response to Katherine Mansfield.*

Susan L. Roberson, instructor of English at Auburn University, has published several articles on the sermons of Ralph Waldo Emerson and has recently completed a book on them, *Emerson in His Sermons: A Man-Made Self.*

S. Bradley Shaw is assistant professor of English at Greenville College. His current research is a study of how popular literature, realism, and domestic ideology intersect in the work of Mary Wilkins Freeman.

Ellen Westbrook, freelance editor and former assistant professor of American literature at the University of Southern Mississippi, has written articles on Nathaniel Hawthorne and is currently working on a study of narratives of Indian captivity. She has been a fellow of the American Antiquarian Society, Worcester.

Helen Petter Westra is assistant professor of English at Grand Valley State University. She is the author of *The Minister's Task and Calling in the Thought of Jonathan Edwards* and has written on David Brainerd, Willa Cather, and Sarah Orne Jewett. Currently she is working on a study of early-twentieth-century Chinese women writers. She has published an essay on Jonathan Edwards in *Early American Literature.*

Isabelle White is professor of English at Eastern Kentucky University. Her most recent publications are on Susan Warner and Harriet Arnow, and she has published an article on Harriet Beecher Stowe in the *American Quarterly.*

# Index

# Index

Bahktin, Mikail, 6, 35 n.1, 69, 282
Baker, Houston, 285, 286
Baldwin, James, 4, 55, 159, 163, 204 n.1, 206–7, 236, 246–49, 265–66, 269, 281–82, 284
Balzac, Honoré de, 286–87; *Sarrazine*, 291
Baraka, Amiri, 286
Bardes, Barbara, 100, 123, 137 n.3
Barlow, Joel, 180, 279
Barthes, Roland, *S/Z*, 291
Baym, Nina, 98 n.9
Beecher, Catharine, 73–74, 103, 124, 125; *American Women's Home*, 119; *Essay on Slavery and Abolitionism*... (1837), 85, 86, 89, 98 n.7
Beecher, Henry Ward, 124–25, 141
Beecher, Lyman, 5, 46, 110, 142, 146–49, 164, 177
Beinecke Library, 158 n.1, 183
Bellamy, Joseph, 142, 182
Bense, James, 6, 7, 278, 280, 283
Bercovitch, Sacvan, *The American Jeremiad*, 177
Berlant, Lauren, 36 n.10
Bernstein, Leonard, 273
Bible, 162; authority of, 21, 23, infallibility of, 141
Biblical language, 177
Biblical narrative, 176
Black Panthers, 273, 284
Bogel, Donald, 235 n.3
Bond, Adrienne, 98
Bowdoin College, 5, 164
Brackenridge, Hugh Henry, 181
Brodhead, Richard, 31
Brown, Elaine, *A Taste of Power*, 271, 284, 286
Brown, Herbert Ross, 36 n.8, 115 n.1
Brown, John, 275
Brown, Richard, 9
Brown, William, *The Power of Sympathy* (1789), 58–59
Brown, William Wells, *Clotel*, 20, 232
*Buds for the Bridal Wreath*, 120
Bunyan, John, 68, 162
Burgess, Anthony, 252
Byron, Lord, 292

Caldwell, Charles, *Thoughts on the Original Unity of the Human Race* (1830), 256
Calhoun, John C., 190

Calvinism, 141, 176, 180, 181; Calvinist logic of exclusive disjunction, 150; Calvinist sermons, 152; New Light Calvinism, 6, 161
Camfield, Gregg, 36 n.4
Canaan, 174, 181; "Canaan's Fields," 173; land of Canaan, 174
Canon, 276–77
Catholicism, 144, 149, 150; Catholic schools, 149
Chafe, William, 102
Chaffin, Jeff, 9
Channing, William Ellery, 125, 259–60
Charlestown, Mass., 149
Child, Lydia Maria, 124, 194–95
Childish beauty, 171
Child-rearing, 122
Chosen people of god, 175
*Chronicle of Higher Education*, 293 n.8
Christ: at Calvary, 175; on the cross, 175; first coming of, 170; and his coming in his kingdom, 170; and his judgment, 171; and his kingdom, 163; and his reign of a thousand years, 161
Christ figure, 160, 175
Christian church, 176
Christianity and humanism in antebellum period, 18, 20
Church of Christ, 178
Cicero, 63
Civil War, 8, 182
Cixous, Hélène, 37, 130
Clark, Mary G., 97 n.4
Clarke, James Freeman, 8, 161, 192–95, 199, 280
Clarke, Lewis, 194–95, 201
Clarkson, Thomas, 87
Clemens, Samuel: *The Adventures of Huckleberry Finn*, 272, 291 n.1; "How to Tell a Story," 202; Mark Twain (pseud.), 256, 287
Cogan, Frances B., 49, 126, 127
Collins, John A., 194
*Columbia Literary History of the U.S.*, 280
Columbian conquests, 274–75
Compromise of 1850, 2, 8, 20, 24, 189; response of ministers to, 20
*Congressional Record*, 160
Constitution, U.S., 24–26, 27, 241; three-fifths compromise, 25, 36 n.6
Cott, Nancy, 36 n.9, 97 n.3

# Index

# Index